The American Idea of Mission

THE AMERICAN
IDEA OF MISSION

CONCEPTS OF NATIONAL
PURPOSE AND DESTINY

by

EDWARD MCNALL BURNS

GREENWOOD PRESS, PUBLISHERS
WESTPORT, CONNECTICUT

The Library of Congress has catalogued this publication as follows:

Library of Congress Cataloging in Publication Data

Burns, Edward McNall, 1897–
    The American idea of mission.

    Bibliography: p.
    1. United States--Civilization. 2. National
characteristics, American. 3. United States--
History--Philosophy. I. Title.
    [E169.1.B943 1973]   917.3   72-11302 5.24.76
    ISBN 0-8371-6648-9

Originally published in 1957
by Rutgers University Press, New Brunswick, New Jersey

Reprinted with the permission
of Rutgers University Press

First Greenwood Reprinting 1973

Library of Congress Catalogue Card Number 72-11302

ISBN 0-8371-6648-9

Printed in the United States of America

To
MARIE BENTZ BURNS
Faithful co-worker and understanding critic

Foreword

About three years ago the Carnegie Corporation issued a quarterly report to which it gave the provocative title, "Who Knows America?" The content of the report led clearly to the conclusion that nobody knows, not even "our lawmakers, journalists, civic leaders, diplomats, teachers, and others." Whether so inclusive an indictment is justified may be open to question, but no one can deny the urgent need for more insight and understanding. According to some interpreters, Americans are the most materialistic people on earth; yet others see them as idealistic and even quixotic in their pursuit of fabulous dreams. Whereas radical critics complain of the conservatism of Americans, conservatives deplore the mania for change and what they regard as revolutionary tendencies. Still other observers classify the inhabitants of our republic as selfish or altruistic, as individualistic or gregarious, as isolationist or interventionist, depending upon the particular vantage point of preconception or prejudice from which they view its intellectual and social history.

It is the author's belief that one of the principal clues to knowledge of America is the sense of mission which has run like a golden thread through most of her history. To a greater extent than most other peoples, Americans have conceived of their nation as ordained in some extraordinary way to accomplish great things in the world. For some of her leaders this mission has been interpreted as ethical and religious. Because of our virtues we have been chosen by God to guide and instruct the rest of the nations in lessons of justice and right. Other leaders have thought of us as having a call to carry civilization to the backward regions of the earth and even to rule over savage and benighted peoples for their own good. To the majority of our spokesmen the mission of America has probably symbolized the dual responsibility of achieving the maximum of liberty and democracy in our own society and at the same time helping in every constructive way the rest of mankind to benefit from our example.

Whether a nation's sense of mission is an asset or a hindrance to its cultural development is an interesting topic for speculation. It is at least arguable that the disadvantages outweigh the advantages. A strong conviction of a call to greatness is almost certain to foster worship of the past. Especially if the call is regarded as in any sense a divine one, the nation must be assumed to have been grand and noble from the beginning. The ideals of its founders therefore become sacrosanct, and its constitution takes on the character of a primitive fetish. In addition, its prophets are very likely to hark back to precursor peoples in some storied epochs of the past. As a result, the ideals and institutions of remote ancestors may also become objects of worship. Even some of our most celebrated re-formers have been backward-looking or illiberal with respect to certain aspects of their philosophy. Examples include William Lloyd Garrison, with his blindness toward the evils of wage-slavery in the industrialized North, William Jennings Bryan, with his ante-diluvian attitudes toward science and religion, Albert J. Beveridge, with his benighted ideas of empire and race, and George W. Norris and Robert M. LaFollette, with their isolationism and xenophobic fears of a League of Nations.

In such tendencies is probably to be found an explanation of the basic conservatism of Americans. Despite superficial evidences to the contrary, we have not been a particularly originative people. Our law is almost exclusively of English origin. Except for Prag-matism, our philosophy is entirely European. Our art and litera-ture copy and perpetuate imported forms. Though advances in technology and in the applied sciences have been numerous on this side of the Atlantic, the foundations of pure scientific achievement have been nearly all European. We have added nothing to the forms or denominations of religion except for Mormonism, Chris-tian Science, and the revivalist sects, and even the underlying theologies of these have sprung largely from Hebrew, Platonist, and Pietist sources. With respect to political institutions a similar story must be told. Except for federalism, the nominating convention, the Electoral College, the independent regulatory commission, the city-manager form of municipal government, and perhaps the Presidency, we have added almost nothing to the forms of organization that free governments cherish. Our system of judicial review was invented by Sir Edward Coke. Our elaborate mechanism of checks and balances represents an engrafting of the ideas of Harrington and Montesquieu on a New World growth. The referendum, woman suffrage, the Bill of Rights, the written Constitution, were likewise importations from various European sources. Our chief claim to originality must lie in the extensive *adaptations* we have made of some of these borrowed institutions and in our establishment of a political milieu free from the relics of feudalism which hampered the development of liberty and equality in the world across the sea.

But neither an assumption of originality nor the lack of it has affected very much the idea of mission. By and large, exponents of the idea have been perfectly willing to grant that America's chief role has been to preserve and continue traditions and institutions inherited from the past. Many of our leading statesmen have exemplified this attitude. Several of the Fathers, notably Hamilton, thought of America as reproducing the achievements of ancient Rome. John C. Calhoun dreamed of a culture duplicating that of Athens, with a true democracy of equals cultivating the arts of leisure with the support of slave labor. Abraham Lincoln thought of himself as a disciple of Jefferson; Theodore Roosevelt and Woodrow Wilson conceived of themselves as perpetuators of the tradition of Lincoln. Even Franklin D. Roosevelt appealed more than once to the heroes of the past—to Jefferson and Jackson in their struggles with the judiciary, to Wilson in his battles with the isolationists, and to both Wilson and the Progressives in their contests with monopolies and the money power. With the exception of the second Roosevelt, none of these leaders departed far from the ancient tradition that free competition is the soul of the republic, and that the sovereign individual is the end of all political endeavor. This fundamental conservatism seems to underlie the major portion of American history, and is both a consequence and an ingredient of the national idea of mission.

In completing this book the author must acknowledge numerous debts of wise counsel and generous assistance. His chief measure of gratitude must go to the Rutgers University Research Council and to its Director, Dr. William H. Cole, for providing the financial aid to make the research possible and for helping to defray the cost of publication. The author is especially grateful to his research assistants, Mr. Raymond D. Bodnar, Mr. Jules Cohn, Mr. John H. Donnelly, and Mr. Harris I. Effross. But this specific enumeration implies no lack of regard for the other graduate students in political theory, who have been a constant stimulus and inspiration. Gratitude is due also to Mrs. Beulah H. Scheer and Captain Robert W. Black for help in obtaining illustrative materials and to Mrs. Sunok Pai for assistance with the index. Most of all, the author is indebted to his wife for her secretarial work on the manuscript, for her valuable achievements in preparing the index, for her painstaking labors in checking references, and for her loyalty, patience, and self-sacrifice. Without her contribution in each of these areas, this book would not have been possible.

EDWARD McNALL BURNS

New Brunswick, New Jersey
January, 1957

Contents

The American Idea of Mission

"And we Americans are peculiar, chosen
people, the Israel of our times; we bear
the ark of the liberties of the world."
—Herman Melville

Chapter One

The Idea of Mission

From time immemorial nations have conceived of themselves as superior and as endowed with a mission to dominate other peoples or to lead the rest of the world into paths of light. The ancient Hebrews were told by their prophets that they were "a holy people unto the Lord," and that God had chosen them to be "a peculiar people unto himself, above all the nations that are upon the earth." [1] For Plato and Aristotle the entire human race consisted of just two branches: Hellenes and barbarians. Plato considered it wrong for Hellenes to burn the houses and slaughter the women and children of other Hellenes, but he found no reason to condemn such atrocities when committed against barbarians. [2] Aristotle thought of barbarians as fit only for slavery by nature and approved of the idea that Hellenes should rule over them. [3] It was a convenient hypothesis which enabled the Greeks to reserve for themselves a priceless heritage of freedom and democracy and to build a fabulous culture upon the labor of their alleged inferiors.

The most elaborate theory in ancient times of mission and superiority was that developed by Confucianist China. According to this theory, the entire world constituted a single unit, and all the people in it were brothers. But they lacked the characteristic of equality. The inhabitants of China proper, who lived by the rules of propriety taught by Confucius, made up the "Middle Kingdom." All who dwelt in the surrounding area were classed as barbarians. This did not necessarily refer to savages. It meant principally peoples who had not adopted Chinese customs and dress, who did not adhere to the proprieties, and whose lives were not governed by reason. In a general way the area was divided into three segments: the peace-seeking domain, where Chinese learning and the proprieties had penetrated half-way; the domain of restraint; and the wild domain. Insofar as possible the relationship of China to this outside world was that of teacher and admonisher. The barbarian nations were viewed by China as younger brothers who needed her wisdom and guidance. Though at times this theory broke down in practice, few would deny that it was one of the most humane conceptions ever entertained by a proud and civilized nation toward its neighbors.[4]

Ideas of mission and destiny have not been confined to ancient nations. In the nineteenth century Slavophil writers and philosophers in Russia portrayed their country as the divinely appointed savior of Europe. The West was anarchic, materialistic, and hypocritical, professing a devotion to "liberalism" for the benefit of the rich. Russia, too, had her faults—sensuality, cruelty to women and children, and a slumbering fatalism which barred the door to the elimination of disease, famine, and filth. But such evils were peccadilloes compared with the arrogance and greed of the West. The redeeming qualities of the Russian peasant were humility, a willingness to share his last morsel with a needy neighbor, and a profound conviction of sin and unworthiness. As some of the philosophers expressed it, these were signs that "God would save Russia" and make her the instrument for the redemption of the world. Such results would be accomplished by transforming the state into a church, creating a theocracy which would bring the peoples of Europe and eventually the world into the Orthodox fold. Russia would take her destined place as the Third Rome with her capital at Moscow. The great Slavic empire was in very truth the "God-bearer" with a messianic mission to the rest of humanity.[5]

Western nations, also, have conceived of themselves as participating in the afflatus which makes them chosen peoples to rescue the benighted of earth from depravity and ignorance. Although the leaders of the French Revolution proclaimed themselves humanitarians and renounced war as a relic of the barbarous past, they gradually came to think of their nation as having the duty to bestow liberty upon its neighbors. In a report to the National Convention in February, 1794, Robespierre asserted that it was time to announce to the world the true aims and principles of the Revolution. He declared these to be, among others, "to accomplish the destiny of mankind," to make France "eclipse the glory of all free peoples that have ever existed," and "become the model to the nations, the terror of oppressors, the consolation of the oppressed, the ornament of the universe." His fellow patriots in the late nineteenth and early twentieth centuries frequently referred to the mission of France as a "civilizer" (*la mission civilisatrice*) in Syria, North Africa, and other parts of the French empire. More typical perhaps was the attitude of British imperialists, who took a kind of masochistic pride in holding, beneath the "awful hand" of God, "dominion over palm and pine."

If it were possible to unearth all of the facts, it would probably be found that every great nation, sometime in its history, has had dreams of destiny and grandeur, and has longed to assume a white man's or a brown or yellow man's supremacy over weak and retarded peoples. Chester Bowles has shown how the Republic of India, under the essentially enlightened rule of Jawaharlal Nehru, has begun to cultivate legends of a glorious past, with more than a suggestion that what has been done before can be duplicated sometime in the future. Children in the schools are taught that India was once the nucleus of a mighty empire, which included not only Ceylon, Burma, and Malaya, but extended to Sumatra, Java, Bali, and Borneo. The creators of this empire did not aim at exploitation or finding new markets but went forth to carry "the light of civilization and the blessings that depend upon it to the more backward regions." The modern Indian writer Chamanlal contends that the Western Hemisphere was discovered and actually colonized by Hindus long before the time of Columbus. He finds evidences for this in supposed similarities between Old and New World cultures. The architecture and sculpture of the Mayas and the highly developed governmental system of the Incas, he argues, were clearly of South Asian origin. Nehru has testified "how excited" he became upon learning of such revelations of India's historic role.[6]

AMERICA THE PEERLESS

Perhaps no theme has ever dominated the minds of the leaders of this nation to the same extent as the idea that America occupies a unique place and has a special destiny among the nations of the earth. It is an idea which characterizes not simply flamboyant orations but pervades the writings of critical philosophers and distinguished historians and social scientists. No period of our history has been free from its seductive influence. Some of the founders of the nation seemed to have been as firmly convinced of their country's exalted role as the statesmen of more stable periods. When James Wilson looked upon the Thirteen States which had lately cemented a Federal Union, he boldly ventured to compare them "with the most illustrious commonwealths" which adorned the records of

Congress voting Independence, 1776. By Robert Edge Pine and Edward Savage. *Historical Society of Pennsylvania*

fame. He opined that when "some future Xenophon or Thucydides shall arise to do justice to their virtues and their actions, the glory of America will rival—it will outshine the glory of Greece." [7] Jefferson, who was sometimes assailed by doubts, conveyed to John Adams on the eve of the War of 1812 his belief that the country would continue to "grow, to multiply and prosper until we exhibit an association, powerful, wise and happy, beyond what has yet been seen by men." [8]

The logic of history would lead one to expect that the most rapturous apostrophes to America's greatness would come from the period when she was cutting her industrial eye teeth in the 1870's and 1880's, or from her period of imperial grandeur after 1898. But such was not entirely the case. During the 1860's Orestes Brownson, the former Universalist and Unitarian who finally became a Catholic, declared that of all the states of the Western Hemisphere, the American republic alone had a destiny, "or the ability to add anything to the civilization of the race." Canada, Mexico, and the whole of South America might be "absorbed in the United States without being missed by the civilized world." The reason for this was that they represented no idea. "The work of civilization could go on without them as well as with them." [9] About 1835 James Fenimore Cooper, who often took a jaundiced view of America's future, inquired: "Where shall we turn to find a parallel to our progress, our energy, and our increasing power?" [10]

More extravagant dithyrambs in the Middle Period of American history were penned by such orators and poets as Edward Everett, Daniel Webster, and Walt Whitman. Addressing the Harvard chapter of Phi Beta Kappa in 1824, Everett declaimed that with the founding of the American nation "in the glittering hills of Hesperian climes," the "farthest Thule" had been reached. There were no more "retreats beyond the seas," "no more discoveries, no more hopes." [11] Celebrating the bicentennial of the landing of the Pilgrims, Webster doubted that anyone possessed an imagination fertile enough to tell what might be the progress of America in half a century to come. Here, he said, was a people of from seventeen to twenty millions, "intelligent, educated, freeholders, freemen, republicans . . . with the world before them! There is nothing to check them till they touch the shores of the Pacific, and then, they are so much accustomed to water, that that's a facility, and no obstruction!" [12] On the eve of the Civil War, Walt Whitman acclaimed the United States as the "custodian of the future of humanity." Long before the second centennial of her independence, there would be "forty to fifty great States, among them Canada and Cuba." The Pacific would be ours, and the Atlantic "mainly ours." There would be daily electric communication with every part of the globe. "What an age! What a land! Where elsewhere one so great?" Like Orestes Brownson, he believed that America's greatness would spring from the fact that she epitomized an idea. For Whitman the idea was *nationality,* the "fused and fervent identity of the individual, whoever he or she may be, and whatever the place, with the idea and fact of AMERICAN TOTALITY, and with what is meant by the Flag, the stars and stripes." [13]

After the War of Secession, despite the welding of the nation into a solider unit than ever, paeans to America's greatness grew less ecstatic. True, there were some echoes of the earlier attitude. Samuel Gompers characterized America as "the apotheosis of all that is right." [14] And, as we shall see, the spread-eagleism of Albert J. Beveridge in glorifying the conquests of Cuba and the Philippines came close to matching anything that came out of Old World empires at the height of their arrogance. But these exceptions may be compared with the modest chauvinism of William Jennings Bryan or Robert M. LaFollette. In his lecture on "America's Mission," the former asserted that the people of this nation could "aspire to a grander destiny than has opened before any other race." He did not describe this destiny as a certainty but merely as an aspiration. Fighting against powerful odds to keep America from ratifying the Treaty of Versailles, Senator LaFollette spoke of his cherished belief that "this was the place for the consummation and the working out of the most perfect Government on earth, the most perfect Government attainable." [15] He asserted that this was true, not because of any inherent superiority of the American people, but because of the best opportunity in the form of virgin soil and a population of immigrants intent upon the quest for freedom and democracy.

As the years passed, the prophets of a glorious and expanding America placed more and more emphasis upon the duties and moral responsibilities of greatness. Increasing power and influence came to be regarded, not as a cause of exultation, but as an inescapable and almost tragic fate. Confronted with the question of what should be done with the newly conquered Philippines, President McKinley went down on his knees and prayed for divine guidance. He told a delegation of Methodist ministers that late one night the answer came to keep the islands as a possession of the United States in order that we might "uplift and civilize and Christianize them." [16] During the same years William Jennings Bryan and Theodore Roosevelt were proclaiming the superiority of the nation which takes upon itself the White Man's Burden of protecting and bestowing good upon backward peoples. The most accurate distinction between Western and Oriental countries, Bryan thought, was that the former conceived that they had a mission "to redeem and to civilize the world," while the latter had no mission and were satisfied to solve their own problems without burdening themselves with the problems of others.[17]

Theodore Roosevelt made even more emphatic the idea that nations like the United States have responsibilities of international stewardship. The civilized peoples, he maintained, have a moral duty to further the progress of history by helping to uplift the laggard peoples. But it is no soft and easy task. "We are a great people," he boasted. At the same time he declared that we must "gird up our loins as a nation, with the stern purpose to play our part manfully in winning the ultimate triumph." We must therefore "turn scornfully aside from the paths of mere ease and idleness, and with unfaltering steps tread the rough road of endeavor, smiting down the wrong and battling for the right, as Greatheart smote and battled in Bunyan's immortal story."[18]

As almost everyone knows, the United States renounced its claims to international leadership after World War I and entered upon a period of self-castigation for being so stupid as to be drawn into a war to solve the problems of a decadent Europe. Power, glory, and responsibility for the welfare of weaker peoples were ridiculed as empty or hypocritical shibboleths. Contrary to a popular impression, idealism did not disappear entirely, for the goal of a warless world remained a reality. But the conception that America had a mission to uplift or civilize was regarded as worthy only of uncritical adolescents. World War II brought an awakened sense of international responsibility, although with overtones of resignation and even humility. As in earlier periods, there were, of course, exceptions. The forthright proprietor of *Life, Time,* and *Fortune* hailed the present and the immediate future as the "American Century." He saw the United States as the "principal guarantor of the freedom of the seas," "the dynamic leader of world trade," "the training center of the skillful servants of mankind," "the powerhouse of the ideals of Freedom and Justice," and "the Good Samaritan, really believing again it is more blessed to give than to receive."[19]

Others of our contemporaries have written in more somber vein. Soon after the outbreak of World War II, Henry Wallace declared confidently that "the world civilization of the next hundred years, at least," depended chiefly upon the United States. But he wondered whether we should "wake up sufficiently" after the war "to conduct ourselves with a wisdom greater than that which we employed after World War I." [20] With the end of the war he saw resting upon the United States a fearsome responsibility of world leadership analogous to that which was assumed by Great Britain following the Napoleonic Wars.[21]

Though disagreeing with Wallace on numerous issues, President Harry S. Truman echoed almost his identical sentiments with regard to America's world responsibilities. In a speech at Wake Forest College during the Korean War, he described our country as "standing before the bar of history in a very conspicuous place." This is because "the world is watching us, because all the world knows that the fate of civilization depends, to a very large extent, on what we do." He portrayed the "positive action for peace" in which the nation was then engaged as a costly effort, involving sacrifices and inconveniences and raising questions in the minds of many as to whether it was worth its cost. But he avowed that it was not only an effort worth making, but that we *had* to make it. It came upon us virtually as a decree of fate, "the result of our entire national experience, over the last few decades."

Probably the most prolific writer on international affairs in America today is the well-known editor and columnist, Walter Lippmann. As early as 1939 he announced his conviction that what Rome was to the ancient world, what Britain was to the nineteenth century, "America is to be to the world of tomorrow." He confessed that he wished it were otherwise, for life would be easier in a country that could live to itself. But when in the course of the great movements of history "the destiny of a nation is revealed to it," it behooves the citizen to accept that destiny and to make ready to meet its demands.[22] America's destiny arises from the fact that she is no longer on the edges of Western civilization, but at the center. If she denies this fact and refuses her destiny, "Western civilization, which is the glory of our world, will become a disorganized and decaying fringe around the Soviet Union and the emergent peoples of Asia." [23] But apparently Lippmann's conception of the mission of America differs considerably from that of the apostles of uplift and stewardship. He deplored the idea of a "persistent evangel of Americanism" taking the form of "meddlesome self-righteousness." For him the glory of America is "to do what the founders and the pioneers always believed was the American task: to make the New World a place where the ancient faith can flourish anew, and its eternal promise at last be redeemed." [24] Taken literally, this would involve no One World idea or Point Four program but a central position of leadership and domination for the United States. America as the New Rome would hold sway over the Atlantic and Pacific regions in much the same way as did the empire of the Caesars over the Mediterranean.

THE HAND OF GOD

No truth is more patent in American history than the fact that this nation is an Old Testament people. Our attitudes toward thrift and success in business, toward Sabbath observance, toward crime and punishment, and toward the taboos of sex morality give convincing evidence of this. The explanation is to be found, no doubt, in the vigor and pervasiveness of the Calvinist influence. Calvinists were not confined to the Puritans of New England but included the Scotch-Irish Presbyterians, who settled the region east and west of the Alleghenies, and also the Dutch Reformed sectaries of New York and New Jersey. Though only a minority of the total inhabitants of the colonies, they were a dynamic and zealous group and disseminated their doctrines widely.

The most common idea deriving from Old Testament sources was the notion that America was divinely appointed to fulfill a great mission in the history of our planet. In the opinion of some of the colonial leaders, the great events of the past had been consummated by God in order to prepare the way for the American triumph. According to Thomas Paine, the Reformation was preceded by the discovery of America in order that the Almighty might provide a sanctuary for the persecuted in future years, "when home should afford neither friendship nor safety." [25] John Adams declared in 1765 that he always considered the settlement of America "with reverence and wonder, as the opening of a grand scheme and design in Providence for the illumination of the ignorant, and the emancipation of the slavish part of mankind all over the earth." [26] To several of the Fathers the victory of the Thirteen States in their struggle

New York from Brooklyn.Heights, 1778. The future metropolis was already
a bustling city. Pen-and-ink drawing by Archibald Robertson. *Spencer Collection, New York Public Library*

with Great Britain was so remarkable an event that they could account for it only by divine intervention. Divine Providence, thought Benjamin Rush, had saved us despite all we had done "to ruin ourselves." [27] Benjamin Franklin related how, in the beginning of the struggle, he and his associates had prayed daily for divine aid to the Revolutionary cause, and how their prayers had been "graciously answered." He said that those who were engaged in the struggle "observed frequent instances of a Superintending providence in our favor." [28] The success of the Constitutional Convention likewise appeared to a number of the Fathers as so improbable an occurrence that an assumption of divine intervention was required to explain it.

Through the period from Washington's inauguration to the extinction of the flames of the Civil War, America's leaders took serene satisfaction in the belief that the destinies of the republic were guided and directed by the God of their Fathers. Two philosophers as disparate as Ralph Waldo Emerson and John C. Calhoun agreed in contending that the American people were charged by Providence, in considerable measure, with the happiness of the human race. [29] Theodore Parker maintained that the virgin continent of North America had been hidden by God, "away off here in the Western ocean," as an ultimate home for the "ideas of Christianity, Protestantism, and Democracy." [30] Even the calamities which befell the nation were interpreted as divine chastisements for the eventual benefit of the chosen people. In proclaiming a national fast day for March 30, 1863, Abraham Lincoln set forth the view that the awful conflict between the states was "but a punishment inflicted upon us for our presumptuous sins," to the end that the whole people might be redeemed. The purposes of the Almighty, he wrote later, are perfect, and therefore some great good must finally come from the mighty convulsion. The war itself was an act of God. No mortal could have brought it to pass or stayed its occurrence. [31]

The belief that America is the chosen instrument of God for the fulfillment of benign and exalted purposes has not died out even in our own day. At the Democratic National Convention of 1952 President Harry S. Truman proudly declared that, under his administration, America had "finally stepped into the leadership which Almighty God intended us to assume a generation ago." In another connection he made clear that the idea he had in mind was the mission of the United States to direct the world toward peace. This it should have done after World War I by entering and leading the League of Nations.[32] But the most grandiloquent expressions of the divine mission were products of the second half of the nineteenth century. They emanated from the minds of religious dreamers like Orestes Brownson and from political idealists like Albert J. Beveridge.

After saturating his mind with Hegelian political philosophy, Brownson came forth with the doctrine that every great nation has a special mission to realize an idea given to it by Providence. Every great nation is in some sense a chosen people of God. The Jews were a chosen people through whom the pure worship of one God was to be preserved, and the Messiah was to come. The Greeks were a chosen people for the development and realization of the beautiful in art and of the true in science and philosophy. The special mission of the Romans was to cultivate the growth of the state, law, and jurisprudence. The United States has a mission not only to continue the work assigned to Greece and Rome but to accomplish a still greater purpose. In art its divinely appointed destiny is to "rival Greece," and in science and philosophy to surpass it. In the realm of the political it "must continue and surpass Rome." Its goal is not so much the achievement of liberty as the realization of "the true idea of the state," which harmonizes the authority of the public and the freedom of the individual. "In other words, its mission is to bring out in its life the dialectic union of authority and liberty, of the natural rights of man and those of society." [33] That the American people were not unaware of this mission was proved by their calmness during the bloody ordeal of the Civil War. This was not arrogance or self-conceit, according to Brownson, but a confidence in their destiny as a providential people, "to whom is reserved the hegemony of the world." [34]

Equally vainglorious was the theological chauvinism of Albert J. Beveridge. Senator from Indiana, amateur historian, and Progressive reformer, Beveridge looked upon the events of 1898 and after as conclusive proof that God had singled out America as the demiurge of His plans. "God has not been preparing the English-speaking and Teutonic peoples for a thousand years for nothing but vain and idle self-contemplation and self-admiration," the Senator shouted. By "English-speaking and Teutonic peoples" he meant primarily the people of the United States, for he went on: "He has made us the master organizers of the world to establish system where chaos reigns. He has given us the spirit of progress to overwhelm the forces of reaction throughout the earth. He has made us adepts in government that we may administer government among savage and senile peoples. . . . He has marked the American people as His Chosen Nation finally to lead in the regeneration of the world. This is the divine mission of America, and it holds for us all profit, glory, happiness possible to man. We are trustees of the world's progress, guardians of its righteous peace. The judgment of the Master is upon us: 'Ye have been faithful over a few things; I will make you ruler over many things.'" [35]

AMERICA, SCHOOL FOR THE WORLD

It was one of the proudest boasts of Pericles in his celebrated funeral oration that Athens was the "school of Hellas." In even more definite measure American statesmen and writers have conceived of the United States as a school for the world. Foreign visitors would come here and take away with them the American concept of love of freedom and American ideals of equality, practical-mindedness, and zeal for achievement. But most of all the American example would fire the imaginations of foreign peoples and stir their countries from sluggishness and from enslavement to outworn habits and institutions.

Scarcely had the Thirteen States gained their independence when it was taken for granted that what they had achieved would be a spur and an inspiration to the victims of tyranny in other countries. As the passing years brought news of revolutions elsewhere, leaders in America rejoiced that the seeds they had scattered were bearing fruit. By the example of her revolution, Charles Pinckney declared, America had "read more useful lessons" to the peoples of the Old World than they had learned by their own experience for centuries. If the American Revolution had not happened, he doubted that Ireland would enjoy "her present rights of commerce and legislation," or that the subjects of the emperor in the Netherlands would have "presumed to contend for, and ultimately to secure, the privileges they demanded." He rightly saw, also, the rumblings of discontent in France as an obedience to the precedent set by the

American colonists.[36] James Wilson held that a glorious privilege had been given to the American people, that of diffusing among all governments a knowledge of the principles of representation and the supremacy of a written constitution.[37] Even Alexander Hamilton thought that the world had its eye upon America. The influence of her example, he averred, had "penetrated the gloomy regions of despotism," and had pointed the way to "inquiries which may shake it to its deepest foundations." Everywhere men were beginning to ask why they should submit to tyrants who build their greatness upon the people's misery and degradation.[38]

Down to the Civil War the thesis was often reiterated that the American example of a revolution for freedom would renovate the life of the civilized world. Edward Everett saw the political regeneration which had begun in the West "going backward to resuscitate the once-happy and long-desired regions of the older world."[39] The historian George Bancroft considered it a certainty that our country would "allure the world to freedom by the beauty of its example." In America, he went on, a new people had emerged, without king, princes, or nobles, "knowing nothing of tithes and little of landlords." They were more religious, better educated, of "serener minds and of purer morals than the men of any former republic." By calm deliberation and friendly agreement they had prepared a constitution which, "in the union of freedom with strength and order," excelled any previously known.[40] Albert Gallatin, immigrant from Switzerland and Secretary of the Treasury under Jefferson and Madison, exhorted the American people that their mission was to improve the state of the world, "to be the model republic," to show that this simple and natural form of government, incorporating the principle of representation, is also productive of the greatest happiness and the highest standards of private and public morality.[41]

Andrew Jackson and William H. Seward gave a religious interpretation to America's role as regenerator of mankind. In his farewell address as President, the former told the American people that God had chosen them as the guardians of freedom, "to preserve it for the benefit of the human race." Seward compared the mission of the American Revolution with that of the Christian religion. As the gospel of peace was gradually improving the moral and social condition of men throughout the world, so the principles of the Revolution would renovate their political condition. Indeed, the principles of the Revolution were "a new and further development of the Christian system, by the introduction of the golden rule of benevolence in the science of human government." [42]

After the Civil War the practice of calling attention to the American Revolution as the galvanizer of nations into seeking freedom and destroying oppression almost disappeared. The scramble of the middle and upper classes for a chance to participate in the Great Barbecue of exploiting the national wealth engendered a spirit of conservatism which made memories of a revolutionary past unpalatable. Moreover, the idea of revolution came to be associated with Marxism, with the violence of the Paris Commune, and with anarchism and terrorism. To encourage revolts against oppression meant cooperation with malcontents who despised not only the capitalist state but religion, the family, and everything else held sacred by the bourgeoisie. Today the Revolution of the 1770's is celebrated as if it were about as sedate an event as a meeting of the Presbyterian synod. The ultrarespectable men and women who devote themselves to cherishing its memory would have more in common with Lord North than with Samuel Adams or Thomas Paine. They seem to believe that if America has any lessons to read to the rest of the world, they are lessons of preserving inherited wealth and social privilege.

THE GLORIOUS FUTURE

Devotion to the idea of mission almost of necessity implied faith in a golden future. The mission of America could not be realized except through the fulfillment of some glorious destiny eternally decreed in the heavens. For this reason most of the apostles of a call to greatness for the American nation have been optimists. Such was particularly the case during the nineteenth century. In a speech in the Senate in 1839 Henry Clay raised the question if every dark spot on our political horizon were not obliterated by the "bright and effulgent and cheering light that beams all around us?" Did any other nation, he continued, "ever contain within its bosom so many elements of prosperity, of greatness, and of glory?" The historian George Bancroft was less magniloquent but more emphatic. The movement of the human species, he told the Adelphi Society of Williams College in 1835, "is upward, irresistibly upward. . . .

"The World is my Market; my customers are all mankind."—Y. Doodle. From the *Daily Graphic*, March 20, 1877. *Courtesy of The New-York Historical Society, New York City*

The world cannot retrograde; the dark ages cannot return. . . . Humanity has always been on the advance; gaining maturity, universality, and power." [43]

After the great ordeal by fire of the 1860's, which left the certainty that the nation was not to destroy itself, forecasts of a roseate future gained in exuberance. Wealth now seemed to be limitless; a whole continent invited conquest; and opportunities for plunder were never more tempting. Typical of those who reveled in such prospects was the prince of ironmasters and canny Scotsman, Andrew Carnegie. "The march of humanity," he proclaimed, "is upward and onward, for all the countless ages to come." International warfare was doomed, and so was its kindred evil, militarism as a profession. Greed would disappear, and likewise intemperance, dissipation, cruelty, and injustice. Even the habit of smoking was destined for an early extinction. Chewing was already a thing of the past, and the pipe and the cigar were fated for the same end. In the movement toward all these accomplishments, the United States led the van. The nations of the Old World crept on at a snail's pace; America thundered past "with the rush of the express." The United States, "the growth of a single century," had already reached the first rank among nations and was "destined soon to out-distance all others in the race." Proof of this was to be found in the fact that Great Britain, the most rapidly growing of European countries, took seventy years to double her population. America had repeatedly doubled hers in twenty-five years. By 1980 the inhabitants of the republic would number about 600 million. [44]

In equally effusive vein Robert G. Ingersoll, celebrated orator and maligned apostle of the Religion of Humanity, acclaimed the new century. The second hundred years of America's history would be grander than the first. They would record the disappearance of ignorance, crime, and exploitation. Prisons would no longer scar the ground, nor the shadow of the gallows curse the earth. And the time would eventually come when liberty, morality, and justice would surround the world "like the rings of Saturn." [45]

The rise of the Progressive movement in the early twentieth century brought a reaffirmation of extraordinarily sanguine beliefs in America's destiny and potentialities. The Progressives were idealists, and the idealist is almost perforce an optimist. Unless he has confidence in the early fulfillment of his ideals, he is not likely to

An Indian farmer learns the advantages of the steel plow-head, under the International Cooperation Administration, Point 4 program. *ICA*

propose them in the first place. He may look upon the present, of course, as a sorry state and bemoan the frivolities and weaknesses of human beings, but he must have some degree of confidence in the ability of men to redeem themselves and to remold the scheme of things closer to their heart's desire—unless, of course, he believes that improvements come only from divine interposition. The Progressives chose to rest their hopes exclusively upon secular foundations.

That the man who was destined to become the foremost leader of the Progressives viewed the future with confidence and hope should occasion no surprise. An ebullient optimism was the heart and soul of Theodore Roosevelt. Except when adverting to the dangers of "race suicide" or excoriating monopolists and radicals, he invariably portrayed the future in rosy hues. In an address at Cairo, Illinois, in the panic year of 1907, he affirmed: "We have as a nation an era of unexampled prosperity ahead of us; we shall enjoy it, and our children will enjoy it after us. The trend of well-being in this country is upward, not downward; and this is the trend in the things of the soul as well as in the things of the body."

Some of Roosevelt's followers fell into even deeper delusions of optimism than did the bubbling Colonel himself. The president of Stanford University, David Starr Jordan, who supported Roosevelt in 1904 but deserted him later on account of disagreement with his foreign policy, proclaimed the dawn of universal peace almost on the eve of World War I. Though he recognized the bullying diplomacy, the screaming headlines in the newspapers, and the piling up of armaments by the two alliances, he found assurance that the deadly implements would remain harmless in the naïve belief that Europe was not rich enough to use them, and was "too human and humane to want to use them." [46] There was "not a shadow of grievance," he declared, separating England and Germany, and he thought that peace-loving people everywhere could rely "on the firm hand of the Emperor of Germany, who, with all his love for the pomp and show of force, had never made its actual use a factor in his policy." [47] The outbreak of war came as a shock to his equanimity, and during the dark days of the stalemate on the Western front he surrendered to the gloomy conclusion that the world was paralyzed by the stupidity of war lords and almost "smothered in the waves of hate." With the end of hostilities, however, his buoyancy returned, and he acclaimed the signing of the Armistice as the "harbinger of a new civilization." [48]

As every student of American history knows, the ideals of Progressivism were not the monopoly of any one party or segment of the population. They were formulated both by men who called themselves Republicans and by adherents of the Democratic party. They embodied the hopes and dreams of prairie Senators and of crusaders for reform in the cities. They numbered among their followers enlightened jurists, muckrakers, social welfare workers, and academicians. Foremost among the last was the chief exponent of Progressive Democracy, Woodrow Wilson. In the campaign of 1912 the prophet of the New Freedom acknowledged his tendency to think of the future, not of the past, "as the more glorious time in comparison with which the present is nothing."

For much of his thinking Wilson was indebted to Louis D. Brandeis, whom he appointed to the Supreme Court in 1916. Brandeis had a broader philosophy of political and social optimism than did the lonely scholar in the White House. In *The Curse of Bigness* the eminent jurist announced his conviction that the "possibilities of human advancement" were unlimited. He prophesied that the world would see a "vastly increased supply of comforts, a tremendous social surplus out of which the great masses will be apportioned a degree of well-being that is now hardly dreamed of." He conceived of business undergoing so great a moral purification that a desire to render the "best Service" would become its objective instead of making money. The eventual outcome would be "a full-grown industrial democracy."

Neither the cynicism of the 1920's nor the hunger and anxieties of the 1930's dampened the enthusiasm of those Americans who refused to look upon the present as pregnant with anything other than bright hopes for the future. Except for H. L. Mencken and the orthodox Marxists, scarcely anyone saw disaster or a fearful day of reckoning as a price that would have to be paid for a better tomorrow. So tough-minded an observer as Charles A. Beard described a host of problems still unsolved—lynching, corruption, periodical industrial crises, slums, waste of natural resources, bigotry, violation of civil liberties—but he betrayed no lack of trust that the nation would "rouse itself, gird its loins, summon its powers of creative imagination, and advance inexorably upon the future, armed with all the instrumentalities of modern science" and make the coming century the fulfillment of its brightest dreams.[49] In spite of three defeats for the Presidency and the frustration of his ambitions as Secretary of State, William Jennings Bryan wrote in his *Memoirs* in 1924 that the American people could aspire "to a grander destiny" than had opened before any other race. The principles of American democracy, he assured his readers, are destined to grow "here and everywhere until arbitrary power will nowhere be known, and until the voice of the people shall be recognized, if not as the voice of God, at least as Bancroft defines it, as the best expression of the divine will to be found upon the earth."

The most comprehensive philosophy of optimism in twentieth century America was that of John Dewey. During the 1920's and the 1930's he issued a series of books and articles arguing the necessity of a benevolent view of human capacities as a condition requisite to a belief in democracy. He did not insist that man's nature is angelic. In fact, he regarded such a conception as naïve and unscientific. But he did maintain, most emphatically, that human behavior admits of improvement. It can be controlled and directed not only for the benefit of the individual but also for the good of society. The vast bulk of what man does, thinks, and feels is socially determined. It is not inborn or instinctive but springs from association with other men. The conclusion follows that it can be shaped and directed by education.

Dewey had strong hopes for the future of American democracy. But he insisted that its survival depended upon *favorable* views of man's capabilities. "Democracy," he argued, "has always been allied with humanism, with faith in the potentialities of human nature." We cannot save ourselves by "rearming morally." We must find out how all the components of our existing culture are operating and then see to it that wherever needed they be modified in order to make them more effective instruments for liberating the possibilities inherent in all of us. To condemn any group of human beings as unworthy of respect and confidence is to open the door for the destruction of democracy. Intolerance begins when criticism is directed at a particular group and is supported by people who suggest or insinuate reasons why that group is not worthy of decent treatment. "But the underlying attitude is one of fundamental distrust of human nature." From limited beginnings it spreads until it

Half Dome, Yosemite, one of the majestic scenes of America. *United Air Lines*

becomes tantamount to the doctrine that no group of persons has any intrinsic rights whatever, except such as may be useful to the dominant group's ambitions and interests. "An anti-humanist attitude is the essence of every form of intolerance." [50] In the light of what is happening in South Africa today, and in many parts of our own country, no words were more truly spoken.

Despite a general predominance of optimism, it would be a mistake to assume that our nation's view of the future has always been suffused with sunshine and sweetness. America has had her Cassandras as well as her prophets of progress. Such was particularly the case during the early history of the country. To a large extent the explanation can be traced to the influence of Calvinism, with its doctrine of the total and innate depravity of man's nature. Even men who had no affiliation or direct contact with Calvinist churches could not entirely escape the overshadowing effects of the Genevan Reformer's teachings. For example, Benjamin Franklin, in a letter to Tom Paine, urging that he burn one of his more heterodox essays, asked him to consider how great a portion of mankind consists of weak and ignorant men and women—who have need of the motives of religion to restrain them from vice and to support their virtue. "If men are so wicked *with religion*," he asked, "what would they be if without it?" [51]

Although John Adams had misgivings and doubts about "frigid John Calvin" and his doctrines, he himself wrote in as lugubrious a fashion as any Puritan concerning the frailties of human flesh. "The first want of man," he grumbled, "is his dinner, and the second want his girl." He complained in a letter to John Taylor that if one gave political power to the common people, they would vote all property out of the hands of the aristocrats. Men are by nature indolent, selfish, cruel, jealous, craving of luxury, and addicted to intrigue, he wrote. Democracy would be impossible even if it were desirable. The masses do not really long for equality. They kiss the feet of those above them and trample the fingers of those beneath. Every society inevitably tends toward oligarchy. No sooner do the common people triumph than a minority appears among them to seize the reins of power. There never was a democracy that did not prepare the way for its own destruction.

No gathering resounded with more doleful animadversions on the nature and destiny of man than the Constitutional Convention of 1787. Such expressions characterized not only the advocates of concentrated government, like Hamilton and Madison, but also the members with more democratic leanings and even those who condemned the Constitution in its final form. Franklin perceived a "natural inclination in mankind to kingly government." The masses prefer this to aristocracy. They would rather have one tyrant than five hundred. For this reason he feared that the government of the United States might, in future times, "end in a monarchy."[52] James Wilson feared a dissolution of the government "from the legislature swallowing up all the other powers." He pointed out that after the overthrow of Charles I in England a "more pure and unmixed tyranny sprang up in the parliament than had ever been exercised by the monarch."[53] George Mason was in doubt whether the new system would end in monarchy or in "a tyrannical aristocracy," but he was sure that it would be one or the other.[54] Fears and suspicions of the most diverse and curious types seemed to obsess the minds of the delegates. They feared that the legislative would draw everything into its "impetuous vortex." They were alarmed lest foreign governments send over their "tools" to capture seats in Congress and carry on machinations among the people. So great was James Wilson's fear of both popular and legislative selection of the President that he proposed an electoral college made up of members of Congress chosen by lot. It was left to George Mason, however, to cap the climax by objecting to that "unnecessary and dangerous officer, the Vice-President, who for want of other employment is made president of the Senate, thereby dangerously blending the executive and legislative powers," and, in addition, giving to one of the states an unjust pre-eminence over the others.[55]

In the light of such rooted suspicions of human character, it was natural that most of the Fathers should take a dim view of the future of the nation. Unlike some of their contemporaries in Europe, they subscribed to no doctrine of permanent progress. Several saw dangerous signs of impending decay in the growth of a proletariat, which they considered inevitable in the United States. The city mob, they believed, had undermined the stability of the Roman Republic and had provided the support for demagogues who eventually destroyed it. A similar danger awaited every republic. In the Philadelphia Convention, John Dickinson and Gouverneur Morris predicted that the time was approaching when America would abound with propertyless multitudes, who would receive their sustenance from their employers. To win their support, politicians would flatter them and appeal to their jealousies and hatreds and thereby bring on civil disturbances.

Of all the Fathers, Madison was probably the one most seriously disturbed by the proletarian danger. With a population which would double itself in twenty years, it would be simply impossible, he argued, for all the inhabitants of the United States to obtain a living from the soil. The majority would flock into the cities and become the tools and dupes of their capitalist employers. They would no longer vote or even express their opinions as free men, but would obey the dictates of those to whom they owed their livelihood. Always on the thin edge which separates privation from comfort, they would secretly sigh for a more equal distribution of life's blessings. The result would be the rise of factions, of sufficient strength to gain control of the government and to trample upon the rights of the more prosperous minority. The latter would attempt to retaliate, and the ensuing disorders would duplicate the conditions which marked the destruction of ancient republics.[56]

Except for the darkest days of the Civil War, American sentiment during the greater part of the nineteenth century reflected an almost universal feeling of optimism. Emerson seems to have set the predominant trend when he proclaimed that our civilization was yet "only at the cock-crowing and the morning star." [57] Only a few bilious critics like Herman Melville and Nathaniel Hawthorne expressed discordant notes. At the end of the century, however, the depression of the 1890's and the Spanish-American War brought a keener awareness of portents and dangers. William Graham Sumner wrote of *The Conquest of the United States by Spain*. Edwin L. Godkin lamented the rise of Populism, with its "anarchistic" creed, and saw nothing but impending disaster in the obscene clamor of the mob for war and colonial conquests.

But the most doleful views of the years ahead were penned by the philosophical historian Henry Adams. Frightened by the effects of war, depression, and possible revolution upon his investments, Adams became almost hysterical. He lived in dread of an imperialistic war among the Great Powers that would result in the collapse of civilization. He feared anarchism and socialism and rejoiced that he would be dead before he could be ruled by the trade unions of the twentieth century. He wavered between fears that Russia would disintegrate and drag the Western world down with her, or that she would conquer and organize China into a colossus of natural wealth and cheap labor with which the free nations could not compete. As he grew older, his attitudes became more and more pathological. In 1906 he wrote that he "loathed mankind." Four years later he fulminated against the Jews and wailed that he couldn't go out of his cheap garret in Paris "without being throttled by some infernal socialist, levelling, humanitarian regulation which is intended to kill me and to keep some syphilitic abortion alive." [58]

Although far removed from the fatalism, to say nothing of the billingsgate, of Henry Adams, the jurist Oliver Wendell Holmes must also be numbered among those who had reservations as to the resplendent future of America. Justice Holmes never joined the chorus of Cassandras who saw disaster stalking the United States behind almost every event, but he was too much of a realist to indulge in predictions of a golden future. In the main he may be described as a cynic and a skeptic, despite the fact that he often found himself on the side of the oppressed and underprivileged. Though popularly regarded as a liberal or even as a radical, his departures from orthodoxy were largely confined to the field of civil liberties and to the belief that the wisdom of legislatures is just as dependable as that of the courts in determining what is good for society. He subscribed to a kind of Social Darwinism or struggle for existence and survival of the fittest among ideas, doctrines, institutions, and nations. The victors in this struggle merit approval, not because they are right in any absolute or ideal sense, but because their triumph is a sign and a token that they are more practical or useful than their competitors. He admitted that when young he used to say that truth was the majority vote of that nation that could lick all the other nations, and it is questionable that he ever advanced very far beyond this position.

In his underlying philosophy as revealed in his letters, Justice Holmes was fundamentally conservative and even defeatist. He had no faith in panaceas and doubted that men could do much by their own efforts to divert the movement of events. In his view the Sherman Act was "a humbug based on economic ignorance and incompetence," and he denied that the Interstate Commerce Commission was "a fit body to be entrusted with rate-making." [59] He was as

callous as any of the classical economists in admonishing the laboring man that "eternal hard work" was the price of a living. The
complaint that wealth was badly distributed and the clamor for
equality left him unmoved. He argued that the masses were already
getting their just entitlement, that in fact they were getting almost
everything, and that the luxuries of the few were "a drop in the
bucket"—not 1 per cent, he guessed, of the total production. He
could think of no better advice to give to socialists than that they
should quit tinkering with the institution of property and take life
in hand and try to build a better race. In his judgment Malthus
was right, and no one could hope for social or economic progress
in the face of "increased and unchecked propagation." [60]

The beliefs of a people in their destiny and greatness do not,
like Jonah's gourd, come up in a night and perish in a night. Instead, they have roots which lie buried deep in the history of the
past and in the economic and cultural conditions which mold a
nation's development. America was, of course, a nation of immigrants from the very beginning. They came to her shores for a
variety of reasons. Some expected to pick up gold from the hills and
valleys. Others were brought over as indentured servants, remaining
as permanent residents after completing their service. But a great
many more migrated thither to escape religious oppression. With
the exception of the followers of Roger Williams, few believed in
religious freedom. Not even the benevolent William Penn would
accord full privileges to atheists, Catholics, and Jews. The freedom
the immigrants demanded for themselves they were not willing
to grant to others who strayed in important particulars from the
path of orthodoxy. But the salient fact about these religious refugees
is that they were men of strong convictions. The Calvinists among
them, at least, conceived of themselves as the veritable instruments
of Providence in effectuating the plan of the universe. With its
abundance of land, vast resources, and stimulating climate, America
seemed like a Land of Promise hidden away by God until, in His
own good time, it was ready to be occupied by His Chosen People.
Here under divine guidance and protection they would work to
bring light and salvation to the rest of the earth.

Whether emanating from divine or earthly sources, the idea of a
call to greatness has not remained a mere wish-fulfillment in Ameri-

can minds. Instead, it has been regarded as an attainable goal. It is a prize within reach, and anyone who seeks to confine it within bounds is a traitor to our national ideals. Americans have always thought and dreamed in large and expansive terms. Our folk heroes have been Paul Bunyans and Davy Crocketts, whose deeds were prodigies of strength and valor. Though the former is now a mere legend of the literati and the latter a hero for juveniles, the nation still thinks of its progress in the future as measurable only by seven-league boots. We not only dream of voyaging beyond the earth's atmosphere but actually plan to do so, and to establish earth satellites which will enable us to command the globe. We spend billions of dollars on the creation of bombs of such devastating power that a single one will destroy a whole city. At the same time we envisage the replacement of our fossil fuels by the limitless resources of atomic energy. It is confidently predicted that atomic power will not only propel our ships and planes but that, supplemented perhaps by solar energy, it will heat and cool our homes, refrigerate our foods, make fresh water out of the briny deep, and provide the energy for draining swamps and irrigating vast Saharas. We still have our pessimists, as we have always had, but they are chiefly novelists, playwrights, and poets. Our statesmen, scientists, and men of affairs are made of more buoyant stuff.

It is of no small significance that America has never produced a Schopenhauer. Her most distinctive philosophers, from Ralph Waldo Emerson to John Dewey, have looked at the world with confidence and hope. It is significant also that the revolt against the fatalistic gloom of Calvinism went farther in America than in any of the countries of Europe. The Old World fathered Arminianism, but it was left to the New to enlarge this into the Great Awakening, with its emphasis upon freedom of the will, the ennoblement of the common man, and the capacity of even the humblest sinner to gain salvation through mystic communion with God. The influence of this and similar movements has been so great that the major elements of Calvinist fundamentalism have been obliterated from American Christianity. Even those churches most directly descended from the Genevan Reformer bear little doctrinal resemblance to the ancestral root. Such sects as the Unitarians and Universalists, the latter especially, with their insistence that ultimately all will be saved, likewise give testimony to our predominantly optimistic temper.

The American idea of mission remains a grandiose conception. In the minds of some of its apostles it has reflected a desire to educate, to liberate, or to improve the world. They have thought of America as the discoverer of great truths that will set men free and as the inventor and practitioner of a way of life far surpassing all others in possibilities for justice and happiness. A few have been impressed by the responsibilities and dangers involved in a role of world leadership. A much greater number have rejoiced in the sense of power and importance conveyed by the idea of a Manifest Destiny. For them the Mission of America is synomymous with a will to dominate, to play the part of a New Rome, to make the next hundred years the American Century with all the pursuit of self-aggrandizement that that name implies.

NOTES TO CHAPTER ONE

1. Deuteronomy 14:2.
2. *The Republic,* Jowett trans. (New York: The Dial Press, n.d.), pp. 206-09.
3. *The Politics,* Jowett trans. (New York: The Colonial Press, 1899), p. 2.
4. M. Frederick Nelson, *Korea and the Old Orders in Eastern Asia* (Baton Rouge, La.: Louisiana State University Press, 1945), pp. 11-16.
5. Sir John Maynard, *Russia in Flux* (New York: The Macmillan Co., 1948), pp. 92-96.
6. Chester Bowles, "The 'Brown Man's Burden' Analyzed," *New York Times Magazine,* September 5, 1954.
7. Bird Wilson, ed., *The Works of James Wilson* (Philadelphia: The Lorenzo Press, 1804), I, 4-5.
8. Albert E. Bergh, ed., *The Writings of Thomas Jefferson* (Washington: Thomas Jefferson Memorial Assoc., 1907), XVII, 123-24.
9. *The American Republic: Its Constitution, Tendencies and Destiny* (New York: P. O'Shea, 1866), p. 392.
10. *New York* (New York: William Farquar Payson, 1930), p. 38.
11. *Orations and Speeches on Various Occasions* (Boston: Little, Brown and Co., 1870), I, 41-42.
12. *The Works of Daniel Webster* (Boston: Little, Brown and Co., 1869), II, 212.
13. *Complete Prose Works* (Boston: Small, Maynard and Co., 1898), pp. 239, 313-14.
14. *Seventy Years of Life and Labor, an Autobiography* (New York: E. P. Dutton and Co., 1925), I, 23.
15. *Congressional Record,* 66th Cong., 1st Session, LVIII, 4755 (1919).
16. Thomas A. Bailey, *A Diplomatic History of the American People* (New York: F. S. Crofts and Co., 1950), p. 520.
17. *Letters to a Chinese Official, Being a Western View of Eastern Civilization* (New York: McClure, Phillips and Co., 1906), pp. 78-79.
18. E. E. Morison, ed., *The Works of Theodore Roosevelt* (New York: Charles Scribner's Sons, 1925), XV, 341.

19. Henry R. Luce, *The American Century* (New York: Farrar and Rinehart, 1941), pp. 36, 39.
20. *The American Choice* (New York: Reynal and Hitchcock, 1940), pp. 49-50. (Quoted by permission of Harcourt, Brace and Company.)
21. *Soviet Asia Mission,* with the collaboration of Andrew J. Steiger (New York: Reynal and Hitchcock, 1946), p. 212.
22. "The American Destiny," *Life,* VI (June 5, 1939), 73.
23. *U. S. War Aims* (Boston: Little, Brown and Co., 1944), pp. 209-10.
24. *Ibid.,* p. 209.
25. Philip S. Foner, ed., *The Complete Writings of Thomas Paine* (New York: The Citadel Press, 1945), I, 21.
26. C. F. Adams, ed., *The Works of John Adams, Second President of the United States* (Boston: Little, Brown and Co., 1856), I, 66.
27. L. H. Butterfield, ed., *Letters of Benjamin Rush* (Princeton: Princeton University Press, 1951), I, 239.
28. Max Farrand, ed., *Records of the Federal Convention* (New Haven: Yale University Press, 1911), I, 451.
29. R. W. Emerson, *Complete Works,* Riverside ed. (New York: Houghton Mifflin Co., 1883-88), XI, 279; Richard K. Cralle, ed., *The Works of John C. Calhoun* (New York: D. Appleton and Co., 1856), II, 152.
30. *Writings,* Centenary ed. (Boston: American Unitarian Assoc., 1907-16), V, 261.
31. Letter to Mrs. Eliza P. Gurney, Sept. 4, 1864, in John G. Nicolay and John Hay, eds., *The Complete Works of Abraham Lincoln* (New York: Francis D. Tandy Co., 1905), X, 215-16.
32. M. B. Schnapper, ed., *The Truman Program* (Washington: Public Affairs Press, 1948-49), pp. 31 32.
33. *The American Republic,* pp. 3-5.
34. *Ibid.,* pp. 434-35.
35. From *The Meaning of the Times and Other Speeches* by Albert J. Beveridge, copyright © 1908, 1936, used by special permission of the publishers, The Bobbs-Merrill Company, Inc., Indianapolis, pp. 84-85.
36. Jonathan Elliot, ed., *The Debates in the Several State Conventions on the Adoption of the Federal Constitution* (Washington: Printed by and for the editor, 1863), IV, 319-20.
37. *Ibid.,* II, 424.
38. J. C. Hamilton, ed., *The Works of Alexander Hamilton* (New York: J. F. Trow, 1850-51), II, 329.
39. *Orations and Speeches,* I, 169-70.
40. *Literary and Historical Miscellanies* (New York: Harper and Brothers, 1865), p. 516; *History of the Formation of the Constitution of the United States of America* (New York: D. Appleton and Co., 1882), pp. 366-67.
41. Henry Adams, ed., *The Writings of Albert Gallatin* (Philadelphia: J. B. Lippincott Co., 1879), III, 581-82.
42. George E. Baker, ed., *The Works of William H. Seward* (New York: Redfield, 1853-54), III, 496.
43. *Literary and Historical Miscellanies,* p. 434.
44. *Triumphant Democracy or Fifty Years' March of the Republic* (New York: Charles Scribner's Sons, 1886), pp. 1-2, 10-11, 196, 314-15.
45. *Complete Lectures* (Philadelphia: David McKay Co., 1935), pp. 34, 206.
46. "The War in Europe," *Harper's Weekly,* LIX (August 15, 1914), 153.

47. "The Suddenness of War," *The Independent,* LXXV (September 18, 1913), 681, 682.
48. E. M. Burns, *David Starr Jordan: Prophet of Freedom* (Stanford, Calif.: Stanford University Press, 1953), p. 34.
49. "Government and Law," in Charles A. Beard, ed., *A Century of Progress* (New York: Harper and Brothers, 1932), p. 232.
50. *Freedom and Culture* (New York: G. P. Putnam's Sons, 1939), pp. 125-27.
51. John Bigelow, ed., *The Complete Works of Benjamin Franklin* (New York: G. P. Putnam's Sons, 1887), IX, 355.
52. Farrand, ed., *Records,* I, 85.
53. *Ibid.,* II, 301.
54. *Ibid.,* II, 652.
55. *Ibid.,* II, 639.
56. *Ibid.,* I, 422-23; II, 203-04; Elliot, ed., *Debates,* III, 87.
57. *Essays* (New York: A. L. Burt, n.d.), II, 214.
58. Newton Arvin, ed., *The Selected Letters of Henry Adams* (New York: Farrar, Straus and Young, 1951), II, 391-92, 393, 466, 541-42.
59. Mark DeWolf Howe, ed., *The Holmes-Pollock Letters* (Cambridge: Harvard University Press, 1941), I, 163.
60. Letter to Dr. Wu, quoted in Max Lerner, *The Mind and Faith of Justice Holmes* (Boston: Little, Brown and Co., 1946), p. 428.

Chapter Two

The National Heritage

Peoples as active and as devoted to material triumphs as Americans generally have been are seldom given to contemplation or self-analysis. Such pursuits are regarded as a waste of time and as fit only for visionaries and impractical idealists. Yet nearly every people with a conviction of glorious destiny has sought to find a rational basis for believing in its purpose or mission. In what sense is it a peculiar people? What attributes mark it off from other nations similarly situated and apparently with like advantages? What factors in its background or heritage endow it with a unique place in the scheme of things? These are the questions we can expect the leaders of any such nation to raise, and rarely have they been left unanswered.

From the time of the Revolution articulate representatives of our own country have sought to probe the hidden sources of the national character and to wonder upon what meat the nation has fed that it has grown so great. Some have traced the attributes of the people to an Anglo-Saxon or British ancestry, others to a Puritan heritage, and still others to factors of climate, topography, pure air, extent of territory, or mysterious causes yet unknown. All who have written on the subject agree that Americans have peculiarities differing in kind or in degree from the qualities of all other peoples. The renowned commentator on American democracy, Alexis de Tocqueville, thought he could discover these characteristics in the very physiognomy of the American people.

A PECULIAR PEOPLE

Since most people discover the characteristics of their nation in the mirror of their own virtues, it is not surprising that ideas of the special qualities of the American people should vary considerably. Yet an underlying uniformity is also discernible. From the Founding Fathers to Harry S. Truman and Dwight D. Eisenhower writers and orators have perceived the genius of the American nation to consist in energy, initiative, inventiveness, self-reliance, and common sense. Thomas Paine thought that his fellow citizens possessed a greater "fund of ability" along these lines than any three million people in any other part of the universe. As a result, the per capita well-being in the United States exceeded by far that in the rest of the world.[1] Jefferson wrote to John Adams on February 28, 1796, that there never was "a finer canvass presented to work on" than his countrymen, all of them engaged in industrious toil, "independent in their circumstances, enlightened as to their rights, and firm in their habits of order and obedience to the laws." Almost a hundred and fifty years later, President Harry S. Truman informed his Democratic cohorts at the Jackson Day dinner that he and they had nothing to fear if they relied upon "the energy, the resourcefulness, and the common sense of the American people." These qualities alone would be enough to defeat the "special interests" in their attempts to undermine the general welfare. A few months afterward Dwight D. Eisenhower, then only a potential candidate for the Presidency, told the audience at the *Herald-Tribune* Forum that the dividing line between government and the citizen must be located at such a point as to provide "full play to the American qualities of initiative, courage, inventiveness," which, he declared, had given the nation a productivity "without a parallel in the world."

That there would be numerous modifications of the initiative-energy-independence theme goes without saying. James Wilson enumerated the superlative qualities of the "children of America" as "activity, perseverance, industry, laudable emulation, docility in acquiring information, firmness in adversity, and patience and magnanimity under the greatest hardships." From such materials, he exclaimed, "what a respectable national character may be raised."[2] To equate energy, industry, firmness, and emulation with self-reliance and independence of government was also a common tendency. Emerson, of course, was noted for this. The wise man, he taught, does not need the state, and with his appearance in large numbers, it ceases to exist. "Every actual State is corrupt. Good men must not obey the laws too well." [3] The argument was often advanced that the greatness of America was achieved in spite of government, not because of it. Henry David Thoreau insisted that the government of the United States "never of itself furthered any enterprise," except by the alacrity with which it withdrew from the scene. Governments, he said, do not "keep the country free." They

The most precious documents of our national heritage, the original Constitution and the Declaration of Independence, on display in the National Archives, Washington. *National Archives*

do not educate. They do not conquer the frontier. Every achievement for which the nation can take credit has been a product of the "character inherent in the American people." [4]

The reader, perhaps, would expect such arguments from Thoreau. They bore no essential difference, however, from the conclusion of William Allen White, liberal editor of the twentieth century. "Free institutions," he avowed, "do not make free men, but . . . free men make free institutions." All that we have and can ever hope to have, he implied, is the "product of our national character." [5] Wendell Phillips refused even to give credit to the Federal Union for the prosperity of American commerce. The genius and energy of the "Yankee race," he contended, were the real parents of commerce and the fountain of wealth, much more than the Union. This race would always be the brain of North America, "united or disunited," and, "harnessing the elements, steam and lightning," to its "car of conquest" would double the value of every prairie acre and garner the wealth of the Western Hemisphere. [6] Although advocating a generous measure of government intervention for the public welfare, Woodrow Wilson nevertheless paid tribute to the capacity of the American people to shift for themselves. He thought that the striking fact about a great country like the United States was that "if the Government neglected everything, the people would do it." They did not need governmental direction; they had "plenty of brains to get together and do for themselves." At any rate, that is what he told the National Grange, on November 14, 1916, urging the production of bigger crops.

Other observers and leaders found the distinctive qualities of the American people to consist in all sorts of peculiar traits. For Henry Clay, as one might expect, the uniqueness of America was founded on the principle of "compromise and concession." This principle gave birth to the Constitution and ever afterward conducted the nation in its onward march "to glory and renown." [7] James Fenimore Cooper discovered that Americans excelled in humanity, in general civility, in hospitality, in an aptitude for ordinary pursuits, and in "an absence of the sophisms that beset older and more artificial systems." [8]

The Hoosier Progressive Albert J. Beveridge seemed to think that it was the quality of "go-ahead" in the make-up of the American that most distinguished him from other "races." Curiously, though, it gave him an affinity with the Russian, for the Russian also, according to Beveridge, likes "to get things done." [9] Therefore, there is "a natural friendship on the part of Russians for Americans." But Beveridge also applauded his countrymen for their exploring, colonizing, and "administrating" qualities. They are the most "self-governing" people in the world. They possess these traits from "irresistible impulse, from instinct, from racial and unwritten laws" inherited from their forefathers. Their archetype is the American businessman, whom Beveridge admired for his "exhaustless initiative," "indomitable will," and "fruitful genius." American men of business constitute the "mightiest force for material greatness in the Nation and the world." They can also constitute the "mightiest force for righteousness." As soon as the businessman understands that he is really "the trustee of the people's welfare," he makes himself "the high priest of the religion of humanity, an agent of God Himself." [10]

Other progressives and liberals defined the spirit of America in more idealistic terms, but at the same time without divorcing it from the practical. Woodrow Wilson proclaimed that it was "something more than the old, immemorial Saxon spirit of liberty from which it sprung." It had been given a more austere and practical twist by the task of conquering a wilderness and covering a vast continent "with a single free and stable polity." It was, above all, "a hopeful and confident spirit—progressive, unpedantic, unprovincial, unspeculative, unfastidious; regardful of law, but as using it, not as being used by it or dominated by any formalism whatever; in a sense, unrefined, because full of rude force; but prompted by large and generous motives, and often as tolerant as it is resolute." [11]

In the first blush of the New Deal, Rexford G. Tugwell, one of the original Brain Trusters, described the core of American character as a kind of Promethean defiance of Fate. "We will not do what we do not want to do," he asserted, "and coercion cannot make us." Americans have a precious inventiveness which gets them out of difficulties. They have a "saving irreverence of authority." Strangely, he then added that no one with the slightest feeling for history would try to impose upon the American people any scheme of regimentation. They must be allowed to think and plan for themselves and to use law, government, and social organization as mere instruments through which their "characteristic actions" can find expression. [12]

The American who developed the most extensive rationalization of his nation's peculiarities was the Social Gospeler of the 1880's, Josiah Strong. Like most of his compatriots, he found these peculiarities to be energy, aggressiveness, perseverance, inventiveness, and a genius for colonizing and expansion. The explanation he posited for these qualities was partly biological and partly environmental. Most of them were inherent traits of the "Anglo-Saxon race," but the "marked characteristics" of this "race" were being accentuated in America to a greater degree than anywhere else. For one reason, the climate was favorable. It was energizing and invigorating. Strong quoted one of the early Pilgrims who wrote that "a sup of New England air" was "better than a whole flagon of English ale." America had abundant resources and a whole continent to exploit. As a consequence, her people were better fed and a greater fluidity of classes prevailed among them. With so vast a territory to move about in, no rigid social stratification could come into being. Everyone was free to make of himself whatever his abilities permitted.

Not only the plethora of resources but the scarcity of labor to develop them had a profound effect in shaping the American character. Labor shortages placed a premium on inventiveness. Machinery consequently multiplied "as if governed by a law of natural increase." The American mind persistently strove for short cuts, albeit they involved "tunneling a mountain or severing an isthmus." Every invention stimulated another invention, and each chemical triumph necessitated a mechanical contrivance to carry its principles into application. Though inventiveness has never been a monopoly of any one people, it distinguishes pre-eminently the Anglo-Saxon, and "Yankee ingenuity" has given to America the highest rank of all. It has enabled this nation to take the lead in money-making, which Strong regarded as another of the cardinal virtues of Anglo-Saxons. Although England was still the richest nation of Europe, America had already outstripped her in the race after wealth, and the marvels achieved thus far would pale into insignificance when compared with the opulence of the future.[13]

Somewhat similar to Strong's environmental explanations was James Russell Lowell's theory of the prevalence of equality in America. Though he admitted that the theory of equality was as old, "among men of English blood," as Jack Cade's rebellion, he denied that it had ever been "practically conceived" by the men who asserted it. Only on the American frontier, where civilized men were brought face to face with nature and compelled to rely mainly on themselves, did the conception of equality acquire the status of a dominant ideal and come to be embodied in the practical relations of men with their neighbors. For a century and a half Americans had the benefit of an apprenticeship in democracy which stimulated self-help and "necessitated helpfulness for others and mutual dependence upon them." "Not without reason did 'help' take the place of 'servant' in the American vocabulary." [14]

THE HERITAGE FROM BRITAIN

A notable fact in the history of thought and culture in the United States is the prevalence of veneration for Britain. To one unacquainted with our past it might almost seem that the American Revolution was a figment of the imagination, that the Thirteen Colonies had never separated from the Mother Country, and that devotion to England and her institutions is as firmly rooted on this side of the Atlantic as in the British Isles themselves. Except for the period of the Revolution and a short time thereafter, admiration for the British and their ways has been almost endemic. De Tocqueville gave currency to the idea of the exclusively British origin of the American nation as early as 1835. Thereafter, with the exception of leaders of Irish origin like Matthew and Henry C. Carey, the vast majority of Americans of the upper strata, at least, cast halos of shining light around the heads of the British. One, however, who refused to be taken in by the dominant hagiolatry was Wendell Phillips. Though a patrician and a descendant of the purest strains of British ancestry, he chided his fellow Americans for looking with "servile admiration" to the institutions their fathers had repudiated. He complained that American literature was but a pale reflection of English models, and he feared that democracy in the United States could never come to a full fruition so long as the literature which constituted the American intellectual diet was "impregnated with English ideas, and every student and every thinker breathed the atmosphere of London." Not until the principles of democracy should enter Temple Bar, he insisted, would Britain be worthy of admiration as the "fount of ideas" for America.[15]

Not all the Americans who celebrated the glories of the British heritage were themselves of English ancestry. Francis Lieber, though born in Berlin and associated in his early life with the patriotic movement for the regeneration of Prussia after her defeat by Napoleon, nevertheless lauded British achievements more ardently than he ever did those of his native land. He hailed the "Anglican race" as one "whose obvious task it is, among other proud and sacred tasks, to rear and spread civil liberty over vast regions in every part of the earth, on continent and isle." It was necessary that Americans, in order to be equipped to solve the problems of their country, should descend from this Anglican race, "should begin as persecuted colonists, severed from the mother country and yet loving it with all their heart and all their soul." American liberty is simply an offshoot from Anglican liberty. It is founded upon the original British achievements of trial by jury, representative government, the common law, self-taxation, the supremacy of the law, and subordination of the military to the civil authority. To be sure, Americans have added some features of their own: federalism, the separation of church and state, "and a more popular or democratic cast of the whole polity," but the fundamental elements of American democracy are mainly British. Throughout his long life in the United States, from 1827 to 1872, Lieber never paid more than casual respects to German institutions, perhaps partly for the reason that, as a young man, he incurred the disfavor of the Prussian government and was twice arrested on suspicion of dangerous intentions.[16]

Even more enthusiastic than Lieber in his admiration for the accomplishments and ideals of the English was the Scotsman Andrew Carnegie. A child of extreme poverty whose father was a Chartist and an agitator against the Corn Laws, the future steel manufacturer had little in his early life to make him enamored of things British. But throughout his long residence in America he retained a curious love for both England and Scotland. Doubtless it stemmed partly from his conviction that the English-speaking nations were the hope of the world. He believed that England and the United States had advanced much farther than other nations, and he cherished the ideal of cementing them closely together as a means of preserving international peace.

It should be noted, though, that Carnegie's ardor for England did not extend to everything British. He loved the English people and English cultural achievements, but he was opposed to monarchy and to hereditary aristocracy. At the height of his career he refused a title offered to him by King Edward VII. In keeping with this, he called for the democratization of England along the lines already adopted by the United States. "When the people reign in the old home as they do in the new," he said, "the two nations will be one people, and the bonds which unite them the world combined shall not break asunder." Such a union would be no more than proper, he argued, for America was indeed a child of the Mother Country. Except for a few Dutch and French, the seed planted upon American soil was "wholly British." Thenceforth the American people "remained loyal to this noble strain" and can still be described as "four-fifths British." It is fortunate that this is so, for the British

"The Mississippi in Time of Peace." Lithograph by Currier and Ives, from a drawing by F. F. Palmer, 1865. *Courtesy Harry T. Peters*

transmitted to America their vigor and enterprise, their talents for colonization, and their capacity for governing. As a result, the American people, descended though they are from the lower ranks of Britons, "have proved themselves possessors of a positive genius for political administration." [17]

Idolization of the heritage from Britain first became noticeable about 1830. It evidently bore some relationship to a growing national pride and to an awakening consciousness of a great future in store for the country. The pessimism of the Founding Fathers had been replaced by a bounding optimism which saw magnificent vistas opening up in the West, and in the expansion of industry and transportation. Great Britain and the United States were the two countries making the most rapid progress along these lines. Therefore, it was assumed that there must be a reason for it, and that that reason must lie in an affinity of the two peoples. Americans and Britons, it was argued, were really members of one family, with a relationship as close as that of children and parents. The only difference was that the children, with their superior advantages, would outstrip their parents. But it seemed natural to suppose that their inborn talents, at least, were derived from the British.

In view of the above, it is not surprising that the first Americans to acclaim the British heritage should have been the nationalist orators and statesmen of the 1830's and 1840's. A characteristic example was Edward Everett. Lauding the heroes of the Revolution, he took pains to disavow any intention of perpetuating hostility to England. England was the home of our forefathers, he asserted, and he professed his shame that Americans should "hang with passion" upon the words of Homer and Vergil and hearken without emotion to the nearer and plainer message of Shakespeare and Milton. True, our fathers were persecuted and provoked into violent rebellion; but the acts of injustice which led to the American Revolution were not perpetrated by England, but by "the English ministerial party of the day, and even a small circle within that party." The rights of America found steady and vigorous defenders in England. Not alone William Pitt, who was "glad America had resisted," but several members of the very ministry that imposed the stamp duties rose in the House of Lords and declared that they had no sympathy for measures proposed by the cabinet.

In another connection, however, the great Boston orator seemed to be saying that the injustices of some of Britain's rulers were acts of kindness to American citizens, albeit unintentional. Had our forefathers not been oppressed and persecuted, they might never have risen to the lofty heights that immortalize their progress; for it is a principle "borne out by the history of the great and powerful nations of the earth . . . that the best fruits and choicest action of the commendable qualities of the national character are to be found on the side of the oppressed few and not of the triumphant many." [18] By more than a hundred years Edward Everett seems to have anticipated Arnold J. Toynbee in developing the theory that "adversity" is a necessary stimulus to the progress of nations.

Everett's more famous contemporary, Daniel Webster, extolled the British inheritance in somewhat different terms but in equally orotund phrases. For more than a century before the settlement at Jamestown, he told his Massachusetts admirers, England had been unconsciously preparing herself, "under the providence of God," for the colonization of North America. She had been cultivating liberty and developing free institutions, and those were her priceless gifts to her sons and daughters who founded new homes for themselves across the Atlantic. The colonists who went out from England to America were a people already free. Whereas Spain descended upon the New World "in the armed and terrible image of her monarchy and her soldiery, England approached it in the winning and popular garb" of free institutions and regard for personal rights. "England transplanted liberty to America; Spain transplanted power." [19]

But Webster refused to admit that the totality of American freedom was derived from England. For reasons he was soon to specify, the British did not transmit all of their institutions to the colonies. "The jury came; the *habeas corpus* came; the testamentary power came; and the law of inheritance and descent came also," except for the rule of primogeniture, which either did not come at all, or was soon superseded by the rule of equal division among all the children. "But the monarchy did not come, nor the aristocracy, nor the church as an estate of the realm." The colonists' acceptance of Britain's gifts was selective. In the main, only those political institutions that conformed to the state of things in the New World were adopted. The others were either modified to make them conform or rejected. And it was not difficult to discover what this conformity involved. "A general social equality prevailed among the settlers, and an equality of political rights seemed the natural, if not the necessary consequence." What Frenchmen gained after bloody years of revolution, violence, and war, the English colonists in America gained "by simply changing their place." [20]

Victory for the North in the War Between the States gave the stamp of approval to the nationalist theories of Everett and Webster. It is not singular that the decades that followed should have witnessed an even more strident acclaim for British achievements.

The trend was fortified by the increasing popularity of racial theories. Under the influence of European doctrines of the superiority of a supposed Aryan race, Americans adopted the theory that the Anglo-Saxon branch of that race was the most gifted of all, and that every political achievement that enhanced the freedom of man could be credited to it. Since Americans and Britons were the foremost representatives of the Anglo-Saxon peoples, and since the latter had a much longer history than the former, it seemed axiomatic that the younger nation should reverence the accomplishments of the older, ancestral one.

It is an ironical fact that racism in America has been a gospel purveyed by liberals and progressives quite as much as by conservatives or reactionaries. We shall see that the racial *mystique* numbered among its adherents such crusaders for reform as Albert J. Beveridge, David Starr Jordan, and William Allen White, who believed in it independently of their attitudes toward Britain. It also attracted the allegiance of some earlier prophets who combined it with an ecstatic devotion to the culture and institutions of the ancestral homeland. Notable among them was George William Curtis, scion of the New England aristocracy and leader of the movement for civil service reform in the last quarter of the nineteenth century.

So enamored was Curtis of English ideals that he was ready to depreciate the attainments of his own countrymen. He advised patriotic Americans that they would do well to remember "that individual freedom seems almost surer and sturdier in England than here," and that they would be wise "to drink at those elder fountains." The Revolutionists who took up arms in 1775 were not fighting to achieve a complete separation from the Mother Country. They were struggling "to defend England against herself, to maintain the principles and traditions of English liberty." The farmers who fired the shots at Lexington and Concord "were the barons of Runnymede in a later day; and the victory at Yorktown was not so much the seal of a revolution as the pledge of continuing English progress." From England the people of the United States inherited nearly every element of their culture of lasting and distinctive value. The Declaration of Independence grew from the seed of Magna Charta. The mechanical ingenuity which produced the steamboat, the telegraph, and all our marvelous machinery was but the fruit of the inventive genius that gave birth to the steam engine and the factory system three thousand miles across the Atlantic. Representative government, trial by jury, the habeas corpus, and freedom of speech and the press are simply "the family heirlooms, the family diamonds, and they go wherever in the wide world go the family name and language and tradition." [21]

Several of the racial theorists of the late nineteenth century traced the political achievements of the English to remote beginnings among the ancient Germans. What Britain did was to bring these achievements to a full-rounded development and to pass them on to her sons and daughters in the New World. But this was no mean accomplishment. Primitive tribal assemblies had to be transformed into a representative parliament and elemental notions of individual freedom refined into charters and bills of rights. No other country but Britain could have done these things. She alone among the nations of Europe had maintained an uninterrupted development of free institutions for a thousand years. The reasons were partly geographic. In contrast with so many of the other countries of Western Europe, England had never been overrun by "fanatical Saracens or beastly Mongols." But to a large extent her progress could be attributed to the fact that her people had Aryan forebears. Germanic blood flowed in their veins and transmitted a heritage of freedom to successive generations, as the branches of a river convey silt from the uplands and deposit it in the valleys below. Such was the reasoning of the historian James K. Hosmer, of the political scientist John W. Burgess, and especially of the Social Darwinist John Fiske.

As a devout disciple of Herbert Spencer, interested in propagating the theories of historical evolution and the survival of the fittest among nations, John Fiske was determined to show that England represented the highest fulfillment of the Teutonic genius inherited from the Middle Ages. She was the only important nation to come out of the medieval crucible with her Teutonic self-government "substantially intact." Two "little spots" on the mainland, Holland and Switzerland, also preserved in purest form rustic Aryan democracy, but they were too small in size to exert much influence. They did, however, form federal unions, an achievement which must be regarded as one of the most significant in universal history.

But it was England alone that attained the political maturity necessary for the preservation and transmission of the heritage of democracy. The boundless vitality of the English enabled them to defeat the last of their great rivals in the French and Indian War and thereby to salvage nearly all of North America for people of their own race. Thenceforth there were two Englands in the world, Motherland and Daughterland, "alike prepared to work with might and main toward the political regeneration of mankind." The conquest of the North American continent by men of English race was unquestionably "the most prodigious event in the political annals of mankind." [22]

Theories of race superiority lent themselves exceedingly well to a justification of imperialism. We shall see that such was one of the cardinal purposes in the minds of Senator Benton of Missouri, Josiah Strong, Albert J. Beveridge, John W. Burgess, and William Allen White, who proclaimed it to be a sacred mission of the noble Aryans or at least of the politically gifted Germanic peoples to extend their civilization to the so-called inferior races.

An equally famous imperialist of the late nineteenth century, Alfred T. Mahan, was more specific. He discovered that in spite of the motley character of recent immigration, the political traditions and racial characteristics of the American people remained English. In particular, they had preserved the true spirit of English freedom, which included as its essential components liberty and law—"not one or the other, but both." This gave to the American nation a warrant for following in Britain's footsteps by extending her dominion to the outermost regions of the earth. As Rome incorporated the other nations of the Italian peninsula, America had already added to her inheritance, spreading and perpetuating everywhere "the foundation principles of free and good government." In her infancy she bordered only upon the Atlantic. In her youth her boundary was extended to the Gulf of Mexico. Her maturity found her upon the shore of the Pacific. But southward her expansion was blocked by the rights of a race completely alien, and to the north by a people of her own tradition. In the light of these facts, the philosophizing admiral asked, "Have we no right or no call to progress farther in any direction? Are there for us beyond the sea horizon none of those essential interests, of those evident dangers, which impose a policy and confer rights?" [23] In view of the admiral's beliefs in the inherent superiority of English blood, there could be little doubt as to his answers.

THE PURITAN HERITAGE

For the most part, the philosophers who found in Puritanism the source of everything good in America were the same men who extolled the heritage from Britain. To a degree this can be attributed to pride in their English ancestry, but it cannot be taken as the sole explanation. Some, at least, acknowledged a broader and earlier source of Puritan virtues. George Bancroft, for example, hailed John Calvin as the father of popular education, the originator of free schools. He sought to identify William Penn as a disciple of the Huguenots and maintained that the ships that brought the first colonists to New Amsterdam were filled with Calvinists. He was prepared to argue that anyone declining to honor the memory and respect the influence of John Calvin knew "but little of the origin of American liberty." [24] At the same time, Bancroft's adoration of Puritanism bordered upon religious worship. The Puritan in his eyes was the incarnation of all the virtues that ennoble a human being and set him apart from his fellows. Every believer who had experienced the raptures of devotion regarded himself as one chosen by God. For him the Almighty had appointed a Savior to die and rise again for the benefit of the elect. How could he help respecting himself, whom God had chosen and redeemed? "As he walked the earth, his heart was in the skies." He could no more become the slave of a despot than he could of a priest. If he feared the powers of darkness and of hell, he feared no power on earth. It is not strange, according to Bancroft, that "the issue of Puritanism was popular sovereignty." [25]

Most of the later admirers of the Puritans were impressed more by the economic and social background than they were by the religious influences that shaped their development. They were likewise interested more in their political contributions. Edward Everett emphasized the hardships suffered by the American members of the sect—their "trials of wandering and exile, of the ocean, the winter, the wilderness, and the savage foe." These kept away from the faithful band all "patrician softness" and prevented any "effeminate nobility" from crowding into their ranks. [26] The researches of John Fiske convinced him that the Puritan settlers of New England were mainly descended from the "Old-English nobility or *thegnhood*" that had been pushed down into a secondary place by the Norman

A nevv and necessarie
Treatise of Nauigation con-
taining all the chiefest principles
of that Arte.

Lately collected out of the best Mo-
derne writers thereof by M. Blundeuile, and by him
reduced into such a plaine and orderly forme of
teaching as euerie man of a meane capacitie
may easily vnderstand the same.

They that goe downe to the Sea in ships, and occupie their
businesse in great waters: These men see the workes of the
Lord and his wonders in the deepe. Psalme, 107

A rare, contemporaneous woodcut of a ship of the *Mayflower* period.

conquerors and had emerged eventually as the backbone of England's strength, the stout gentry and independent yeomanry. The leaders of the New England migration were country gentlemen from these classes. A large proportion of them were graduates of universities. Even the rank and file were intelligent and prosperous, and no idle, shiftless, or disorderly folk were represented among them. Out of so select a body of colonists, distinguished as they were by sober restraint and "unflinching adherence to duty," no form of society other than one of freedom and equality could be expected to come, except perhaps "in case of a scarcity of arable land." To Fiske it was no more strange than it had been to Bancroft that immediately upon their arrival in New England, the settlers should have "proceeded to form for themselves a government as purely democratic as any that has ever been seen in the world." [27]

Fiske's older contemporary, George William Curtis, lauded the Puritan spirit as "the master influence of American civilization." Though he admired the religion of the Puritans and warned that the decay of that faith would blast the hopes of mankind, he was more keenly interested in their political legacy. In the inspiring air of the American continent, the spirit of Puritanism, he believed, had been modified and enlarged, so that government by sectaries became government by the people. "John Pym became James Otis." The modified Puritanism of America fired the Revolution. Puritan guns echoed at Bunker Hill, and the Puritan spirit was embodied in the Declaration of Independence. "It was to the Puritan idea that Cornwallis surrendered at Yorktown; and eighty-three years later, it was the Cavalier who again surrendered to the Puritan under the Appomattox apple-tree." Those stern, unyielding sons of Calvin, whom frivolous modern men sometimes disdain to honor, "were the indomitable vanguard of moral and political freedom. If they snuffled in prayer, they smote in fight; if they sang through their noses, the hymn they chanted was liberty; if they aimed at a divine monarchy, they have founded the freest, the most enlightened, the most prosperous, the most powerful republic in history." [28]

During the heyday of Progressivism, admiration for the Puritans seemed to swing back to praise for their religious and moral qualities. Perhaps this can be attributed to the fact that many of the Progressive leaders were moral idealists or reformers who had been shocked by the corruption and vice unearthed by such muckrakers as Lincoln Steffens and Upton Sinclair. A capital example was the bustling president of Stanford University, David Starr Jordan. Jordan traced his ancestry to Puritan forebears, and in his early life was deeply influenced by the bloodless asceticism of Emerson and Thoreau and by the towering intolerance of John Brown. When he went to California in 1891, he took his Puritanism with him and sought to transplant it on the tawny hills that slope down to the Pacific. The degree of his success may be questionable, but no one can doubt the intensity of his efforts. He strove to indoctrinate both faculty and students with the idea of total abstention from alcohol and tobacco and even from coffee and tea. "From the 'beer bust' of the college," he wrote, "to the red-light district of the town the way is short and straight, and thousands of young men find themselves ruined for life from a single night of excesses." [29] His reasons for frowning upon human frivolity were partly scientific. He alleged that stimulants like tobacco and coffee and depressants like alcohol "caused the nervous system to lie," gave a false sense of excitement or well-being, and thereby encouraged activity or indulgence when the body needed rest. But he justified other forms of asceticism which could hardly be reduced to a scientific explanation. Though he deplored the brutishness of some of the athletic sports of his time, he declared that a young man was safer on the football field than on the floor of a modern ballroom. The chastity of women he regarded as "society's most precious jewel," and he taught that the pure woman "will turn from the man who touches her hand in wantonness as she would turn from a rattlesnake." [30]

Jordan described the Puritan conscience as "the most precious political heritage of the republic and the backbone of American culture." Nearly all the great spokesmen for freedom in the country's history, he maintained, with the exception of Thomas Jefferson and James Madison, had Puritan blood in their veins. As examples he mentioned Thoreau, Emerson, Channing, Garrison, Wendell Phillips, James Russell Lowell, Oliver Wendell Holmes, and Charles W. Eliot. The Puritans derived their great power, Jordan argued, from the austerity of their practices. It was not their stiff-necked dogmatism that deserved praise but the fact that they were ready to resist whatever they thought wrong. Resistance augmented their strength of character and produced the only happiness worth pursuing. The modern man who would aspire to the same benefits

Statue of John Harvard, founder of Harvard College, 1636. *Standard Oil Co. (N. J.)*

must cultivate the Puritan's hatred of evil. His pattern of life must be as restricted as theirs, for it is still true that the road which leads to achievement in life is narrow and rocky, while the path which leads to failure and wretchedness is broad and flowery. "There is no real happiness that does not involve self-denial." [31]

But happiness to Jordan as to most other Puritans was almost synonymous with the fulfillment of personal ambition. Anything that stood in the way of this was *ipso facto* immoral. He frowned upon smoking, for instance, because he considered it a disguise for idleness. The person who smokes is frittering time away that he might otherwise use for a valuable purpose. Even such subjects as literature and art should be judged by the same standards of avoiding a waste of time and contributing to personal success. The twentieth century, Jordan thought, would have a superior culture, but the books it would publish would not be "idle books written for idle people." Instead of what is ordinarily classified as literature, the twentieth century would demand "the real thoughts of real men." [32]

Jordan's younger associate in the Progressive movement, Albert J. Beveridge, voiced no admiration for a Puritan background. This is not strange, for none of his ancestors had Puritan lineage. His paternal grandfather belonged to a Virginia family of slave-owners. The nearest approach to Puritan influence could be found in the fact that most of his paternal ancestors were of Scottish descent, and some at least were Presbyterians. But a much more important condition shaping Beveridge's mind in the direction of ideals similar to those of the Puritans was his personal success in overcoming the privations and hardships of his early life. His boyhood and youth were devoted to rugged toil on farms in Ohio and Illinois and to cutting and hauling lumber for the construction of railroads. From the age of twelve he worked regularly in the fields and at fifteen was placed in charge of a gang of lumbermen, whose respect he could command only by doing a full share of the manual labor. Yet in the midst of these austerities he found time for considerable reading, in such works as Emerson's essays, Gibbon's *Decline and Fall of the Roman Empire,* and the novels of Dickens, Scott, and George Eliot. He also managed to save nearly all of his nominal wages with a view to obtaining a college education. At the age of nineteen he entered Asbury (now DePauw) University with total assets of fifty dollars. He carried his trunk on his back through the streets of the town to his lodging place. In 1885 he was graduated from the university laden with all the honors and prizes that campus life afforded.

Senator Beveridge characterized the Puritan principle as "the very breath of life" of the American republic. The Puritan, he declared, was the foremost citizen of history. His destiny was to build free institutions, and to tear asunder the rotten fabric of civil abuses. At the same time, he had an instinct for governing. When he overthrew existing systems, his methods were more orderly than the conditions he attacked. Men have supposed that the Puritans set their course into the inky horizon because of their fanatical ambition for religious freedom. Beveridge preferred to believe that they "obeyed a divine impulse to found the everlasting commonwealth of liberty." He insisted that what America needed was a rebirth of Puritan virtues. The nation was suffering from the worship of Mammon, from "epicureanism," from public and private immorality, and from the decline of religion. The people were losing sight of the "eternal" and lavishing too much attention upon material success. Only the Puritan principle could save the country as it had saved England two centuries before.[nn]

Although Puritanism might seem to be the complete antithesis of the widespread revolt against Victorian standards that set in after World War I, the contradiction applies almost exclusively to the realm of sex morality. In the worship of business and personal achievement, the Puritan spirit is still regnant. Not many pay deference any longer in their actual conduct to frugality or self-denial, but few of the nation's pundits have ever spoken or written openly against such practices. Thrift, denial, sacrifice, and hardship have always been and continue to be extolled as the qualities that make a nation great and provide the keys to security and prosperity for individual citizens.

Only a small number of critical observers, mostly unorthodox, have suggested that perhaps the Puritan economic approach is outmoded. In the New Deal era Henry Wallace classified Puritan ideals as admirably adapted to a period of "rapidly expanding wealth production," but he doubted that they were as well suited to "wealth distribution and wealth consumption in line with the doctrines of the New Testament." Our need, he suggested, is not to learn how to compete with each other in a mad scramble for a limited supply of worldly goods but "to learn how to live with each other in abundance." [34]

When Henry Wallace was still a callow freshman at Iowa State College, another economic thinker published a book expounding in more elaborate fashion a similar conception of the anachronism of Puritan ideals. The title of the book was *The New Basis of Civilization,* and the author was Simon N. Patten. Nations, according to Patten, had lived long enough under conditions of poverty, privation, sacrifice, and hardship. Such conditions degraded men to the level of animals and lowered the tone of civilization. The time had arrived when a deficit economy should be replaced by an economy of surplus. Men must learn that the morality of sacrifice is the antithesis of progress, and that "cooperation can abolish poverty by saving men instead of spending them." Disease, insecurity, premature old age, starvation, and class conflict were the hastening ills of the period when surplus workers competed with each other for a limited number of jobs at pitiful wages. The remedy, he argued, was to increase opportunities for employment by procedures of social planning and thereby to enlarge the national income available for the purchase of goods. Income generates capital, and a rich environment is the cardinal stimulus to social progress. The surplus energy of the well-paid worker spills over into new desires and fresh enthusiasms. Some of these broaden and deepen and are eventually transformed into ideals of "goodness, of patriotism, of culture, and of art." When imperfect civilization frustrates and distorts the free play of pleasurable desires, "toil becomes a monstrous, incalculably evil thing; we call it drudgery, and the man condemned to it reverts to a lower kind of creature, unpliant, crudely limited in passions, early matured, and prematurely decayed." [35] It would be difficult to conceive of a more emphatic repudiation of the Puritan gospel of sacrifice, denial, and hard work as the regenerating forces in civilization. In this respect Patten's philosophy was almost unique in American history.

Americans have devoted much time and energy to rationalization of their idea of mission. And the most impressive result is the degree of unanimity that has prevailed among their more active spokesmen. This has been notably true with regard to the assumption of special attributes of the American character. Nearly every speaker and writer, whether liberal or conservative, has assigned the credit for our national superiority to such qualities as initiative, independ-

Engraving by Paul Revere, in the *New England Psalm-Singer or Chorister*, composed by William Billings, 1770. *William L. Clements Library, University of Michigan*

ence, aggressiveness, perseverance, industry, frugality, and enterprise. That a nation might experience a call to greatness for its generosity, humanity, tolerance, or justice seems never to have crossed their minds. Though America is officially proclaimed a Christian nation, it is not the virtues of Christianity that are credited with making her great. It is the ethics of the Book of Proverbs and of the Books of Kings and Chronicles that is exalted above all others. In this fact we have additional evidence of the strength of the Old Testament influence.

Two other elements entering into the formation of our national ethos, the heritage from Britain and the Puritan influence, have also been widely acclaimed as foundations of our country's greatness. The former was undoubtedly a factor in propelling the United States toward intervention on the side of the Allies in World War I. President Wilson himself admitted that his strong emotional interest in a British victory made the steering of a neutral course extremely difficult. Yet the actual effects of both the heritage from Britain and the Puritan influence are not easy to assess. Unquestionably, America inherited her law from Great Britain, and likewise her language and many of her customs and governmental institutions. But the same cannot be said of her ideal of social equality, of her belief that the voice of the people is the voice of God, of her multiplicity of elections, or of such basic institutions as the town meeting, the national convention, the federal system, or the initiative, referendum, and recall. Frederick Jackson Turner and his followers undoubtedly went too far in insisting upon the indigenous character of our democratic institutions. But it is just as erroneous to trace all of them to British origin. Some go back to ancient German and particularly to feudal custom. Others exemplified by the higher law and inviolable rights have their roots in Stoicism.

The notion that Puritanism put a rod of iron into the American character and thereby made the nation strong and great also requires qualification. There can be no doubt that industry, frugality, ambition, and glorification of material success are deeply imbedded in our folkways, but Puritanism is not necessarily their only source. They could have germinated in part, at least, from the conditions and requirements of life on the frontier. The religions of the frontier bore little relation to Puritan ideology. Eventually crystallizing into such sects as Methodists and Baptists, they reflected the influence of Arminianism and the Great Awakening much more than they did the theological determinism of the Calvinists. The non-Calvinist sects of Methodists, Baptists, Episcopalians, Unitarians, and Quakers have produced more than twice as many Presidents of the United States as have the combined offshoots of Puritanism. Among the movers and shakers of American social and intellectual history at least half have had antecedents essentially non-Puritan. The list includes Benjamin Franklin, Thomas Paine, Thomas Jefferson, Ralph Waldo Emerson, Abraham Lincoln, William James, and Justices Brandeis and Holmes. They undoubtedly exalted the individual and the virtues associated with ambition and self-assertion. But it was an individualism derived from the Enlightenment, from German Idealism, from Darwinism, and from the humanism fostered by an increasing awareness of man's helplessness in a complex society. It had nothing to do with the Puritan conception of man as the instrument of divine omnipotence.

NOTES TO CHAPTER TWO

1. Philip S. Foner, ed., *The Complete Writings of Thomas Paine* (New York: The Citadel Press, 1945), I, 203.
2. Jonathan Elliot, ed., *The Debates in the Several State Conventions on the Adoption of the Federal Constitution* (Washington: Printed by and for the editor, 1863), II, 527.
3. *Essays* (New York: A. L. Burt, n.d.), II, 205, 213.
4. "Civil Disobedience," *The Writings of Henry David Thoreau* (Boston: Houghton Mifflin Co., 1906), IV, 357.
5. *The Old Order Changeth* (New York: The Macmillan Co., 1910), p. 169.
6. *Speeches, Lectures, and Letters,* First Series (Boston: Lothrop, Lee and Shepard Co., 1891), p. 361.
7. Calvin Colton, ed., *The Works of Henry Clay* (New York: Henry Clay Publishing Co., 1897), V, 546.
8. *The American Democrat* (New York: Alfred A. Knopf, 1931), p. 156.
9. *The Russian Advance* (New York: Harper and Brothers, 1903), p. 252.
10. From *The Meaning of the Times and Other Speeches* by Albert J. Beveridge, copyright © 1908, 1936, used by special permission of the publishers, The Bobbs-Merrill Company, Inc., Indianapolis, pp. 113-14, 280-81.
11. *Mere Literature* (New York: Houghton Mifflin Co., *ca.* 1896), pp. 199-200.
12. Address delivered before the American Society of Newspaper Editors, April 21, 1934.
13. *The New Era or the Coming Kingdom* (New York: The Baker and Taylor Co., 1893), pp. 59, 65-66; *Our Country* (New York: The Baker and Taylor Co., 1885), p. 221; *Expansion under New World Conditions* (New York: The Baker and Taylor Co., 1900), pp. 73-74.
14. *Works* (New York: Houghton Mifflin Co., *ca.* 1892), VI, 205-06.
15. *Speeches, Lectures, and Letters,* Second Series (Boston: Lee and Shepard, 1905), pp. 42-43.
16. *On Civil Liberty and Self-Government* (Philadelphia: J. B. Lippincott Co., 1877), pp. 21, 256; *The Stranger in America* (Philadelphia: Carey, Lea and Blanchard, 1835), p. 33.

17. *Triumphant Democracy or Fifty Years' March of the Republic* (New York: Charles Scribner's Sons, 1886), pp. 12, 72-73.
18. *Orations and Speeches on Various Occasions* (Boston: Little, Brown and Co., 1870), I, 65-66, 75.
19. *The Works of Daniel Webster* (Boston: Little, Brown and Co., 1869), I, 93, 97-98.
20. *Ibid.*, I, 101.
21. Charles Eliot Norton, ed., *The Orations and Addresses of George William Curtis* (New York: Harper and Brothers, 1894), I, 393-96; III, 129-30, 211.
22. *American Political Ideas, Viewed from the Standpoint of Universal History* (Boston: Houghton Mifflin Co., 1911), pp. 79-80, 83-84, 116-17, 120-21.
23. *The Interest of America in Sea Power, Present and Future* (Boston: Little, Brown and Co., 1898), pp. 34-36.
24. *Literary and Historical Miscellanies* (New York: Harper and Brothers, 1865), p. 406.
25. *History of the United States of America* (New York: D. Appleton and Co., 1885), I, 318.
26. *Orations and Speeches*, I, 67.
27. *American Political Ideas*, pp. 20-22.
28. Norton, ed., *Orations and Addresses*, I, 370-71; III, 6-7, 204.
29. "The Care and Culture of Freshmen," *The North American Review*, CXCI (1910), 443.
30. *The Strength of Being Clean* (San Francisco: Viavi Press, 1898), p. 9.
31. *Ibid.*, pp. 4-5.
32. *The Call of the Twentieth Century* (Boston: American Unitarian Assoc., 1903), pp. 25-26.
33. From *The Meaning of the Times and Other Speeches* by Albert J. Beveridge, copyright © 1908, 1936, used by special permission of the publishers, The Bobbs-Merrill Company, Inc., Indianapolis, pp. 20, 24-25.
34. *Whose Constitution? An Inquiry into the General Welfare* (New York: Reynal and Hitchcock, 1936), p. 302; *New Frontiers* (New York: Reynal and Hitchcock, 1934), p. 254. (Quoted by permission of Harcourt, Brace and Company.)
35. *The New Basis of Civilization* (New York: The Macmillan Co., 1907), pp. 156, 178-79. (Quoted by permission of the publishers.)

Chapter Three

The Promised Land

That a people should derive a sense of mission, in any important degree, from factors of geography may seem strange. Yet no one can read very far in the folklore of America without discovering that many of her leaders have done just that. Long before Ellen Semple and Ellsworth Huntington developed their theories of geographic determinism, American statesmen and publicists were celebrating the greatness and promise of their country as products of its area, salubrious climate, and wealth of resources. They had few authorities to buttress their conclusions, with the exception of Montesquieu, but they made the most of what they had. They considered this continent so richly adorned with natural advantages that God must have reserved it for His Chosen People. It was a Land of Canaan meant only for the Children of Israel. When the time was ripe, He had led them thither and charged them with the role of guide and exemplar to all other nations. Even the very remoteness of the country had enabled it to develop this role uncorrupted by the influence of effete peoples.

LOCATION AND CLIMATE

Although geography is broadly defined as the science of the earth and its life, the term can be taken to include, first of all, the importance of location and its effects in molding the conditions of life. From early times Americans have rejoiced in the favored location of their country. On the eve of the Declaration of Independence, Gouverneur Morris voiced his conviction to the Continental Congress that the "great gulph which rolls its waves between Europe and America" would be a major factor guaranteeing "a full and lasting defence" to the Thirteen Colonies.

Soon after the adoption of the Constitution, both Hamilton and Madison took occasion to emphasize the advantage to America of her remoteness from Europe. Hamilton argued that the conquest of America by a European power would require such exertions as to be "ruinous to the undertaker." And even if it could be accomplished, enormous occupation forces would be necessary to prevent its undoing.[1] Madison thought the advantages that would result in the securing of liberty were even more important than military security. Just as the rulers of Britain had never been able, "by real or artificial dangers, to cheat the public into an extensive peace establishment," so the United States, by its even greater distance from the centers of aggression, would "enjoy the same happy security." There would be no excuse for a standing army, which "perfidious governments" might use to overawe the citizens. A navy and coastal fortifications might be necessary, but their weapons could not be conveniently employed for the destruction of liberty.[2]

Ironically, the arguments of Hamilton and Madison were revived in the twentieth century, despite the progressive narrowing of the oceans by modern inventions. In his *Republic*, published in 1943, Charles A. Beard cited the benefits accruing to Great Britain over several centuries as a consequence of her insular position. This enabled her to rely upon a navy for protection instead of a powerful army. An open and dangerous land frontier would have necessitated a large military establishment with consequent domination by an army class and "an iron solidarity" in the nation. In similar fashion, protection of the United States by two oceans fostered the development of diversity in economics, politics, and religion and helped to educate Americans in toleration and respect for one another's rights. There was no dominant military clique to impose uniformity upon them.[3]

During almost the same period, Walter Lippmann was classifying the United States as "for all practical purposes an island." She enjoyed therefrom the advantage that if wars had to be fought, they could be fought at a safe distance from the nation's homes, churches, hospitals, and schools. They could be fought by the armed forces of the nation and not by the women and children and by the aged and helpless. As in the case of Great Britain, America needed sea power, but navies were "weapons of freedom." They could not be used to occupy, subjugate, and rule over foreign territory. Although he subsequently repudiated the idea of a Fortress America relying upon passive defense behind impregnable frontiers, as late as 1948 he could still describe the United States as the least vulnerable of the powers to invasion, to blockade, or "with existing weapons, to decisive assault." [4] Neither Lippmann nor any other American appeared to recognize the significance of an additional consequence of the country's isolation. Separation from the military powers of Europe had enabled the United States to devote her major energies and resources to peacetime industry, and eventually to achieve the world's highest standard of living.

At least one American saw advantages quite different from military and political security in America's insular position. To Albert J. Beveridge, America's location was an "imperial location." He avowed that if the brains of all the statesmen who ever lived were gathered into one "vast intellect of world-wisdom," and if this composite brain took an eternity to plan, it could not conceive a land "better located for power and world dominance than the American Republic." This nation, he declared, is "enthroned between two great oceans of the world," its seat of power commanding both Europe and Asia. The very harbors of the United States show how cunningly "the Master Strategist" has provided the means of communication with the ends of the earth. The ocean currents, also, flow in relation to American coasts as if in accordance with a benevolent plan devised for our benefit. Every American citizen should carefully ponder these incomparable advantages and sink to his knees "in prayerful gratitude" that an all-wise Father has given him such a land for his earthly habitation. [5]

A number of prophets of American destiny have found the key to their country's greatness in climate. That only a temperate climate can nourish the progress of civilization has long been a popular doctrine in the Northern Hemisphere. Some of our meteorological philosophers have gone further and insisted that howling winds and bitter cold are almost indispensable factors. William Cullen Bryant maintained that "variable, capricious, and severe" weather enabled the United States and other northern nations to carry the arts and sciences to their highest perfection. [6] Ralph Waldo Emerson and Robert G. Ingersoll taught that the foundations of civilization rested upon snow and frost. The former argued that "four months of snow make the inhabitant of the northern temperate zone wiser and abler than his fellow who enjoys the fixed smile of the tropics." The southerner may loaf all day, sleep at night on a mat under the moon, and awaken to find that Nature has "spread a table for his morning meal." The northerner is by necessity a householder. He must brew, bake, salt and preserve his food, and pile up reserves of wood or coal. Each of these activities involves from time to time novel experiences and, as a consequence, new accumulations of wisdom.[7]

Similar theories were contained in the mellifluous prose of Ingersoll. You can't have civilization, he declared, except where there is snow "and an ordinarily decent winter." "Where man needs no bedclothes but clouds, revolution is the normal condition of such a people." Winter necessitates homes and firesides, and the stability and other conditions requisite for the advancement of society flow from the labor and prudence essential to the maintenance of the home. "Civilization, liberty, justice, charity and intellectual advancement are all flowers that bloom in the snow." If you should take 5,000 ministers from New England, 5,000 college presidents, and 5,000 solid businessmen and transfer them to the tropics, in the second generation you would see "barefooted boys riding bareback on a mule, with their hair sticking out of the top of their sombreros, with a rooster under each arm going to a cockfight on Sunday."[8]

Additional postulates of America's greatness in terms of climate can easily be found in the writings of such men as Carl Schurz and David Starr Jordan. Both regarded tropical and subtropical climes as inimical to human progress. Schurz was ready to explain the persistence of slavery in the South until after the Civil War as a product of climatic causes generating "those passions and propensities of human nature which, in the gratification of its appetites, lead to the arbitrary employment of force in preference to a just recognition of the rights of others." He attributed despotism and revolution to the same causes. Tropical heat stimulates the imagination and inflames the passions. "The consequences are natural: there is a tendency to government by force instead of by argument; revolutions are of chronic occurrence, like volcanic outbreaks," and political life continually oscillates between extremes of anarchy and despotism.[9]

David Starr Jordan espoused the doctrine of Ambrose Bierce that the tropics were "nature's asylum for degenerates." He argued that

Anglo-Saxons could not live there for more than a short time without deteriorating mentally, morally, and physically. Life in the tropics fostered laxity and indolence, fatalism, and indifference to moral standards. Where it was too warm or too uncomfortable to be conventional, it was "too much trouble to be decent." Excessive heat discouraged physical and mental activity, while the lavishness of nature favored the weak and inert. With the decline of effort went a deterioration of the will, an unwillingness to compete, and a contempt for time. Such qualities could never give birth to a high civilization. The great nations were products of hard times. They rose through struggle and never succumbed to the defeatist doctrine that it is the will of God that man should live in filth and "die of rottenness." The strength of Anglo-Saxon civilization lay in productive energy and activity and in the growth of the home. But the home could not endure in the climate of the tropics.[10] He seemed to forget that in many tropical countries unchastity, at least on the part of females, is more severely reprobated than in temperate regions. At the same time, husbands and fathers appear to guard more jealously the honor of their families—as long as their own freedom is not limited thereby.

LAND AND MINERAL RESOURCES

If in the writings of American philosophers one could discover a single formula to account for the greatness of our country, that with the most nearly universal appeal would doubtless be the abundance of cheap and fertile land. From the beginning of our national history this factor has been widely credited as a source of prosperity, democracy, and freedom. John Adams declared in 1785 that the United States, with her wealth of valuable territory, was "destined beyond a doubt to be the greatest power on earth, and that within the life of man."[11] Gouverneur Morris was only a trifle less modest when he predicted in 1801 that "the proudest empire in Europe is but a bauble compared to what America will be, must be, in the course of two centuries; perhaps of one." The reason he gave was that the interior of the country contained inexhaustible riches "in soil, in climate, in everything."[12]

More philosophical than most of his contemporaries, Jefferson sought to prove that great land area was favorable to the growth of democracy and to refute the contention of Montesquieu that republics could prosper only in countries of limited size. He went so far as to argue that a "just republic" was not merely compatible with a large territory but could scarcely exist on any other basis. It was imperative, he thought, that the area should be sufficiently extensive that "local egoisms" could never reach its greater part. Like Madison, he believed that extending the sphere of government would bring into the public councils a majority of representatives free from particular interests and thereby promote a "uniform prevalence to the principles of justice." The smaller the society, he argued, the greater the susceptibility to "violent and convulsive schisms." [13]

Jefferson had another reason for urging the importance of a large area for the state. This was to offset the Malthusian principle that population growth rapidly outruns the means of subsistence. Writing to the French economist J. B. Say in 1804, he asserted that the American republic had a capital advantage over the countries of Europe. In the latter the quantity of food was fixed, or increasing in no more than an "arithmetical ratio." A large proportion of the additional births each year went merely to swell the mortality rates. But in America "the immense extent of uncultivated and fertile lands enables everyone who will labor, to marry young, and raise a family of any size." As a consequence, food supply "may increase geometrically" with the number of laborers, and the total births, "however multiplied, become effective." [14] Although Jefferson had his moods of pessimism, most of them antedated the Louisiana Purchase. With so great an addition to the land supply guaranteeing an agrarian society for several decades, the future looked brighter.

As the nation grew in size and prosperity during the nineteenth and twentieth centuries, Americans became more and more deeply impressed with the quantity of cheap and fertile soil as a factor in the country's greatness. For some it was the exclusive factor. Henry George, for instance, attributed nearly every aspect of the American character—the general intelligence, the genius for invention, the power of adaptation, the free independent spirit, and the energy and hopefulness—to the vast extent of "unfenced land." He would allow no particular credit to the people for their achievements in social and political democracy, for their separation of church and state, or for their avoidance of a titled aristocracy. Any other nation with the same advantage of an "enormous common" would have accomplished as much.[15]

Almost identical theories emanated from William Graham Sumner, though they were invested with a stronger academic flavor. According to the Yale sociologist, the path of American development was predetermined by the two conditions of abundant land and a small population to inhabit it. "If you have abundance of land and few men to share it,. the men will all be equal." Social classes will disappear. Wages will be high. The masses of men, apart from those who succumb to laziness, folly, and vice, will be prosperous. But it will not be theories of ethics or political philosophies that will make them prosperous. Instead, their creeds will be the results of prosperity. Democracy itself, "the pet superstition of the age," will be the natural and inevitable product of the economic conditions. "The orators and constitution-makers do not make democracy. They are made by it." Liberty comes easy when the struggle for existence is easy, and there is no problem in maintaining a fluidity of classes where land is abundant and the population is sparse.[16]

Efforts to credit democracy to the free and supposedly independent life of the spacious West have been popular in American history. Frederick Jackson Turner was only one of a large number who expounded such theories. The idea was implicit, at least, in the writings of Lincoln, of Daniel Webster, and of Theodore Parker. Others traced to the same source of vast and open spaciousness additional abstractions, some of them almost mystical. Edward Everett hailed the expansion of the republic for the effect it would have in giving "elevation and dignity" to literature and to every species of mental effort.[17] Josiah Strong discovered occasion for profound rejoicing in the alleged fact that "for the first time in the records of history the greatest race" had come to occupy "the greatest home." "What a conjunction, big with universal blessings," he exclaimed; "the greatest race, the greatest civilization, the greatest numbers, the greatest wealth, the greatest physical basis for empire!" [18]

Strong and Everett seemed to be expressing the sentiments of a number of Americans who believed that somehow the very magnitude of their country exalted the people who occupied it. The idea was most clearly expressed, perhaps, by Woodrow Wilson. Indeed, he was so enamored of it that he repeated his conclusions in several of his writings. Rebuking Europeans for criticizing Americans for boasting of their country's size, he contended that every race and every man is as big as the thing he dominates or takes possession of. Therefore, the size of America is "in some sense a standard of the size and capacity of the American people." Their greatness, the elasticity of their institutions, and the adaptability of their lives are worthy of being measured "by the scale of a continent." The conquest of the nation's "proper territory" from nature is a herculean task, and a "bold race" derives inspiration from the difficulties and dangers of the enterprise. Expansion means "nationalization," and nationalization means "strength and elevation of view." [19]

Although most Americans who have written economic appraisals of the nation's greatness have found the clue in extent and richness of territory, writers and publicists of the more recent period have tended to emphasize industrial resources. Typical have been the

Reckless exploitation in the early days of the oil industry. The Spindletop Field near Beaumont, Texas, discovered in 1901.

Two great apostles of conservation—President Theodore Roosevelt and Chief Forester Gifford Pinchot—on the Inland Waterways Commission trip down the Mississippi River in October, 1907. *U. S. Forest Service*

theories of Thorstein Veblen, Henry Wallace, and Harry S. Truman. Veblen believed that with the full and free use of "its unexampled natural resources," the American people as a whole would enjoy a material abundance and a leisure for cultural development unparalleled in history. But the great obstacle was absentee ownership. The chances of overcoming this obstacle did not appear to him particularly bright. What stood in the way was the "moral sense" of American citizens, which put them in close accord with the "working bias" of their constituted authorities.[20]

Henry Wallace considered the United States so rich in material things that, "with ordinary common sense," a high standard of living was almost inevitable. In fact, he maintained that for quite a considerable period her people could do "nonsensical things, things which in almost any other nation would be immediately disastrous." [21] Some thirteen years later President Truman advised Congress that our natural resources were the foundation of our national life. He made it clear that by natural resources he meant primarily mineral resources. The nation's productive capacity, he affirmed, was dependent upon these, and he cautioned that shortages of critical materials were already developing. He foresaw the rapid emergence of the United States as a "have-not" nation, with respect to copper, steel, lead, and petroleum. He implied that an "expanding return of mineral discovery" and "improved methods of recovery" would be the only appropriate means of insuring the economic progress and security of the country. Had he realized at that time the tremendous possibilities of nuclear science, his warnings would probably have been milder. Few Americans seem concerned any longer with the depletion of our energy resources. And it is a common assumption that atomic power will ultimately make feasible the substitution of the more abundant light metals for copper, steel, and lead.

Though countless Americans have stressed the importance of the possession of resources, comparatively few have recognized the value of their provident use. Through most of our history the prevailing practice has been one of reckless exploitation. The land has been "mined" instead of farmed, while overgrazing, the depletion of forests, and ignorant methods of cultivation have caused precious inches of top soil to be blown away or to be washed down the rivers into the sea. The attitude of the frontiersmen was to regard timber as a nuisance. They must get rid of it as quickly as possible in order to have more land to cultivate. The federal and state governments encouraged this attitude by the prodigality with which they disposed of extensive tracts for little or nothing. Railroad companies and lumber and mining companies were permitted to acquire free of charge, or to steal, millions of acres. To make matters worse, forest fires added to the reckless waste, and scarcely a citizen mourned the losses. Major John Wesley Powell, chief of the United States Geological Survey in the 1890's, described in print how he had set fire to a great alpine tree just to see it burn. The resulting conflagration that went roaring off through the western mountains seemed to cause him no pang of regret.[22]

If any one man could be called the father of conservation in America, he would undoubtedly be Gifford Pinchot, Chief Forester of the United States from 1898 to 1910. A devout believer in the identity of democracy with the interests of the common citizen, Pinchot perceived as the most dangerous threat to the nation the unscrupulous greed of corporations in monopolizing the resources of the earth. Though they professed to be practicing free enterprise, they were actually depriving the people of privileges rightfully theirs and at the same time plundering the heritage of future generations. To Pinchot the social and cultural advancement of the republic could be measured only in terms of the common prosperity of all. Monopoly threatened not merely economic welfare; endangered also were the moral and intellectual interests of the people— their freedom, their education, and their individuality. None of these could be maintained except by a systematic program of conservation which would guarantee privileges to all and not simply to a few. Finally, according to Pinchot, conservation was "the key to the future" because of its relation to the maintenance of peace. Most wars, he argued, were the result of exhaustion of natural resources and the need for a new supply. He considered a just and permanent peace to be vital to the interests of all nations. But such a goal could be attained only by a wise and frugal use of nature's bounty in all countries. He admitted that no nation is completely self-sufficient, but he contended that an intelligent exploitation of the wealth of the richer countries would provide an abundance not only for them but for their poorer neighbors as well.[23]

HUMAN RESOURCES

Nearly every vocal American has recognized that land, forests, and mineral wealth are not enough to account for the greatness of America in the past or to exalt her destiny in the future. Numbers and quality of people are even more necessary to make certain that physical possessions will be used effectively. Yet the attitude toward human resources has been ambivalent. On the one hand there has been a tendency to rejoice as each decennial census showed increases mounting into the millions, and particularly as the population of America gave promise of surpassing that of the sluggish and decadent nations of the Old World. But some of the same leaders who hailed the rate of growth found themselves wondering from

time to time what would happen when the nation became overcrowded, especially when it filled up with less assimilable immigrants from the more backward countries of Europe and Asia. Concern over excess population was as old as the Founding Fathers, and
antiforeignism was a recurrent phenomenon from the Know-Noth-
ing movement of the 1850's to the revived Ku Klux Klan in the
1920's.

Rousseau contended that the most valid test of a good government was the tendency of the population to increase, unaided by
immigration. Numerous Americans have agreed with him, although
some of them forgot to add his qualifying phrase. Even before the
adoption of the Constitution, John Adams exulted in a "50 per cent
growth" of the American population since the beginning of the War
for Independence. This he regarded as a testimony to the beneficence of our institutions and a harbinger of future greatness.[24]
Addressing the Senate in 1832, Henry Clay predicted that the un-
occupied lands on the western frontier would soon "teem with people, and be filled with monuments of civilization." Such results
would be inevitable with the extension thither of the government
and laws of the greatest republic on earth. In 1850 he again regaled
the Senate with an account of the marvelous growth of the nation,
from four millions at the "commencement of this Government" to
"upward of twenty millions." The cause could be none other than
the matchless blessings of liberty and equality under the sovereignty
of the people.

Similar implications underlay the confident predictions of numerous others. In 1788 Hamilton forecast a national population of six
millions in twenty-five years, with a further increase to nine millions
in forty years. At the time of the Virginia Constitutional Convention
of 1821, Madison predicted that the inhabitants of the nation would
double every twenty-five years, until in 1929 they would equal 192
millions. But these prophecies were modest compared with some
that were to follow. In a message to Congress on December 3, 1861,
Lincoln declared that some of his own contemporaries would live
to see the Union contain 250 million people. John Fiske thought it
"an extremely moderate" estimate that by the end of the twentieth
century "the English race in the United States" would number at
least 600 or 700 millions.[25]

From the viewpoint of most Americans who have written on the subject, increase in population is a boon to a nation. In his seventh annual address, George Washington informed the Senate and the House of Representatives that the celerity of increase in the number of inhabitants augmented the strength and resources of America and guaranteed its future security. In 1801 Gouverneur Morris asserted in a letter to Jefferson that the rapid increase in population fostered such "pleasing hopes" that no doubt could be reasonably entertained of the "prosperity, power, and glory" of the country.

The middle of the century witnessed the appearance of thoughtful disquisitions attempting to prove defects in the Malthusian theory. Henry C. Carey, recognized by some as America's first professional economist, thought it an insult to God to suppose, as Malthus did, that the Creator had doomed the great mass of human beings to suffer misery and want because the increase in the food supply would never keep pace with the multiplication of births. Refusing to concede that hunger and privation inevitably followed the crowding of people into limited areas, Carey contended that the true situation was almost the reverse. "When population increases and men come together," he affirmed, "even the poor land is made rich." When population declines, and men are forced to live in isolation remote from each other, "even the rich lands become impoverished." At other times, he did recognize a reciprocal relationship between the two factors. In order that man may increase, he admitted, there must be an increase in the supply of food. And in order that the latter may increase, "mankind must grow in numbers." [26]

Almost identical conclusions were drawn by Henry George. He professed to see no connection whatever between the prodigality of nature and the wealth of nations. The richest countries, he said, are not those with lush environments but those where labor is efficient. To point his argument he contrasted Mexico with Massachusetts and Brazil with England. He denied, moreover, that increase in population brought squalor and misery as unavoidable consequences. "The countries whose population is densest and presses hardest upon the capabilities of nature," he argued, "are, other things being equal," the countries with the largest proportion of their national income available for luxury, for capital investments abroad, and for the support of culture and the amenities of life. As evidence, he cited the example of the United States with her population doubling every twenty-nine years but with wealth increasing in the same proportion at much shorter intervals. It was not the increase of wealth, he concluded, that brought about this increase of men. Instead, the increase of economically productive people caused the increase of wealth, in the form of food supply and everything else.[27]

Among political leaders who have expressed their views on the growth of population, the one with the most elaborate theory has been Henry Wallace. Writing at the end of the Great Depression, he conceded that surplus population was in some respects a problem in the United States. But not in the Malthusian sense. There was no population pressure resulting from inadequate food supply. Instead, there was an altogether different pressure produced by technological development. Advances in mechanization had made such rapid headway that the 50 per cent of farmers who were most efficient in the United States grew about 90 per cent of the farm products sold on the market. As a consequence, the "Okies" and "Arkies" and other marginal cultivators were "tractored" off their farms.

At the same time, the New Deal Secretary of Agriculture was acutely aware of the evils accruing to a nation when growth of population slows down or diminishes to the vanishing point. The immediate effects are a reduction of births, a decrease in the proportion of young people to the total population, and a marked increase in the percentage of aged and elderly folk. For a time these effects may create an illusion of well-being. In a rapidly aging community "there is usually more money, more wisdom, more caution, and for a time a greater opportunity to cultivate the arts." But such conditions are transient. Soon the predominance of the aged leads to a slowing down, an excess of caution and conservatism, and a hardening of the intellectual arteries. Ultimately the nation takes on the characteristics of New England, France, or Sweden. The future belongs to the growing nations, with high enough birth rates to insure a preponderance of younger people in their populations. Youth alone can provide the buoyancy, the spirit of adventure, and the zest for achievement essential to national progress. "The fundamental trend of all great civilizations takes form . . . among populations where the children under fourteen outnumber the old people by around three to one." It is necessary to add that Wallace did not regard the aging nations as decadent or dying. Recognizing that some, at least, could grow old "gracefully," he paid tribute to Sweden for her achievements in economic and social democracy. But he still maintained that the peoples with the "nascent energy" of youth would become the world leaders of the future.[28]

From acclaiming the advantages of a growing population to urging a liberal immigration policy is an easy step; and numerous Americans can be found who were willing to take it. In the Convention of 1787, Madison asserted that he wished to invite foreigners "of merit and republican principles" to settle in America. That part of the nation which had given the greatest encouragement to immigration had "advanced most rapidly in population, agriculture & the arts." Emerson believed so firmly in the principle of heterogeneity that if he had had his way he would have welcomed immigrants in unlimited numbers from all countries. The Irish, the Swedes, the Poles, the Russians, and even the Africans and the Polynesians, he thought, would infuse new life into America and give it a civilization as vigorous as that "which came out of the melting pot of the Dark Ages." [29]

Almost as generous was the attitude of Wendell Phillips. "Let every oppressed man come," he exclaimed; "let every poor man come; let every man who wishes to change his residence come,—we welcome all; frankly acknowledging the principle that every human being has the right to choose his residence just where he pleases on the planet." Curiously, though, this principle did not seem to apply to the Chinese. They were to be admitted under annual quotas, lest the nation be unable to absorb great quantities of mere "human freight." [30]

Near the end of the century Grover Cleveland vetoed a bill providing for a literacy test in the form of ability to read twenty-five words of the Constitution in any language as a basis for admitting immigrants into the country. His conservative prejudices led him to see much less danger in admitting a hundred thousand illiterates who sought merely a home and opportunity to work, than one educated but "unruly" agitator who would come here to stir up discontent.

The twentieth century witnessed the influx of much greater numbers of immigrants than ever before, and clamor for a tightening of restrictions inevitably increased. Yet advocates of a liberal policy continued to preach their doctrines. Albert J. Beveridge wrote in

1908 that the drawing of blood from the veins of the most virile
nations constantly renewed the American republic and kept its
people "normal, sane and steady." [31] Woodrow Wilson conceived of
the United States as being continually reborn out of all the sources
of human energy in the world. She was constantly drinking new
strength by absorbing into the national organism "the strong men

Bound for the Klondike Gold Fields, over Chilcoot Pass, Alaska, 1898.
Library of Congress

and forward-looking women" of other lands. It was almost as if the human race itself had determined to make sure "that this great nation, founded for the benefit of humanity, should not lack for the allegiance of the people of the world."

Contemplating these facts, the noted apostle of the New Freedom was inspired to some lofty thoughts. Because we were made up out of all the great family of mankind, he averred that we were especially equipped to understand all peoples and serve as champions of the rights of mankind. It gave us, moreover, a solicitude for the interests of peoples no matter where they might live. We had no designs upon other nations' territory. If in the past we had been "obliged by circumstances" to take possessions from other countries, we did this in the interest of the natives involved. We acted in the capacity of trustees for those to whom the territory really belonged, and we were ready to turn it over to them when conditions seemed feasible.[32] How this could be reconciled with more than a small proportion of the examples of American imperialism, he did not make clear.

Another Democratic President, Harry S. Truman, expressed sentiments similar to those of Wilson, but with an idealism that did not soar so high. Pleading for the admission of displaced persons, he reminded the nation that it was founded by immigrants and that it had "thrived on the energy and diversity of many peoples." He considered it a capital source of America's strength that she numbered among her people "all the major religions, races—and national origins."[33]

But in the midst of the rejoicing over growth of population, by immigration or otherwise, there were not a few discordant notes. The critic who made the broadest and most discerning observations was none other than the Father of the Constitution. Long before the theories of Malthus became popular in America, Madison was writing in Malthusian terms. In 1791 he commented in the *National Gazette* on the tendency of every plant and animal species to reproduce surplus offspring. The human species, he pointed out, is no exception. It, too, propagates far beyond the capacity of nature to provide for subsistence. The surplus human beings are disposed of in a number of ways: (1) they are destroyed by infanticide, "as among the Chinese and Lacedemonians"; (2) they are slowly starved to death, as among other nations where food supply is barely sufficient for a stationary population; (3) they are "consumed by wars and endemic diseases"; or (4) they are weeded out by emigration "to places where a surplus of food is attainable." The parallel between the foregoing discussion and the Malthusian thesis of population increasing faster than the means of subsistence except where checked by war, disease, famine, and vice is too obvious for comment.

In 1818, in a letter to Richard Rush, Madison referred to the Malthusian theory by name for the first time. He said he had been looking over Malthus, and thought the world much indebted to him for the views he had given of an interesting subject. In subsequent writings he advanced a number of criticisms. He thought Malthus vulnerable for assigning an arithmetical ratio as a universal principle for the increase of food. In a country thoroughly cultivated, as China was supposed to be, there could be *no* increase. In one partially cultivated, and as fertile as the United States, the increase might actually *exceed* the geometric ratio. He criticized Malthus also for his fatalism, for refusing to recognize that man is a reasoning creature and can certainly do something by his own ingenuity to augment his means of subsistence. In the final analysis, however, he continued to walk pretty closely in the shadow of the English rector. He believed that it was the inexorable fate of the United States to become, in little more than a century, as overcrowded as Great Britain or France, and he considered misery inseparable from "a high degree of populousness." He looked with special concern upon the tendency of "the laboring part of mankind" to increase their numbers after the increase of food had reached its limit. The ensuing competition for jobs would reduce wages to a minimum and augment privation to a maximum. Should the results of this tendency be curbed by either physical or moral checks, the checks themselves were "but so many evils." The only antidote seemed to be a stoic resignation to the impossibility of banishing evil altogether from human affairs. Men must console themselves with the belief that evil is "overbalanced by the good mixed with it," and direct their efforts to increasing "the good proportion of the mixture." [34]

Several Americans of later years saw evils in excess population more serious even than those depicted by Madison. By way of example, William Graham Sumner found excess population to be the cause not only of poverty and war but of despotism and tyranny. The only reason the United States had enjoyed democracy thus far was the fact that she was a young and underpopulated country. When overcrowding set in, liberty would be supplanted by authority, and democracy would give way to imperialism and war.[35]

The equally cynical individualist and Social Darwinist, Justice Oliver Wendell Holmes, agreed with Sumner in emphasizing the population factor and the increasing acerbity of the struggle for existence as territories fill up with inhabitants. Writing to his friend, John C. H. Wu, in 1925, he affirmed his belief that "Malthus was right in his fundamental notion." "Every society," he continued, "is founded on the death of men. In one way or another some are always and inevitably pushed down the dead line." He denounced as "manifest humbug" the idea that tinkering with property or changing forms of government could do any good so long as every social improvement was "expended in increased and unchecked propagation."

Even the collectivist enemies of individualists like Sumner and Holmes agreed with them, for the most part, on the population issue. Edward Bellamy, for example, discovered a close connection between poverty on the one hand and prolificity, on the other. He reversed Malthus, however, in regarding the former as the *cause* of the latter. Where poverty and squalor abound, he wrote, human beings multiply like rabbits, while in proportion as the economic level of a class is raised its prolificity declines.[36]

Other social planners, notably Simon Patten and Edward Alsworth Ross, espoused a kind of Neo-Malthusianism based upon the assumption that man should control his rate of increase to avoid the disadvantages of overpopulation, in the same way that he should control every other important aspect of his social and economic life. The former ridiculed the old religious imperative to increase and multiply and the insistence of rulers and priests that men should blindly obey it.[37] At the end of World War I, Ross exulted over the fact that the proportion of children among Americans had fallen by 25 per cent in forty years. What did this mean, he asked, but a sign of release—"release of women from the 'home' sphere, of wives from the yoke of husbands," of married couples from the demand for continuous child-rearing? The alacrity with which the masses were repudiating the old shibboleths was to him a symbol of "hope for a Golden Age when the specter of overpopulation will be laid forever." His interest in this consummation was both social and economic. He thought that a falling birth rate in the modern age might have economic results for the common people comparable to those of the Black Death. The great epidemic of the fourteenth century, by decimating the population, so "enhanced a man's worth that serfdom came to an end." [38]

THE SALT OF THE EARTH

It goes without saying that Americans who have applauded the growth of their nation have been interested not merely in mounting numbers. The deprecators of "race suicide," for instance, from Theodore Roosevelt to Madison Grant, have not been disturbed by falling birth rates in general but by a disproportionate decline of births among the "better classes." Some of the opposition to birth control has also been fathered by the belief that it would be used chiefly by the educated and more provident elements, and that the ignorant and shiftless would continue their spawning as recklessly as ever.

But the deepest concern over the quality of the population has probably sprung from the agrarians. It is commonly believed that the tone of agrarianism in America was set by Jefferson. Soon after the adoption of the Constitution he expressed to James Madison his conviction that the nation would continue to be virtuous as long as agriculture remained its "principal object." When Americans got piled upon one another in large cities, as people were in Europe, they would become corrupted and start "eating one another" after the manner of Europeans. Shortly before, in his "Notes on the State of Virginia," he had been even more emphatic. The "chosen people of God," he declared, are "those who labor in the earth." Corruption of morals in the mass of cultivators is a phenomenon of which no age or nation had yet furnished an example. Generally speaking, the proportion which the number of nonagriculturists in any state bears to the number of farmers is "the proportion of its unsound to its healthy parts." He hoped, therefore, that he should never see America's citizens "occupied at a work-bench or twirling a distaff." It was better to let the workshops remain in Europe and not run the risk of transforming a large part of our own population into urban proletarians, tarnished by "subservience and venality." The mobs of great cities contributed about as much to the support of pure government "as sores do to the strength of the human body."

But Jefferson was not always so zealous a votary of the agrarian life. In his first annual message as President he referred to agriculture, manufactures, commerce, and navigation as "the four pillars of our prosperity." Eight years later he described the embargo laws as having promoted the desirable result of "an equilibrium" among agriculture, manufactures, and commerce, and of having simplified "our foreign concerns to the exchange only of that surplus which we cannot consume for those articles of reasonable comfort and convenience which we cannot produce." [39] By 1816 he was almost as much of an economic nationalist as Hamilton. The reason he gave for reversing his earlier position was the British and French depredations upon American commerce which had led to the War of 1812. The two nations most distinguished for science and civilization had covered "earth and sea with robberies and piracies, despoiled the United States of a thousand ships, enslaved her citizens, and completely excluded her commerce from the ocean." She was left with no alternative but to "place the manufacturer beside the agriculturist." To be independent for the comforts of life, she must fabricate them herself. He who would recommend otherwise must be for reducing her citizens to dependence on foreign nations or for living like wild beasts in dens and caverns. The former President considered the encouragement of manufacturing the only course for the immediate future. Subsequent events, though, might dictate a different policy; "for in so complicated a science as political economy," no one axiom could be accepted as wise and practicable for all circumstances. [40]

Jefferson, of course, was only one of a number of early Americans who, at one time or another, were apostles of an agrarian economy. Madison also despised large cities and acclaimed the toilers in the earth as "the best basis of public liberty and the strongest bulwark of public safety." At the age of twenty-one he wrote that "impertinent fops . . . breed in towns and populous places as naturally as flies do in the shambles." It is not the rural population, he averred, that furnishes inmates for the Bridewells and Bedlams. [41] Yet in his later career he appeared to feel that a well-rounded economic life was essential to national strength and safety, and he advocated protective tariffs to enable manufacturing to keep pace with the growth of agriculture and commerce. He seemed to have visions of a national self-sufficiency in which the manufactures of the North would complement the agriculture of the South. Moreover, he was disturbed by the prospect of a time when it would be difficult to find export markets for American agricultural products. He repeatedly adverted to the fact that foreign and domestic markets alike were glutted with the products of the soil, and he feared that this condition would become worse unless surplus labor in this country could be diverted into manufacturing.[42] In short, like Jefferson, he saw no solution except in the adoption of measures of self-sufficiency very similar to those recommended by Hamilton.

With the exception of Hamilton, and of Jefferson and Madison in their later years, there were few political thinkers from the American Revolution to the Populist Revolt who did not idolize the American farmer and his way of life. Benjamin Franklin enumerated three ways by which nations acquire wealth. The first, he said, is by war, "which is robbery." The second, by commerce, "which is usually cheating." And the third, by agriculture, "the only honest

Brush dams are a simple but effective means of checking erosion resulting from wasteful farming and destruction of forests. In this scene in California's Keswick Watersheds, willow cuttings will now grow in the eroded gullies. *Bureau of Reclamation*

way, wherein man receives a real increase of the seed thrown into the ground, in a kind of continual miracle, wrought by the hand of God in his favor, as a reward for his innocent life and his virtuous industry." [43] For Emerson, there was something peculiarly wholesome in the life of a man "who by real cunning extorts from nature its sceptre." From his viewpoint a sturdy lad from New Hampshire or Vermont was "worth a hundred of these city dolls." [44] In the opinion of Henry Clay and Andrew Jackson, agriculture was of such transcendent importance that commerce and industry deserved the attention of government only insofar as they increased the value of agricultural production. [45] The irrepressible agitator Wendell Phillips regarded cities as a noisome blight on the republic. They were "nests of great vices" and victims of some hidden disease. Modern civilization simply could not tolerate such cesspools of iniquity. [46]

Not until the great era of railroad building and industrialization had been under way for several decades did any notable American place industry and agriculture, or the worker and the farmer, on a plane of equality. Grover Cleveland seems to have been one of the first to adopt this attitude. In 1888 he told the participants in the annual picnic of the Pennsylvania Grange that the farmers were the most stable support of the nation's prosperity and the most reliable source of its greatness and strength. But the following year he informed the New York Chamber of Commerce that the "business of a country" was its life blood, and that those directly or indirectly connected with it were the best of all citizens. He quickly explained that by business he did not mean the "selfish scurry and sordid clutching after wealth which we see about us every day." Instead, he was referring to the "active, strong impulse which, starting from important centers, steadily permeates the entire land, giving to our tradesmen, everywhere, healthy prosperity, to our toilers remunerative labor, and to our homes comfort and contentment. . . ." This was the type of activity which the people loved to recognize as proof of the value of their free institutions. If his rhetoric meant anything, it meant that he considered the great corporations as major benefactors of the American people.

Fortunately, some of Cleveland's contemporaries regarded the interests of the working classes more benevolently. During the campaign of 1896, William Jennings Bryan declared the farmers and the laboring men to be the "foundation of society." "Upon this foun-

Large-scale mechanized farming in the State of Washington. *Caterpillar Tractor Co.*

dation," he said, "the commercial classes rest, and the financier acts as a sort of roof over the structure." The roof might be taken off and another put on in its place, "but you cannot destroy the foundation without destroying the whole building." [47]

Long after industry, commerce, and finance had gained a predominance in the American economy, and even after a majority of the people had abandoned the farms and villages for urban living, philosophers and publicists continued to proclaim the nobility of agriculture and those who took part in it as the guardians of civic virtue. As President, Theodore Roosevelt hailed the farming folk as the backbone of the nation and asserted that "the permanent greatness of any state must ultimately depend more upon the character of its country population than upon anything else." [48] The views of Woodrow Wilson were not dissimilar. The vitality of America, he declared at the peak of the Progressive movement, does not lie in her great cities. Instead, it is to be found in "the brains, the energies, the enterprise of the people throughout the land . . . in the wealth they extract from nature and originate themselves." In proportion as America's self-contained towns and her countrysides were "happy and hopeful," the nation would realize the "high ambitions which have marked her in the eyes of the world."⁴⁹ It is generally recognized that the early New Deal, which owed considerable to the Progressivism of both Wilson and Theodore Roosevelt, also had a strong agrarian flavor. Franklin D. Roosevelt liked to think of himself as an enlightened squire and probably did more for the farmers of America than all of his predecessors in the White House since the beginning of the century. The agrarian philosophy of the New Deal, however, was chiefly the work of Henry Wallace and Rexford G. Tugwell.

As a practitioner of scientific agriculture and a member of a long line of editors of farm journals, Henry Wallace had a realistic respect for farmers of America as the most active group in the quest for economic democracy. He did not argue that this was because they were more intelligent, more virtuous, or more courageous than other classes. Rather it was because they had "suffered more," and because they still lived in "the simpler and plainer environment wherein this democracy was born." But Wallace was no partisan of peasant agriculture or of the hard-scrabble family farm. He admitted that "way-of-life" farmers deserved recognition. In spite of a miserable standard of living, their contact with the earth "kept them human beings" at a time when industrial capitalism was exerting a dehumanizing effect upon all its workers and upon many who distributed its wares. But "way-of-life" farming was something out of the past. The future belonged to the commercial farmers, who were "coming closer and closer in their thinking to the business men in the towns." Only through the development of scientific and mechanized agriculture on farms large enough to produce a substantial cash income could the farmers of America obtain their share in the good things that city life affords.⁵⁰

Wallace's erudite Under-Secretary of Agriculture Rexford G. Tugwell probably agreed with his chief in most of his agrarian theories. At any rate, he was bold enough to tell the New York State Bankers Association in 1934 that "intelligent use of the land is the first criterion of any civilization." The country that neglects the soil and the interests of its cultivators as the ultimate source of its wealth, he added, is paving the road to decay.⁵¹

Our study of ideas about land and resources reveals a vision of

America destined to be a beacon to the world because of the magnificence of her material endowments. God must have intended that it be so, for He conferred no such blessings upon any other nation. Here were soil, minerals, and forests enough to sustain the population of the globe. Yet a mere handful of venturesome immigrants were invited as guests to so lavish a banquet. They were given, moreover, an invigorating climate to stimulate their ambition to make the most of their new opportunities. What theory could be more logical than the supposition that an all-wise Providence had chosen these people and set them apart for an exalted purpose? Perhaps it was His will that they should expand and conquer and become rulers over many nations. It would at least be their mission to create an example that would bring light and healing to the rest of mankind.

That American thinkers would draw identical conclusions from the geographic phenomena of their country would be more than anyone should expect. For some its insular location was a source of protection and a haven for the growth of democracy. For others it was the foundation of empire. For Jefferson its vast expanse was a safeguard against the dangers of overpopulation. For Woodrow Wilson it was the basis of bold conceptions and elevated views. The very size of the country, he believed, somehow exalted the thoughts of the people who inhabited it. To a small number of our molders of opinion the hope of America is to be found in her wealth of mineral resources, providing the basis of a flourishing industry. To the vast majority, however, predestined greatness has always had its roots in the soil. They have seen in the virtue and self-reliance of the independent farmer the elixir of life for the nation. But despite these conflicts of opinion, one underlying assumption has retained the fixity of a polar star: The American territory has been endowed by nature or by some higher power with geographic features which give to the people who inhabit it exceptional advantages in fulfilling their mission of democracy and liberty.

NOTES TO CHAPTER THREE

1. J. C. Hamilton, ed., *The Works of Alexander Hamilton* (New York: J. F. Trow, 1850-51), VII, 152-53.
2. *The Federalist*, Modern Library ed. (New York: Random House, n.d.), No. 41.

3. *The Republic* (New York: The Viking Press, 1943), pp. 149-50.
4. "Weapon of Freedom," *Life*, IX (October 28, 1940), 45, 110, 112; "The Rivalry of Nations," *Atlantic Monthly*, CLXXXI (February, 1948), 18.
5. *The Young Man and the World* (New York: D. Appleton and Co., 1905), pp. 339-40.
6. Parke Godwin, ed., *The Prose Writings of William Cullen Bryant* (New York: D. Appleton and Co., 1884), II, 376.
7. *Essays*, First Series (Boston: Houghton Mifflin Co., 1876), II, 213-14.
8. *Complete Lectures* (Philadelphia: David McKay Co., 1935), pp. 29-30.
9. Frederic Bancroft, ed., *Speeches, Correspondence and Political Papers of Carl Schurz* (New York: G. P. Putnam's Sons, 1913), II, 81-83, 89.
10. *The Question of the Philippines* (Palo Alto, Calif.: John J. Valentine, 1899), pp. 24-25; *The Heredity of Richard Roe* (Boston: American Unitarian Assoc., 1911), pp. 127-29; *Imperial Democracy* (New York: D. Appleton and Co., 1899), pp. 44-45.
11. C. F. Adams, ed., *The Works of John Adams, Second President of the United States* (Boston: Little, Brown and Co., 1856), VII, 246.
12. Jared Sparks, *Life of Gouverneur Morris* (Boston: Gray and Bower, 1832), III, 144.
13. Albert E. Bergh, ed., *The Writings of Thomas Jefferson* (Washington: Thomas Jefferson Memorial Assoc., 1907), IX, 299-300.
14. *Ibid.*, XI, 2.
15. *Progress and Poverty*, Modern Library ed. (New York: Random House, n.d), p. 390.
16. Albert G. Keller, ed., *Earth-Hunger and Other Essays* (New Haven: Yale University Press, 1913), pp. 42-43; Albert G. Keller, ed., *War and Other Essays* (New Haven: Yale University Press, 1913), pp. 324-25.
17. *Orations and Speeches on Various Occasions* (Boston: Little, Brown and Co., 1870), I, 27-28.
18. *The New Era or the Coming Kingdom* (New York: The Baker and Taylor Co., 1893), p. 74.
19. *Division and Reunion, 1829-1889* (New York: Longmans, Green and Co., 1893), pp. 3-4; R. S. Baker and W. E. Dodd, eds., *College and State* (New York: Harper and Brothers, *ca.* 1925), p. 406; R. S. Baker and W. E. Dodd, eds., *The New Democracy* (New York: Harper and Brothers, *ca.* 1926), I, 56.
20. *Absentee Ownership and Business Enterprise in Recent Times* (New York: The Viking Press, 1923), pp. 119-65.
21. *New Frontiers* (New York: Reynal and Hitchcock, 1934), pp. 7, 87.
22. Gifford Pinchot, *Breaking New Ground* (New York: Harcourt, Brace and Co., 1947), p. 24.
23. *Ibid.*, pp. 368-69.
24. C. F. Adams, ed., *Works*, VIII, 385.
25. *American Political Ideas, Viewed from the Standpoint of Universal History* (Boston: Houghton Mifflin Co., 1911), pp. 123-24.
26. *Principles of Social Science* (Philadelphia: J. B. Lippincott Co., 1868), I, 311; III, 313.
27. *Progress and Poverty*, Modern Library ed., pp. 131, 143, 146-47.
28. *The American Choice* (New York: Reynal and Hitchcock, 1940), pp. 43-46. (Quoted by permission of Harcourt, Brace and Company.)

29. E. W. Emerson and W. E. Forks, eds., *The Journals of Ralph Waldo Emerson* (Boston: Houghton Mifflin Co., 1909-14), VIII, 316.
30. *Speeches, Lectures and Letters,* Second Series (Boston: Lee and Shepard, 1905), pp. 145-46.
31. *Work and Habits* (Philadelphia: Henry Altemus Co., 1908), pp. 94-95.
32. Baker and Dodd, eds., *The New Democracy,* I, 194, 299-305, 318.
33. *Vital Speeches,* Vol. XIII, No. 19 (July 15, 1947).
34. *Letters and Other Writings of James Madison,* Published by Order of Congress (Philadelphia: J. B. Lippincott Co., 1865), III, 74, 102, 209-10, 577; IV, 30.
35. *Folkways* (New York: Ginn and Co., 1906), pp. 162-63, 194.
36. *Equality* (New York: D. Appleton-Century Co., 1934), p. 411.
37. *The New Basis of Civilization* (New York: The Macmillan Co., 1907), p. 76.
38. *Changing America* (New York: The Century Co., 1919), pp. 10-11.
39. Saul K. Padover, ed., *The Complete Jefferson* (New York: Duell, Sloan and Pearce, 1943), p. 557.
40. *Ibid.,* 374-75.
41. *Letters,* Cong. ed., IV, 476; Gaillard Hunt, ed., *The Writings of James Madison* (New York: G. P. Putnam's Sons, 1900), I, 12; *National Gazette,* March 8, 1792.
42. *Letters,* Cong. ed., IV, 567; III, 170-71; IV, 264-65.
43. John Bigelow, ed., *The Complete Works of Benjamin Franklin* (New York: G. P. Putnam's Sons, 1887), IV, 19.
44. *Essays,* First Series, II, 75.
45. Calvin Colton, ed., *The Works of Henry Clay* (New York: Henry Clay Publishing Co., 1897), V, 263; F. N. Thorpe, *The Statesmanship of Andrew Jackson As Told in His Writings and Speeches* (New York: The Tandy-Thomas Co., 1909), p. 47.
46. *Speeches, Lectures and Letters,* First Series (Boston: Lothrop, Lee and Shepard Co., 1891), p. 496; *Ibid.,* Second Series, pp. 163-64.
47. *The First Battle* (Chicago: W. B. Conkey Co., 1896), p. 360.
48. E. E. Morison, ed., *The Letters of Theodore Roosevelt* (Cambridge: Harvard University Press, 1951-54), VI, 1225; E. E. Morison, ed., *The Works of Theodore Roosevelt* (New York: Charles Scribner's Sons, 1925), XVIII, 176.
49. *The New Freedom* (New York: Doubleday, Page and Co., 1913), pp. 289-90.
50. *New Frontiers,* p. 137; *The Price of Freedom* (Washington: The National Home Library Foundation, 1940), p. 9; *Technology, Corporations and the General Welfare* (Chapel Hill: University of North Carolina Press, 1937), p. 25.
51. *The Battle for Democracy* (New York: Columbia University Press, 1935), pp. 238-39.

Chapter Four

Democracy and Mission

It has long been assumed that if America were to fulfill her dream of liberating and renewing the world she must set an example within her own borders of free and enlightened institutions. Indeed, most of her leaders have taken it for granted that such an objective was long since accomplished. They have looked upon free government, for example, as almost an American patent. In 1792 Madison wrote that in Europe charters of liberty had been granted by power. America had set the example of "charters of power granted by liberty." This revolution in the practice of the world he thought should be pronounced "the most triumphant epoch of its history, and the most consoling presage of its happiness." [1] A half-century later Theodore Parker declared that the American government, in nation, state, and town, was "an original thing." The parts, he admitted, were old, but the organism which represented the parts in combination was the "most original thing" that could be found "in the political history of the world for many an age." To illustrate, he referred to the fact that the idea of the sacredness of man had germinated in the bosom of the early Christian, but without enough force to prevent Paul from justifying slavery. Only in America could the doctrine come to full fruition. Here a new nation "could develop the idea into institutions, and ultimately found an empire on the proposition that 'all men are created equal and endowed by their Creator with certain unalienable rights.'" [2]

According to James Wilson, the principle of representation in government was "altogether unknown to the ancients," and even the British recognized it only to a limited extent, for they applied it neither to the executive, nor to the judiciary, nor to the House of Lords. To America was "reserved the glory and the happiness of diffusing this vital principle throughout the constituent parts of government." [3] Jefferson seemed almost willing to share the credit for representative government with a number of modern nations, but he ended by describing the achievement in such terms as would fit the facts in his own country exclusively. In a letter to A. Coray, in 1823, he wrote that "modern times have the signal advantage" of having discovered the only device by which the rights of man can be secured, "to wit: government of the people, acting not in person, but by representatives chosen by themselves, that is to say, by every man of ripe years and sane mind, who either contributes by his purse or person to the support of his country." A few years later Edward Everett added the weight of his learning and orotund phrasing to the same idea. It was no contribution from British sources, he declared, that gave the Thirteen Colonies their representative assemblies. They were established by the ingenuity of the colonists themselves, on the model of boards of directors of trading corporations. Thus without benefit of charter provisions or fine-spun theories of philosophical statesmen, the resourceful colonists, "in a simple, unpretending manner, introduced to the world the greatest discovery in political science." [4]

The passage of time did not diminish the regard of Americans for their form of government or their self-esteem for having originated it. William H. Seward hailed the establishment of the republic of the United States as "the most important secular event in the history of the human race." [5] Contemplating the wonders of the American system and the prosperity it had vouchsafed to the country, Daniel Webster was moved to pronounce it "a Divine interposition in our behalf." [6] In 1842 Lincoln conveyed to the Springfield Temperance Society his pride in the "political revolution of '76." It gave rise, he said, to a governmental system which provided a degree of freedom far exceeding that of any other nation of the earth. The spirit that animated it would eventually "grow and expand into the universal liberty of mankind." About fifty years later Grover Cleveland enjoined the Commercial Club of Providence, Rhode Island, to reverence their government "as the perfect work of the highest patriotism"; to love it "as the fountainhead of their national life"; to have "confidence in its justice and equality"; and to have "pride in its ownership and management." The final phrase was perhaps not too indelicate, since the year was 1891 and the speaker was not then in the White House.

Not only did Americans claim credit for having invented the most perfect system of government on earth, but they also prided themselves upon having originated constitutionalism. It was a com-

Democracy at work. A town meeting in Vermont. *Standard Oil Co.* (*N. J.*)

mon doctrine at the beginning of the nation's history that America occupied a place of unusual distinction in being the only country governed under a constitution. James Wilson seems to have fathered the thesis. In the Pennsylvania ratifying convention of 1788, he argued that Britain, in reality, had no constitution. The so-called British Constitution was simply the will of Parliament. "To control the power and conduct of the legislature, by an overruling constitution, was an improvement in the science and practice of government reserved to the American states." [7]

The same theory was echoed by Thomas Paine in his *Rights of Man*. Defying Edmund Burke to produce the British "Constitution," Paine sought to clinch his contention by insisting that a constitution has a "real existence, and wherever it cannot be produced in a visible form, there is none." He defined a constitution as "a thing antecedent to a Government." The government, he said, is only the creature of a constitution, not its creator.[8] Although Jefferson found defects in the Constitution as it came from the Philadelphia Convention, he expressed himself a few years later as willing to revere it for incorporating the "collected wisdom of our country." He would even consider it competent "to render our fellow citizens the happiest and the securest on whom the sun has ever shone."[9] John Adams esteemed the new instrument so highly that he urged his fellow citizens to fall on their knees "in gratitude to heaven" for having destined them to live under its aegis. Nowhere in the world was power so nicely balanced, the press so free, or the laws so nearly supreme.[10]

Until comparatively recent times, the march of the years did not lessen the veneration of Americans for their Constitution. Emerson praised it as "the hope of the world."[11] Webster described it as the most glorious instrument of a free government with which it had pleased Providence, "in any age, to bless any of the nations of the earth." He regarded it, in fact, as "complete and perfect" and denounced attempts to amend it as almost the equivalent of treason. The duty of the citizen was to be content with it in its existing form and to resist all proposals for change from whatever quarter they might come.[12] As a member of Congress, Abraham Lincoln voiced much the same sentiments. He admonished his colleagues in the House in 1848 not to get into the habit of amending the Constitution. It was better to leave it untouched, in a form as close to the original as possible. The men who made it had done their work, and who would presume to improve upon it? If Webster, Lincoln, and their predecessors venerated the Constitution, the attitude of Grover Cleveland was one of idolatry. Speaking at the centennial of its adoption, in 1887, he admonished his countrymen to revere their Constitution as an Ark of the Covenant, and to take upon themselves the solemn duty of shielding it "from impious hands." It had been found sufficient in the past, he asserted, and he doubted not that it would be fully adequate for the indefinite future.

Dramatic events in the early twentieth century made the first important breach in the wall of constitutional idolatry. The first was the annexation of the Philippine Islands and the subjugation of the natives to American rule. Statesmen who approved these projects soon found the letter of the Constitution ill adapted to the ends they hoped to accomplish. The Bill of Rights, for example, and guaranties against suspension of habeas corpus could not be easily extended to jungle-dwellers but little removed from the Stone Age. As a consequence, a tendency developed to refer to the "spirit" of the Constitution and to draw a distinction between its "formal" and its "fundamental" provisions.

One of the foremost exponents of such views was the polished Senator and rabid imperialist from Indiana, Albert J. Beveridge. He characterized the nation's fundamental law as "better than any other yet conceived," but he refused to regard it as divine, and he insisted that anyone who wished to change it should be allowed to state his views. More significant, he justified overriding the Constitution when it stood in the path of great national objectives. The security of our citizens, the security of our "island wards," and the security of liberty, he wrote, are not in the written word of the Constitution alone but also in our institutions, "which are the Spirit of the Constitution." The secret of American success is the willingness of the nation to look the facts squarely in the face, regardless of maxims and theories and even of "the letter of the Constitution itself when it stood in the way." [13]

A more important influence in promoting a realistic approach to the Constitution was the Progressive movement. In 1907 J. Allen Smith, of the University of Washington, published his *Spirit of American Government*, which deeply interested Theodore Roosevelt, Robert M. LaFollette, and other noted Progressives. Smith attempted to prove the undemocratic character of the original Constitution, castigating the Fathers for their doctrines of checks and balances and judicial review and especially for their concern with the protection of property. Six years later the substance of this book became the basis of Charles A. Beard's *Economic Interpretation of the Constitution*.

But long before Smith and Beard published their theories, the man who was destined to make the most successful application of Progressive doctrines had adopted a cool, analytical view of the

Constitution. In 1889 while a professor at Wesleyan University, Woodrow Wilson spoke at the centennial of the inauguration of George Washington. Chiding his hearers for being too prone to worship the past, the future apostle of the New Freedom asserted that the genius of America lay not in the forms but in the essence of her institutions. "We are not great in popular government," he said, "because we invented written constitutions; for we did not invent them. . . . We are great because of what we perfected and fulfilled," and such real achievements are not found in legal documents. On the eve of his nomination for President in 1912, he informed the celebrants at a Jefferson Day banquet that constitutions do not create liberty. "They are not the condition of our liberty but its expression." He considered the Constitution of the United States superior to that of Great Britain only in being more definite and more difficult to amend. There could be no doubt at any time as to the main intent of the American Constitution. But much of the British Constitution did not even have the support of a common statute. It could be "interpreted or understood in half a dozen different ways, *and amended by prevalent understanding.*" But according to Wilson, this did not make the English less free than the Americans, only less secure.[14]

One other component of the American political system impressed some observers as a marvelous invention. This was federalism. Madison, who was one of its principal originators, described it as "essential to the complete success of republicanism in any form."[15] John Fiske denominated federalism "the finest specimen of constructive statesmanship" the world had ever seen. It alone made it possible for the affairs of a great people, spreading over a vast continent, to be kept in a condition of permanent peace. But Fiske conceived for it an even grander mission. He saw no reason why the entire human race should not constitute one great federation, each little group managing its local affairs independently, but relegating all questions of international concern to the decision of a central tribunal. He looked forward to the time when it would be possible "to speak of the UNITED STATES as stretching from pole to pole,—or, with Tennyson, to celebrate the 'parliament of man and the federation of the world.'"[16]

Despite his general disdain for political forms and mechanisms, Woodrow Wilson was also ready to boast of federalism as an American achievement. Never before had any nation given to popular liberty "the scope of empire." Democracy for the ancient Greeks and for the "snug Swiss cantons" had received no more than a narrow, local application. Through federalism the American republic had bestowed upon liberty its highest confirmation: the extension of its principles over an entire continent.[17]

WHAT DEMOCRACY MEANT TO THE FATHERS

The founders of our political system left little doubt as to what they meant by democracy. For the most part they conceived it as rule by the people directly, in contradistinction to popular rule through representatives. But most of them thought of it also as a synonym for the sovereignty of the masses or the supremacy of the majority. Defined in either sense, it was viewed by nearly all of them in a distinctly unfavorable light.

Madison, for example, as chief architect of the Constitution and author of the most notable essays of the *Federalist*, left such a legacy of hostility to the rule of the masses that he appeared to many in later times as virtually a prophet of oligarchy. To his credit it must be said that after the new government was established, he fought for the Bill of Rights, condemned the Alien and Sedition Acts, and sought to limit judicial review to a defense of the prerogatives of the Court against encroachments by Congress and the Executive. But shortly before, during, and immediately after the Federal Convention he seldom referred to the rule of the majority except to condemn it. In 1786 he wrote to James Monroe that no maxim was more contemptible than "the current one that the interest of the majority is the political standard of right and wrong." It could only lead to the supremacy of the vicious principle that force is the measure of right. He urged his colleagues in the Constitutional Convention to adopt long terms of office for members of the national legislature, in order that they might have the requisite firmness and independence to "intervene against impetuous counsels." In addition, he advocated a Presidential veto, to be overridden only by a three-fourths vote in both houses of Congress. In Number 52 of the *Federalist*, which he claimed to have written, he referred to the tendency of all single assemblies to yield to sudden and violent impulses "and to be seduced by factious leaders into intemperate and pernicious resolutions." He warned the country also against the "symptoms of a levelling spirit" which had already appeared and advised the establishment of an agency in the government "sufficiently respectable for wisdom and virtue" to counterbalance the ambitions of the mob. Even after his retirement from public life he occasionally returned to the idea of a proletarian majority menacing the rights of the minority. The time would come, he cautioned, when the majority of the citizens would be without property, and without much hope of obtaining it. Class conflict would then develop, and the rights of the minority of landholders would be in danger.[18]

The antidemocratic proclivities of Alexander Hamilton are almost too well known to require comment. True, he recommended manhood suffrage, and he opposed slavery. But in the Federal Convention of 1787 he acknowledged himself no friend even of *republican* government. In presenting his plan for a federal union to the convention, he lavished praise upon the British system. He thought the House of Lords "a most noble institution." As for the executive, the "English model was the only good one on this subject." Only a monarch could be considered as above the danger of being corrupted from abroad. But since the American people were determined to have a republic, let the executive at least be chosen for life. Senators also should hold their places for life, or, at the minimum, during good behavior. The convention should go as far in the direction of stability and permanency as republican principles would permit. He saw nothing antithetical to free government in life terms for public officials. As long as the magistrates were appointed, and vacancies filled, by the people, or by a process of election originating with the people, the government was still a republic. In the *Federalist*, Hamilton wrote of the operation of government in terms unflattering to men in the mass. When great numbers of them got together, passion never failed "to wrest the sceptre from reason." If every Athenian citizen had been a Socrates, the Athenian assembly "would still have been a mob." The reason for this, he argued, was that regard for reputation had less effect when the shame of misconduct was divided among a number than when it fell singly upon one. Moreover, a spirit of faction, which is likely to infect all bodies of men, will often plunge their members into "improprieties and excesses, for which they would blush in a private capacity." [19]

By common conviction Jefferson is regarded as the most democratic of American statesmen in the early history of the republic. It is universally agreed that he deserves everlasting renown for his success in overthrowing such relics of aristocracy as primogeniture and entails, for his efforts to extend the suffrage, for his defense of intellectual and political freedom, and for his opposition to slavery. He has been somewhat less enthusiastically acclaimed for his condemnation of judicial oligarchy, his praise for the spirit of rebellion, his opposition to militarism and to government by force, and his demand for periodic referenda on constitutions and laws. All of these elements would have to be included in any broad ideal of democracy.

Yet Jefferson cannot be fitted to the Procrustean bed of the majority-rule democrat. In his first inaugural address he reminded his followers that "though the will of the majority is to prevail in all cases, that will, to be rightful, must be reasonable; that the minority possess their equal rights, which equal laws must protect, and to violate which would be oppression." Much earlier he wrote in his "Notes on Virginia" that "an *elective despotism* was not the government we fought for, but one which should not only be founded on free principles, but in which the powers of government should be so divided and balanced among several bodies of magistracy, as that no one could transcend their legal limits, without being effectually checked and restrained by the others." [20]

Two other documents seem especially significant in explaining Jefferson's views on democracy: his letters of December 20, 1787, and October 28, 1813, to James Madison and John Adams, respectively. In the first, Jefferson set forth his attitude toward the new Constitution, adopted during his absence in France. He liked it because of the compromise of the claims of the large and small states, the control over taxation given to the lower house, the provision for direct election of members of the lower house, the substitution of voting by persons for voting by states, and the organization of the government into legislative, executive, and judicial branches. There were only two features he disliked: the omission of a Bill of Rights and absence of the principle of rotation in office for the President. He said nothing about indirect election of the

President, choice of the Senators by state legislatures, or any of the provisions for the protection of the interests of the propertied and creditor classes.

In his letter to John Adams, Jefferson committed himself to the support of a "natural aristocracy of virtue and talent." This type of aristocracy he declared "the most precious gift of nature, for the instruction, the trusts, and government of society." "May we not even say," he went on, "that that form of government is the best, which provides the most effectually for a pure selection of these natural aristoi into the offices of government?" He made it clear that he would delegate the function of selection to the people themselves. They would separate the wheat from the chaff and, most of the time, succeed in making a proper choice of "the really good and wise." In some instances wealth might corrupt them and ancestry blind them; "but not in sufficient degree to endanger the society." It should be noted also that he envisaged an extensive system of public education as an accompaniment of this natural aristocracy. The ordinary citizens would need instruction to select their rulers wisely. And education of a higher order would be necessary for the training of talented youth whom the people might eventually choose for the work of governing.

In the popular mind of today Jefferson's political philosophy was distinguished by "boundless faith in the masses" and by confidence in the wisdom of majorities. Some of his expressions do seem to comport with such views. In his famous letter of 1813 to Samuel Kercheval he avowed himself "not among those who fear the people. They, and not the rich," he maintained, "are our dependence for continued freedom." He urged that all public officers, including the judges, be chosen by popular vote, by "every man who fights or pays." He proposed also that the counties be divided into wards, "of such size as that every citizen can attend, when called on, and act in person."

But against such assertions must be placed his regard for the farmers as the chosen of God, and his contempt for "the class of artificers as the panders of vice, and the instruments by which the liberties of a country are generally overturned." [21] He would apparently have had no more confidence in the rootless mobs of present-day cities than he had in the tycoons of industry and finance of his own time. It should not be forgotten either that Jefferson was a disciple of Locke. As such, he believed in limited government and endorsed the idea of divided sovereignty, with the powers of the legislature restricted to enforcement of the law of nature. He approved also of the system of checks and balances, including the executive veto; and while his theory of judicial review was not so broad as that of Hamilton, he nevertheless accorded to the judiciary the right to nullify laws, at least those necessary for protecting the coordinate status of the three branches of the government. He argued, in addition, that one of the chief reasons for desiring a Bill of Rights was the "legal check" it would put into the hands of the judiciary.[22]

We may conclude, then, by way of summary, that the Fathers had a conception of democracy different in many respects from that which prevails at present. Much of what we think of as democracy they denominated republicanism. The latter term meant to most of them stability above everything else. Madison thought that the chief need in every government was security against "fluctuating and undigested laws." Hamilton contended that "inconstancy and mutability in the laws" was the chief blemish of popular rule. He would give praise to "every institution calculated to restrain the excess of law-making and to keep things in the same state in which they happen to be at any given period." [23] Even James Wilson, with all his affection for popular sovereignty, informed the Pennsylvania ratifying convention that "in order to give permanency, stability, and security to any government," he conceived it of "essential importance that its legislature should be restrained; and that there should not only be what we call a *passive,* but an *active* power over it; for of all kinds of despotism this is the most dreadful, and the most difficult to be corrected." [24]

It was this passion for stability which dictated a large proportion of the components of the new governmental system: the executive veto, the division of Congress into two houses, judicial review, the aristocratic Senate, the Electoral College, and the whole elaborate system of checks and balances. The purpose was not merely to curb the rash and impulsive actions of the masses but, as Madison explained it, to banish unwholesome economic activity and create a favorable environment for the man of prudence and industry. Unsteady and capricious government gave an advantage to the "moneyed few," the shrewd and enterprising speculators, who were always eager to gamble on changing trends. It worked to the detriment of the conservative, industrious farmer, artisan, or small businessman by denying him the rewards of perseverance, thrift, and useful labor.[25]

By republicanism the Fathers also meant universal manhood suffrage, the subordination of the military to the civil authority, opposition to hereditary privilege, representative government, a federal system, and the sovereignty of law. Each of the last three requires a word of comment. Madison regarded representative government as so valuable an invention that he thought it might well happen "that the public voice, pronounced by the representatives of the people, will be more consonant to the public good than if pronounced by the people themselves, convened for the purpose." [26] Hamilton affirmed that the welfare of the people could be adequately protected by representatives as few in number as the five ephors of Sparta or the three tribunes of Rome. In fact, he believed that the smaller the number the greater their capacity for wise deliberation.[27] The marvelous achievement of a federal system meant to the Fathers an arrangement under which the sovereignty originally held by the people in the states was divided, with a portion being given to the central government, a portion to the governments of the states, and the remainder reserved by the people. As a result, both the central government and the governments of the states became truly sovereign authorities, each in its own sphere, with power to act upon individuals. This feature made the United States a real state in the juridical sense, as contrasted with the union under the Articles of Confederation, which was a mere league of states.

Especially characteristic of republicanism as the Fathers conceived it was the principle of the sovereignty or supremacy of law. Stemming from the teachings of such revered philosophers as Sir Edward Coke, James Harrington, and John Locke, it assumed the existence of a higher law beyond the enactments of legislatures and the decrees of magistrates. Much of this higher law was contained in the Constitution, but it was embodied also in certain vague principles of absolute justice and eternal right commonly regarded as the law of nature. To maintain and enforce the higher law was the special responsibility of the courts. Such had already been done when a number of colonial courts declared the Stamp Act unconstitutional and directed that it need not be obeyed. Many of the Fathers believed that the same principle should operate under the new Constitution. Madison, for example, informed the Convention that a statute "violating a constitution established by the people themselves would be considered by the judges as null and void." In defending the Bill of Rights as a member of the First Congress, he declared that the courts would "consider themselves in a peculiar manner the guardians of those rights." [28]

James Wilson and Alexander Hamilton sponsored a still broader interpretation of the higher law. The former avowed that the power of judges to declare laws unconstitutional was not enough. "Laws may be unjust," he argued, "may be unwise, may be dangerous, may be destructive; and yet not be so unconstitutional as to justify the judges in refusing to give them effect." He wanted to make the judges members, with the executive, of a council of revision, in order that they might lend the weight of their learned opinions in "counteracting the improper views of the legislature." [29] Hamilton expressed a similar view in Number 78 of the *Federalist*. He declared that the power of the judicial veto should extend, not merely to "infractions of the Constitution," but to invasions of private rights of the citizen "by unjust and partial laws." Perhaps he was thinking of property rights primarily, but the principle was susceptible of logical extension to any of the unalienable rights supposed to be derived from the law of nature.

THE EVOLUTION OF THE DEMOCRATIC IDEAL

One of the most surprising facts about the history of democracy in the United States since Jefferson's time is the dearth of emphasis upon absolute popular sovereignty. The idea that the majority has an unlimited right to rule, or that the voice of the people is the voice of God, has seldom found expression in the writings of those who have molded our ideology. Even during the age of Jackson, when the doctrine was supposed to have been regnant, few men of prominence avowed it. Emerson referred to frontier democracy as "that ill thing, vain and loud, which writes lying newspapers, spouts at caucuses, and sells its lies for gold." [30] The only equality among men he would recognize was the presence in all of them of the divine Reason. Even William Leggett, editor of the New York *Evening Post* and the *Plaindealer* and spokesman for the "mechanics" and small merchants, affirmed his belief in majority rule only to the "extent of the moral maxim that it is the duty of the majority

A national convention, an American contribution to the democratic process.
Republican National Committee

so to govern as to preserve inviolate the equal rights of all." He
hoped that rulers would "confine the interference of legislation to
the fewest possible objects, compatible with the preservation of
social order." [31] It would almost seem that the only prominent individual of the Jacksonian era who ever paid more than lip service
to the idea of majority supremacy was Chief Justice Roger B. Taney.
In helping to decide such cases as City of New York *v.* Miln, and
Charles River Bridge Co. *v.* Warren Bridge Co., he held fast to the
principle that the people, through their representatives, have the
right to take steps for the protection of their health, safety, and
welfare, even though the interests of individual persons may sometimes be infringed.

To find vigorous champions of democracy in the sense of majority rule it seems necessary to come down to the middle decades of
the nineteenth century. One of its most voluble apostles of this time
was Wendell Phillips. Most of the opponents of slavery appealed
to a higher law of justice and right to bolster their arguments. Not
so Phillips. He had a sublime faith in the moral judgment of the

people to correct a wrong if their noble instincts were allowed free exercise. "The people never err," he told the Massachusetts Anti-slavery Society in 1852. "The voice of the people is the voice of God." He hastened to add that he did not mean the people of any particular day or week. No single verdict of the masses could provide a definitive solution. But the people in the long run always judge and determine rightly. According to Phillips, their wisdom and virtue greatly exceed those of their leaders. "The accumulated intellect of the masses," he said, "is greater than the heaviest brain God ever gave to a single man." The race would be better off without its leaders, who often turn out to be "dried mummies of dead intellects," too heavy to be dragged forward.[32]

Even more passionately than Wendell Phillips, the "Good Gray Poet" of *Leaves of Grass* and *Democratic Vistas* glorified the average man and applauded the rule of the masses. For Walt Whitman the leading men of America were "not of much account" and never had been, but the average of the people was "immense, beyond all history." When he did acclaim a leader, it was someone like Lincoln, whom he regarded as the supreme incarnation of the mass character. He eulogized even Grant, who, with no more genius than the average farmer or mechanic, commanded armies of a million men, ruled the nation for eight years, and then retired and toured the world with a cigar in his mouth "as phlegmatically as he ever walk'd the portico of a Missouri hotel after dinner." Whitman thought this an epic worthy of Plutarch. How those old Greeks, he exclaimed, would have seized upon Grant!

Nothing seemed to gratify Whitman more than evidences of the solidarity and collective zeal of the masses. The great effort of the people of the North during the Civil War was to him an august spectacle, which justified the proudest claims and wildest hopes of democracy. He profoundly admired the alacrity with which the "peaceablest and most good-natured race in the world" sprang "at the first tap of the drum, to arms—not for gain, nor even glory, nor to repel invasion—but for an emblem, a mere abstraction—for the life, *the safety of the flag.*" The docility and obedience of the soldiers in confronting the hopelessness, mismanagement, terror, and incredible suffering of the war conveyed to him eloquent testimony of the invincible greatness of the common people. He saluted the masses also for what he considered their wisdom and competence in choosing their rulers. In his judgment the "sublimest part of political history" was a national political campaign and its culmination in a national election. The actions of average Americans listening to their candidates, standing off and observing them, and "always giving, finally, the fit, exactly due reward" impressed him as a grand and dramatic exhibition of the success of democracy.[33]

The heyday of democracy conceived as the absolute sovereignty of the people was the period of Populism and Progressivism from about 1890 to the early 1920's. This was the age when it was confidently assumed that the cure for the ills of democracy was more democracy. It was a period of sublime faith in ingenious devices to transfer control over government from the bosses and party machines to the people themselves. Such was the motivation for the direct election of United States Senators, the initiative, referendum, and recall, the direct primary, the short ballot, and most of the movements for reform of municipal government. Typical of the leaders who personified the agitation for such doctrines were William Jennings Bryan and Robert M. LaFollette.

Bryan maintained early in his career that the people of the United States had sufficient patriotism and intelligence to pass judgment on every question that had ever arisen or that ever would arise. The great political issues, he argued, were essentially moral issues, and who could doubt the capacity of the people to decide between right and wrong? In the autumn of his life he took a stand in the Scopes evolution trial which proved that he had not departed one iota from his earlier conviction. As an attorney for the prosecution, he argued that a teacher is a representative and an employee of the people, and is required to act as his employers dictate. "A man cannot demand a salary," he pontificated, "for saying what his employers do not want said." [34]

Although part of a broader and more discerning philosophy, LaFollette's ideas on the sovereignty of the people did not differ markedly from those of Bryan. The Wisconsin Senator decided early that the rule of the people, with all its faults and shortcomings, in the final analysis provided better government than was attainable by any other system. In a letter to his constituents in 1910 he affirmed his confidence in their intelligence and patriotism, and declared that "the common, average judgment of the community is always wise, rational and trustworthy." He hoped to see the people clothed with the largest power to say the final word on both public officers and public issues. To achieve this it would be necessary to abolish caucuses and conventions, to substitute nomination by direct primary, to throw the full light of publicity on conduct in office, and to reorganize government to make it more truly responsive to majority opinion.[35] But in at least one respect the theory of LaFollette differed from the dogmas of Bryan. The Wisconsin Progressive recognized the need for expert counsel to enable representatives to legislate the people's will intelligently. Accordingly, he sponsored a Legislative Reference Bureau and fact-finding commissions and advocated the use of the resources of the state university in pointing the need for economic and social reform.

The decline of the Progressive movement in the 1920's and the descent of America into the slough of depression brought a re-examination of the nature and possibilities of democracy. The result was a series of new interpretations more profound and comprehensive than any that had appeared hitherto. Pre-eminent among them was the theory of John Dewey. In the mind of the Columbia philosopher, democracy meant primarily the antithesis of aristocracy. He regarded it, in fact, as almost synonymous with equality. He did not for a minute maintain that human beings are equally endowed with innate ability, but he held it to be part of the democratic creed that intelligence is sufficiently general to enable each individual to contribute something. He conceived of democracy also as requiring democratic means as well as democratic ends. Such elements as universal suffrage, frequent elections, and responsibility to constituents, he maintained, *are* important, not as ends in themselves, but as factors "expedient for realizing democracy as the truly human way of living." They rest upon the conviction that "no man or limited set of men is wise enough or good enough to rule others without their consent." They are important, moreover, for their educative value. They force a recognition of common interests. They involve consultation and discussion, which generally contribute to enlargement of views and to clarification of issues. Finally, according to Dewey, democracy embodies the idea of experiment. Its meaning must be continually explored afresh. "It has to be constantly discovered and rediscovered, remade and reorganized." And the institutions in which it is embodied have to be rebuilt to meet the changes that are taking place in the development of new needs of the citizens.[36]

The monumental events of the New Deal, World War II, and the "cold war" against Russia also necessitated some extensive revisions of the democratic ideal. As architect of the New Deal, Franklin D. Roosevelt sought to emphasize the strength and adequacy of democratic government to solve the problems of the hour. In his second inaugural address he affirmed his conviction that democracy had the "innate capacity to protect its people against disasters once considered inevitable." No matter what storms assailed, he never wavered in his robust optimism. With dictatorship riding the crest of the wave in Europe, he hailed democracy in his third inaugural as "the most humane, the most advanced, and in the end the most unconquerable of all forms of human society." At the height of the great struggle against Germany and Japan he declared the "power of the American people expressed through the free ballot" to be the "surest protection against the weakening of our democracy by 'regimentation' or by any alien doctrines." [37]

But democracy for Roosevelt was not a mere matter of universal suffrage and free expression of the popular will. He insisted that it must also be a positive force in the daily lives of the people. It must make the ordinary citizen feel that it really cares for his security. It must be "an affirmative, up-to-date system," never adopting a defeatist attitude. In the midst of tense and dangerous situations it would save itself with the average man and woman only by "proving itself worth saving." [38] In other words, it must provide not merely for political but for economic needs. If men are forced to choose between liberty and bread, they will choose bread. The real reason for the collapse of democracy in several European countries was not that the people disliked democracy but because they had "grown tired of unemployment and insecurity and of seeing their children hungry." [39] Although the New Deal President maintained that democratic government could accomplish everything necessary to preserve the balance of economic justice and eradicate oppression without impairing any of the liberties guaranteed by the Constitution, he showed little interest in the sovereignty of law. What he ardently desired was *effective* government, and he was not impressed by the supposed sanctity of any legal obstacles that stood in the way. In common with John Dewey, he refused to recognize any rigid principles binding upon government in all circumstances. No President went further in justifying experiment and expediency as cardinal political policies.

The function of interpreting democracy to the American people during World War II was performed not so much by President Roosevelt as by his Vice-President, Henry Wallace. Wallace conceived of democracy partly as an element of the welfare state and partly as a defense of the dignity and rights of the individual. Under the former he included economic democracy, which he defined as the "promotion of a stable but ascending general welfare by increasing the productivity of the people and distributing the income as evenly as possible without destroying incentives." Concern for the social welfare also necessitated ethnic democracy, or equality of opportunity for the different races and minority groups. Wallace contended that Soviet Russia had gone further in this direction than any other nation—so far, in fact, that she had much to teach Anglo-Saxons. The latter had persisted too long in an attitude of superiority toward other races. Britons and Americans had not sunk to the "lunatic level" of the Nazis, but they had sinned enough to cost them "the blood of tens of thousands of precious lives."

A final ingredient in social democracy, as Wallace conceived it, was education. He accepted the principle of majority rule, but only on the premise that the people should have the opportunity to inform themselves as to the facts. Here again he believed that Soviet Russia could hold a mirror to much of the rest of the world. For generations the Russian people had had a great hunger to learn to read and write. When Lenin and Stalin gave them the opportunity, they changed in twenty years from a nation with "ninety per cent" illiteracy to a nation in which "nearly ninety per cent" were able to read and write. If Russia could continue her educational progress at the same rate, in another twenty years she would surpass the United States.[40]

But democracy for Wallace was inseparable from the Bill of Rights and the idea of the sacredness of the individual personality. With the Nazi hordes rampaging through Europe and imposing their brutal dominion upon weaker nations, he insisted that the democratic body of faith must honor the right of the individual to use the motive power within him for the full attainment of whatever "great and glorious conception" his mind had developed. He spoke also for "tolerance and humor in recognizing the right of all men to be different"; for freedom of speech, press, art, science, and religion; for "stability, order, and the avoidance of violence, bloodshed, and anarchy"; and for a "joyous faith in a progressive future based on the intelligent and constructive efforts of all the people to serve the general welfare." He affirmed his belief that the unlimited possibilities of both man and nature could be realized if those who were talented in science, art, and religion would "approach the unknown reverentially" and not under the compulsion of glorifying some particular despot, race, or nation.[41] In none of his wartime writings did he show evidence of perceiving any conflict between his lofty ideals of individualism and his admiration for the "democracy" of Russia. Perhaps he was deceived by the propaganda of the Soviets or the paper guarantees in their constitution. Possibly he assumed that Communist tyranny was a mere excrescence that would be worn away with the passage of time and the achievement of a stable, productive economy.

The beginning of the "cold war" in 1947 required some reorientation of the democratic ideal. No longer could Russia be praised as the shining exemplar of economic justice or as the gallant defender of the rights of minorities. Although President Truman had professed a liking for "Old Joe" after meeting him at the Potsdam Conference, he soon took a position in the vanguard of those who were denouncing the Soviet dictator and his minions as the incarnation of everything Satanic. But as a preacher of democracy, he voiced sentiments almost identical with those of his predecessors. He extolled the Bill of Rights as the "most important part of the Constitution." He declared that "unless citizens have rights against the government, no one can be safe or secure." The history of the Fascist, Nazi, and Soviet tyrannies, he said, had shown us how vital and necessary these guarantees are. The unrestrained use of force by government, he went on, "is just as great a danger to human progress now as it was ages ago." But in common with Roosevelt and Wallace, he did not consider that protection of individual rights exhausted the purposes of democracy. It must also be a "vitalizing force to stir the peoples of the world, not only against their human oppressors, but also against their ancient enemies—hunger, misery, and despair." [42]

DOUBTS AND MISGIVINGS

If we review the whole history of the country, America has had almost as many critics of democracy as stalwart defenders. In

"The Great American Game of Public Office for Private Gain." The "Plumed Knight" is James G. Blaine. By Thomas Nast. *Harpers Weekly, 1884*

colonial times, with the exception of a few notables like John Wise, Thomas Hooker, and Roger Williams, proponents of the ideal were nonexistent. Most of the founders of our national system had so strong a distrust of popular rule that they can scarcely be regarded as democrats in the modern sense. Since their time, the number of advocates of at least limited popular sovereignty has increased, but among them are several who had grave doubts, on occasions, of the merits of the system in actual practice. Woodrow Wilson, for example, referred to democracy as "the clumsiest form of government in the world." [43] During World War I, Senator LaFollette became so disgusted with the surrender by Congress of the authority and responsibility committed to it by the Constitution that he declared that the "soul of representative democracy" had been destroyed. The government was no longer a government "by the people for the benefit of the people," but a government "dominated in every department by wealth, primarily to increase the profits of wealth." [44]

The most trenchant critics of democracy in the United States since the early 1800's can be divided into three categories. That of first significance perhaps would include the advocates of intellectual aristocracy. Articulate among these, after the time of Jefferson, were Emerson, Edwin L. Godkin, and Oliver Wendell Holmes, Sr., but none of them went far in developing their aristocratic postulates. The first of the major philosophers of intellectual aristocracy was William Graham Sumner. Although he never condemned democracy as an evil, Sumner denied its importance and questioned its adequacy for the changing times. Conceiving it as almost synonymous with equality, he regarded it as a natural and inevitable product of the infancy of the nation when land was abundant and cheap. But he branded it as inadequate for the nation that was growing up. He did not see how, in an old country, it could be "anything but a short road to Caesarism." He denied that democracy had ever done anything, in politics, in social affairs, or in industry, "to prove its power to bless mankind." All great achievements, he argued, are made by the élite of the race. The masses provide little but muscle power. In every community those who carry on the work of society are those who "use reflection and forethought, and exercise industry and self-control." Therefore the dogma that all men are equal is the most flagitious falsehood and the most immoral doctrine ever propagated. It means that the man who has shirked or neglected his responsibilities is as good as the man who has honored and observed them, and it thereby "takes away all sense from the teachings of the moralists." Truth, wisdom, and righteousness can be attained only by painstaking, study, and striving. These things are so difficult that it is only the few who achieve them. "These few carry on human society as they always have done." [45]

Equally influential among the advocates of intellectual aristocracy, although less truculent and dogmatic, was William James. In fact, his ideas were so loosely expressed that it is difficult to determine what types he had in mind for an intellectual élite. He had a firm conviction that genius should rule, but he was undiscriminating in his preferences for different embodiments of genius. A Bismarck or a Napoleon seemed to him as worthy of esteem as a Jeremy Bentham or a John Stuart Mill. It was the great men and not the common people who determined the course of history. What would have been the future development of the British Empire, he asked, if Robert Clive had shot himself, as he tried to do at Madras? If Bismarck had died in his cradle, "the Germans would still be satisfied with appearing to themselves as a race of spectacled *Gelehrten* and political herbivora." For ordinary individuals to gain either virtue or wisdom, someone must be there to teach them—some Rembrandt to show them the struggle of light with darkness, some Wagner to teach them to enjoy musical effects, some Emerson to kindle a moral fire within them. As with individuals, so with nations. If shown a particular way, a nation may take it; if not shown, "it will never find it." Some nations have advanced more rapidly than others solely because of genius. Great epochs of civilization can be accounted for by an "exceptional concourse of genius" within a limited time. Mankind does nothing except through the initiative of leaders, great and small, and "imitation by the rest of us." Individuals of genius point the way, and set the patterns, which ordinary folk then adopt and follow. The problem of democracy, therefore, can be reduced to a simple question: What kinds of men are going to be charged with the responsibility of giving the cue to the masses? [46]

A second category of severe critics of democracy comprises the contemporary advocates of limited government. They propose not merely a few ordinary restrictions, like checks and balances, but such stringent limitations as practically to make the rule of the people impossible. Typical of the exponents of such views are Peter

Viereck, Russell Kirk, Eric Voegelin, and Walter Lippmann in the more recent formulations of his philosophy. The first three have attracted attention lately as prophets of a New Conservatism based upon a worship of tradition, a distrust of human nature, and a contempt for democracy as the enthronement of incompetence.

As early as 1922 Walter Lippmann in *Public Opinion* began casting aspersions upon the common man. The mass man, he alleged, is a victim of "stereotypes," of mental pictures grotesquely distorted

"Don't Expect Me To Get This Real Accurate, Bub." *From the Herblock Book (Beacon Press)*

by advertisers, journalists, and demagogues. This attitude was re-affirmed and elaborated about fifteen years later in the *Good Society*, with its references to "the sovereign but incompetent people." But the most emphatic assertion of such doctrine is to be found in Lippmann's most recent book, *The Public Philosophy.* The title refers to a supposed objective order of law and tradition embodied in Magna Charta, the Bill of Rights of 1689, the Declaration of Independence, the first ten amendments of our Constitution, and certain "traditions of civility" that have guided men of reason and integrity through the ages. The public philosophy, according to Lippmann, should actually govern. Both the people directly and their elected representatives are incompetent. They are too intimately concerned with the needs of the hour and with the placation of selfish interests. Someone, however, must apply the public philosophy. The official best fitted for this is the executive. He alone has the wisdom and patriotism to discern the welfare of the entire state. He embodies, as in Burke's conception, the interests, not simply of the people now living, but of those who lived in the past and of those yet unborn. He is "honor bound not to consider himself as the agent of his electors." How wide a gulf separates this doctrine from the faith of the Fathers in representative government and the separation of powers as a cure for the defects of democracy should be readily apparent.

Finally, the opponents of democracy in the United States must be taken to include the advocates of minority government. Obviously, the members of this group are related to the intellectual aristocrats, since any form of rule by the few is minority government. But the writers now under consideration are men who developed special theories to control or counteract the supremacy of the majority. John Fiske, for example, relied upon the independence of the executive, the judicial veto, and the checks and balances and other mechanisms of the Constitution to prevent the majority from using its power "tyrannically and unscrupulously, as it is always tempted to do." [47] Francis Lieber described the majority as "an unorganic multitude," addicted to impulsive actions. The true friend of freedom, he asserted, knows that the majority may err, and he has the right and the duty to try to convince them of their error, and "to bring about a different set of laws." [48]

The most elaborate theory of minority government was that of John C. Calhoun. The dour and implacable nullificationist denied that governments based upon majority rule could preserve their liberty even for a single generation. The history of all had been the same: "violence, injustice, and anarchy—succeeded by the government of one, or a few, under which the people seek refuge from the more oppressive despotism of the many." The appropriate remedy was to provide for a representation of interests, with a veto power accorded to each. Calhoun called this the "concurrent majority," but in actuality it would be the will of the minority that would generally prevail since every interest would have a negative on a proposed action. The South Carolina statesman contended that the requirement of unanimity would promote a spirit of compromise and conciliation, but how such a result could be expected from conflicts over explosive issues like slavery and the tariff he never made clear. There was perhaps more validity to his argument that the concurrent majority would improve the quality of statesmanship, since each competing interest would have the incentive to choose as its representatives men "whose wisdom, patriotism, and weight of character would command the confidence" of the other interests.[49]

DEMOCRACY AND THE REIGN OF LAW

Through most of American history the reigning concept of democracy as an ideal has not been that of unlimited popular sovereignty but of majority rule subject to the restrictions of a higher law. Such was the conception of the Fathers, and of Emerson, Channing, and most of the Jacksonians. Such, with a vengeance, was the doctrine of Thoreau and William Lloyd Garrison. The former exalted the moral law and the law of conscience above all political enactments and declared a single individual in the right more worthy of allegiance than an overwhelming majority in the wrong. Garrison proclaimed the standard that "that which is not just is not law, and that which is not law should not be in force." For him the Declaration of Independence came close to being an epitome of perfect justice. He publicly burned the Constitution of the United States as "a covenant with death and an agreement with hell." Similar in his basic assumptions but less radical in his conclusions was Abraham Lincoln. He also made the Declaration of Independence a part of the fundamental law of the nation. An underlying principle of his philosophy, moreover, was the existence of an absolute, unchange-

able moral law. If he sometimes departed from this in dealing with
opponents of the war, it was because he regarded the Union he
was fighting to preserve as no ordinary political system but as one
founded upon justice and right.

The most eloquent statement in Lincoln's time of the ideal of
democracy under the reign of law came from the man who provided Lincoln with some of his slogans. Theodore Parker defined
democracy as "government over all the people, by all the people,
and for the sake of all." But he insisted that it must also be "government according to the natural law of God, by the eternal justice to
which you and I and all of us owe reverence." American democracy,
he said in another connection, rests on the idea that "the substance
of manhood, the human nature in which all are alike, is superior to
any human accident wherein all must differ. Democracy can exist
only on condition that this human substance is equally respected
in the greatest and the least. Each man's natural rights are to be
sacred against the wrongdoing of any other man, or of the whole
nation of men." [50]

More famous but by no means more cogently expressed than
the preachments of Parker were those of William H. Seward. Referring to the constitutional provision for the return of fugitive
slaves, Seward declared that "there is a higher law than the Constitution." All laws governing property and personal rights within
the states, he insisted, "must be brought to the standard of the laws
of God, and must be tried by that standard, and must stand or fall
by it." [51]

The ideal of the reign of law has meant many other things. Some
noted Americans have given it the meaning of slavish allegiance to
every law on the statute books, regardless of its quality. In 1850
Daniel Webster deplored an increasing spirit of disobedience to
the laws, and he urged "good men" to resist it. He condemned the
"still more extravagant notion" that individuals may judge of their
own rights and duties and determine on the basis of some "higher
law" which ones they will fight for and observe. Obedience to established government, he avowed, is more than a mere matter of expediency; "it is a Christian duty." [52]

As a youthful member of the Illinois legislature, Abraham Lincoln was even more explicit. "Let every American," he exclaimed,
"every lover of liberty, every well-wisher to his posterity swear by

the blood of the Revolution never to violate in the least particular the laws of the country, and never to tolerate their violation by others . . . let every man remember that to violate the law is to trample on the blood of his father, and to tear the charter of his own and his children's liberty." He hoped that reverence for the law would become the "political religion" of the nation, and that all manner and classes of men would "sacrifice unceasingly upon its altars." Although after the outbreak of the Civil War he praised the concept of a higher law of right and justice, while the embers of the conflict were still smoldering he apparently adhered to a quite opposite view. Rebuking Seward for his proclamation of a higher law, he declared that that doctrine, insofar as it encouraged disobedience to the Constitution, "or to the constitutional laws of the country," had his "unqualified condemnation." [53]

The reign of law as a concept of American democracy includes one other element of signal importance. This is constitutionalism. As an operating principle, constitutionalism involves the supremacy of a body of rules constituting a fundamental law binding upon all officers and agencies of the government and guaranteeing rights and the protection thereof to individuals. It is the opposite of arbitrary or despotic government, whether of the few or of the many. Few writers caught the spirit of constitutionalism more accurately than did Alexander H. Stephens in condemning the arbitrary exercise of executive power by Jefferson Davis. Declaring that he would not turn on his heel "to exchange one master for another," the Vice-President of the Confederacy insisted that constitutions were made for war as well as peace. Under none of them could there be any such thing as martial law, for martial law "in its proper sense" was "nothing but an abrogation of all laws." When the laws were set aside, despotism resulted, and no proclamation by the highest officer in the land could make it otherwise.[54]

Many years after Stephens' death, John W. Burgess, the most eminent political scientist of his day, described constitutionalism as "the consciousness of the American people that law must rest upon justice and reason," and that a fundamental law is a "more ultimate formulation of justice and reason than mere legislative acts." [55] Later still, an equally eminent and more critical political scientist incorporated in a philosophical dialogue imitating the manner of Plato a definition of constitutionalism as "the civilian way of living together in the Republic, the way of preserving our liberties and the decencies of social intercourse against the frenzies of the despotic and violent temper." The author, Charles A. Beard, made clear his conviction that constitutionalism is not synonymous with the supremacy of the majority. The majority could vote themselves a despotism, dangerous to, if not destructive of, individual rights. But in doing so they would be waging war upon democracy, in the sense of free and enlightened rule. The essence of constitutional government is "restraint on power." [56]

To the majority of articulate Americans, constitutionalism has been almost synonymous with judicial review. Such was the prevalent assumption during the post-Revolutionary period, during the period of preparation and adoption of the Constitution, and during the era of John Marshall. It was even more the prevailing assumption during the nationalist epoch that followed the Civil War. Political theorists and constitutional lawers took it for granted that a supreme judicial tribunal must interpret and uphold the fundamental law. To John Fiske it was a truth as simple as the fact of evolution that legislatures were prone to violate the Constitution. When any of them did so, their laws could be brought before the Supreme Court, which would properly annul them and render them of no effect. This feature of civil government, he taught, could hardly be overrated. It marked a "momentous advance in civilization." [57]

John W. Burgess did not hesitate to call the government of the United States an "aristocracy of the robe," the truest aristocracy the world had yet produced. His logic was as disarmingly simple as that of Fiske: The law must rest upon justice and reason. The Constitution is a "more ultimate formulation" of justice and reason than ordinary laws. The judiciary is a "better interpreter" of the justice and reason embodied in the Constitution than can be said to be true of the legislature. Good citizens should therefore be grateful for the rule of the courts as the surest guaranty of intelligent and civilized government. [58]

It has been noted already that the tendency of Americans to worship their Constitution as an Ark of the Covenant began to break down soon after the beginning of the twentieth century. A similar change occurred with respect to judicial review. The appointment of Oliver Wendell Holmes, Jr., as an Associate Justice of the Supreme

Court by Theodore Roosevelt in 1902 foreshadowed an increasing popularity of the doctrine of judicial continence, under which the Justices themselves are supposed to restrain their tendency to veto laws properly enacted, unless in direct and palpable conflict with the Constitution. Time and again in his court opinions, Justice Holmes affirmed the right of the people through their representatives to adopt measures necessary to advance their welfare. Though

The United States Supreme Court Building, home of the nation's highest judicial body. *National Park Service*

he doubted the wisdom of many of their enactments, he argued that progress comes only through trial and error, and that social experiments "in the insulated chambers afforded by the several States" are the best means of obtaining knowledge and experience for the good of society.

In few respects was Holmes either a democrat or a liberal. Though he sometimes wrote as if he had faith in the wisdom and virtue of the masses, such was not really the case. His philosophy was deeply imbued with the cynicism of the Social Darwinists. The law of the universe was competition and conflict, a struggle for existence and survival of the fittest. Ideas and projects for social welfare were subject to this iron law. Those which emerged victorious in the struggle were the ones that would be best for a particular time and condition. The others would suffer elimination as ruthless as the destruction of summer insects by an autumn frost. Holmes's paramount concern was to make sure that the struggle went on unimpeded. For this reason the courts should not interfere with the activity of legislatures in experimenting or with the tendency of individuals to express unorthodox ideas. But he had almost no sympathy with reform and none at all with panaceas or nostrums. He scoffed at proposals for tinkering with the economic system, and doubted that the condition of the lower classes could be much improved except by "taking life in hand" and building a better race.[59]

As one would expect, opposition to the judicial veto took a more radical form outside the Supreme Court. In 1912 Theodore Roosevelt, as candidate for President on the Progressive ticket, advocated the recall of judicial decisions. If the courts annulled a law involving social issues, the people would have the right in an election to reverse the decision of the court and uphold the law. Ten years later Robert M. LaFollette rose in his wrath in the United States Senate to condemn "judicial oligarchy." The fundamental question, he said, was whether "all progress should be checked by the arbitrary dictates of five judges." He made no specific proposals for correcting the evil, but he seemed to imply that a two-thirds or perhaps a three-fourths majority should be required to enable the Court to nullify a law.

The most formidable attack on the power of judicial review awaited the advent of the New Deal. In 1935 two of the laws which President Roosevelt considered most basic to his program—the NIRA and the AAA—were pronounced unconstitutional by the Supreme Court. The President was stunned and aghast. He denounced the Court for throwing the nation back into the "horse and buggy age." After several additional defeats, he startled the nation by proposing to "reform" the Court in February, 1937. For every justice who had reached the age of seventy and refused to retire, a new justice would be added to the bench, up to a maximum of six. By this means Roosevelt hoped to accomplish an infusion of younger blood into the Court to counteract the influence of the aging conservative members appointed by his Republican predecessors. In his message to Congress proposing the reform, the New Deal President indicted the judges for rigidity of outlook and indifference to the changing times. They were wearing "old glasses, fitted for the needs of another generation." Only by the addition of younger men could the Court be revitalized and given the resilience necessary to enable it to take into account the complicated facts of a revolutionized world.

Roosevelt's scheme for judicial reform brought an avalanche of wrath upon his head. He was accused of trying to "pack" the Supreme Court and of plotting to destroy the separation of powers and the independence of the judiciary. Newspaper editors, eminent lawyers, and conservative deans of law schools denounced him for undermining constitutionalism. For some of his opponents the reform proposal could have no other effect than the ultimate destruction of republican government. So vehement was the opposition that when the bill was presented to the Senate, the Judiciary Committee killed it by a vote of 10 to 8. Nevertheless, Roosevelt achieved most of the aims of his plan. While the project was still being considered, one of the Justices announced his retirement, and his example was soon followed by several others. Within a few years the President was able to appoint seven new members to the supreme bench. The reconstituted Court proceeded to approve legislative measures no less revolutionary than AAA and NIRA. Among them were the Social Security Act, the Fair Labor Standards Act, and laws providing for a death sentence on public utility holding companies and prohibiting the use of injunctions in labor disputes. The results amounted virtually to a constitutional revolution, but a very necessary one from the viewpoint of the President. He regarded the effects of his Court plan as "a turning point in our modern history." He believed that "unless the Court had changed, or unless some quick means had been found" to give the government the power it needed to solve the nation's problems, there was "grave doubt" that democracy could have survived the crisis "which was bearing down upon it from within, to say nothing of the threat against it from abroad." [60]

By way of summary it can be said that American thinkers have conceived of both the greatness and the destiny of their country largely in terms of its democratic institutions. But their conceptions of the meaning of democracy have varied widely. Comparatively few have envisaged the ideal in the literal sense of government by the masses, directly or through their representatives. Some have thought of it as the repudiation of aristocracy or as the embodiment of equality. A small number have regarded it as not inconsistent with the rule of an intellectual élite chosen by a discriminating citizenry. Except during the flowering of the Populist and Progressive movements, the overwhelming tendency has been to interpret the democratic ideal as synonymous with limited popular sovereignty. Those adhering to this view have conceded that the majority should rule, but only with a due regard for the rights of minorities.

As a restriction upon popular sovereignty, exponents of democracy have assumed the existence of a higher law, reigning over all and sundry like "a brooding omnipresence in the sky." To embody such a law a written constitution, revered almost as a sacred charter, has been considered necessary. The homage it has received derives not merely from the checks and obstacles it places in the way of impetuous majorities, but more especially from its safeguards of individual rights. As the shadow of totalitarianism has lengthened, more and more emphasis has been given to such elements of free government as protection of minorities, the sacredness of the individual, and the importance of safety and security under the reign of law. To uphold and foster such values is recognized by an increasing number of thoughtful Americans as the true mission of our republic in a darkening world.

NOTES TO CHAPTER FOUR

1. *Letters and Other Writings of James Madison,* Published by Order of Congress (Philadelphia: J. B. Lippincott Co., 1865), IV, 467.
2. *Writings,* Centenary ed. (Boston: American Unitarian Assoc., 1907-16), VIII, 281.
3. Jonathan Elliot, ed., *The Debates in the Several State Conventions on the Adoption of the Federal Constitution* (Washington: Printed by and for the editor, 1863), II, 423-24.
4. *Orations and Speeches on Various Occasions* (Boston: Little, Brown and Co., 1870), I, 161-62.
5. George E. Baker, ed., *The Works of William H. Seward* (New York: Redfield, 1853-54), III, 78.
6. *The Works of Daniel Webster* (Boston: Little, Brown and Co., 1869), I, 404.
7. Elliot, ed., *Debates,* II, 432.

8. *The Rights of Man,* Modern Library ed. (New York: Random House, 1943), p. 124.
9. Albert E. Bergh, ed., *The Writings of Thomas Jefferson* (Washington: Thomas Jefferson Memorial Assoc., 1907), X, 292; XIII, 403.
10. C. F. Adams, ed., *The Works of John Adams, Second President of the United States* (Boston: Little, Brown and Co., 1856), IV, 382.
11. R. W. Emerson, *Complete Works,* Riverside ed. (New York: Houghton Mifflin Co., 1883-88), VII, 267.
12. *Works,* I, 336; II, 382, 402.
13. *The State of the Nation* (Indianapolis: The Bobbs-Merrill Co., 1924), pp. 44-45; from *The Meaning of the Times and Other Speeches* by Albert J. Beveridge, copyright © 1908, 1936, used by special permission of the publishers, The Bobbs-Merrill Company, Inc., Indianapolis, pp. 109, 171.
14. R. S. Baker and W. E. Dodd, eds., *College and State* (New York: Harper and Brothers, *ca.* 1925), II, 182-83, 428-29; *An Old Master and Other Political Essays* (New York: Charles Scribner's Sons, 1893), pp. 143-44.
15. *Letters,* Cong. ed., IV, 66-67.
16. *American Political Ideas, Viewed from the Standpoint of Universal History* (Boston: Houghton Mifflin Co., 1911), pp. 125, 143-44.
17. Baker and Dodd, eds., *College and State,* I, 179-80.
18. Gaillard Hunt, ed., *The Writings of James Madison* (New York: G. P. Putnam's Sons, 1900), II, 273; Max Farrand, ed., *Records of the Federal Convention* (New Haven: Yale University Press, 1911), II, 214, 421, 587; *Letters,* Cong. ed., IV, 23.
19. *The Federalist,* Modern Library ed. (New York: Random House, n.d.), Nos. 15, 55.
20. Saul K. Padover, ed., *The Complete Jefferson* (New York: Duell, Sloan and Pearce, 1943), pp. 648-49.
21. H. A. Washington, ed., *The Writings of Thomas Jefferson* (Washington: Taylor and Maury, 1853), I, 403.
22. Padover, ed., *The Complete Jefferson,* p. 123.
23. *The Federalist,* Modern Library ed., No. 73.
24. Elliot, ed., *Debates,* II, 445.
25. *The Federalist,* Modern Library ed., Nos. 37, 42.
26. *Ibid.,* No. 10.
27. Elliot, ed., *Debates,* II, 254.
28. *Annals of Congress,* I, 439.
29. Farrand, ed., *Records,* II, 22.
30. E. W. Emerson and W. E. Forks, eds., *The Journals of Ralph Waldo Emerson* (Boston: Houghton Mifflin Co., 1909-14), IV, 95.
31. Theodore Sedgwick, ed., *A Collection of Political Writings of William Leggett* (New York: Taylor and Dodd, 1840), II, 109.
32. *Speeches, Lectures, and Letters,* First Series (Boston: Lothrop, Lee and Shepard Co., 1891), 44-45, 177.
33. *Complete Prose Works* (Boston: Small, Maynard and Co., 1898), pp. 146, 210, 218.
34. From *The Memoirs of William Jennings Bryan.* Edited by Mary Bryan and reprinted by permission of the publishers, The John C. Winston Company (Philadelphia, 1925), p. 528.
35. Belle Case and Fola LaFollette, *Robert M. LaFollette* (New York: The

Macmillan Co., 1953), II, 842; *LaFollette's Autobiography* (Madison: The Robert M. LaFollette Co., 1913), pp. 760-61.

36. Joseph Ratner, ed., *Intelligence in the Modern World* (New York: The Modern Library, 1939), pp. 400-04; *Problems of Men* (New York: The Philosophical Library, 1946), pp. 47, 59; *The Public and Its Problems* (New York: Henry Holt and Co., 1927), pp. 206-07.

37. Samuel I. Rosenman, compiler, *The Public Papers and Addresses of Franklin D. Roosevelt* (New York: Random House, 1938-50), XIII, 322.

38. *Ibid.*, VII, 586.

39. Fireside Chat, April 14, 1930.

40. *The Price of Freedom* (Washington: The National Home Library Foundation, 1940), pp. 31-32; Russell Lord, ed., *The Century of the Common Man* (New York: Reynal and Hitchcock, 1943), pp. 37-39.

41. *The Price of Freedom*, pp. 31-32.

42. *Vital Speeches*, Vol. XVII, No. 24 (October 1, 1951); *A New Era in World Affairs* (Washington: Department of State Publications 3653, 1949), p. 8.

43. *Robert E. Lee, an Interpretation* (Chapel Hill, N. C.: University of North Carolina Press, 1924), pp. 19-20.

44. *Congressional Record*, 65th Cong., 3rd Session, LVII, 4984 (1919).

45. Albert G. Keller, ed., *War and Other Essays* (New Haven: Yale University Press, 1913), pp. 204-05; Albert G. Keller, ed., *The Challenge of Facts and Other Essays* (New Haven: Yale University Press, 1914), p. 275; Albert G. Keller, ed., *The Forgotten Man and Other Essays* (New Haven: Yale University Press, 1918), p. 364; Albert G. Keller, ed., *Earth-Hunger and Other Essays* (New Haven: Yale University Press, 1913), pp. 362-63.

46. *The Will to Believe* (New York: Longmans, Green and Co., 1897), pp. 227-30, 242-43; *Memories and Studies* (New York: Longmans, Green and Co., 1912), p. 318.

47. *Civil Government in the United States* (Boston: Houghton Mifflin Co., 1904), p. 176.

48. *On Civil Liberty and Self-Government* (Philadelphia: J. B. Lippincott Co., 1877), p. 407.

49. Richard K. Cralle, ed., *The Works of John C. Calhoun* (New York: D. Appleton and Co., 1856), VI, 33; *A Disquisition on Government* (New York: Political Science Classics, 1947), pp. 66, 69.

50. *Writings*, Centenary ed., XII, 436; XIV, 169-70; S. B. Stewart, ed., *Sins and Safeguards of Society* (Boston: American Unitarian Assoc., n.d.), pp. 6-7.

51. Baker, ed., *Works*, I, 66, 74.

52. C. H. Van Tyne, ed., *The Letters of Daniel Webster* (New York: McClure, Phillips and Co., 1902), pp. 442, 747.

53. John G. Nicolay and John Hay, eds., *The Complete Works of Abraham Lincoln* (New York: Francis D. Tandy Co., 1905), I, 42-43; Paul M. Angle, ed., *New Letters and Papers of Lincoln* (Boston: Houghton Mifflin Co., 1930), pp. 108-09.

54. *A Constitutional View of the Late War between the States* (Philadelphia: The National Publishing Co., ca. 1868-70), II, 786-87.

55. John W. Burgess, *Political Science and Comparative Constitutional Law* (Boston: Ginn and Co., 1890), II, 365.

56. Charles A. Beard, *The Republic* (New York: The Viking Press, 1943), pp. 26, 37-38.
57. *Civil Government in the United States,* p. 195.
58. *Political Science and Comparative Constitutional Law,* II, 365.
59. Truax *v.* Corrigan, 257 U. S. 312, 343 (1921); Noble State Bank *v.* Haskell, 210 U. S. 104, 575 (1911); Tyson *v.* Banton, 273 U. S. 418, 445 (1927); Max Lerner, ed., *The Mind and Faith of Justice Holmes* (Boston: Little, Brown and Co., 1946), pp. 390, 393, 428.
60. Rosenman, comp., *Public Papers and Addresses,* VI, Introduction, lxvi-lxvii.

Chapter Five

Freedom and Equality

M ost Americans who believe that their nation has been called by Destiny to redeem and enlighten the world have assumed that this call bears a close relation to the ideals of freedom and equality which are supposed to have characterized the republic from the beginning of its history. Both these ideals have been regarded as inseparable from democracy, and the former has been thought of as virtually a synonym for it. Theodore Roosevelt referred to freedom of the individual as the distinguishing principle of our American governmental system. He declared it to be quite as important to prevent the individual from "being oppressed by many men as it is to save him from the tyranny of one." [1] Much earlier Daniel Webster identified "American liberty" with representative government, the reign of law, and the supremacy of a written Constitution, founded upon the authority of the people, and "regulating and restraining all the powers conferred upon government." [2] Theodore Parker conceived of love of freedom as the very heart of American life. Americans, he said, "have a genius for liberty," and this liberty he identified with natural rights, with impatience of authority, contempt for tradition, and indifference to precedents. He saw his countrymen as rash, restless, forever changing, impatient, and addicted to the intensity of life. He thought it significant that, alone of all peoples, Americans had added rockers to their chairs—"because we cannot sit still." [3]

Perhaps in the whole history of our country no one brought out the substantial identity of democracy and freedom more clearly than did Justice Louis D. Brandeis in Gilbert *v.* Minnesota. "The right of a citizen of the United States," he said, "to take part . . .

in the making of Federal laws and in the conduct of the Government, necessarily includes the right to speak or write about them;
to endeavor to make his own opinion concerning laws existing or
contemplated prevail; and, to this end, to teach the truth as he sees
it." Were this not so, he went on, the right of the people to petition
the government for a redress of grievances "would be a right totally
without substance." In a later case the noted jurist reaffirmed his
views with even greater cogency. The Fathers of the nation, he
asserted, believed that freedom of thought and discussion are indispensable means to the discovery and spread of political truth,
that public discussion is a political duty, and that "the greatest
menace to freedom is an inert people." They realized that order
cannot be secured by force alone or by fear of punishment. Believing
in the power of reason, they held that the path of safety "lies in
the opportunity to discuss freely supposed grievances and proposed
remedies." It was one of their profoundest convictions that "the
fitting remedy for evil counsels is good ones," dispensed through
the medium of untrammeled debate both inside and outside the
government.[4]

Our political and intellectual leaders have not only thought of
liberty as the quintessence of our national being; they have conceived it as a foundation of greatness. For some it was a source of
moral and spiritual greatness. As North and South prepared for the
awful plunge into war, Abraham Lincoln sought to convince an
audience in Illinois that the strength of the republic lay in the love
of liberty. "Destroy liberty," he said, "and you have planted the
seeds of despotism at your own doors. Familiarize yourselves with
the chains of bondage and you prepare your own limbs to wear
them."[5] During the same years Carl Schurz, in a letter to a friend,
rejoiced that in America "anarchy" existed in full bloom. "Here,"
he declared, "are governments but no rulers—governors, but they
are clerks." Yet he saw in this superabundance of liberty the basis
of nearly all the nation's vitality. The churches, the universities, the
hospitals, and other charitable institutions springing up wherever
the need existed owed their origin, in nearly all instances, to the
"productivity of liberty." They were organized not by the governments, as in Europe, but by the spontaneous enterprise of private
individuals. The very possibility of doing something inspired a
desire to do it.[6]

On the eve of another great ordeal of battle Woodrow Wilson made devotion to liberty the key to the preservation of the soul of America—with a suggestion that if she saved her soul, she might reap some material benefits also to sweeten the spiritual morsel. He declared that he "would rather belong to a poor nation that was free than to a rich nation that had ceased to be in love with liberty." "But we shall not be poor," he continued, "if we love liberty, because the nation that loves liberty truly sets every man free to do his best and be his best, and that means the release of all the splendid energies of a great people who think for themselves." [7]

Other statesmen and publicists have proclaimed unequivocally their faith in liberty as the basis of material greatness. Robert G. Ingersoll wished that the signers of the Declaration of Independence could see what a century of freedom had produced—"the fields we cultivate, the rivers we navigate, the railroads running over the Alleghenies, far into what was then the unknown forest, on over the broad prairies, away over the mountains of the West, to the Golden Gate of the Pacific." [8] That quite a few people were deprived of their liberty and even of their lives as a result of the extension of these grandiose projects was of no moment to him. Some of our contemporary prophets have also paid homage to freedom as the source of material splendors. Herbert Hoover described in flowing metaphor the "garden of Liberty, which produces fine blossoms of enterprise and invention." He admitted that a few weeds of economic abuse might also be found there, but he argued that it was better to extirpate them "than to lose the whole garden through the blight of tyranny" and thereby destroy forever the hope of increased prosperity. [9]

THE MEANING OF FREEDOM

It seems to be an axiom of history that as a society increases in complexity its ideal of liberty undergoes a progressive constriction. To be sure, in some overripe or decadent societies, as in France before the Revolution, a considerable measure of freedom may exist on sufferance. But such cases are exceptions resulting from the indifference of rulers intent upon luxury and self-indulgence. In America the characteristic pattern of a gradual whittling away at the borders of freedom has been the rule.

The Sully portrait of Thomas Jefferson, painted in 1821. *American Philosophical Society*

The founders of the nation reverenced liberty as the most valuable of man's enjoyments. Even Hamilton described it as "the greatest of terrestrial blessings." He was convinced that the "whole human race is entitled to it; and that it can be wrested from no part of them without the blackest and most aggravated guilt." [10] As every schoolboy knows, Jefferson bracketed liberty with life and the pursuit of happiness as an inalienable right of man; what is not so well known is that he sometimes substituted "property" for the pursuit of happiness, as in his message to the General Assembly of Virginia, February 16, 1809. So profound was his concern for liberty that he once raised the question whether the condition of the American Indians, without any government at all, was not the most desirable.[11] Madison's opposition to a Bill of Rights in the Constitutional Convention is sometimes taken to mean that he cared little about freedom. But such a view is not consistent with the facts. His attitude did not spring from indifference to liberty, but from a desire to avoid confusion and delay in ratification, and from a concern for preventing every possible opportunity for an abuse of power. In the Virginia ratifying convention he argued that the inclusion of a charter of rights might be dangerous, to the extent that if an imperfect enumeration should be made, some people might draw the inference that everything omitted had been given to the general government. It is significant that after the new government went into operation, Madison became the foremost leader of the movement to add a Bill of Rights to the Constitution. He even proposed to include, along with restrictions upon the national government, prohibitions upon the states against violating freedom of conscience and the press and against deprivation of jury trial in criminal cases.[12]

Madison and Jefferson had scarcely been gathered to their fathers when American pundits began to narrow the concept of liberty in various ways. William E. Channing spoke of "moral freedom," which was not a "lawless liberty," not freedom from all restraint, but liberty united with law. This, he contended, had been the watchword of the Revolution, "the grand idea on which all our institutions were built." [13] John C. Calhoun went out of his way to heap scorn upon Jefferson's idea that liberty is an inalienable right of all men. Instead of being a right, he contended, it is "a reward to be earned, not a blessing to be gratuitously lavished on all alike;—a reward reserved for the intelligent, the patriotic, the virtuous and deserving;

—and not a boon to be bestowed on a people too ignorant, degraded, and vicious to be capable either of appreciating or of enjoying it." [14] In the opposite camp of northern nationalists interest in hedging freedom about with special restrictions was just as intense. Webster informed the Charleston Bar in 1847 that liberty was the creature of law, "essentially different from that authorized licentiousness that trespasses on right." "Liberty," he avowed, "exists in proportion to wholesome restraint; the more restraint on others to keep off from us, the more liberty we have."

When it came to professions of devotion to liberty as an ideal, perhaps no one was more voluble than President Lincoln. Yet some of his applications of the ideal appeared in strange contrast with his preachments. In defiance of the Constitution he suspended the writ of habeas corpus. He proclaimed martial law in areas far removed from the scene of fighting. He authorized his generals to suppress newspapers and to imprison their editors without a trial. Of course, he justified these actions on the ground that they were necessary to preserve a nation which was the citadel of freedom for all mankind. But whether he did not establish some dangerous precedents in taking a position above the law and setting the Constitution aside in time of emergency is a debatable question.

Although the Supreme Court, in 1866, sought to restore the Constitution to its honored place by proclaiming it "a law for rulers and people, equally in war and in peace," liberty did not suddenly recover the inclusive meaning it had had in the early history of the nation. Those who would contract it both in its content and its application continued to be active. The tough-minded Yale sociologist William Graham Sumner pilloried the romantic notion that liberty is a natural, indestructible right. Neither beasts nor savages, he declared, possess it, for they have neither the intelligence to understand it nor the sense of obligation to deserve it. Instead, liberty is found only at the summit of civilization, and only those are free who have the resources of civilization at their command. Liberty is not given to man as a boon from nature; it has to be earned by hard and incessant effort. Nature cares no more for the individual human being than she does for an animal. She allows either to die with complete indifference. To speak of rights emanating from nature or from nature's God is supreme folly. Nature does not even grant a right to life; as for liberty and happiness, man wins them if he can. The only real liberty that is possible or conceivable on earth is a product of law and institutions.[15]

Two other philosophically minded Americans in the so-called Gilded Age rejected the conception of liberty as freedom from moral and legal restraint. Paradoxically, one of these was Walt Whitman, commonly thought of as an archindividualist. Whitman described liberty as freedom from custom, from social and political convention, but, most of all, "a general freedom of One's-Self from the tyrannic domination of vices, habits, appetites, under which nearly every man of us is enslaved." But he denied that true freedom consists in escape from law. In a curious metaphysical fashion, he conceived the whole universe as "absolute Law." Only by understanding and obeying the laws could one maintain true liberty. Liberty was itself the "Law of Laws," the fusion of conscious individual interests with the eternal, universal, unconscious principles which run through all history, prove immortality, and give moral purpose to the objective world.[16]

Whereas Whitman wrote after the manner of a Hindu mystic, his younger contemporary, John W. Burgess, derived his inspiration from Hegel. "There never was, and there never can be," declared the Columbia constitutional theorist, "any liberty upon this earth and among human beings outside of state organization." Human beings did not begin their earthly existence in possession of liberty. They acquired it by becoming civilized and entering upon the obligations of political society. "Liberty is as truly a creation of the state as is government." And the higher the citizens rise in civilization, the more will the state expand their freedom and through them realize its material and also its spiritual destiny. Meanwhile, the state alone has authority to define individual liberty, limit its scope, and protect its enjoyment. Against that authority, the citizen has no defense. The state can give and the state can take away.[17]

Few Americans have made more serious inroads upon the meaning of liberty than have some who are commonly thought of as liberals. Denying that freedom is absolute, they have repudiated the Jeffersonian doctrine that government should not interfere with freedom of expression until "principles break out into overt acts against peace and good order." Justice Holmes declared that the right of free speech "would not protect a man in falsely shouting fire in a theater and causing a panic"—as if a parallel could be drawn between such a harebrained act and the expression of un-orthodox opinions. For a surprisingly large number in modern times freedom has been put into the category of what is expedient. By way of example, Woodrow Wilson advocated giving to agitators free rein to shout their ideas from the housetops because "it is pent-up feelings that are dangerous, whispered purposes that are revolutionary, covert follies that warp and poison the mind." The smart way to dispose of a fool, he said, is to encourage him to hire a hall and broadcast his folly to all who will listen. "Nothing chills nonsense like exposure to the air; nothing dispels folly like its publication; nothing so eases the machine as the safety valve." [18]

Since World War I the attitude of the Supreme Court in defining liberty has also been grounded primarily upon expediency. Freedom has not been regarded as a natural, or even a constitutional right, to which man is entitled because he is a human being, but rather as something to be granted or withheld, contracted or expanded, as the conditions of the moment may seem to warrant. To be sure, there have been apparent exceptions. Justice Brandeis, at times, came close to the view of eighteenth century philosophers that liberty is an indestructible right because it is essential to the life of reason. Those who won our independence, he pointed out, believed that the primary purpose of the state was to give the citizen freedom to develop his faculties. They prized liberty both as an end and as a means. It was an essential ingredient of happiness and also the instrument whereby happiness could be gained. They believed that unhampered debate of political issues was an indispensable element of free government, and that public discussion ordinarily affords adequate protection against noxious doctrines. But he went on to assert that freedom is not absolute. Its exercise is subject to restriction if necessary in order to protect the state from destruction, or even from serious injury. He did say, however, that the danger must be "so imminent that it may befall before there is opportunity for full discussion." If there is time to refute the falsehood or fallacies by argument, or to combat the evil by education, the remedy is more discussion, not silence. "Only an emergency," he added, "can justify repression." [19]

Likewise an apparent exception to most of the precedents set by the Court was the opinion of Justice Robert H. Jackson in West Virginia State Board of Education *v.* Barnette in 1943. The Justice declared: "If there is any fixed star in our constitutional constellation, it is that no official, high or petty, can prescribe what shall be orthodox in politics, nationalism, religion, or other matters of opinion or force citizens to confess by word or act their faith therein." He asserted also that "freedom to differ is not limited to things that do not matter much. . . . The test of its substance is the right to differ as to things that touch the heart of the existing order." Despite this last assertion, the impression lingers that he *was* referring to things that do not matter much. The case grew out of the refusal of children of Jehovah's Witnesses to salute the flag in the public schools. The Witnesses were a small and relatively obscure sect, noted for their eccentricities rather than for socially dangerous heresies. Refusal of children to salute the flag constituted no grave threat to the existing order. What the Justice would have said if the sect had been accused of advocating the overthrow of the economic system or of the government by force and violence is another question.

The sovereign basis of the Supreme Court attitude toward liberty in the period following World War I was the opinion of Justice Holmes in Schenck v. United States. The case involved the conviction of a Socialist agitator for distributing leaflets condemning the Conscription Act during World War I. Conscription was arraigned by the defendant as despotism in its worst form, a monstrous wrong against humanity in the interest of Wall Street, and the conscript was held to be little better than a convict. In the judgment of Holmes the propagation of such doctrine under the circumstances described was a heinous offense. It amounted virtually to criminal obstruction of the draft. Although no specific obstruction could actually be traced to the leaflets, such was their tendency and intent. Success was not necessary to make the distribution a crime. Freedom of expression, the Justice averred, is not absolute but relative. "The question in every case is whether the words used are used in such circumstances and are of such a nature as to create a clear and present danger that they will bring about the substantive evils that Congress has a right to prevent. It is a question of proximity and degree." When a nation is at war, many things that might be said in calmer times will be regarded as so dangerous to its safety and its chances of victory that their utterance will not be tolerated. In short, it was not the content of the leaflets which made their author liable to punishment; it was rather that they were distributed under conditions which gave a reasonable and probable prospect of leading to results that Congress had defined as criminal.

The new attitude of the Court received an emphatic reinforcement from the opinion of Holmes in the Debs case. Debs was convicted of violating the Espionage Act in 1917 and was sentenced to ten years in prison. His specific offense consisted in making a speech in Canton, Ohio, in which he proclaimed himself a pacifist and expressed sympathy for some other Socialists who, he alleged, had been unfairly convicted of obstructing the draft. He declared his opposition to America's war against Germany because he abhorred *all war*, and argued that the master class had always made a practice of exploiting the common people by forcing them to fight its battles. In upholding the conviction of Debs, Holmes said nothing about the "clear and present danger" test, but he made emphatic his belief that Debs's speech had a natural and probable tendency to obstruct recruiting for the armed forces and therefore to interfere with the war effort. Although Holmes's opinion was severely criticized as a departure from the premises of the Schenck case, its author did not consider it such. He wrote to Sir Frederick Pollock that he hoped that the President would pardon Debs, but only because of his age and poor health and because of the aura of martyrdom that was beginning to surround him. He did not for a minute concede that the Canton speech was a justifiable exercise of freedom of expression in a national emergency.

That the clear and present danger doctrine of Justice Holmes diluted the conception of liberty sanctified by early American tradition seems almost indisputable. But its weakening effect was minor compared with that of more recent opinions of judges of the highest court. In 1951 Chief Justice Vinson, appointed to the supreme bench by President Truman, delivered the majority opinion in Dennis *et al. v.* United States. The case involved the conviction of eleven Communist leaders for conspiring to form a political party and other assemblages and groups which would teach and advocate the overthrow of the government by force and violence. The defendants were not charged with overt acts of force and violence or even with conspiracy to commit such acts. Their behavior was exclusively verbal. What they had done was to organize people to teach Marxist-

Leninist doctrine contained chiefly in four books: *The Communist Manifesto, History of the Communist Party of the Soviet Union, Foundations of Leninism* by Stalin, and *The State and Revolution* by Lenin. It was established that the defendants took these books as gospel, and since the books themselves preached revolution by violence, the Court assumed that anyone urging their use must have the *intent* that everything they contained should be put into practice.

The majority opinion came close, as Justice Douglas pointed out in a dissenting opinion, to an argument for thought-control. It would result "in probing men's minds for motive and purpose." They would become "entangled in the law not for what they did but *for what they thought.*" They would be convicted "not for what they said but for the purpose for which they said it." The Chief Justice argued, however, that the government has the authority to protect itself. It must not be required to restrain itself "until the putsch is about to be executed, the plans have been laid, and the signal is awaited." He deduced from this that it is time for the government to strike whenever it learns that a group is attempting to indoctrinate its members with a revolutionary philosophy and to commit them to action when the leaders feel that conditions are ripe. In a concurring opinion Robert H. Jackson denied that even an individual has the right to teach or advocate the overthrow of government by force or violence. He implied that suppression of the free speech of anarchists in the late nineteenth century would have prevented the Haymarket riots of 1886, the attempted murder of Henry Clay Frick in 1892, and the assassination of President McKinley in 1901.

Liberals outside the Court have also contributed to the process of attenuating liberty. Chief among them was John Dewey. At the end of World War II he took it upon himself to emphasize that civil liberties are not absolute but are dependent upon the social needs of particular situations. He applauded Holmes and Brandeis for placing their defense of liberty, not upon anything inherent in the individual, but upon "the indispensable value of free inquiry and free discussion to the normal development of the public welfare." Earlier he had insisted upon a positive definition of freedom, rather than the old negative idea of freedom of the individual to do as he pleases, provided he does not interfere with the equal right of other individuals to do the same. The basic freedom, he contended, is that of freedom of *mind*, together with such freedom of action and experience as is necessary to produce freedom of intelligence. Freedom of speech and of the press are liberties of this character. They should be recognized as belonging to individuals, not by inherent right, but because the citizen needs them in order to develop his potentialities and make his contribution to society. Freedom of mind is not produced by the mere absence of restraint. It is essentially a matter of education. "It is a product of constant, unremitting nurture of right habits of observation and reflection." The chief obstacles to its supremacy are taboos, prejudice, intolerance, and the errors which spring from inadequate knowledge and neglect of the scientific method in dealing with social problems. The object to be attained by the removal of these obstacles is not so much the good of the individual as it is the welfare of the social organism to which he belongs.[20]

A few thoughtful liberals of our time have sought to broaden liberty, not by repudiating exceptions to it, but by extending it into new areas of social purpose. The celebrated Four Freedoms of Franklin D. Roosevelt provide a cardinal example. These were contained in a speech which the President delivered to Congress on January 6, 1941. They reflected both his deepening concern for the security of America and his growing determination to halt the march of fascism. He couched his ideal in international terms—that is, he appealed for liberty not only in the United States but "everywhere in the world." The four essential freedoms he declared to be freedom of speech and expression, freedom of every person to worship God in his own way, freedom from want, and freedom from fear. The last two rested exclusively upon an international basis. Freedom from want was to be attained by economic agreements which would secure to every nation "a healthy peacetime life for its inhabitants." Freedom from fear meant "a world-wide reduction of armaments to such a point and in such a thorough fashion" that no nation would be able to commit aggression against its neighbors.

Three years after the Four Freedoms were enunciated, America had emerged from a dark Gethsemane in which defeat by the forces of fascism was a dire possibility. Victory was still many months in the future, but the war had entered its decisive phase. President Roosevelt now went before Congress to emphasize the duty of laying plans for a lasting peace and "the establishment of an American standard of living higher than ever before known." Declaring that as the nation had grown in size and stature the old guarantees of life and liberty in the first ten amendments had proved inadequate, he called for a new Bill of Rights "to assure us equality in the pursuit of happiness." Genuine freedom, he said, cannot exist without economic security and independence. "People who are hungry and out of a job are the stuff of which dictatorships are made." Accordingly, he appealed for a second or supplementary Bill of Rights, which would include the following:

The right to a useful and remunerative job.

The right to earn enough to provide adequate food and clothing and recreation.

The right of every farmer to raise and sell his products at a return which will give him and his family a decent living.

The right of every businessman, large and small, to trade in an atmosphere of freedom from unfair competition and domination by monopolies at home or abroad.

The right of every family to a decent home.

The right to adequate medical care and the opportunity to achieve and enjoy good health.

The right to adequate protection from the economic fears of old age, sickness, accident, and unemployment.

The right to a good education.[21]

THE PERILS AND SNARES OF FREEDOM

Traditional liberty in the United States has included a large number of specific elements, all contained in the Declaration of Independence and in the Constitution and its first ten amendments. But aside from freedom of speech, only three—freedom of the press, freedom of religion, and the right of revolution—have received much attention. Each has been warped and misinterpreted to a surprising degree.

The Founding Fathers exalted freedom of the press as the palladium of our liberties, the indispensable means whereby an informed public opinion could guide the destinies of the nation. If forced to make a choice, Jefferson, as is well known, would have preferred newspapers without government to government without newspa-

"Mad Tom in a Rage." In 1801 some Federalist opponents insinuated that Jefferson was pulling down the pillar of government. *New York Public Library*

pers. He would tolerate no restraint upon the press except the ordinary laws of libel whereby an individual might recover damages for the publication of false statements injurious to himself. In condemning the Alien and Sedition Acts, Madison declared that "to the press alone, chequered as it is with abuses, the world is indebted for all the triumphs which have been gained by reason and humanity over error and oppression." He regarded the prohibition upon Congress in the First Amendment as absolute, and denied the possibility of drawing a distinction between freedom and "licentiousness" of the press. No means have ever yet been devised, he insisted, by which the press can be corrected without being enslaved. A supposed freedom that admits of exceptions is not freedom at all.[22]

The degree of attenuation and distortion of freedom of speech has already been surveyed in the section on the meaning of liberty. Misinterpretation of freedom of religion has been much more extreme. By any decent standard of accuracy the term must be defined as the right of the individual to believe anything he chooses to believe regarding a world of unseen powers. It must include a right of disbelief as well as full liberty to hold orthodox or unorthodox convictions. It must also include freedom to teach and practice religious doctrines, whatever their character, and to profess and attempt to convert others to one's unbeliefs. As Justice Robert H. Jackson expressed it, "The day that this country ceases to be free for irreligion it will cease to be free for religion—except for the sect that can win political power." [23] Yet religious freedom, defined in this fashion, has been a rarity in America. Its lone exponent during the colonial period was Roger Williams. The other so-called advocates demanded exceptions. Lord Baltimore granted toleration to all who believed in the Trinity. William Penn allowed free exercise of religion to all who reverenced "almighty God," but he made faith in Jesus Christ the test of eligibility for holding office.

Two of the Founders of the republic came close to a genuine philosophy of religious freedom. As early as 1776 Jefferson argued against interference with any religious practice unless it conflicted with the ordinary civil and criminal requirements of the state. He did not insist that its practitioners be Christians; he was ready to give equal privileges to pagans, Moslems, and Jews. He would in no wise forbid free argument, raillery, or even ridicule of religious dogma—on the ground, however, that such would preserve the purity of religion. In 1797 he drafted a Bill for Establishing Religious Freedom in Virginia, which declared religious liberty to be one of the natural rights of mankind. The bill incorporated the principle that no person should be compelled to frequent or support any system of religious worship, or be penalized on account of his religious opinions or beliefs. All should be free "to profess, and by argument to maintain, their opinions in matters of religion."

It is significant that Jefferson regarded this bill as one of the major accomplishments of his life. In organizing the University of Virginia he refrained from establishing a professorship of divinity lest the public authorities exert some influence upon the formation or evolution of creeds and observances. His philosophy was summed up by the famous phrase "a wall of separation between church and State," which meant in his mind that the government, under the First Amendment to the Constitution, had no authority to assist, promote, restrict, or interfere with the religious activities or doctrines of any sect or individual. Although he described himself as a Christian, in the sense of being a believer in the "human excellence" but not the divinity of Jesus, he regarded religion as exclusively a matter of individual conscience, and boasted that he had never attempted to make a convert or change another's creed.[24]

The views of Madison on religious freedom paralleled those of Jefferson more closely perhaps than on any other subject. Like Jefferson, he rejected adherence to any branch of Christian orthodoxy. He referred to belief in God as "essential to the moral order of the world and to the happiness of man," but he considered official Christianity an intellectual impossibility. His earliest contribution to religious liberty was a change he procured in the Virginia Declaration of Rights of 1776, substituting a phraseology which declared freedom of conscience to be a natural right and not merely an object of toleration. Like Jefferson, also, he insisted upon the absolute exemption of religion from control, assistance, or restriction by the state. He condemned the doctrine that some alliance or coalition between church and state is necessary for the health of both. So far did he carry his opposition to any mingling or collaboration of the two that he disapproved of the appointment of chaplains to be paid out of the public treasury. He objected also to proclamations by public authorities of religious fasts and festivals, unless in the form of mere recommendations to the people.[25] On the other hand, he differed from Jefferson in being more cynical as to the basis of religious liberty. Instead of crediting it to the idealism of the people or their leaders, he traced it to the multiplicity of sects in America. This, he said, "is the best and only security for religious liberty in any society." [26]

After the time of the Fathers, enthusiasm for genuine religious liberty seemed to pass into limbo. True, the phrase was often mouthed as a slogan but with such modification as to divest it of most of its meaning. The chief reason was probably the revival of emotional religion in the early decades of the nineteenth century. The movement took fire in the back-country regions and on the frontier and spread with the winds of Jacksonian Democracy. It lost little of its force or intensity until well into the 1900's. The whole course of the movement was marked by a tendency to equate freedom of religion with freedom to believe and practice some form of Christianity. To illustrate, Daniel Webster informed the Pilgrim Festival in New York in 1850 that it was America's mission and destiny to show that "all sects and all denominations" could be "safely tolerated without prejudice to our religion or to our liberties." The only requirement was that they profess "reverence for the authority of the Author of our being, and belief in his revelations." Six years earlier he had pleaded in the Supreme Court in an attempt to invalidate the will of Stephen Girard, on the ground that the latter's bequest of $6,000,000 to educate orphan boys was not a genuine charity, since it forbade instruction in religion before the age of eighteen. "No religion till eighteen!" the great orator shouted. "What would be the condition of all our families, of all our children, if religious fathers and mothers were to teach their sons and daughters no religious tenets till they were eighteen? What would become of their morals, their character, their purity of heart and life, their hope for time and eternity?" The Christian religion, he went on, "must ever be regarded among us as the foundation of civil society." Any plan of education which derogates from that religion, weakens men's reverence for it, or impairs its authority is in defiance of the public interest and can no more produce genuine charity "than evil can spring out of the Bible." [27]

Insistence upon the identity of religious liberty and loyalty to Christianity subsided but little in the decades that followed the

Civil War. The new period witnessed the revivalism of Moody and Sankey and the enormous popularity of Henry Ward Beecher. Even the compromised morality of the latter did not seem to impair the authority of his preaching. But belief in the indispensability of Christian doctrine was also prevalent in secular and less orthodox circles. The Social Gospeler Washington Gladden declared that a monarch believing himself ordained to rule by God was infinitely preferable to "a republic with no sense of divine vocation." "American democracy," he pontificated, "is not atheistic." [28]

The noted imperialist and naval expansionist Alfred T. Mahan declared Christianity to be "an essential factor in developing in nations the faculty of self-government, apart from which fitness to govern does not exist." [29] Mahan's bellicose disciple Theodore Roosevelt was superficially more ambiguous, but a critical reading leaves little doubt of what he meant. He called for "absolute religious liberty" and urged all to realize that "conduct is of infinitely greater importance than dogma." But he cautioned that no democracy could afford "to overlook the vital importance of the ethical and spiritual, the truly religious, element in life." The average good man, he continued, "grows clearly to understand this, and to express the need in concrete form by saying that no community can make much headway if it does not contain both a church and a school." [30]

As in the nineteenth and early twentieth centuries, the existence of complete religious freedom in America today is open to doubt. It often seems that what we really have is a kind of multisectarianism which accords toleration to every conceivable organized group adhering to a body of belief and practice. But rarely does anyone vigorously assert the right of every individual to believe or not to believe, and to express his beliefs, either positive or negative, in accordance with his own conscience, experience, or knowledge. What we mostly hear are admonitions to accept a belief in God as a foundation of morality and an element in the priceless heritage of American democracy. Two recent pronouncements of the New York State Board of Regents will serve as examples. In 1951 the board recommended that in every school the day be inaugurated with prayer as part of a program to stress the importance of moral and spiritual values. Four years later the board supplemented this by urging that moral and spiritual values be developed "through all activities and lessons of the school day." To support their urging of this program the Regents cited these words of President Eisenhower: "Without God there could be no American form of government, nor an American way of life. . . . Each day we must ask that Almighty God will set and keep His protecting hand over us so that we may pass on to those who come after us the heritage of a free people, secure in their God-given rights and in full control of a Government dedicated to the preservation of those rights." [31]

Another element in traditional American liberty that has undergone a progressive deterioration is the right of revolution. That a people had the right to overthrow a government grown tyrannical or which failed to protect life, liberty, or property was taken for granted by the men who founded the republic—not merely by such radicals as Samuel Adams and Thomas Paine but also by conservatives like John Adams and Alexander Hamilton. It was a doctrine necessary to justify the action of '76, but it had a broader basis than that. Government was assumed to be a product of a contract, under which the people delegated to their rulers power to enforce the law of nature and to judge violations of it. Essentially, this meant the power to preserve and protect life, liberty, and property. If a government abused or exceeded this authority, it followed by simple logic that it made itself oppressive and no longer deserved the people's allegiance. In the language of the Declaration of Independence, it then became not only the right but the duty of the people to rebel against their government and to set up a new one of such form "as to them shall seem most likely to effect their Safety and Happiness." The moderately conservative James Madison justified not merely the War for Independence but the revolutionary action of the Philadelphia Convention in scrapping the Articles of Confederation and providing for a new system of government, by referring to "the transcendent law of nature and of nature's God, which declares that the safety and happiness of society are the objects at which all political institutions aim, and to which all such institutions must be sacrificed." [32]

The most noted defender of the right of revolution, in the history of this country, was, of course, Thomas Jefferson. For him the right existed not just for the protection of the individual against tyranny but as a valuable device for keeping the citizens alert and aware of the importance of free government. A little rebellion, now and then, he maintained, was a good thing, "as necessary in the political world as storms in the physical." It helped to prevent the degeneracy of government and to nourish "a general attention to the public affairs." Apropos of Shays's Rebellion of 1786, he wrote: "God forbid, we should ever be twenty years without such a rebellion." If people remain quiet under discontent, "it is a lethargy, the forerunner of death to the public liberty." A few years later he declared: "The tree of liberty needs to be refreshed from time to time with the blood of patriots and tyrants." Nor did increasing responsibilities and the accumulation of power make him more conservative. Upon assuming the Presidency in 1801 he incorporated in his inaugural address the refreshing statement: "If there be any among us who would wish to dissolve this Union or to change its republican form, let them stand undisturbed as monuments of the safety with which error of opinion may be tolerated where reason is left free to combat it." [33]

For sixty years after Jefferson was inaugurated President, the right of revolution was rarely questioned. When discontented classes and oppressed nationalities in Europe and Latin America rebelled against their rulers, the events were hailed in the United States with almost universal rejoicing. With reference to the Hungarian revolt against the Hapsburgs, Abraham Lincoln introduced the following resolution in the Illinois legislature on January 9, 1852: "Resolved, that it is the right of any people, sufficiently numerous for national independence, to throw off, to revolutionize, their existing form of government, and to establish such other in its stead as they may choose." [34] Even as the chasm of civil war yawned in the faces of prominent Americans, their attitude did not change. Wendell Phillips justified the right of the seceding southern states to organize their government as they chose—just as freely as he acknowledged the right of four million slaves and freedmen to organize *their* government "and to vindicate that right by arms." He denied that there was a constitutional right of secession, but he insisted that the Declaration of Independence guaranteed to the people an "inherent, paramount, inalienable right to change their government" whenever *they* think that such a change will "minister to their happiness." [35]

Southern leaders also contended that what they were doing was nothing more than giving effect to the philosophy of the Founders. Upon resigning from the United States Senate in January, 1861,

Jefferson Davis reminded his colleagues that, according to the Fathers, "governments rest on the consent of the governed, and that it is the right of the people to alter or abolish them at will whenever they become destructive of the ends for which they were established." In seceding from the Union, the southern states were simply affirming their revolutionary right in accordance with the Declaration of Independence. If they should be compelled to resort to force, it would only be because this revolutionary right was wrongfully denied.

By a strange irony Abraham Lincoln lent his endorsement to almost the identical doctrine of Jefferson Davis. In his inaugural address of March 4, 1861, Lincoln affirmed: "This country, with its institutions, belongs to the people who inhabit it. Whenever they shall grow weary of the existing government, they can exercise their constitutional right of amending it, or their revolutionary right to dismember or overthrow it." From this assertion he went on to counsel patience on the part of his dissatisfied countrymen, and to urge them to refrain from reckless action. He adjured them to believe that in their hands, and not in his, was "the momentous issue of civil war." He pledged that his government would not assail them, and he admonished them that there would be no conflict unless *they* were the aggressors. Thus did each side attempt to fasten responsibility upon the other for beginning hostilities. So eager was Lincoln to achieve this that he seemed almost willing to accept Horace Greeley's advice to "let the erring sisters go in peace." After war broke out, however, he adopted an ingenious revision of the theory of revolution. When the Fathers proclaimed the right of revolution, they meant, he said, revolution against tyranny. There is no right to rise up against the freest government on earth. Consequently he felt justified in treating the southern secession movement as a criminal resistance of the authority of the Union. He denied both the right and the fact of secession. The Constitution recognized no privilege of a state to withdraw from the Union. The rebellion was therefore the work of individuals and could legally be suppressed by the military power of the federal government.

After the debacle at Appomattox the right of revolution practically disappeared from the folklore of America. From the fiery crucible of war came a swaggering nationalism that exalted the

Union above both individuals and subdivisions. Lincoln's conception of the Union as older than the states and the American republic as the citadel of freedom appeared to be vindicated. Seventeen months after Lee's surrender, as enlightened a liberal as Carl Schurz could say that he still considered the rebellion "one of the great crimes in history"; and he added that "victorious Liberty, firmly planting her heel upon the neck of defeated crime, would have been no unwelcome sight to me." [36] As time passed, the nationalism generated by the war was strengthened by new conceptions of sovereignty imported largely from Germany. Sovereignty was held to be indivisible and to be vested exclusively in the nation. Despite the fiction of federalism, the American republic was denominated a fully sovereign state in no less degree than France, Great Britain, or Russia. Finally, the preaching by anarchists and Marxists of violent overthrow of governments aroused the full hatred of reactionaries, and of many substantial and conservative citizens also, against the idea of rebellion. As a result, revolution came to be associated in the popular mind with bloody riots, bomb-throwings, and assassinations.

Since the close of the nineteenth century, both liberals and anti-liberals have spoken as if with one voice in condemnation of revolution. As strikes and radical movements swept through the industrial cities, Theodore Roosevelt bewailed the fact that a section of the population deified what he called "violent homicidal lawlessness." If ever the people as a whole adopted these views, he warned, "then we shall have proved that we are unworthy of the heritage our forefathers left us; and our country will go down in ruin." [37] So firmly convinced was he that the dangers he foresaw were imminent that he refused to meet John P. Altgeld personally lest he might soon have to face him sword in hand on the field of battle. Many years later the Supreme Court of the United States upheld the constitutionality of an act which made it a crime merely to "advocate" the overthrow of the government by force and violence. The Chief Justice, in delivering the opinion of the Court, argued that advocacy signified intent to accomplish the result "as speedily as circumstances would permit." In a concurring opinion Associate Justice Robert H. Jackson supported this view. He admitted that, according to Communist doctrine, "an established government in control of modern technology cannot be overthrown by force until it is about ready to fall of its own weight." But he contended that advocacy would be the initial step in a long chain of preparations for revolution. The probable or immediate success of the initial step was not an issue.[38] Why such reasoning could not be extended to make criminal the advocacy by Communists of government ownership of public utilities, or of any other reform that might weaken capitalism, is not readily apparent.

It remains to consider one final viewpoint in opposition to revolution. This is the forceful argument of John Dewey that it is impossible to separate ends and means. The means, he said, condition and often control the ends or purposes it is hoped to achieve. He declared that he knew of no greater fallacy than the claim of those who hold to the dogma that the use of brute force will bring into existence some noble conception of a New Jerusalem. "Force breeds counterforce," he maintained. "The Newtonian law of action and reaction still holds in physics, and violence is physical." He demonstrated, moreover, that a reliance upon force, in the belief that violence is inevitable, "limits the use of available intelligence." The method of democracy, he contended, is not the resolution of conflicts by bludgeoning the opposition into silence but by bringing the claims of both sides into the open, discussing, investigating, and analyzing them and arriving at solutions by scientific consideration of evidence.[39] The Dewey approach would undoubtedly eliminate the evils of revolutionary violence. But the problem of how to induce a brutal tyranny like that of Hitler or Stalin to accept the methods of scientific analysis would still remain.

EQUALITY, SOCIAL AND ECONOMIC

Few subjects in American lore have elicited more general agreement than the idea that equality is a distinguishing element of our national character. James Madison advised the delegates to the Federal Convention that the people of the United States were "perhaps the most singular" of any known. The reason he adduced was that they had "fewer distinctions of fortune and less of rank" than characterized the inhabitants of any other nation. He refused to admit Greece or Rome, or any other ancient state, as an exception. He scoffed, moreover, at the supposition that American equality might be ephemeral. The vast extent of unpeopled territory, he opined, would effectively prevent for a considerable time "an increase of the poor and discontented."

John Adams thought it significant that in every country of considerable size, where the arts and sciences were cultivated and commerce or agriculture improved, an aristocracy had risen up, consisting of a few rich and honorable families who had wrested power from the people and had hoodwinked the latter into believing and confessing them a "superior order of beings." Only in America, and to some extent in England, had the people preserved a share of power. Elsewhere popular rule was limited to "the tops of a few inaccessible mountains, among rocks and precipices in territories so narrow that you may span them with a hand's breadth." [40] Though contemptuous of the masses and their Jacobin radicalisms, he urged a bridle upon the rich lest they use their economic power to maintain a ruthless oligarchy. What he really preferred was a government of the mean based upon a wide distribution of property, with checks and balances to curb the ambitions of particular classes. He would suppress relentlessly all such leveling movements as Shays's Rebellion, but he had no sympathy for Hamilton's schemes to give free rein to speculative capitalists in using the government for their own enrichment.

Among the founders of the republic, the most celebrated exponent of equality was Thomas Jefferson. That Jefferson condemned monarchy and aristocracy, that he was an agrarian, and that he opposed the financial schemes of Alexander Hamilton is well known. On the basis of these facts it has been assumed that he was a radical egalitarian, that he aspired to abolish concentrated wealth and transform America into a nation of petty tradesmen and small freeholders. There can be no doubt that he did accomplish the abolition of entails and primogeniture in Virginia, and he proposed in 1776 that the state should grant fifty acres of land to every white male adult who had less than that amount. There can be no doubt also that he condemned aristocracy of birth or wealth. He did not oppose but warmly favored a *natural* aristocracy of virtue and talent. He denounced the fiscal schemes of Hamilton, but for antimercantilist rather than for anticapitalist reasons. Even his agrarianism he was able to modify drastically after he became President. In his last year in office he recommended "the encouragement of manufactures to the extent of our own consumption at least, in all articles of which we raise the raw material." As for measures to promote equalization of wealth, the appeal was never strong. In his second inaugural address he urged that the government adopt as one of its objectives maintaining "that state of property, equal or unequal, which results to every man from his own industry, or that of his fathers." He seems even to have been opposed to surtaxes of any kind to level down the fortunes of the rich. In his "Prospectus on Political Economy" written in 1816, he asserted that to take from one, because he is thought to have acquired or inherited too much, "in order to spare to others, who, or whose fathers have not exercised equal industry or skill" is to violate a law of nature. The only concession he would make to equality in such cases was to suggest a "law of equal inheritance to all in equal degree."

More modern in his outlook than Jefferson, and at the same time more radical, was his well-known disciple Thomas Paine. Never the possessor of much property himself, Paine could perhaps sympathize more keenly with the fate of the lower classes. Though untinged by extremism, he argued that the miseries of the poor were generally not of their own making but were the product of bad laws, obsolete customs, and cruel strokes of fortune. On the other hand, the possessions of the rich were not entirely things they could rightfully claim as rewards of their talent or industry; to a large extent they were profits from the labor of others or bounties resulting from the progress of society. He proposed, therefore, to redress the balance by expropriating the rich of some of their unmerited surplus and using it for the benefit of the poor. In his *Rights of Man* he advocated progressive taxes on unearned incomes and steeply graduated inheritance taxes. The revenues obtained would be used to provide subsidies for the support of children and the aged, public works for the relief of unemployment, and benefits for education and similar purposes. In a shorter work entitled *Agrarian Justice* he recommended a special tax on land, similar to a levy on the unearned increment. "It is the value of the improvement only," he wrote, "and not of the earth itself, that is individual property." He would therefore require every owner of cultivated land to pay to the community a *ground-rent* as his contribution to society for wealth he did not create.

Through the remainder of the nineteenth century and into the twentieth American leaders continued to give generous endorsement to the idea of equality, and some of them obviously meant it. Wendell Phillips declared for the "equalization of property—nothing else." The nearest approach to his ideal of civilization was a New England town of two thousand inhabitants, "with no rich man and no poor man in it, all mingling in the same society, every child at the same school, no poorhouse, no beggars, opportunities equal.

A sod house in Custer County, Nebraska, about 1887. This humble dwelling contrasted sharply with the marble palaces of the rich in New York, Chicago, and Newport. *Nebraska State Historical Society*

. . . " [41] Walt Whitman wrote in terms of "millions of comfortable city homesteads and moderate-sized farms, healthy and independent, single separate ownership, fee simple, life in them complete but cheap, within reach of all." Democracy, he said, looks with dissatisfied eye "upon the very poor, the ignorant, and on those out of business. She asks for men and women with occupations, well-off, owners of houses and acres, and with cash in the bank. . . ." But exceptional wealth, luxury, "immense capital and capitalists," "five-dollar-a-day hotels," artificial improvements, "form, more or less, a sort of anti-democratic disease and monstrosity. . . ." [42]

Daniel Webster, also, paid verbal tribute to the ideal of a wide distribution of ownership. Though in his professional and political life he spent much time lusting after the fleshpots, he devoted a large portion of his intellectual energy to attempts to prove the merits of limited ownership. America, he claimed, owed her greatness and her democratic institutions to the fact that her first settlers divided the soil into small freeholds. They came to these shores as men of limited resources with no capital to acquire large estates. None could become landlords and none needed to accept employment as tenants or laborers. In reclaiming the wilderness from barbarians, all were on the same level. This fact, according to Webster, fixed the future frame and form of the government. With property divided as it was, "no other government than that of a republic could be maintained." If we can believe his assertions, he hoped that this condition would continue. The freest government on earth, he admonished, could not long endure "if the tendency of the laws were to create a rapid accumulation of property in few hands, and to render the great mass of the population dependent and penniless." When the indigent become numerous, they grow clamorous. They look on property as their prey and plunder, and are "naturally ready, at all times, for violence and revolution." His outlook, however, was optimistic, for he contended that the people of America still possessed property in more even distribution than could be said of the people of any other country.[43]

But most eminent Americans have conceived of equality as something far different from a substantial equalization of possessions. For Francis Lieber it meant the absence of a peasant class. The American farmer was not a member of a subject caste. He was a citizen "not only as to political rights but as to his whole standing and social connection." No peculiar views, manners, or dress distinguished him from the inhabitant of the towns. He might be rich or he might be poor, but no one could look down upon him as a rustic, villein, or boor.[44] Andrew Jackson and Andrew Carnegie found the meaning of equality in the absence of special privileges and of titles and distinctions of rank. The former vetoed the bill for rechartering the United States Bank on the ground that it would create just such distinctions and privileges. In his *Triumphant Democracy* Carnegie rejoiced in the alleged fact that this country had "no ranks, no titles, no hereditary dignities, and therefore no classes." Surprisingly, the interpretation given to equality by a twentieth century liberal—John Dewey—was not greatly dissimilar.

Dewey explained equality as a way of saying "that there is no 'natural' inherent difference between those of one social caste, class, or status and those of another caste, class, or status; that such differences are the product of law and social customs." [45]

As one would expect, America has also had her critics and contemners of equality. Some, like William Graham Sumner and John C. Calhoun, ridiculed the concept as arrant nonsense. The former referred to it as "the purest falsehood in dogma that was ever put into human language." He insisted that "five minutes' observation of facts" would show that men are unequal in a wide variety of respects, including inequality before the law. [46] Calhoun described the doctrine of equality as "so destitute of all sound reason" that it was difficult to understand "how it ever could have been so extensively entertained." He maintained that there never had existed a wealthy and civilized society in which one portion of the community did not live off the labor of the other. Even in primitive societies, the same was largely true. Men are not born into the com-

Living conditions among the American Indians scarcely fit the ideal of equal opportunity for all. Shown here is a typical "hogan," or mud and log house, of a Navajo family. *Central Library, Department of the Interior*

munity in a condition of equality with the other members. Instead, they are born into whatever condition of wealth or poverty, rank or status, their parents possess. They are not born free but subject to parental authority and to the laws and institutions of the country of their birth. As for a so-called state of nature, endowing the individual with freedom and equality, nothing of the sort ever existed. Man's natural state is the social and political—"the one for which his Creator made him, and the only one in which he can preserve and perfect his race." [47]

Other critics have been less dogmatic but just as positive in rejecting equality. In March, 1854, Abraham Lincoln made a point of reminding a committee from the Workingmen's Association of New York that he deprecated a war upon property. Property, he said, is the "fruit of labor"; it is desirable; it is a "positive good in the world." That some should be rich, he argued, is proof that others may become rich, and wealth, therefore, is a proper encouragement to ambition and industry. He then unburdened himself of the following homily: "Let not him who is houseless pull down the home of another, but let him work diligently and build one for himself, thus by example assuring that his own shall be safe from violence when built." [48]

Lincoln's verbose contemporary Edward Everett argued not merely that property is a positive good but that wealth in superabundance, when properly used by its owner, is a boon to society. He was not in favor of perpetuating vast estates through primogeniture, but he maintained that nothing but public good could result from the accumulation of large fortunes through industry, enterprise, and frugality, and their wise expenditure and prudent investment. In admonishing the rich to use their capital for the benefit of humanity, he anticipated the Gospel of Wealth made famous by Andrew Carnegie some thirty years later. The possessor of millions, in spending and investing his money to give "life to industry and employment to labor," is serving, whether he wills it or not, as the "steward" of society.[49]

EQUALITY OF OPPORTUNITY

If equality *as a leveling concept* has not received hearty approval from very many Americans, the same cannot be said of equality of opportunity. From Franklin to Truman the doctrine that every man should have his chance to make what he can of himself has been given almost unanimous endorsement, except in the South under slavery. It has made its appeal to both individualists and collectivists and has seemed to fit in with the very genius of democracy. James Russell Lowell, on one occasion, defined democracy as "that form of society, no matter what its political classification, in which every man has a chance and knows that he has it." [50] But the ideal of equality of opportunity, of course, is much older. Jefferson subscribed to it when he crusaded against primogeniture and entails, when he condemned the aristocratic implications of the Society of the Cincinnati, and when he drafted plans for free public education for the state of Virginia. Paine endorsed it when he proposed that each child of a poor family be given at government expense six months of schooling a year for six years. Equality of opportunity was the watchword of Jacksonian Democrats, especially of such men as William Cullen Bryant and William Leggett in campaigning against monopolies, the United States Bank, and the American System with its subsidies and protective tariffs.

As the settlement of western lands continued apace and the influence of the frontier penetrated eastward, American writers and orators gave an increasingly conspicuous place to equality of opportunity as a national ideal. Theodore Parker related having seen "a thousand young Irish women" coming out of a Catholic church on Sunday, bedecked with ribbons and cheap ornaments, "to help elevate their self-respect." He recalled the condition of these same women in their native land, "barefoot, dirty, mendicant, perhaps thievish," glad of an opportunity to work as scullery maids at two pounds a year. It was then that he began to see the importance of America to the world, as a haven for the hopeless, as a place where the humblest of life's victims could gain some self-esteem as one among equals and not be forever dependent upon the charity of his "betters." [51] Daniel Webster saw America as a refuge for the oppressed of all nations because of its free laws, its "comparative exemption from taxation," its low prices, and its "just and adequate" wages. "Is it not true," he queried, "that sobriety, and industry, and good character can do more for a man here than in any other part of the world?" [52] He was at least frank in recognizing the importance of material objectives in bringing immigrants to American shores.

The most persuasive of all the exponents of equality of opportunity in the middle decades of the nineteenth century was Abraham Lincoln. His own career, of course, was a living exposition of what this equality can produce, and he frequently emphasized the point. Opportunity for the lowly to raise themselves above their station, to achieve the highest goals consistent with their natural endowments, seemed to him the most sacred of rights. It was chiefly because of its violation of this right that he condemned slavery. He rejected completely the southern contention that slaves were better off than hired laborers because of the security and protection they enjoyed. The trouble with this was that they were *permanent* hired laborers, with no opportunity for advancement or improvement in condition. Twenty-five years earlier, he proudly reminded his hearers, he himself was a hired laborer, "mauling rails, at work on a flatboat." He wanted each man to be free to work or not to work and to have full liberty "to acquire property as fast as he can." The humblest man should have "an equal chance to get rich with everybody else." The black man should have a chance as well as the white to better his condition—"when he may look forward and hope to be a hired laborer this year and the next, work for himself afterward, and finally to hire men to work for him. That is the true system." [53]

Lincoln regarded the Civil War as in large part a struggle to maintain and extend equality of opportunity. The conflict was barely three months old when he informed Congress that, on the side of the Union, it was "a struggle for maintaining in the world that form and substance of government whose leading object is to elevate the condition of men—to lift artificial weights from all shoulders; to clear the paths of laudable pursuit for all; to afford all an unfettered start, and a fair chance in the race of life." Eight months before the end of the war he told the 166th Ohio Regiment that the main reason for fighting on to victory was in order that each one of them might have "an open field and a fair chance" for his industry, enterprise, and intelligence; that all might have "equal privileges in the race of life"; and that any one of their children might have the same opportunity that he had had to occupy the White House. It was for these things, he concluded, that the struggle should be maintained, for two or three years longer, if neces-

The University of North Carolina, one of the oldest state universities in the country. An early print, probably made in the 1840's. *North Carolina Collection, University of North Carolina Library*

sary. The nation was worth fighting for, "to secure such an inestimable jewel."

In more recent times the attention given to equality of opportunity as a basic American ideal has diminished, possibly for the reason that the growth of collectivism has divested of some of its luster what was originally an individualist doctrine. Yet it is still set forth occasionally as a true expression of the national genius. In his Freedom Train address of 1948, Justice William O. Douglas declared that the only real aristocracy known in America is the "aristocracy of individual initiative and achievement." Men who toil in working clothes today, he boasted, "can become corporation executives tomorrow. There is no station in private or public life closed to any man or woman, no matter how lowly his start. The lists are open to all, and the ribbons go to the fleet." In 1951 President Truman told the Foreign Ministers of the American Republics, assembled in Washington, that the free nations were growing in strength, and that they were "going forward along the road of greater economic opportunity for all." He proffered the assurance that their governments were holding out to all their citizens the "prospect of bettering their condition, not in the dim future, not after some terrible and bloody upheaval, but steadily through the years in the simplest activities of their daily life."

Though freedom and equality today have somewhat different meanings from what they had during the eighteenth and nineteenth centuries, they remain components of the American dream. And our sense of a mission to the rest of the world is still predicated upon the assumption that they are distinctive features of our national life. Freedom no longer has the implications it carried for Jefferson or for the authors and sponsors of the Bill of Rights. It has ceased to be freedom to defy or to rebel and has become identical with what Rousseau meant by liberty in obedience to "a law which we ourselves have made." Though it is not the same as conformity, it nevertheless sets rather definite limits to the individual's range of expression and action. In effect, freedom is no longer regarded as a fundamental right of man, but is something which the state grants or withholds depending upon the degree of danger to its own survival. Equality, on the other hand, has been broadened in meaning. Whereas in early times it signified the absence of privilege and of extremes of wealth and poverty, it has now come to mean such things as subsidies to farmers to lessen their inequality with industrialists, collective bargaining for workers, minimum wage laws, and graduated taxes on incomes and inheritances. No one of these nor all in combination have established complete equality. The gap between professions and practices is still the American Dilemma described by Gunnar Myrdal in 1944. Nevertheless, enough progress has been made to convince the unprivileged in other countries that the ideal in America is but another name for the reality.

NOTES TO CHAPTER FIVE

1. E. E. Morison, ed., *The Works of Theodore Roosevelt* (New York: Charles Scribner's Sons, 1925), VIII, 92.
2. *The Works of Daniel Webster* (Boston: Little, Brown and Co., 1869), II, 602.
3. *Writings*, Centenary ed. (Boston: American Unitarian Assoc., 1907-16), XI, 126-45.
4. Whitney *v.* California, 274 U. S. 357 (1927).
5. John G. Nicolay and John Hay, eds., *The Complete Works of Abraham Lincoln* (New York: Francis D. Tandy Co., 1905), XI, 110.
6. Frederic Bancroft, ed., *Speeches, Correspondence and Political Papers of Carl Schurz* (New York: G. P. Putnam's Sons, 1913), X, 77-82.
7. R. S. Baker and W. E. Dodd, eds., *The New Democracy* (New York: Harper and Brothers, *ca.* 1926), I, 68-69.
8. *Complete Lectures* (Philadelphia: David McKay Co., 1935), p. 206.

9. *The Challenge to Liberty* (New York: Charles Scribner's Sons, 1934), p. 167.
10. J. C. Hamilton, ed., *The Works of Alexander Hamilton* (New York: J. F. Trow, 1850-51), II, 125.
11. Saul K. Padover, ed., *The Complete Jefferson* (New York: Duell, Sloan and Pearce, 1943), p. 270.
12. *Annals of Congress*, I, 431-32.
13. *The Works of William E. Channing* (Boston: American Unitarian Assoc., 1877), p. 889.
14. *A Disquisition on Government* (New York: Political Science Classics, 1947), p. 55.
15. Albert G. Keller, ed., *Earth-Hunger and Other Essays* (New Haven: Yale University Press, 1913), pp. 141-47, 160.
16. *Complete Prose Works* (Boston: Small, Maynard and Co., 1898), pp. 331-32.
17. *Political Science and Comparative Constitutional Law* (Boston: Ginn and Co., 1890), I, 88-89, 176-77.
18. *Constitutional Government in the United States* (New York: Columbia University Press, ca. 1908), p. 38.
19. Whitney *v.* Calif., 274 U. S. 357 (1927).
20. *Problems of Men* (New York: The Philosophical Library, 1946), p. 121; Joseph Ratner, ed., *Intelligence in the Modern World* (New York: The Modern Library, 1939), p. 404; *Characters and Events* (New York: Henry Holt and Co., 1929), II, 463-64.
21. Samuel I. Rosenman, compiler, *The Public Papers and Addresses of Franklin D. Roosevelt* (New York: Random House, 1938-50), XVIII, 41.
22. Gaillard Hunt, ed., *The Writings of James Madison* (New York: G. P. Putnam's Sons, 1900), VI, 334-36, 389-92.
23. Dissenting opinion in Zorach *v.* Clauson, 343 U. S. 306 (1952).
24. Padover, ed., *The Complete Jefferson*, pp. 945, 947, 948n., 957.
25. Hunt, ed., *Writings*, II, 88-89; IX, 99, 127, 230.
26. Jonathan Elliot, ed., *The Debates in the Several State Conventions on the Adoption of the Federal Constitution* (Washington: Printed by and for the editor, 1863), III, 330.
27. *Works*, II, 521; VI, 138-67.
28. *The New Idolatry* (New York: McClure, Phillips and Co., 1905), p. 161.
29. *The Major Operations of the Navies in the War of American Independence* (Boston: Little, Brown and Co., 1913), p. 2.
30. Morison, ed., *Works*, VI, 56.
31. New York *Times*, March 29, 1955.
32. *The Federalist*, Modern Library ed. (New York: Random House, n.d.), No. 43.
33. Padover, ed., *The Complete Jefferson*, p. 270; Thomas J. Randolph, ed., *The Writings of Thomas Jefferson* (Boston: Gray and Bowen, 1830), II, 267-68.
34. Philip Van Doren Stern, ed., *The Life and Writings of Abraham Lincoln* (New York: Random House, 1940), p. 334.
35. *Speeches, Lectures, and Letters*, First Series (Boston: Lothrop, Lee and Shepard Co., 1891), pp. 383, 403.
36. Bancroft, ed., *Speeches*, I, 381.
37. Morison, ed., *Works*, XV, 5-6.

38. Dennis *et al. v.* United States, 341 U. S. 494 (1951).
39. Ratner, ed., *Intelligence in the Modern World*, pp. 443-44, 449.
40. C. F. Adams, ed., *The Works of John Adams, Second President of the United States* (Boston: Little, Brown and Co., 1856), IV, 380-81.
41. *Speeches, Lectures, and Letters*, Second Series (Boston: Lee and Shepard, 1905), p. 163.
42. *Complete Prose Works*, pp. 215, 332.
43. *Works*, I, 35-40.
44. *The Stranger in America* (Philadelphia: Carey, Lea and Blanchard, 1835), pp. 269-70.
45. *Problems of Men*, p. 115.
46. Keller, ed., *Earth-Hunger*, p. 88.
47. Richard K. Cralle, ed., *The Works of John C. Calhoun* (New York: D. Appleton and Co., 1856), I, 57-58; II, 631.
48. Nicolay and Hay, eds., *Works*, X, 54.
49. *Orations and Speeches on Various Occasions* (Boston: Little, Brown and Co., 1870), II, 301-02.
50. *Works* (New York: Houghton Mifflin Co., *ca.* 1892), VI, 33.
51. *Writings*, Centenary ed., XII, 219.
52. *Works*, I, 229.
53. Nicolay and Hay, eds., *Works*, II, 184-85; V, 360-61.

Chapter Six

The Gospel of Individualism

Probably no political and social ideal is more characteristic of the American culture pattern than individualism. The nation had its birth during a period when the whole Western world was attempting to throw off the restraints imposed by a paternalistic state, the medieval guilds, and the mercantilist economy. The individual was exalted as never before. Government was considered a necessary evil, and the less of it the better. The new economics of the Physiocrats and Adam Smith posited the existence of natural economic laws and condemned political interference with these laws as worse than useless. If each individual were allowed to pursue his self-interest, it was claimed, the world would be guided "as by an invisible hand" to maximum prosperity and happiness. The dominant philosophy of the time stemmed from the Enlightenment, which had as its cardinal purpose the liberation of the individual from reliance upon authority, from dogma, and from superstition. It envisaged man as a reasoning being, capable of solving his problems in isolation through the exercise of his rational faculties in organizing the impressions gained from his senses. The most popular political theory was that of Locke, which also conceived of man as originally a self-sufficing creature, living according to the law of nature and enforcing his own rights under that law. When the inconveniences of the latter function became too burdensome, he as an individual entered into a compact with other individuals to establish a government and to vest it with certain powers. But the authority delegated was limited strictly to maintenance and enforcement of the law of nature. With that one exception the individual was as sovereign as he had been before.

As the western territories of the United States filled up with settlers, the individualist influence from Europe was supplemented and strengthened by the influence of the frontier. At times the effects were contradictory. In some of its aspects the frontier could produce a drab uniformity which was the very antithesis of individualism. Most of the settlers were obscure, untutored folk, with no skill or attainments to set them apart from their neighbors. They tended therefore to regard the exceptional person with suspicion, unless his achievements were the product of some bodily endowment like physical strength. This attitude, however, was compensated by the fact that the frontier promoted self-reliance. The settler and his family made their own clothing, built their own house (with some limited help from the neighbors), and cleared the trees from their own plot of ground to plant a scraggling crop among the stumps. Each family lived in virtual isolation, cultivating a rugged independence and trusting to its own efforts to conquer hardships and solve its problems. Hard work, self-denial, physical skill, and Yankee ingenuity were the keys to whatever comfort and prosperity one might obtain. Government was a thing apart, with little meaning except when canals needed to be dug or turnpikes built to provide transportation to eastern markets. Law for the frontiersman was largely a matter of his own making, and justice was often administered with scant regard for formal procedure. Whatever seemed expedient in a given circumstance was likely to pass for both law and justice. It must not be supposed that the western settlers completely ignored the law or lived in defiance of it. Yet partly because the courts and enforcement officers were remote and inadequate, a spirit of lawlessness did develop and gradually insinuated its influence into all sections of the country.

The idea of the free individual has survived as a fundamental ingredient of the American ethos. It continues to be a part of the messianic illusion that this nation can be a guide and example to the rest of the world. Here it is supposed that the individual is free in a measure unparalleled anywhere else. He is not a slave to some despot or dictator, nor is he held down by the weight of time-worn custom or by the absurdities of hereditary privilege and class domination. There are no limits to what he can make of himself, except his own inadequacies and lack of willingness to sacrifice immediate satisfactions for future prosperity. Periods of depression make a temporary dent in this Horatio Alger concept, but it recovers with business revival and is still an important article of faith to the majority of our citizens.

FREE ENTERPRISE AND FREE COMPETITION

Free enterprise and free competition have long been among the sacred cows of American individualists. They have an ingratiating sound to a people brought up on ideas of a fair fight and no favors, let the best man win, and the devil take the hindmost. They have also served as a convenient screen to enable tycoons and buccaneers to pile up their riches under the pretext that they are doing no more than any other individual might do if he possessed their foresight and ability. Much of the trumpeting of free enterprise and free competition has obviously been for such deceptive purposes. Nonetheless, many who have professed the ideals have certainly believed in them with a faith to move mountains. One such was Benjamin Franklin. Though he preferred an agrarian to an industrial society, he thought that all branches of the economy would be better off if the government did no more than protect them. Most of the statutes, edicts, and decrees for regulating, restraining, or promoting trade were "either political blunders, or jobs obtained by artful men for private advantage, under pretense of public good." He wished that commerce between all the nations of the world were as free as between the counties of England. "Those counties," he said, "do not ruin one another by trade; neither would the nations." [1]

Although they eventually came to advocate a considerable degree of paternalism, both Madison and Jefferson had theoretical preferences for a policy of laissez faire and unhampered trade. Jefferson espoused it in his first inaugural, when he called for a "wise and frugal government, which shall restrain men from injuring one another, which shall leave them otherwise free to regulate their own pursuits of industry and improvement, and shall not take from the mouth of labor the bread it has earned."

Madison thought that, in general, government should limit its functions to protecting and educating its citizens, and to providing the conditions under which every person might garner the legitimate rewards of his industry, frugality, and talent. The most important conditions for this purpose were confidence, justice, and security,

William Gropper's conception of Paul Bunyan, legendary hero of the frontier. Bunyan's prodigious feats exemplified American individualism and self-confidence. *Metropolitan Museum of Art*

and government alone could successfully provide them. He did not consider it desirable that the state should intervene directly for the benefit of the less fortunate members of society. Compassion was due them, he conceded, but not direct assistance. In the main, he conceived of the condition of the lower classes in Malthusian and Ricardian terms. Like the two great English exponents of the "dismal science," he feared that a degree of poverty would always be inseparable from congestion of population. He doubted the value of all plans to improve the lot of the poor because of what he considered their persistent tendency to increase their own numbers with every amelioration of their economic condition. The increase in numbers would result in a more intense competition for employment, thereby forcing wages down again to the bare subsistence level.[2]

To the end of his life Madison continued to affirm a theoretic devotion to freedom of trade, though admitting the desirability of many exceptions in practice. He argued that if industry and commerce were allowed to take their own course, they would in the main be directed to those objects for which they were best suited. Whenever manufacturing promises more profit than agriculture or commerce, its establishments will increase rapidly enough without the assistance of the state. "It would be of no advantage," he observed, "to the shoemaker to make his own clothes to save the expense of the tailor's bill, nor of the tailor to make his own shoes to save the expense of procuring them from the shoemaker. It would be better policy to suffer each of them to employ his talents in his own way. Thus all are benefited by exchange, and the less this exchange is cramped by the government, the greater are the proportions of benefit to each." During the years of depression that followed the Napoleonic Wars, he complained that attempts of Great Britain and France to achieve "self-subsisting" systems would produce similar efforts elsewhere, and that the final result must be disastrous to those whose prosperity depended most on the freedom and extent of international trade. He thought that the best remedy for depressed conditions in any country was "freedom of commerce among all nations." The "aggregate fruits of the earth" would then be available for all.[3]

From the period of the Fathers until after the War of Secession free enterprise and free competition were taken almost for granted.

Great monopolies such as the United States Bank had been broken, and new ones had not yet risen to take their place. Agitation for protective tariffs steadily increased, but few seemed to think of these as inconsistent with an individualist economics. Besides, the great age of protectionism had not yet dawned. The Civil War and the extension of railroads gave an impetus to industrialization that enabled the United States to surpass every country in the world by 1900 in the production of manufactured goods. Success imbued the captains of the system with pride in their achievements and a conviction that special virtue resided in their methods. To a plundering age they were heroes, and it was natural that millions of their admirers should endorse their ideas as standards of value. Moreover, the introduction of Marxism and collectivistic anarchism from Europe focused attention upon economic individualism as a means of preserving the *status quo*. Free enterprise became a watchword for conservatives.

Noted among the conservative apologists for economic individualism was Charles A. Dana, erstwhile colleague of George Ripley at Brook Farm and subsequent cynic and ranting imperialist. About 1850 Dana journeyed to Europe and after observing the machinations of Louis Napoleon and other demagogues, turned sour against the idealism of his youth and devoted the remainder of his life to pursuit of the main chance for himself and to glorification of the buccaneering activities of his capitalist associates. Though professing adherence to Manchesterism, he departed from that gospel sufficiently to advocate protective tariffs for industrialists and huge grants of public land for the railroads. He did insist, however, that the role of the government should be reduced to that of a policeman to keep the peace, and he scoffed at ideas for pure food legislation, for an income tax, and for the regulation of business. When in 1896 the Democrats adopted Populist demands for nationalization of the railroads, prohibition of "government by injunction," the free coinage of silver, and reorganization of the Supreme Court, Dana's wrath flamed into hysteria. He talked about "absurd, unpatriotic, and dangerous" experiments and referred to the "approval of lawless violence" and the "wild light of anarchy shining through." He did not stop to consider that his own jingoism and irresponsible clamor for Cuba, Mexico, and Canada might ultimately do more to promote a spirit of lawlessness than any of the schemes of the Populists.

Abraham Lincoln's philosophy of no interference with the freedom of the individual to accumulate property helped to prepare the way for the great age of industrial free enterprise after the Civil War. Photo by M. Brady or A. Berger. *Library of Congress*

Equally dogmatic in his conservatism, though less violent in language, was Grover Cleveland. Inaugurated President for a second term in 1893, he cautioned those who listened to him under the lowering clouds of depression, that they must actively seek to expose and destroy the evils "which are the unwholesome progeny of paternalism." These, he said, were the "bane of republican institutions and the constant peril of our government by the people." The citizens must be encouraged to unlearn the lessons of paternalism and to embrace the "better lesson" that "while the people should patriotically and cheerfully support their government, its functions do not include support of the people." He advised particularly against any tendency to regard frugality and economy as virtues which we may safely outgrow. Such a tendency would result in reckless waste of the people's money by their chosen servants and would encourage useless extravagance by the citizens themselves in their private lives.

Quite a number of thinkers and political leaders of liberal reputation also espoused an individualist economics. Among the most prolific in ideas was Edwin L. Godkin, British-born apostle of classical theories and dour critic of most of the trends of his time. In 1887 he wrote in the new *Princeton Review* that the existing state of things was one which no thinking person could contemplate without concern. If protectionism were continued as a cardinal policy, American society would become more and more like that of Europe. Concentration of wealth in the hands of a few corporations and individuals would rapidly increase. More serious, he thought, was the growth of political corruption. Hundreds of manufacturers were going down to Washington every year to influence members of Congress to retain or increase the duty on particular articles. Godkin was convinced that such methods were not only vicious but unnecessary. Under a policy of free trade and free competition all the manufacturing essential to a healthy economy would have been brought into existence. There would have been a constant overflow from the farms of the "most quick-witted, sharp-sighted, and enterprising men of the community." They would have "toiled, contrived, invented, copied," until they had brought under the aegis of an industrial regime every resource of the country. Godkin was as vigorously opposed to socialism as he was to protectionism and other forms of paternalism. The great law of nature, he taught, is that "the more intelligent and thoughtful of the race shall inherit the earth and have the best time." Socialism teaches the reverse of this.[4]

Some of Godkin's younger contemporaries who could also lay claim to recognition as liberals were just as emphatic in endorsing economic freedom. The Hoosier Progressive Albert J. Beveridge, for instance, solemnly warned against government ownership as un-American. Ownership of business by the government was the "European theory." He was for the "American theory," which had suited American conditions in the past and was good enough for the future. Government ownership violated the American principle "that government enterprise ought not to own and manage what individual ownership can own and manage." Moreover, it fostered bureaucracy and multiplied abuses of incompetence and mismanagement which nothing could cure. Much better was the alternative of government supervision, "which leaves business in individual hands but requires that individual to act as a trustee for the people."[5] A few years later, however, Beveridge decided that "self-regulation" would be preferable to government supervision. Why not turn over the ordinary regulation of business and the maintenance of ethical standards, he inquired, to "voluntary organizations of citizens"? He referred to the fact that almost all branches of business had such associations—grocers and druggists, farmers and bankers, merchants, and manufacturers of various kinds.[6] His proposal represents what seems to have been the first scheme for a kind of cartelization of the American economy, a limited forerunner of the NRA.

Despite the broad collectivism of the New Freedom, the New Deal, and the Fair Deal, the habit of paying tribute to economic individualism did not die out. One would expect such tributes from Calvin Coolidge, John W. Davis, Herbert Hoover, and Wendell Willkie, but to find them emanating from Woodrow Wilson, Franklin D. Roosevelt, Henry Wallace, Harry S. Truman, and Adlai E. Stevenson is not so understandable. Yet there were almost as many from one group as from the other. The explanation resides in the fact that the leaders in the second group often found themselves in the camp of small business, crusading for equality of opportunity against huge combines and monopolies. Such a position necessitated a defense of free competition, if not of free enterprise and freedom of trade. Woodrow Wilson, in particular, assumed the role of champion of the middle class. He charged that this class was being squeezed out by ruthless monopolists. But he denied that this was the result of free competition. The aim of the monopolists was to destroy *all* competition.[7] He constantly reiterated that his program of reform contemplated no radical alterations in the economic system. Instead, its objective was to preserve some of the most vital elements in the American heritage—individualism, free competition, enterprise, and opportunity.

The New Deal and the Fair Deal far surpassed the New Freedom in pursuing the goal of collectivism. But the old shibboleths of individualist economics lost none of their emphasis. In a campaign address in Chicago in 1936, President Roosevelt affirmed his undying belief in private enterprise as "the backbone of economic well-being in the United States." A few months earlier at the Texas Centennial he declared that "the very nature of free government" demands a line of defense for the "yeomanry of business and industry and agriculture." By these he explained that he meant "the average men" who own their establishments and assume the responsibility for running them. To eliminate these "dependable defenders of democratic institutions" and to permit the concentration of control in the hands of a few powerful groups would be "directly opposed to the stability of government and to democratic government itself."

Henry Wallace, as we shall presently see, tinctured his individualism with numerous suggestions for government interference in the interest of society. In his applications of policy President Truman did the same. But when theorizing on public issues, he often gave forth the same individualist clichés as would be mouthed by a spokesman for the United States Chamber of Commerce. He had been in office only a few months when he urged Congress to enact legislation to promote freedom of competition, especially for the benefit of the small entrepreneur. He gave as his reason the following proposition: "The American small business is the backbone of our free enterprise system." At Baylor University in 1947 he associated freedom of enterprise with freedom of worship and freedom of speech and counseled that the last two were closely dependent upon the first. Freedom of conscience and freedom of expression, he argued, are incompatible with highly centralized power. Therefore, the devotion of our citizens to freedom of enterprise is not motivated merely by a desire to protect the profits of business. "It is part and parcel of what we call America." In 1948 he informed Congress:

"Growth and vitality in our economy depend on vigorous private enterprise." As was his wont, he interpreted the last phrase to mean primarily free competition.

In the campaign of 1952, Adlai E. Stevenson courted the support of liberal voters on a platform heartily endorsing the Truman policies. With respect to free enterprise and free competition, however, he seemed to move a degree or two farther to the right. Perhaps he sensed an increasing revolt against the regimenting tendencies of Roosevelt and Truman. In any case, he affirmed his allegiance to free enterprise as the "basic structure" of American society. He announced that he would dedicate his efforts to a healthier, more secure, and more prosperous America; but at the same time he declared: "Our national commitment is to a free economy—to the belief that an economic system based on freedom of choice, freedom of opportunity and freedom of decision is more productive and creative than any system devised by man." Not only did he pledge that he would not abandon our free enterprise system, but he declared that he would oppose all attempts to limit its freedom, whether by centralized government or by private monopoly.[8]

INDIVIDUALISM, OLD STYLE

Individualism in American history has not been confined, of course, to advocacy of free enterprise and free competition. There has also been a broader theory which has championed independence, self-reliance, and the right to follow preferences and interests in a number of spheres. Philosophers almost without number have sponsored this broader individualism, but none more vigorously and appealingly than the two great Transcendentalists of the last century, Emerson and Thoreau. In defending moral and intellectual freedom, Emerson characterized society as a "conspiracy against the manhood of every one of its members." Whoso would be a man, he declared, "must be a nonconformist." As for the state, "it must follow and not lead the character and progress of the citizen." Its function is to produce the wise man, and his actual appearance will be the signal for the state to dissolve. Its facilities, and those of society as well, will no longer be needed. Meanwhile, the fewer laws the better; and even those which are necessary, good men should not obey too well.[9]

Thoreau carried his revolt against both society and the state so far as to assert a doctrine of individual nullification. No government, he said, can have any "pure right over my person or property but what I concede to it." He would not have men cultivate respect for the law, but rather respect for the right. One man standing for the right was worth more than the largest of majorities in the wrong. Government Thoreau compared to a timid old woman alone with her silver spoons. That government was best which governed not at all; and when men were ready for it, that would be the kind of government they would have.[10]

The individualist philosophy of Jacksonian Democracy and of the turbulent decades of sectional controversy preceding the Civil War was forcefully expressed by William Leggett, Theodore Parker, and Walt Whitman. As a crusader against monopolies, William Leggett logically opposed paternalism in all its forms. He demanded that the authority of the state be restricted to the "protection of person and property from domestic and foreign enemies." The only exception he would countenance was the promotion of education. "See that the people are educated," he counseled, "and then leave every man to take care of himself and of those who have a natural claim on his protection." He would not even approve government assistance to the poor, to the sick and disabled, or to the insane. "Public charities," he thundered, "are founded on erroneous principles, and do infinitely more harm than good." Regulations of morality also came under his ban. For gambling and other vices, he argued, "the great and only salutary corrective" is public opinion. If the moral sense of the community cannot suppress them, they cannot be suppressed at all, no matter how many statutes and edicts may be issued against them. Even such public functions as inspecting and gauging, Leggett considered unnecessary and potentially vicious. He would have been glad to see the whole army of collectors, snoopers, examiners, and "lickspittles" swept off the earth or forced to join the line of march into some "democratic" occupation. The nation, he hoped, would finally discover that the "true democratic principle, and the true principle of political economy, is 'Let us alone.'"[11]

As a foremost crusader against slavery, the liberal New England philosopher Theodore Parker essayed the role of a defender of northern initiative and ingenuity and even of Yankee acquisitiveness. Instead of deploring northern materialism in contrast with southern "chivalry" and "devotion to culture," he gloried in it. He declared the acquisition of property to be almost a *summum bonum.* "No nation," he exclaimed, "was ever too well fed, clad, housed, adorned, and comforted in general." The peoples of the world "*must* think chiefly of what they shall eat and drink and wherewithal be clothed." If they do not, civilization will perish. He advised all men to shun

End of the Union Pacific track, near Archer, Wyoming, 1867. Railroad-building was one of the principal interests of speculators and promoters in the Gilded Age that followed the Civil War. *Union Pacific R.R.*

poverty, to seek a generous competence for themselves and their families. There is nothing shameful in this, provided the competence is acquired honestly. The idea that men should spurn wealth and deny themselves luxuries and comforts is a relic of an outworn asceticism. America would never have become great on any such basis. "Much and permanent property is the indispensable condition for the advance and development of mankind, in mind and conscience, heart and soul." Parker did set, however, one limitation to the acquisition of wealth—"A man must earn all he takes." "If a man fully pay in efficient, productive toil and thought, he is entitled to all he gets, one dollar or many million dollars." The author saw no contradiction between this and his doctrine that property must rest upon justice and that ownership must be widely distributed.[12]

For Walt Whitman individualism was almost entirely an ideal of the spirit. As a democrat he glorified man in the mass, but he believed that to democracy was surely joined another principle, indispensable to it but opposite and complementary, as one sex to the other. This second principle was individuality, or personalism, forming a "compensating balance-wheel of the successful working machinery of aggregate America." To aid in the development of strong individuality is the primary purpose of a democratic republic. It is this which gives character to the nation and provides the basis of its civilization. "What does civilization rest upon," inquired Whitman, "but rich, luxuriant, varied personalism?" It is this that makes possible the entire esthetic culture of a nation and thereby gives it its genuine greatness. So earnest was Whitman on this score that he suggested the establishment of a science of personalism, "the object of which should be to raise up and supply through the States a copious race of superb American men and women, cheerful, religious, ahead of any yet known." He wanted them to emerge as "clear-blooded," erect, healthy specimens, with sound digestion, voices like music, and "eyes of calm and steady gaze." He pictured them as ardent, aspiring, and full of adventure in youth, and brave, perceptive, and restrained in maturity.[13] How he would prevent them from becoming a ruling élite, in the early stages when they would be only a minority, he did not make clear.

The period from 1865 to 1900 is commonly regarded as the Golden Age of American individualism. But it was an individualism which emphasized initiative, enterprise, aggressiveness, industry, and frugality. Few writers had much to say about the importance of freedom for self-development or to enable the individual to make a larger contribution to culture. Almost none said anything about the ultimate sovereignty of conscience or the right of the individual to defy authority when morally convinced that a statute or edict was wrong.

The most fully developed philosophy of individualism in this age of bold and bearded plunderers was that of William Graham Sumner. As a crusty and cynical Social Darwinist, Sumner plunged into the sea of theory from two basic assumptions. The first was the premise that poverty is the natural condition of mankind, and the second was the doctrine that struggle is the law of the universe. Because of the niggardliness of nature, human beings, like all organic species, must struggle for the necessaries of life. This struggle, if allowed to proceed unhindered, results in the elimination of the unfit and the survival of the strongest and best. Socialism and all other forms of paternalism would reverse this process and, by supporting and assisting the weak, would preserve the "unfittest." Sumner, therefore, would tolerate nothing but a rigorous application of economic individualism. He wanted to abolish all monopolies, protective tariffs, and regulatory agencies, and institute a regime of dog-eat-dog competition. Like William Leggett, he would repeal all laws for the regulation of morality—not because they are futile, but because they are worse than futile. Nine tenths of the measures for preventing vice are really "protective towards it, because they ward off the penalty." If government will let nature alone, she will cure vice by her own frightful penalties. The drunkard should be left in the ditch, so that nature may "work away at him to get him out of the way." No laws should be passed against gambling "and less mentionable vices" lest the persons weak enough to succumb to such sins be preserved to procreate offspring like themselves. Without the laws, the vices will "cure themselves by the ruin and dissolution of their victims." [14] Sumner was using almost the same language as did Heinrich von Treitschke in justifying war as "a terrible medicine for the human race." The two men seemed equally oblivious of the frightful toll of innocent victims that would have to be charged to their peculiar therapeutics.

In common with most individualists, Sumner regarded private ownership as one of the great blessings of mankind. Unlike some, he did not insist that ownership be widely distributed. For him it was sufficient that property be acquired by one's own efforts or lawfully inherited. He would raise no question as to the amount. Indeed, he was quite impatient with "wailings about the danger of the accumulation of great wealth in few hands." Many of the needs of society, he contended, require large accumulations of capital. And capital, to be effective, "must be in few hands, for the simple reason that there are very few men able to handle great aggregations of capital." He had another purpose, also, for not wishing to challenge anyone's right to extensive possessions. "The reason why I defend the millions of the millionaire," he wrote, "is not that I love the millionaire, but that I love my own wife and children, and that I know no way in which to get the defense of society for my hundreds except to give my help, as a member of society, to protect his millions."

No Israelites ever yearned for the fleshpots of Egypt more ardently than did Sumner for the comfort and security symbolized by the possession of property. Property was dear to him not only for the sensual pleasure it could afford but also as a support for everything else he held dear. He regarded it as the shield and buckler of civil liberty, which "begins and ends with freedom of production, freedom of exchange, and security of property." The man he considered the most valuable bulwark of civilization was the Forgotten Man, "the clean, quiet, virtuous," hard-working citizen, who pays his debts and taxes, and has a bank account which becomes a part of the store of capital available for the progress of society.[15]

An individualism much less deeply rooted in economics was propounded by William James. In his judgment society was completely atomistic, and nothing was of any consequence except the welfare of its component members. Since the progress of nations is directly proportional to the variation of individuals from the mass, complete tolerance should be accorded to every individual or set of individuals with a unique idea from which any conceivable good may come. Anarchists, nihilists, free silverites, free lovers, socialists, single-taxers, prohibitionists, antivivisectionists—all should be allowed to preach and practice their doctrines. They and their conservative opponents arrayed against them "are simply deciding through actual experiment by what sort of conduct the maximum amount of good can be gained and kept in this world." In the competition the freakish ideas will generally be weeded out. But once in a while some genius will bring forth a revolutionary idea that will be found to yield "more prosperous fruit" than the "truth" it displaces. But only by keeping the competition open can such discoveries be made. James would not even approve of a system of compulsory licensing of physicians lest it result in a rigid orthodoxy maintained by the mandarins of the profession. He had no confidence in the faith healers who would be debarred by such licensing, but he deplored the shutting down on the "extremely important experiences" "these peculiar creatures" were rolling up.[16]

There remains a consideration of the Gospel of Wealth as an expression of nineteenth century individualism. Though the name given to it implies an economic content, such was not wholly the case. Most of its exponents believed in the moral authority of the doctrines they preached, and some traced them to a divine sanction. The basis of the theory of the Gospel of Wealth was Puritanism, and still farther back, Calvinism. To be diligent, frugal, self-reliant, and ambitious was to walk in a path pleasing to God, according to the Geneva Reformer and his New England disciples. Such conduct would keep one immune from the wiles of the Devil and would be calculated to produce a surplus of wealth for the glory of the Kingdom. If great wealth came into the possession of an individual, he must regard it as a trust placed in his hands for the doing of good. This was the doctrine of stewardship, which was at least as old as Cotton Mather. From early New England sources it was carried into the nineteenth century by such doughty theologian-philosophers as Noah Porter, James McCosh, and Mark Hopkins, presidents of Yale, Princeton, and Williams, respectively.

The first formulation of the Gospel of Wealth for popular consumption seems to have been the work of Russell H. Conwell, a Baptist minister of Philadelphia who later founded Temple University. Conwell set forth his economic message in a clumsily worded, ungrammatical lecture entitled "Acres of Diamonds," which he is supposed to have delivered six thousand times from platforms throughout the nation. Its central theme was the religious duty of getting rich because money is a badge of honesty and diligence and because it will enable its possessor to do good in the world. Poverty, on the other hand, is not merely an evidence of sloth, but is a sign of God's punishment for sin. Good people, therefore, should have no sympathy for the poor, for "there is not a poor person in the United States who was not made poor by his own shortcomings, or by the shortcomings of some one else." A man who has been in business for twenty years and has not made at least $500,000 ought to be shunned by his neighbors or driven from the community as a moral leper.[17] The Gospel of Wealth received even more attention when it was made the subject of an article by Andrew Carnegie in the *North American Review* in 1889. Carnegie had the merit of investing his opinions with more humanity for the poor than did Conwell, or at least he had more grace in expressing them. But the dominant

According to many historians, unrestrained individualism, based upon Social Darwinist principles, and supported by high tariffs, was bound to result in monopoly. *Courtesy of The New-York Historical Society, New York City*

theme was essentially the same. Ruthless competition is the basic law of industrial society. All progress depends upon it. This law soon operates to bring into existence wide disparities of wealth. Huge fortunes, more than can be judiciously expended by one man and his family, come into the possession of the few, while the many share what is left in proportion to their lower degrees of ambition and ability. Though this may seem unjust, it is a necessary provision to stimulate the race to improve its condition. The rich man, however, must not consider that his wealth is his own to do with as he likes. Instead, it is a trust which he is given to administer for the welfare of society.

The canny steelmaster preached his ideal with a fervor almost evangelical. He described it as "the true antidote for the temporary unequal distribution of wealth." He portrayed it as a means for the reconciliation of the rich and the poor—a reign of harmony—"a Utopia, superior to that of the Communist," yet differing from communism "in requiring only the further evolution of existing conditions, not the total overthrow of our civilization." It would usher in an ideal state, "in which the surplus wealth of the few will become, in the best sense, the property of the many."

As the nineteenth century faded into the past, ideas of individualism in America began to give place to what appeared to be a robust collectivism. The Populists advocated government ownership of railroads, grain elevators, and telegraph and telephone lines. They also recommended licensing and control of corporations and government guarantees of bank deposits. The Progressive movement, in both its Republican and Democratic phases, included in its reform program the prohibition of child labor, the enactment of more stringent antitrust legislation, federal control of banking, and the use of inheritance and income taxes to level down great fortunes. The "collectivist" proposals of the New Deal are so well known as to make enumeration unnecessary. Suffice it to say that in such fields as labor legislation, public utility regulation, and social security they went far beyond the recommendations of the earlier movements.

Yet none of these reform programs sponsored the type of collectivism demanded by Socialists and Communists. There was not one clamor for the abolition of capitalism, the destruction of free enterprise, or the supplanting of the wage system by some other means of compensation. Underlying all of the platforms was a strong conviction of the importance of the individual. What the reformers wanted was not the submergence of the individual in a collectivist economic regime but the restoration and, if possible, the enlargement of his opportunities. It was the restriction of these opportunities by trusts and interlocking directorates and by the grasping overlords of transportation and finance that had deprived the individual of his rightful chance to gain for himself a place in the sun. The chief victims of exploitation in the eyes of both Populists and Progressives were the farmers and small businessmen. The New Dealers added the industrial worker, not with a view to making him the owner of the means of production, but simply to gain for him better terms as a hired laborer.

Prophets of a new individualism, in the years that make up our century, have been numerous and important. And a surprising unanimity has prevailed among them. With rare exceptions they have conceived of individuality as equality of opportunity. There was nothing particularly novel in this, for Lincoln had presented the same conception long before. But the prophets of the new age were ready to go to much greater lengths to give effect to the ideal. They would clip the wings of the rich and powerful in almost any degree necessary to accord to the little man a chance to get off the ground. They were not revolutionists, however. They had not come to destroy but to fulfill. They believed that capitalism could be made to work for the good of the many and not chiefly for the enrichment of the

A Bessemer furnace during a "blow." The development of giant industry, with a wide distribution of stock ownership, constitutes to some theorists a new phase of "individualism," in which the big corporation has become a public service agency. *Photo by Bethlehem Steel Corp.*

few. Typical of their viewpoint were the ideas of such diverse figures as Franklin D. Roosevelt, Henry Wallace, Wendell Willkie, and Walter Lippmann.

The great architect and executive of the New Deal affirmed his belief in the "sacredness of private property" and avowed his intention of making "American individualism what it was intended to be—equality of opportunity for all, the right of exploitation for none." [18] His Secretary of Agriculture and, subsequently, Vice-President and Secretary of Commerce insisted that "the spirit of free competition will and must continue to be one of our main driving forces." This spirit, or something closely akin to it, he identified with Horatio Alger, who "is not dead in America and never will be." [19] But in an earlier context he seemed to entertain some doubts, for he asserted that "liberty of opportunity is not automatic in a country whose frontiers are closed and in which 90 per cent of jobs in industry are controlled by corporations." [20]

As the white hope of the liberal Republicans to spike the Roosevelt ambitions for a third term, Wendell Willkie nevertheless committed himself to much of the New Deal philosophy. He told the Toledo Civic Forum and Rotary Club in March, 1940: "If the Government of the United States will sincerely dedicate itself to the purpose of making men free to carry on their economic enterprises, and of making it posisble for 'the man with brains to get into the game,' then this country . . . will resume an economic progress which will be even greater in the future than it has been in the past." A month later he gave a thinly veiled warning before the American Newspaper Publishers Association: "If free economic enterprise is unable to provide jobs and products for this country, then, obviously, some other system should be tried." [21] Walter Lippmann wrote in similar vein during the years when the bloom was still on the New Deal. The surest way to kill individualism, he cautioned, was to put upon the individual person burdens too great for him to carry. It followed that the true defenders of the ideal were those who were "laboring to distribute justly the social risks of our immensely complicated society." [22]

In popular legend the exemplar of rugged individualism in the twentieth century is Herbert Hoover. Without doubt he is a foe of regimentation, of a planned society, of currency-tinkering, and of attempts to promote prosperity by restricting production. Yet as

President, he approved the setting up of Grain and Cotton Stabilization Corporations to take surplus wheat and cotton off the market, the Reconstruction Finance Corporation to rescue railroads and other business corporations from bankruptcy and to lend money to land banks and agricultural credit corporations, and the Commodity Credit Corporation to make loans directly to farmers for the purpose of pegging prices. He even approved plans for limited construction of public works, though he condemned proposals of sufficient size to provide effective unemployment relief lest they involve "pork-barrel" legislation. Nine years before he became President he expounded his philosophy that individualism is the equivalent of equality of opportunity. We must safeguard to every individual, he wrote, an equality of opportunity to take that position in the community which he clearly merits on the basis of intelligence, character, ability, and initiative. Individualism is the one source of human progress, the primary force which has motivated American civilization for three centuries. Progress to even greater perfection is certain if we will "hold an abiding faith in the intelligence, the initiative, the character, the courage, and the divine touch in the individual." [23]

The most evocative and original advocates of a revised individualism after 1900 were not Presidents or cabinet members but an eminent philosopher and a brilliant lawyer, who later became a Supreme Court justice. The philosopher was John Dewey. At the beginning of the depression when waves of radical discontent were lapping at the foundations of the American economy, Dewey published his *Individualism, Old and New*. In it he deplored the growth of a "corporate" society, destroying initiative and independence and requiring more and more conformity. The emergence of vast combinations for the production and distribution of goods, the mechanization of industry, and the integration of sports and amusements and of transportation and communication, were reducing the individual to a cog in a machine. Even crime, he pointed out, was becoming organized and syndicated. Added to all these were the effects of mass unemployment and insecurity in producing fear and a sense of bewilderment. The old idea of a sovereign individual making his way to the top by sheer initiative, industry, and ability under a regime of free competition had become largely meaningless. The individualism of the future must take into account the changing conditions of society. The citizen cannot be left to struggle for himself as a confused and helpless being in an alien world. He must be freed from anxiety and insecurity by the collective intelligence of the group.

The problems of modern times, according to Dewey, are not primarily physical; they involve human and social relations rather than the conquest and control of the natural environment. They are problems of war, unemployment, poverty, insecurity, and race and class conflict. The obstacles standing in the way of their solution are prejudice, ignorance, fear, and the persistence of outworn ideas. Nothing can remove such obstacles but the consistent application of the scientific method to all branches of education. We must analyze causes and attempt to predict and control consequences instead of continuing to think and act in "prescientific 'moral' terms." Only in this way can the individual be saved from the mass pressures destroying his independence and be set once more on the road to an equal chance with his fellows.

More keenly critical of the ravages of modern economic developments upon the independence of the individual was Justice Louis D. Brandeis. He saw the growth of giant corporations as a menace not only to equality of opportunity but to every value that makes life worth living. They were creating a mode of existence so inhuman as to "make our former Negro slavery infinitely preferable." The master, at least, owned the slave and therefore had an incentive to care for his property. The trusts considered their employees as something to be worked to the point of exhaustion and then thrown aside. The result was physical and moral degeneracy and the divesting of human beings of every quality that raised them above the animal level. The reason for this was not the innate depravity of their employers but the fact that excessive power corrupts those who wield it. The very size of a great corporation deprives those who manage it of a sense of responsibility for their workers. They become the agents of a multitude of absolute owners, the stockholders, who care for nothing but increased dividends. The stockholders are remote, often hundreds of miles from the people who toil for them, and know nothing of the conditions under which their dividends are actually earned. Such a system, Brandeis believed, made economic democracy impossible and industrial despotism almost inevitable. He wondered how long under the circumstances political democracy could really endure.[24]

Brandeis proposed numerous expedients to preserve the kind of individualism he prized so highly. To begin with, he would abolish all forms of corporate giantism that fostered monopoly and irresponsibility. He admitted that competition involves waste, but so, he contended, does democracy. The gains in both cases cancel the losses. He recommended also positive measures for preserving the freedom and self-reliance of the individual. One would be the maintenance of private property and private enterprise. He was opposed to all forms of government ownership, and he doubted that any man can be really free unless he has a substantial measure of economic independence. He proposed further that labor unions be fully protected in their right to use collective bargaining as a check upon the arbitrariness of capitalists. He believed that power must always be set to curb power, and that bringing representatives of capital and labor together in direct negotiation would force each side to see the other's point of view. He recognized the need for shorter hours and regular days of rest, in order that men and women may conserve their health and "fit themselves to be citizens of a free country." Like the ancient Athenians, he equated freedom with leisure.

But Brandeis was just as deeply concerned with a higher standard of living for the masses in order to abolish the misery that comes from poverty. To this end he recommended a guaranteed annual wage, which would be a fixed charge upon the operations of industry, in the same class with interest on bonds or other indebtedness. In his judgment, irregularity of employment was one of the worst features of the industrial system. The time had come, he maintained, when society and labor should demand continuity of employment. The best way to ensure it was to insist that workingmen be paid throughout the year, on the same basis as the officers of a corporation. If the employees had to be paid at regular intervals whether they worked or not, they would undoubtedly be kept working. The result would be greater productivity and more wealth for distribution equitably throughout the population.[25]

Finally, Justice Brandeis presented a strong case for industrial democracy. He pointed out that, politically, the individual is about as free as it is possible for him to become. Every man, he claimed, has his voice and his vote, and "can therefore secure an adequate part in the government of the country in all of its political relations." But the position of the worker in his industrial relations is that of a mere subject bound to submit to the will of an untempered oligarchy. He has no control whatever over company policy and little or no voice in determining his own fate. But democracy in the industrial sphere is just as important as political democracy. It is essential for the proper education and development of the individual and for giving him the status of a free man rather than a human tool. The solution is to be found in participation by labor representatives in all important company decisions. Competent representatives of the workers should sit on the board of directors and grapple with the complicated problems of profit and loss, hiring and firing, supplying and creating markets. They would acquire in this way a sense of dignity and a knowledge of how difficult it is to run a business without suffering disastrous losses. It would be an expedient better than profit-sharing, for it would give to its beneficiaries a consciousness of responsibility and make them citizens of the realm most vital to them—that which provides their livelihood. In no other way can the destiny of the great mass of our people be fulfilled. Democracy must be concerned not merely with the provision of social justice but with the perfection of manhood.[26]

Individualism as an expression of mission has evoked less disagreement than almost any other American ideal. Though by no means all of our spokesmen and prophets have accepted the ruthlessness of the Social Darwinists, few indeed have been outright collectivists. The overwhelming majority have set their faces sternly against treating the individual as a means to some social end. They have subscribed almost instinctively to the sacredness of human personality and have taken it for granted that this is a basic element in the American tradition. The chief divergence of opinion lies between those who have insisted that unrestricted competition is the key to both the happiness of the individual and the good of society and those who have maintained that neither can enjoy maximum benefits unless the government intervenes to assist in the solution of social problems. But for both schools of theorists the welfare of the individual is a dominant concern.

NOTES TO CHAPTER SIX

1. John Bigelow, ed., *The Complete Works of Benjamin Franklin* (New York: G. P. Putnam's Sons, 1887), II, 401.
2. Gaillard Hunt, ed., *The Writings of James Madison* (New York: G. P. Putnam's Sons, 1900), VI, 102; II, 247-48; Jonathan Elliot, ed., *The Debates in the Several State Conventions on the Adoption of the Federal Constitution* (Washington: Printed by and for the editor, 1863), II, 394; *Letters and Other Writings of James Madison*, Published by Order of Congress (Philadelphia: J. B. Lippincott Co., 1865), III, 587.
3. *Annals of Congress*, I, 111-12; *Letters*, Cong. ed., III, 577; Hunt, ed., *Writings*, VIII, 438.
4. *Problems of Modern Democracy* (New York: Charles Scribner's Sons, 1896), pp. 110-11, 120-21, 208.
5. From *The Meaning of the Times and Other Speeches* by Albert J. Beveridge, copyright © 1908, 1936, used by special permission of the publishers, The Bobbs-Merrill Company, Inc., Indianapolis, pp. 268, 273-74.
6. *The State of the Nation* (Indianapolis: The Bobbs-Merrill Co., 1924), pp. 179-81.
7. *The New Freedom* (New York: Doubleday, Page and Co., 1913), pp. 17-18.
8. *Major Campaign Speeches, 1952* (New York: Random House, 1953), pp. 57-58, 114.
9. *Essays* (New York: A. L. Burt, n.d.), I, 52; II, 198, 205, 213.
10. *The Writings of Henry David Thoreau* (Boston: Houghton Mifflin Co., 1910), IV, 356.
11. Theodore Sedgwick, ed., *A Collection of Political Writings of William Leggett* (New York: Taylor and Dodd, 1840), I, 81, 82, 116, 162, 252; II, 68-69.
12. *Writings*, Centenary ed. (Boston: American Unitarian Assoc., 1907-16), XIV, 170-71, 188-89; XIII, 364-65.
13. *Complete Prose Works* (Boston: Small, Maynard and Co., 1898), pp. 208, 221, 223-25.
14. Albert G. Keller, ed., *Earth-Hunger and Other Essays* (New Haven: Yale University Press, 1913), pp. 132-33, 275; Albert G. Keller, ed., *The Forgotten Man and Other Essays* (New Haven: Yale University Press, 1918), pp. 10, 480.
15. Keller, ed., *Earth-Hunger*, pp. 268-69, 351; Keller, ed., *The Forgotten Man*, pp. 230-31.
16. *The Will to Believe* (New York: Longmans, Green and Co., 1897), pp. 207-08; Henry James, ed., *The Letters of William James* (Boston: The Atlantic Monthly Press, 1921), II, 67.
17. *Acres of Diamonds* (New York: Harper and Brothers, 1915), pp. 15-25, 49-59.
18. F. D. Roosevelt, *Looking Forward* (New York: John Day Co., 1933), pp. 224-25.
19. Russell Lord, ed., *The Century of the Common Man* (New York: Reynal and Hitchcock, 1943), p. 57.
20. *Whose Constitution? An Inquiry into the General Welfare* (New York:

Reynal and Hitchcock, 1936), p. 103. (Quoted by permission of Harcourt, Brace and Company.)

21. *This Is Wendell Willkie* (New York: Dodd, Mead and Co., 1940), p. 204.
22. Allan Nevins, ed., *Interpretations 1933-1935* (New York: The Macmillan Co., 1936), p. 82.
23. *American Individualism* (Garden City, N. Y.: Doubleday, Page and Co., 1922), pp. 8-10, 48, 71-72.
24. O. K. Fraenkel, ed., *The Curse of Bigness* (New York: The Viking Press, 1934), pp. 38-39, 77, 171; A. T. Mason, *The Brandeis Way* (Princeton: Princeton University Press, 1938), pp. 35, 67-68.
25. Fraenkel, ed., *The Curse of Bigness*, pp. 45, 51; A. T. Mason, *Brandeis: A Free Man's Life* (New York: The Viking Press, 1946), p. 429.
26. Fraenkel, ed., *The Curse of Bigness*, pp. 73, 91-92, 270-71; Alfred Lief, ed., *The Social and Economic Views of Mr. Justice Brandeis* (New York: The Vanguard Press, *ca.* 1930), p. 383.

Chapter Seven

The Ethnic Rationalization

A conviction of race superiority may be both a cause and a consequence of a nation's consciousness of mission. If a people already feel that they have been endowed by God or by nature with talents surpassing those of their neigbhors, they will almost inevitably conclude that it is their destiny to redeem or to dominate their inferior brethren. Conversely, if they start out, as the ancient Hebrews did, with the idea of a divine appointment to lead and regencrate the nations of the earth, they will seek to justify their exalted mission by claims to a superior inheritance. Pride in ethnic endowments makes a tempting appeal to a people feeling themselves called to some glorious purpose. As Emerson expressed it: "Men hear gladly of the power of blood or race. Everybody likes to know that his advantages cannot be attributed to air, soil, sea, or to local wealth as mines and quarries, nor to laws and traditions, nor to fortune; but to superior brain, as it makes the praise more personal to him." [1]

Ideas of race superiority in the United States have shown a tenacity almost unmatched by that of any other doctrine. From colonial times until well into the twentieth century there has never been a period when men of influence and prominence could not be found in substantial numbers arrayed on the side of ethnological prejudice. And it is a melancholy fact that their ranks have included some of the most liberal and humane thinkers in American history.

In his "Notes on the State of Virginia," written between 1781 and 1785, Thomas Jefferson characterized the Negroes as a race with "a strong and disagreeable odor," lacking the capacity for affection, and much inferior to the whites in reasoning. He doubted that any

Negro existed with an ability to trace and comprehend the "investigations of Euclid." He declared that he had never found one capable of uttering a thought "above the level of plain narration." Comparing the American slaves with the more intelligent slaves of the Romans, he contended that it was nature and not bondage that accounted for the difference between them. A few years before his death James Madison incorporated in a letter to Lafayette an acrid criticism of Miss Fannie Wright for her "universally obnoxious" opinions in favor of "amalgamating the white and black population." [2] Both Madison and Jefferson regarded slavery as an evil and hoped for its ultimate extinction, but neither believed that the Negro could ever rise to the intellectual level of the Caucasian, and they denied that the two races could live in harmony on a plane of equality. The only solution they could envisage was gradual emancipation followed by deportation to Africa.

Many other Americans of broad sympathies clung to the notion that ineradicable differences between Negroes and Caucasians allocate the former to an inferior status and condemn them as forever unfit to share the social and political privileges accorded to the latter. In his famous debates with Stephen A. Douglas before the Civil War, Abraham Lincoln referred to "a natural disgust in the minds of nearly all white people at the idea of an indiscriminate amalgamation of the white and black races." He admitted that he did not know what should be done with the institution of slavery. His first impulse was to free all its victims and send them to Liberia, but a moment's reflection convinced him that this was impracticable. He then asked in consternation, "What next? Free them and make them politically and socially our equals?" His innermost feelings revolted against this. He contended that nature had fixed a gulf between the two races which would probably forbid forever their living together in perfect equality. And inasmuch as there had to be differences between them, he was in favor of the race to which he belonged "having the superior position." [3]

Some fifty years later William Jennings Bryan, foremost spokesman of agrarian democracy, scolded Theodore Roosevelt for giving, and Booker T. Washington for accepting, the first invitation to a Negro to dine at the White House. He feared that the motive on the part of both was an attempt to wipe out race lines. He criticized the Negro leader for deserting those of his own color "in order to shine in white society." As for the President's part in the affair, it seemed to the Great Commoner an incomparable folly to add to domestic race problems "while we must meet another greater and more complicated race problem in the Orient." [4]

THE IMPORTANCE OF RACE

To understand why race should have been regarded as so important by molders of opinion in America it is necessary merely to call to mind the circumstances of her history. To begin with, the settlers for the most part were a proud and ambitious lot. Though many of them had been persecuted or deprived of privileges, their conviction of righteousness and self-esteem had not been impaired. They sought all the more the justification to be obtained from pride in ethnic origins. It should be emphasized also that the settlers of America and their descendants for several generations were a conquering people. Not only when they first landed but as they pushed their way into the western wilderness they found their path blocked by aborigines who often retaliated in dangerous and unorthodox ways against the seizure of their lands. Slaughtering the natives and despoiling them of their property were crimes which the perpetrators could justify only on the ground that the Indians were an inferior people and that the progress of civilization required them to give way to the more richly endowed Caucasians.

Racism was strengthened further by the development of slavery. The ideological defense of the institution was elaborated in the South, especially after the invention of the cotton gin produced an extension of the plantation system and thereby increased the use of slave labor. But long before these developments the enslavement of the Negro was regarded by the majority of Americans in both North and South as the logical status for members of his race. It would appear that Roger B. Taney was essentially correct when he argued in the Dred Scott opinion that at the time the Constitution was adopted the Negro was generally considered an inferior being in no sense entitled to the rights and privileges of white citizens. He was, in fact, "so far inferior" that he was assumed to have no rights "which the white man was bound to respect." The Chief Justice went on to point out that in the early nineteenth century one State after another, including Massachusetts, Connecticut, New Hampshire, and Rhode Island, had passed laws discriminating against the Negro. It seemed, therefore, that members of the African race, whether free or slave, could never have been intended to enjoy the privileges and status accorded to whites.[5]

Affirmations of the importance of race have been so numerous in American history as to make one wonder whether those who expressed them were not trying to convince themselves. Such statements were founded almost exclusively upon ignorance and upon specious reasoning, though uttered by men of wide reputation for learning and wisdom. Emerson, for example, argued that it was race which put "the hundred millions of India under the dominion of a remote island in the north of Europe." He advanced the preposterous claim that ethnic factors were the primary reasons why all Celts were Catholics and all Saxons Protestants. As one would expect, he considered the Jews a separate race and contended that race accounted for their keeping "the same character and employments" for two millenniums regardless of climate and changing conditions. Though he doubted the survival of many pure races and referred to the mingling of peoples as "the most potent advancer of nations,"

The Statue of Liberty in New York Harbor, figure of hope and deliverance to immigrants and refugees of many races. *Port of New York Authority*

he still found "plenty of well-marked types." Among these he distinguished a "Norman" type, an "American" type, and a "Roman" type.[6]

Emerson's Transcendentalist colleague Theodore Parker was in some respects more realistic and practical minded; but on the subject of race he professed a sentimentalism almost mystical. Every people, he declared, "has a peculiar character in which it differs from all others that have been, that are, and possibly from all that are to come." He discovered the Ionian Greeks to have been characterized by "a devotion to what is beautiful," the Romans by hardness and materialism, skill in organizing men, a turn for affairs, and a genius for legislation. The Saxon race he described as practical; less pious than moral; trusting to experiment, facts, and precedents; not philosophical but commercial, warlike, obstinate, grasping, ambitious to colonize, devoted to liberty and law, and possessing an aptitude for "political confederations." These qualities, he averred, were not mere idiosyncrasies but sacred gifts, "given for some divine purpose to be sacredly cherished and patiently unfolded."[7] He refused to concede any capacity for cultural progress to the colored races. All the "great, permanent, and progressive" civilizations, he wrote, were Caucasian. Caucasians alone had produced "civilized" religions and the great works of science, literature, poetry, and the fine arts. Liberal governments—"democracies, republics, aristocracies, limited monarchies"—were likewise Caucasian achievements. "No other race ever got beyond a despotism limited by fear of assassination."[8]

The South, of course, produced its full complement of exponents of the importance of race. For reasons not easy to explain, many of them drew their arguments from the Bible. Possibly it was because religion generally has a stronger hold upon an agrarian society, since the farmer is more isolated and more dependent upon the whims of nature. Doubtless it had a relationship also to the fact that a master class lives in a state of fear and cultivates religion for its uses in lulling the victims of domination into accepting their servile status. In any event, the Bible was found to contain various passages which seemed to justify distinctions on an ethnic basis between masters and slaves. Old Testament heroes were commanded by Yahweh to make slaves of foreigners whose ancestors had hindered the ambitions of the Chosen People in achieving their destiny.

True, members of the Chosen Race themselves sometimes became slaves for debt, but Hebrew law prescribed for them a more liberal treatment. At the end of six years they were to be set free, and they were not to be "sent away empty." The portions of the Old Testament which seemed to make the strongest appeal to the southern aristocratic mind were those relating to the murder of Abel by Cain and the indignities committed by Ham, the son of Noah, against his father. Jefferson Davis expressed the common interpretation as follows: "When Cain, for the commission of the first great crime, was driven from the face of Adam, no longer the fit associate of those who were created to exercise dominion over the earth, he found in the land of Nod those to whom his crime had degraded him to an equality; and when the low and vulgar son of Noah, who laughed at his father's exposure, sunk by debasing himself and his lineage by a connection with an inferior race of men, he doomed his descendants to perpetual slavery." "

Davis, of course, was merely reiterating the theories of a whole school of apologists for Negro slavery. In some fashion it had been deduced that Ham was the father of the Negro race (apparently because the word "ham" was sometimes given the meaning of "that which is black") and that when Noah cursed him and decreed that he and his descendants should be "a servant of servants" unto their brethren, he placed a stigma of inferiority upon that race for as long as the earth should last. It was a barbarous and benighted theory conceived in ignorance and born of prejudice, but it undoubtedly had a powerful effect in buttressing the faith of the master race in its own superiority.

It would be too much to suppose that southerners would confine their views on the importance of race to theories derived from the Bible. Jefferson Davis himself referred to a "natural" inferiority of the Negro which caused him to sink into crime and to fill the jails of those areas where he was not a slave. Servility was stamped upon his very nature, and from that he could never rise. Throughout history the only factor that had saved him from barbarism was servitude. Davis even suggested that slavery might ultimately produce such an improvement in members of the black race that in God's good time they might safely be made free men: for slavery not only protected the Negroes in sickness and old age and kept them out of poorhouses and penitentiaries, but it "advanced them in intelligence." [10] John C. Calhoun extended the alleged inferiority of the Negro to all the colored races. He avowed that there was no instance in history of any colored race, "of any shade, being found equal to the establishment and maintenance of free government." In his view it was degrading, and fatal to American institutions, for white men to associate themselves as "equals, companions, and fellow-citizens" with any people of color, whether Negroes, Indians, or the mixed races of Mexico. [11]

That apologists for the planter aristocracy should have stressed the importance of race is hardly a source of wonder. What is really surprising is the fact that so many intellectuals in the North, after the Civil War, should have continued and even redoubled their efforts to make race appear to be the magic answer to the riddle of civilization. Thorstein Veblen found that the "dolicho-blond" stocks were "perceptibly more efficient in the machine industries," more materialistic, "more given to radical innovations," and more "socialistic" than other breeds. They were also "more industrially advanced," and Protestant rather than Catholic. [12] Henry Adams poured out his doleful prophecies that the "dark races" would soon overwhelm a large part of the earth by force of numbers. In another fifty years, he lamented, the whites "would have to reconquer the tropics by war and nomadic invasion, or be shut up, north of the fortieth parallel." At other times the racial menace appeared to him in the guise of the Jews. Like the Nazis of later years, he conceived of the Jews as the chief bulwark of both socialism and international capitalism. Though he admired them for their vigor and enterprise, he loathed them as a threat to the stability of the Western world. He thought of nearly all of them as either radicals or gamblers. Their agitation against capitalism was undermining confidence and impairing the value of investments. Their operations as moneylenders were squeezing the lifeblood out of industry and trade in both Europe and America. Soon we should all be in the hands of the Jews, and they would be able to do what they pleased "with our values." [13]

One of the most decisive developments in American history was the beginning of large-scale immigration from the Orient and from southern and eastern Europe during the very period when the racial theories derived from Social Darwinism were gaining converts by the thousands. It is a fact, of course, that the popularity

Immigrants in the 1880's awaiting distribution to the coal mines of Pennsylvania. Most were Poles, Italians, and South Slavs. By W. A. Rogers. *Harpers Weekly, 1888*

of these theories was directly related to the increased immigration, but their introduction came earlier. Social Darwinism was derived from the philosophy of Herbert Spencer. It represented an attempt to apply the Darwinian principle of natural selection to the sphere of institutions, customs, traditions, and ideas. Just as there was a struggle for existence among plants and animals, resulting in the elimination of the weak and unadaptable and the preservation of the fittest, so it was assumed that the competition of culture elements and of civilizations themselves had similar results of weeding out the inferior and preserving the best.

Although Spencer was interested primarily in the clash of social systems and institutions, some of his disciples extended the theory to a struggle among races and nations. For example, the American historian John Fiske energetically promoted the doctrine that those peoples who had achieved the greatest success in conquest and in the development of political organization necessarily represented superior types. John W. Burgess, constitutional lawyer and political philosopher at Columbia, warmly seconded Fiske's contentions. He endorsed the superior "morality" which Bismarck and Cavour employed to justify their use of force in unifying their nations. He lauded the peoples with an extraordinary genius for self-government as "nations *par excellence*" and taught that they should not hesitate to "clear out" barbarous populations, by force, if necessary, and "righteously assume sovereignty" over any that failed to meet high standards of political stability.[14]

Theodore Roosevelt rejoiced that Anglo-Saxon democracy had preserved the two "best portions" of the earth's surface, temperate America and Australia, for the white race. Aristocratic governments would have encouraged Chinese immigration precisely as the southern slaveholding oligarchy had encouraged the slave trade. But democracy, "with the clear instinct of race selfishness, saw the race foe, and kept out the dangerous alien." Though as President he sought more than once to protect the Japanese against discrimination, apparently because he admired their warlike qualities and their skill as colonial administrators, he expressed the opinion privately that no greater calamity could befall the United States "than to have the Pacific slope fill up with a Mongolian population." [15]

The American philosophers whose thinking seems to have been most deeply affected by the coming to American shores of hordes of alien immigrants were the two Progressive reformers David Starr Jordan and Edward Alsworth Ross. Both professed to repudiate important elements in Social Darwinism. The former rejected the thesis that war results in the survival of the fittest among nations, and the latter condemned the rugged individualism of Spencer and most of his followers. Yet when it came to race, both were in accord with the theories of the most rabid of the Social Darwinists. Jordan considered the blood of a nation the cardinal factor determining its history. America, he contended, was essentially a Nordic nation, and no other quality could account for so much of its progress. "Its freedom was won and its integrity maintained by Nordic methods." In the life of any people, he wrote, the vital differences are not matters of education but of "hereditary potentialities." "A good stock is the only material out of which history can make a great nation." Jordan was firmly convinced that races differed from one another as radically as flocks of sheep or herds of cattle. He recognized an almost infinite variety of ethnic types. In his book, races included not merely Caucasians, Mongolians, and Negroes but Saxons, Jews, Greeks, Serbians, Montenegrins, Frenchmen, Italians, and numerous others. Each had its characteristics marking it off as a separate breed. Knowing its nature would make possible a forecast of its achievements. The Saxon would make Saxon history wherever he went, the Jew would make Jewish history, and the Italian in whatever clime he might settle would "do deeds after his kind."

Like all racists, Jordan believed that the peoples of the world could be divided into superior and inferior types, and that the problem of distinguishing them was a relatively simple one. In general, he considered the best stocks to be those which most closely approximated the blond, Nordic type and the worst to be those at the opposite end of the scale. He thought that he found scientific evidence for this distinction in a record he kept of the number of arrests in a nearby county in California. More than half of the persons accused of crimes were individuals with Italian names, "presumably Sicilian," and a large proportion of the others were Mexicans and Chinese. He could not escape the conclusion that the southern and eastern European "races" were distinctly below the cultural and moral level of such peoples as the British, the Scandinavians, and the Dutch. He despised the French as dissolute and slovenly and the Spaniards and southern Italians as mentally backward. Even lower in the scale were the Mexicans, whom he described as "ignorant, superstitious, ill-nurtured, with little self-control and no conception of industry or thrift." Orientals he regarded as also beyond the pale, except the Japanese, whom he profoundly admired for their charming manners, their capacity for drawing pleasure from simple things, and their genius for "order and discipline." But it is significant that he made efforts to prove that the Japanese people were basically Aryan, though mixed with Chinese and Malay elements. Their earliest ancestors, he thought, were the now degenerate Ainus, "a branch of the Aryan race, belonging to the group vaguely known as Turanian and remotely allied to the tribes of the Caucasus." [16]

On a number of issues Jordan differed markedly from Edward Alsworth Ross, so markedly in fact that there was not room for both at Stanford. Ross antagonized Mrs. Stanford, and developments reached such a stage in 1900 that either President Jordan or his brilliant sociologist must go. When Ross refused to play the game of being eased out of Stanford "with dignity," and being shifted quietly to another university, Jordan fired him. Ross was disposed toward socialism and ridiculed Jordan's economic individualism.

Both were reformers; but where Ross favored direct benefits for the working classes, Jordan recommended that the worker be trained in vocational skills and then forced to shift for himself. On the subject of race, however, their views were almost identical, except that Ross had a stronger antipathy toward the immigrant types then flooding the country. He cast what he called his "practical eye" over the hordes of eastern Europeans who were settling in American industrial towns and found "from ten to twenty per cent" to be "hirsute, low-browed, big-faced persons of obviously low mentality." He was sure that they ought to be garbed in skins and to be living "in wattled huts at the close of the Great Ice Age." He looked at other gatherings of the foreign-born and discovered that "narrow and sloping foreheads were the rule." Short and small craniums were very noticeable. "Among the women, beauty, aside from the fleeting, epidermal bloom of girlhood, was quite lacking. In every face there was something wrong—lips thick, mouth coarse, upper lip too long, cheek-bones too high, chin poorly formed, the bridge of the nose hollowed, the base of the nose tilted, or else the whole face prognathous." He saw so many "sugar-loaf heads, moon-faces, slit mouths, lantern-jaws, and goose-bill noses" that he was almost ready to believe that some demon had "amused himself by casting human beings in a set of skew-molds discarded by the Creator." [17]

With respect to the foregoing description, one wonders if Ross ever looked at the high cheek bones and broad, hirsute face of Thorstein Veblen, the moon-shaped physiognomy in a picture of Horace Greeley, or the tilted nose in a portrait of Thomas Jefferson. Yet he employed such meaningless data to support his demands for a restrictive immigration policy similar to that sponsored later by the Ku Klux Klan. He feared that the foreigners of the types described would "lower the general plane of intelligence, self-restraint, refinement, orderliness, and efficiency." He criticized them for their intemperance and for their sexual irregularities, which he was a good enough sociologist to ascribe to the excess of men among them. He noted that in the mining towns the women went about their homes barefoot, and that their clothing reeked with the odors of cooking and uncleanliness. He was shocked to discover that the miner bathed in the kitchen before the females and children of the household, and that women soon to become mothers appeared in public "unconcerned." [18] It did not seem to occur to him that some of these alleged moral deficiencies were the products of substandard economic conditions. But it was doubtless as easy then as it is now for the uncritical mind to be disturbed by radical departures from an accepted norm.

It would be inaccurate, of course, to assume that leaders of thought in America were unanimous in considering blood to be the determining factor in a nation's progress. Long before the Nazis repelled every person of humane sympathies with the grotesqueries of their racial theories, a few noted Americans had rejected the superstition that a people's characteristics are ineradicably fixed by the nature of their ancestors. Before the end of the eighteenth century the enlightened physician Benjamin Rush expressed doubts that the innate intelligence of the Negroes was inferior to that of Caucasians. He was sure that most of the vices charged against Negroes were the offspring of slavery, which debased their understanding and rendered their moral faculties torpid.[19] The Swiss-American Albert Gallatin, Secretary of the Treasury under Jefferson and Madison and founder of the American Ethnological Society,

Students of many ethnic backgrounds mingle freely, under Quaker influence, at the Westtown School, Westtown, Pennsylvania. *Photo by Philadelphia Inquirer*

denounced all theories of race superiority as pretexts for "covering and justifying unjust usurpation and unbounded ambition." He contended that the progress of mankind should be credited much more to religious and political institutions than to race.[20]

After the Civil War few Americans seemed to recognize any inconsistency between demands for equality of rights for Negroes and assertions of the inborn superiority of the white race. One who did see the contradiction was George William Curtis, civil service reformer and man of letters. "Inferior race!" he exclaimed. "Was it they [the Negroes] who carved the skulls of our boys into drinking-cups and their bones into trinkets? Was it they who starved and froze our brothers into idiocy and madness at Andersonville and Bell-Isle? Was it they who hunted our darlings with bloodhounds, or hung faithful Union men before the very eyes of their wives and children?" He then called upon his Caucasian brothers, North and South, to "clasp hands in speechless shame, and confess that manhood in America is to be measured not by the color of the skin, but by the quality of the soul." Regrettably, these assertions were tied in with atrocity propaganda against the South, but there is evidence that Curtis was capable at one time of broader reasoning. On the eve of the Civil War he had said that "national characteristics continually blend and mingle, and gradually lead us to the reflection that . . . the races are but one race, human nature is everywhere endowed with the same rights and duties, and thus Christianity, or the doctrine and practice of universal brotherhood, becomes simply the ethical statement of a scientific fact." [21]

THE NOBLE ARYANS AND GODLIKE TEUTONS

From the dawn of their history Americans seem to have taken it for granted that members of the Caucasian race had been miraculously endowed by God or by nature with qualities of mind and of morals which gave them a marked superiority over men with darker skins. But eventually the idea spread that not all Caucasians were alike—that after the manner of George Orwell's animals, some were "more superior" than others. As early as 1846 Senator Thomas Hart Benton of Missouri proclaimed the "Celtic-Anglo-Saxon" division to be the van of the Caucasian race with a mission to spread over all the Americas and to reanimate the torpid peoples of the Old

World. The popularity of such notions rapidly increased after 1853-1855, when the Frenchman Joseph Arthur de Gobineau published his *Essay on the Inequality of the Human Races*. This work purported to show that all the significant achievements of civilization had been made by members of the so-called Aryan division of the Caucasian race. Aryans, it was claimed, included the Greeks and Romans, the Hindus, the ancient Persians, and most of the peoples of northern and western Europe. Soon Aryanism was refined into Teutonism, which glorified the Germanic peoples as the paragons of civilization and the purest representatives of the Aryan strain. Some of the prophets of the new doctrine worked themselves into a mystic frenzy over the peerless virtues of the godlike Teutons. Houston Stewart Chamberlain, British expatriate who lived in Germany and became active as a leader of the Wagnerian Circle, described the "great, radiant, heavenly eyes" of the Teutons, and their lengthened skulls, "which active brains, tortured by longing, had changed from the round lines of animal contentedness and extended towards the front." He insisted upon classifying Dante as Teutonic because of his "expressive countenance and cupola-like forehead."

American prophets of the racial *mystique* did not lag far behind their European brethren, and some of the things they said were just as nonsensical. Few of them tarried long over the Aryan thesis, and fewer still gave recognition to any other branch of the Caucasian race. James Russell Lowell suggested that the Jews were "perhaps the ablest," and he was sure that they were the "most tenacious," race inhabiting the earth. He thought that ability was as natural and hereditary with them "as the curve of their noses," and he deplored the fact that they had not been given a greater share in the government of the world.[22] Lewis H. Morgan, lawyer turned anthropologist, who exerted an enormous influence through the publication of his *Ancient Society* and other works between 1850 and 1880, taught that only two branches of the human race, the Semitic and the Aryan, had ever become civilized "through unassisted self-development." The Aryan branch, he argued somewhat circuitously, "represents the central stream of human progress, because it produced the highest type of mankind, and because it has proved its intrinsic superiority by gradually assuming the control of the earth." [23]

The idea that "assuming control over the earth" or a considerable

During the 1920's a revived Ku Klux Klan flourished as an anti Catholic, anti-Jewish, anti-Negro organization. It wielded political and religious influence in many sections, both North and South. Here some of its members are shown in a Northern church, with the Exalted Cyclops, and the Kleagle in the pulpit. *United Press Photo*

portion thereof demonstrated the superiority of a race proved to be a popular one in American ethnological lore. With the vast majority of writers, however, it was applied to the so-called Anglo-Saxon race rather than to any such broad category as Aryans. The term Anglo-Saxon was used almost as a synonym for British, and sometimes even for English. Emerson, for example, found "on the English face" decision and nerve combined with the "fair complexion, blue eyes, and open and florid aspect." These gave rise, he believed, to "love of truth," "sensibility," "fine perception," and "poetic construction." "The fair Saxon Man," he continued, "is not the wood out of which cannibal, or inquisitor, or assassin is made, but he is moulded for law, lawful trade, civility, marriage, the nurture of children, for colleges, churches, charities, and colonies." [24] Why this description would not fit almost any of the civilized nations of northern and central Europe he did not make clear. He maintained that members of the English race alone could be trusted with freedom—"freedom which is double-edged and dangerous to any but the wise and robust." Their moral superiority armed them "with the sceptre of the globe." [25]

Theodore Parker likewise referred to the Anglo-Saxons as if they were identical with the English, though he also made allowance for the considerable infusion of Norman blood into the English stock after 1066. He admired all Teutonic peoples, but he considered the elements that had produced the English nation, and the American also, to be superior to the others. He praised them for their love of individual liberty, modified by decorum and a zeal for law and order; for their practical-mindedness; for their interest in Christianity and democracy; for their "invasive and aggressive disposition"; and, curiously, for their "intense materialism." [26]

The most powerful voice upholding the identity of Anglo-Saxon and English civilizations and peoples was that of the Reverend Josiah Strong, Social Gospeler and drum major of the missionary movement in the 1870's and 1880's. Contemplating the products of the Anglo-Saxon mind as preserved in the English language, he did not see how anyone could question "that the destruction of these treasures would be a greater loss to the world than would the destruction of all the thought embodied in any other language." "And may we not correctly infer," he asked, "that on the whole, the Anglo-Saxons are the intellectual leaders of the world?" Language, he affirmed, is "a wonderfully truthful expression" of the thoughts, ideals, character, institutions, and civilization of a people. Since the English language is one of the most pervasive on earth, it followed that the Anglo-Saxon was doing for the modern world what the Greek did for the ancient. "They each produced a civilization characterized by a high development of the individual; they each produced an unequalled language and literature; and as the restless Greek carried his language and civilization around the Mediterranean, so the more restless Anglo-Saxon is carrying his language and civilization around the globe." He did not argue that the Anglo-Saxons duplicated the Greeks in every particular. But in those respects in which the Greeks "rendered supreme service to the world," notably in the development of individualism, "in the centrifugal or colonizing tendency," and in their power to impress their civilization upon the world, the Anglo-Saxons were certainly the "modern representatives" of the Greeks.[27]

Paradoxical as it may seem, the two most eminent political thinkers in the United States of German origin also paid homage to the supposed identity of Englishmen and Anglo-Saxons. Francis Lieber thought that the "Anglican race" had been divinely appointed as the original workmen to build the temple of liberty, and that to learn true freedom, nations must go to America and England, in the same way that they would go to Italy to study music and the fine arts, to France to study science, or to Germany to "learn how to instruct and spread education." At the same time, he was no stickler for race purity. Most of the noblest nations, he asserted, had arisen from the mixture of others.[28] Carl Schurz agreed with Lieber in extolling the qualities of the Anglican breed. No other race, at so early a date, would have founded the "stern democracy" of the Plymouth colony. No other race possessed the bravery, the hardihood, and the stubborn enterprise to carve a civilization out of the wilderness. The members of this race had the enviable talent of acting when others merely think, of promptly executing their ideas, and of appropriating the ideas of others. The Anglo-Saxon spirit he regarded as the "locomotive of progress," but it had made itself effective only insofar as it drew behind it a train consisting of the vigorous elements of all nations. The true greatness of the Anglo-Saxon race lay in the fact that it established and maintained its ascendancy without, at the same time, completely absorbing the other national elements. They modify each other, and their peculiar characteristics are "blended together by the all-assimilating power of freedom."[29]

A number of noted Americans, in the days when racism was in its prime, preferred to include in the chosen people a broader category than Anglo-Saxons. Henry Adams was willing to give credit to the "Aryans" as the creators of civil law. Woodrow Wilson thought it a deeply significant fact that democracy was to be found only in countries "begotten of the English race" and in Switzerland, "where old Teutonic habit" had been as firmly established as in England.[30] John Fiske expressly denied that the history of British institutions actually began with the English people. Instead, it descended "in unbroken continuity from the days when stout Arminius in the forests of northern Germany successfully defied the might of imperial Rome." In fact, he convinced himself that so many examples of primitive self-government existed throughout the

Aryan world "as to make it apparent that in its essential features it must be an inheritance from prehistoric Aryan antiquity." [31] William James was so enamored of Germany that he never visited the country "without delight." He loved the beauty and order; "the smiles of the chambermaids"; the perfect carriage of the men, "taught to walk in the army"; the "moral earnestness and readiness to take you seriously"; the "loquacity"; the "simplicity." He was convinced that the "uncivilized" parts of the earth would be as safe under German as under British control. He could see no excuse for regarding the "Anglo-Saxon race" as the "sole providential vehicle" of colonial salvation. [32]

The most enthusiastic champion of the Germans as the élite of the Caucasian race was John W. Burgess. Completing his education in Germany when the Hohenzollern empire was at the height of its grandeur, he returned to his homeland imbued with deep respect for what he regarded as the distinctive qualities of the Germanic race. It was Germans who had accomplished the difficult feat of reconciling "Government and Liberty." This was an achievement of the purest of the Teutonic tribes, the Angles, Saxons, and Jutes, all of whom migrated to the British Isles before they had become modified "in the slightest degree by contact with the civilization of the Roman Empire and of the Christian Church." Moreover, the Germans, according to Burgess, were the founders of political liberty as distinct from civil liberty. The former he defined as liberty of the subject to "participate in the operations of government," rather than a sphere of anarchic freedom beyond the control of government. The Germanic peoples were unique also in being guided in their political activities by *reason*. With them it was not mere will that was considered as sovereign, but will guided by reason. While the peoples of Latin Europe were recklessly destroying the old ruling classes, "which contained most that there was of intelligence, character, and capacity," the Teutonic nations were discovering how, "under the rule of reason," to conserve all classes, to give to each its proper place in the social and political order and to employ the talents and energies of each for the highest development of the individual and the welfare of the whole community. Instead of mounting the barricades of revolution, the Teutonic nations followed the method of moderate change and constant repair. They learned how to fit the new into the old, instead of completely demolishing the old and replacing it with the "crude and untried new." [33]

The most valuable of all the Germanic accomplishments, according to Burgess, was the national state. This he regarded as the *ne plus ultra* of political achievements. The national state came nearer to solving all the problems of political society than any other institution ever devised. To begin with, it rescued the world "from the monotony of universal empire." Like a good Social Darwinist, Burgess believed that human beings advanced politically as well as individually by "contact, competition, and antagonism." But the universal state suppressed this competition in its pursuit of a universal reign of peace, which meant, in the long run, "stagnation and despotism." In the second place, the national state solved the problem of the reconciliation of sovereignty and liberty. This became possible because such a state permits the participation of the governed in the work of governing. Thus while the national state is the strongest on earth, it is also the freest. To be sure, it does not allow an extensive freedom in the sense of immunity from government; but its laws are recognized by the people who share in making them as expressions of what is necessary for the common rights and interests. Obedience to such laws is realization of the truest liberty. Although the facts of history did not always support Burgess' optimism, even in the empire he most admired, there can be no doubt of his enthusiasm for the national state. In his view, it was the

In some parts of the South desegregation has been markedly successful. Here are Negro and white pupils in the cafeteria of a large city school. *Wide World*

supreme achievement of mankind, and the nations that produced it could be justifiably applauded as the political nations par excellence.[34]

For almost a century after 1840 the tendency of American writers to glorify the northern European peoples as bearers of the torch of civilization was overwhelming. It made little difference whether or not Anglo-Saxons were singled out as a special élite among the Teutons, for both peoples were almost universally believed to possess the same characteristics. They were revered alike as the exemplars of liberty, obedience to law, representative democracy, and respect for the individual. Theodore Parker, who venerated the English, also acclaimed the Germans as the "noblest of earth's noble nations." For had they not invented printing and originated the Protestant Revolution? All the "generous glories" which had accumulated "from fighting Arminius 'down to the thoughtful von Humboldt" wove a halo round the head of the humblest Fritz and Gretchen.[35] Jefferson Davis held that the principle of self-government, "generated in the German forests before the days of the Caesars," had given the ancient Teutons a "self-reliance and patriotism" which enabled them to check the flight of the Roman eagles and to become the guardians of liberty for central and northern Europe. Through the Saxons the principle of self-government was transplanted in England, and was carried thence into the wilds of America. All the great benefits in the form of free institutions enjoyed by both North and South could be traced ultimately to German origins.[36]

THE GREAT RACE AND ITS DESTINY

Even in the days when ethnic dogmas were at their peak, Americans seldom thought of themselves as a separate race. Indeed, it was practically impossible to do so, since most of their institutions, to say nothing of their language and culture, had obviously been imported from across the sea. It seemed more logical to speak of an Anglo-Saxon race, of which Americans were merely the youngest but undoubtedly the most promising branch. A few theorists, however, were not satisfied with this and proposed to take in the whole Germanic breed as the people destined to inherit the earth. For instance, John W. Burgess maintained that the Teutonic nations were "intrusted, in the general economy of history, with the mission of conducting the political civilization of the modern world." In particular, they were called to extend political civilization into those parts of the world inhabited by "unpolitical and barbaric races." They should also consider themselves authorized to "interfere" in the affairs of nations not wholly barbaric, which have made some progress in state organization, but which are manifestly incapable of solving political problems "with any degree of completeness." Such nations are a threat to civilization everywhere. The Teutonic peoples should never regard the exercise of political power as a right of man. It must be based upon capacity to "discharge political duty," and the Teutonic peoples themselves are the best judges of when and where that capacity exists. Indifference on the part of these peoples to political failure and incapacity is not only a mistaken policy but disregard of a solemn obligation. The Teutonic nations are "the political nations of the modern era." To them has been given the noble mission of organizing the world politically. If less gifted peoples resist, their political superiors have the right to "force organization upon them by any means necessary, in their honest judgment," to accomplish the beneficial result.[37]

Most other Americans who wrote on the subject conceived of racial destiny in terms of the Anglo-Saxons. John Fiske, for example, assigned to the "two great branches of the English race" the common mission of establishing over the greater part of the globe the highest civilization and the most perfect political order mankind had ever seen. He drew the conclusion that the work which the Anglo-Saxon race began when it colonized North America was destined to go on until every country on the earth's surface that was not already the center of an old civilization would become "English in its language, in its political habits and traditions, and to a predominant extent in the blood of its people." The day would soon dawn, he thought, when four fifths of the human race would trace its descent to English ancestors.[38]

The ink was scarcely dry on John Fiske's predictions when Josiah Strong began to suggest that the American branch of the Anglo-Saxon race was the one really armed with the scepter of the world. The reasons for this were partly geographic and economic. The American homeland surpassed all other Anglo-Saxon domains in resources and population. It had a better climate, and it lay in the "pathway of the nations." But these were not the sole explanations. The American race had been honored, "not for its own sake, but for the sake of the world." The nation had been made powerful, rich, exalted, and free for no purpose of aggrandizement but to serve the true interests of civilization. The call to so noble a mission came from no less an authority than God Himself. For this reason the chosen race, representing the "largest liberty," the "purest Christianity," and the "highest civilization," would move with righteous assurance "down upon Mexico, down upon Central and South America, out upon the islands of the sea, over upon Africa and beyond." Before its triumphant advance, inferior peoples would give way, for they were only "precursors of a superior race, voices in the wilderness crying: 'Prepare ye the way of the Lord!' " [39]

Strong helped to prepare the way for even more vainglorious affirmations of the exalted mission of the Anglo-Saxons and of their highest representatives, the Americans. With the Spanish-American War opening vistas of imperial grandeur and kindling hopes of fabulous profits, racial theorists grasped eagerly at the opportunity to expound the claims of the Saxon élite. In the debate over annexation of the Philippines, Albert J. Beveridge proclaimed to an enraptured Senate that America would not renounce her part in the mission of her race, "trustee under God, of the civilization of the world." Instead, she would rejoice in the White Man's Burden and give thanks to Almighty God that He had marked the nation "as His Chosen people to lead in the regeneration of the world." The Senator concluded his speech with the grandiloquent flourish that God had given to Americans the paramount position among Anglo-Saxon peoples, to serve as the "master organizers" of the world, to establish order where chaos reigned, and to advance the cause of civilization. This was the divine mission of America. Her people were appointed "trustees of the world's progress, guardians of its righteous peace."

During the same war that whetted the appetites of American imperialists, another well-known liberal sounded the clarion for race supremacy. He was William Allen White, editor of the Emporia *Gazette*. On March 20, 1899, he avowed in his paper that only Anglo-Saxons could govern themselves. Cubans would therefore have to be governed despotically for many years by Uncle Sam until the island was "filled with Yankees." It was the Anglo-Saxon's manifest destiny, he continued, to "go forth in the world as a world conqueror." The members of this race were the chosen people. They were destined to "take possession of all the islands of the sea" and to "exterminate" the peoples they could not subjugate. Ten years later he was still convinced that Americans of Anglo-Saxon stock were the hope of the world. "The best blood of the earth," he announced, "is here." But this blood would remain "a clean, Aryan blood," because there were no hordes of inferior men gathered about to debase the stock. Anglo-Saxons in the United States were separated by two oceans from the lower races, and by "that instinctive race revulsion to cross breeding that marks the American wherever he is found." [40]

Americans are fond of thinking of themselves as the most tolerant and broad-minded people on earth. But in the hundred and eighty years of their independence as a nation, astonishingly few of them have rejected racial exclusiveness or championed the view that all men are brothers entitled to the same rights and privileges, regard-

An American Point 4 technician greets a chief of a Liberian village. *ICA*

less of the color of the skin, shape of the head, or any other physical peculiarities. Not a single one of the great popular heroes of democracy—neither Jefferson, Jackson, Lincoln, nor Woodrow Wilson— rose much above the common prejudices. George William Curtis, as we have seen, came close to doing so, but his conclusions were tarnished by the aim of indicting the southern whites. Perhaps purer in motive was Henry George, who taught that "human nature is human nature all the world over," and attempted to show that "the influence of heredity is as nothing compared with the influences which mold the man after he comes into the world." [41]

By 1900 a number of American anthropologists, notably Franz Boas and William Z. Ripley, had published cogent criticisms of the prevailing race mythology, calling into question the whole idea of superior and inferior stocks. But these criticisms had little influence outside the realm of science. A few philosophers, among whom John Dewey was pre-eminent, gave them generous recognition, but political, social, and even educational leaders took little notice. Albert J. Beveridge, William Allen White, John W. Burgess, and David Starr Jordan went blandly ahead with their preachments of Aryan, Teutonic, and Anglo-Saxon superiority. As late as 1952 Harry S. Truman could proclaim that diversity of races and peoples was the clue to American greatness. Although he repudiated "false ideas of racial superiority," he affirmed that the United States, "better than any other country," could reach out through its "diversity of races and origins," and help other nations to higher levels of prosperity and happiness.[42] Without question this was more commendable doctrine than the theories of Aryan or Teutonic supremacy, but it was still a far cry from the scientific hypothesis that mankind is a single species, and that race is of no more consequence than stature or the length of the nose in determining capacities or moral qualities.

NOTES TO CHAPTER SEVEN

1. *Complete Works*, Riverside ed. (New York: Houghton Mifflin Co., 1883-88), V, 49.
2. Gaillard Hunt, ed., *The Writings of James Madison* (New York: G. P. Putnam's Sons, 1900), IX, 311.
3. John G. Nicolay and John Hay, eds., *The Complete Works of Abraham Lincoln* (New York: Francis D. Tandy Co., 1905), II, 207, 329; III, 229.
4. *The Commoner Condensed* (New York: The Abbey Press, 1902), pp. 293-94.

5. Dred Scott *v.* Sandford, 19 Howard 401-16 (1857).
6. *Complete Works*, Riverside ed., V, 49-51, 56-57.
7. *Writings*, Centenary ed. (Boston: American Unitarian Assoc., 1907-16), XI, 120-23.
8. *Ibid.*, VIII, 412.
9. Dunbar Rowland, ed., *Jefferson Davis, Constitutionalist, His Letters, Papers and Speeches* (Jackson, Miss.: Dept. of Archives and History, 1923), IV, 231.
10. *The Rise and Fall of the Confederate Government* (New York: D. Appleton and Co., 1881), I, 534.
11. Richard K. Cralle, ed., *The Works of John C. Calhoun* (New York: D. Appleton and Co., 1856), IV, 411.
12. *The Theory of Business Enterprise* (New York: B. W. Huebsch, 1923), p. 354.
13. Harold D. Cater, ed., *Henry Adams and His Friends* (Boston: Houghton Mifflin Co., 1947), pp. 467, 482-84; Worthington C. Ford, ed., *Letters of Henry Adams* (New York: Houghton Mifflin Co., 1930-38), II, 111; Newton Arvin, ed., *The Selected Letters of Henry Adams* (New York: Farrar, Straus and Young, 1951), p. 183.
14. *Political Science and Comparative Constitutional Law* (Boston: Ginn and Co., 1890), I, 39, 41.
15. E. E. Morison, ed., *The Works of Theodore Roosevelt* (New York: Charles Scribner's Sons, 1925), VIII, 118; XIV, 245-46.
16. David Starr Jordan's ideas on race are discussed fully in E. M. Burns, *David Starr Jordan: Prophet of Freedom* (Stanford, Calif.: Stanford University Press, 1953), Ch. IV.
17. *The Old World in the New* (New York: The Century Co., 1914), pp. 285-86.
18. *Ibid.*, p. 228.
19. Dagobert D. Runes, *The Selected Writings of Benjamin Rush* (New York: The Philosophical Library, 1947), pp. 4-5.
20. Henry Adams, ed., *The Writings of Albert Gallatin* (Philadelphia: J. B. Lippincott Co., 1879), III, 585.
21. Charles Eliot Norton, ed., *The Orations and Addresses of George William Curtis* (New York: Harper and Brothers, 1894), I, 42, 174.
22. *Works* (New York: Houghton Mifflin Co., ca. 1892), VI, 18-19.
23. *Ancient Society* (New York: Henry Holt and Co., 1907), p. 553.
24. *Complete Works*, Riverside ed., V, 68.
25. *Ibid.*, V, 288, 294.
26. *Writings*, Centenary ed., VI, 349.
27. *The New Era or the Coming Kingdom* (New York: The Baker and Taylor Co., 1893), pp. 59, 64-65.
28. *On Civil Liberty and Self-Government* (Philadelphia: J. B. Lippincott Co., 1877), pp. 295-96.
29. Frederic Bancroft, ed., *Speeches, Correspondence and Political Papers of Carl Schurz* (New York: G. P. Putnam's Sons, 1913), I, 54-57.
30. *An Old Master and Other Political Essays* (New York: Charles Scribner's Sons, 1893), p. 118.
31. *American Political Ideas, Viewed from the Standpoint of Universal History* (Boston: Houghton Mifflin Co., 1911), pp. 5, 29.

32. Letter to Hugo Münsterberg, June 18, 1900, in R. B. Perry, *The Thought and Character of William James* (Boston: Little, Brown and Co., 1935), II, 148.

33. *The Reconciliation of Government with Liberty* (New York: Charles Scribner's Sons, 1915), pp. 113, 124-25, 251-52.

34. *Political Science and Comparative Constitutional Law*, I, 37-39.

35. *Writings*, Centenary ed., XIV, 279, 330.

36. *The Rise and Fall of the Confederate Government*, I, 116.

37. *Political Science and Comparative Constitutional Law*, I, 44-48.

38. *American Political Ideas*, pp. 5-6, 135-36.

39. *Our Country* (New York: The Baker and Taylor Co., 1885), pp. 76, 165-66; *Expansion under New World Conditions* (New York: The Baker and Taylor Co., 1900), p. 213.

40. *The Old Order Changeth* (New York: The Macmillan Co., 1910), p. 252.

41. *Progress and Poverty*, Modern Library ed. (New York: Random House, n.d.), pp. 489, 497.

42. *Vital Speeches*, Vol. XVIII, No. 18 (July 1, 1952).

Chapter Eight

Religion and Morality

If a nation is to play the role of messiah to a benighted humanity, the demands of logic would seem to require that it be armed with the scepter of righteousness and be clad with the garments of superior virtue. In the opinion of most of her prophets America has not failed in these requirements. Religion was the source of much of her political theory and has entered into the warp and woof of her laws and many of her institutions. No other nation in modern times has produced a Dwight L. Moody, a Billy Sunday, or a Billy Graham. It would also be difficult to find anywhere else so great a profusion of Holy Rollers, Bible literalists, and religious primitives. Though some of these phenomena may be doubtful evidences of spirituality, they do indicate at least an uncommon religiosity.

But a halo of piety is not enough to justify the efforts of the world deliverer. He who would preach redemption to a slavish mankind must also be attired in the spotless robes of innocence and probity. Americans have donned such garments from the beginning of their history. Scarcely any other nation even in our own day has so extensive a catalogue of remedies for sin. Our blue laws, our laws against gambling, and our rules against profanity and obscenity are among the strictest in the world. Though censorship of books, plays, and movies has been relaxed somewhat by court decisions recently, we still have such unique institutions as Watch and Ward Societies, Societies for the Suppression of Vice, and Legions of Decency.

But moral fervor in the United States does not express itself merely in the form of restrictions and prohibitions. Several of our wars have taken on the character of great moral crusades. It was our duty to wipe out such evils as slavery, militarism, persecution, and oppression. Rarely did we go to war solely for the defense or even for the extension of national interests. Ironically, much of our isolationism has also been the result of moral fervor. In numerous instances apostles of withdrawal within our own borders have sought to justify their policy by the argument that Old World politicians were cynical and corrupt, and that their methods could never be anything but a stench in the nostrils of sincere and honest Americans. Such was the attitude of many of the Progressives during the early twentieth century, notably, of Robert M. LaFollette, George W. Norris, Herbert Croly, and Oswald Garrison Villard in opposing ratification of the Versailles Treaty.

THE SPIRITUAL FOUNDATION

Nearly every American who has ever acclaimed the greatness of his country or announced his belief in its glorious destiny has grounded his enthusiasm to some extent upon devotion to religion. He has assumed that the republic was founded for religious purposes and that divine favor has been its guide and companion ever since. Not only does he regard America as a Christian nation but he thinks of it as more Christian than any other. For this reason he considers his nation peculiarly well qualified to instruct other peoples by both precept and example as to the ways in which they should go.

To stress the importance of religion in the early history of our country would be almost superfluous, at least with respect to New England and some of the Middle Colonies. For Calvinists the chief end of man was "to glorify God and enjoy him forever." The magistrate ruled as the vicegerent of God, and the law was the supposed decrees of Moses contained in the Old Testament. The state was essentially the secular arm of the church, and the maintenance of the true religion and the true morality was its primary function. The Great Awakening, with its encouragement of dissent from orthodoxy and the development of mystical and emotional attitudes, promoted the democratization of religion and a breaking of the link with the state. But in no sense did it destroy the feeling that religion is a necessary ingredient of the well-ordered society. Even in the period when the influence of the Enlightenment permeated most rational minds, an appearance of piety, at least, was considered essential to social stability. The attitude of American intellectuals of this time was similar to that of Voltaire, who, after being robbed by some peasants, attended church for a season to persuade the country bumpkins that he still believed in God.

Nor did the stress upon religion diminish appreciably with the termination of colonial dependence and the establishment of the Federal Union. Suspicious as they were of human nature, nearly all of the Fathers of the republic subscribed to the theory that governments were constantly menaced by the innate depravity of citizens and subjects. In their view corruption and licentiousness were primary causes of the downfall of ancient Rome. Since they assumed that virtue required for its support a supernatural sanction, they urged that at least the fundamental doctrines of a belief in God and in rewards and punishments be zealously maintained. In a report to the General Assembly of Connecticut, in 1802, Oliver Ellsworth recommended that the state give generous support to religious institutions as "eminently useful" agencies for the promotion of good morals so essential to the preservation of society. In 1811 John Adams expressed his devotion to religion as one of the true foundations, "not only of republicanism and of all free government, but of social felicity under all governments and in all combinations of human society." [1] Madison referred to a belief in God as "essential to the moral order of the world and to the happiness of man." [2] Although Jefferson approved of the harshest criticism and even ridicule of religious dogmas, he did so with the thought that the purity of religion might thereby be enhanced. [3]

With the exception of a few who came under the influence of scientific materialism toward the end of the nineteenth century, American leaders continued to preach the importance of religion from Jefferson's time to the present. For the most part, they meant the importance of Christianity, though occasionally they extended their precepts to cover almost any supernatural system. The gentle evangel William E. Channing declared that the Christian religion was "singularly important to free communities." In fact, he doubted whether political freedom could subsist without it. Equal rights and an impartial administration of justice, he maintained, had always been inseparable from it. But he was much more deeply disturbed over the direful effects of no religion at all. "The whole social fabric

Camp Meeting about 1835. In frontier communities camp meetings often extended over a period of weeks. Religion was highly emotional, with shouting, swooning, and "talking in tongues." Lithograph by Kennedy and Lucas from a painting by A. Rider. *Courtesy of The New-York Historical Society, New York City*

would quake," he said, "and with what a fearful crash it would sink into hopeless ruins, were the idea of a Supreme Being, of accountableness, and of a future life, to be utterly erased from every mind. . . . Once let men thoroughly abandon religion, and who can conceive or describe the extent of the desolation which would follow?" The French Revolution was a failure, he alleged, because the apostles of French liberty had thrown off all the supernatural sanctions which control and exalt the mind. "How could we believe," he demanded, "that a liberty of which that heartless scoffer, Voltaire, was a chief apostle, could have triumphed?"[4] The noted orators and statesmen William H. Seward and Daniel Webster were more positive in their conviction that nothing else but Christianity could provide the proper bulwark of a free society. Both believed that the foundations of democracy must surely crumble without the support of Christian principles.[5]

The beginning of the quest for overseas empire in the late nineteenth century seemed to heighten the interest in religion as a basis for national greatness. Perhaps the conquest of distant territories and alien peoples needed a divine sanction to make it reputable. More likely, it was subconsciously felt that the new vistas of power and glory were so magnificent that they could only be accounted for as signal manifestations of God's favor and sublime purposes for His chosen nation. Whatever the explanation, spiritual interpretations of American history and government took on a new life. The harbinger of the imperialist era, the Reverend Josiah Strong, described in 1885 the matchless blessings which American expansion would bring to the benighted natives of distant regions. "A Christian civilization," he said, "performs the miracle of the loaves and fishes, and feeds its thousands in a desert." It brings new industries and replenishes the earth, so that a thousand civilized men may thrive where a hundred savages starve. It appeared, however, that the advantages would not be one-sided, for with such vast continents as Africa added to our market, "what is to prevent the United States from becoming the mighty workshop of the world, and our people 'the hands of mankind'?" [6]

By a curious paradox the leading exponent of naval supremacy who was the real father of the new imperialism wrote more like a Christian idealist than did the famous divine just quoted. In the opinion of Alfred T. Mahan, Christianity was an essential factor not only in developing in nations the capacity for self-government but in making them fit to govern. The chief element which operates for the latter purpose is conscience, which can only be of divine origin. It is conscience that enables nations to choose the path of honor rather than that of submission, and to fight for the right as a sacred duty instead of compromising with evil. As long as evil exists in the world, it will be justifiable to use force to combat it. For this reason the great literary sea dog opposed the signing of treaties which would require America to arbitrate her disputes with other countries. The nation must be free to obey the higher law of God, which invalidates any statute or agreement of men involving a concession to unrighteousness. [7]

Mahan's ebullient disciple Theodore Roosevelt also conceived of a religious and moral order of the world in which nations would be called upon from time to time to stand at Armageddon and battle for the Lord. They could not afford "to overlook the vital importance of the ethical and spiritual, the truly religious, element in life." If confronted by a conflict between righteousness and peace, they must invariably choose the former. The Christian, civilized peoples of the earth have a moral duty to rescue and uplift their backward brethren. If the latter have the intelligence to assimilate and profit by the ideas of civilization and Christianity, all will be well; but if they lack this intelligence, they should be forced to submit to the rule of the superior peoples.

The racial chauvinism of Senator Beveridge, to say nothing of his imperialism, also had a religious rationalization. Discussing the conquest of the Philippines, he declared that we would "not renounce our part in the mission of our race, trustee under God, of the civilization of the world." For God had "marked us as His chosen people to lead in the regeneration of the world." It was not enough that the English-speaking and Teutonic peoples had developed a capacity for making their own countries the freest and best governed on earth. God had appointed them to a higher calling. He had made them adepts in government in order that they might "establish system where chaos reigns" and administer the affairs of "savage and senile peoples." And of all the Teutonic race He had singled out the American people for the most exalted destiny. Their mission was nothing less than "trustee of the world's progress, guardian of its righteous peace." Like the profitable servant of the Bible, the people of this nation had taken the talents given to them, labored hard and shrewdly and gained additional talents, and now were ready for the Master's judgment: "Ye have been faithful over a few things. I will make you ruler over many things." [8]

By common supposition, involvement of a nation in war produces a need for spiritual sustenance and a sense of dependence upon God in the face of uncertainty and tragedy. World War I appeared at times to have been an exception so far as the great leader of America's crusade was concerned. In most of his speeches President Wilson referred to the war as a political rather than a moral or religious struggle. America was fighting for liberty, for democracy, for the rights of small nations, for the collective peace of the world, and against militarism and autocracy. There is evidence, however, that the renowned apostle of the New Freedom steadily cherished in the back of his mind the comforting thought that God was waiting in the nearby shadows ever ready to come to his rescue if help should be needed. Moreover, he had long entertained a theocentric interpretation of his nation's history. America was a special ward of Providence, subject to the divine blessing or chastisement in accordance with her virtues or deficiencies. In September, 1919, he predicted that if the United States rejected the League of Nations, "the vengeful Providence of God" would bring a new war in which not a few hundred thousand but many million Americans would die. For Wilson the word religion was virtually synonymous with Christianity. As far back as 1911 he told an audience assembled in Denver to celebrate the tercentenary of the translation of the Bible into the English language that "America was born a Christian nation" and commissioned "to exemplify that devotion to the elements of righteousness which are derived from the revelations of Holy Scripture." Addressing the Federal Council of Churches in December, 1915, he lauded Christianity as "the most vitalizing thing in the world" and declared that nations advanced "not by material but by spiritual means."

If religiousness of such proportions was to be expected of a man like Wilson, born in a Presbyterian manse and rising to eminence in the midst of the sentimental influence of Progressivism, different anticipations might well have been entertained for his successors. Most of them had worldly backgrounds and reached their political maturity during the cynicism of the 1920's. Nevertheless, assertions of the importance of religion during the 1930's, 1940's, and 1950's were just as numerous as they had been earlier. In his Madison Square Garden campaign address of 1936, Franklin D. Roosevelt expressed his "deep conviction that democracy cannot live without that true religion which gives a nation a sense of justice and of moral purpose." In 1940 Henry Wallace insisted that "the American ideal is as definitely religious as the ideal of any church." [9] On the eve of the Korean War, President Truman told an assemblage of law-enforcement officers, convened to plan a drive against organized crime, that "the fundamental basis of this nation's law was given to Moses on the Mount." "The fundamental basis of our Bill of Rights," he continued, "comes from the teachings which we get from Exodus and St. Matthew, from Isaiah and St. Paul." Unfortunately he failed to make clear to his audience just how the Bill of Rights could be reconciled with Paul's teachings: "The powers that be are ordained of God" and "Let every soul be subject unto the higher powers." To his credit, the Fair Deal President was more realistic in the latter part of his speech, when he stressed the point that "human misery breeds most of our crime." He urged the wiping out of slums, improving the health of our citizens, and eliminating the inequalities of opportunity "which embitter men and women and turn them toward lawlessness." [10]

The outbreak of the "cold war" against Russia undoubtedly stimulated a stronger interest in religion in American political circles. It could easily be shown that Communism is atheistic; therefore, it was convenient to emphasize the spiritual aspects of democracy in order to heighten the contrast between the two systems. Soon after his retirement from the Presidency, Harry S. Truman took comfort in the prospect of an early collapse of Russian power, because of a fatal flaw in Soviet society. Their system was a "godless system" and consequently a system of slavery, with no freedom in it. [11]

During the campaign of 1952, the New York *Times* requested each candidate to tell how he would expect the precepts of his religious faith to influence his official acts as President of the United States. In his reply General Eisenhower indicated his belief that the whole struggle against Communism could be boiled down to "a fight between anti-God and a belief in the Almighty." Since the Communists know this, he said, they must eliminate God from their system; for "when God comes in, communism has to go." Democracy, by

The three chapels at Brandeis University, for Catholic, Jewish, and Protestant students. *Brandeis University News Bureau*

contrast, gives a central place to religious faith. Indeed, free government on any other basis is inconceivable. "Our forefathers proved that only a people strong in Godliness is a people strong enough to overcome tyranny and make themselves and others free." The Democratic candidate, Adlai E. Stevenson, reduced his conception of American spirituality to a Christian framework. "Christian faith," he averred, "has been the most significant single element in our history and our tradition." From the beginning it has been "the most powerful influence in our national life" and "has inspired our highest achievements." He thought of it also as a protection against moral confusion, which he characterized as "too often the moral nihilism of this age." "The blight of moral relativism," he concluded, "has not fallen destructively upon us." Which nation or nations it had fallen upon, he did not specify, but he doubtless meant the Russians, since the relativity of morality to property relations is a Marxian dogma.

THE MORAL FOUNDATION

Most spokesmen for American ideals have considered morality of equal importance with religion as a foundation of national mission. Usually the two have been considered as interrelated, though a few of our staunchest moralists have been skeptics with regard to the supernatural. From the Founders of the republic to those who give counsel to the troubled minds of the present, virtue has been regarded as essential to the survival of the land of the free. At the beginning of the Revolution, Samuel Adams wrote to James Warren that while "we may look up to armies for our defense," virtue is "our best security." He added: "It is not possible that any State should long remain free, where virtue is not supremely honored." [12] Thomas Paine contended that America was unique in being perhaps the only nation in history whose record had never been sullied by any dishonor. Her cause was always good, her principles just and liberal. He contrasted America with Rome, "once the proud mistress of the universe," but "originally a band of ruffians." America need never be ashamed to tell her birth, nor relate the stages by which she rose to empire.[13] For James Madison, John Adams, Benjamin Franklin, and Gouverneur Morris religion *and* virtue were the mainstays of the republic.

The predominant tendency of our exponents of morality as a key to superiority was to give it a Puritan frame of reference. That is, they stressed such qualities as diligence, frugality, restraint, and ambition. Shortly before he became President, George Washington wrote to his friend Lafayette: "Nothing but harmony, honesty, industry, and frugality are necessary to make us a great happy people." [14] One of Alexander Hamilton's reasons for emphasizing the blessings of a national debt was that it would be a spur to industry. Americans labored less than any civilized people of Europe, he complained, and he argued that a habit of labor was not only essential to the health and vigor of minds and bodies but "conducive to the welfare of the State." He recommended also the development of manufactures partly in order to give employment to persons who might otherwise be idle, including women and children. He thought it especially desirable that the latter should make themselves useful at an early age. [15]

The second half of the nineteenth century witnessed what seems to have been a major revival of Puritan morality. This revival came about apparently because the Puritan virtues of diligence, thrift, and self-denial tied in well with the aggressive competition sancti-

Eliza's escape from her captors. A chapter in the ethical folklore of America, with a strong suggestion of divine intervention for the help of the innocent and the defeat of the wicked. Lithograph in color by Bettannier, Paris. *Courtesy of The New-York Historical Society, New York City*

fied by Social Darwinism and the Manchester theories of economics. Between his two terms as President, Grover Cleveland gave out strong intimations that the government ought to be placed in the hands of those who had been made responsible and self-reliant by denial and "by the surroundings of an enforced economy." "Thrift and careful watchfulness of expenditure among the people," he argued, "tend to secure a thrifty government." [16] The most perfect exemplification of Puritan ideals was to be found in the philosophy of David Starr Jordan, who sought to inculcate on the Pacific Coast doctrines of diligence and self-abnegation worthy of a medieval monk. Jordan condemned almost every form of self-indulgence that had ever been reckoned among the vices, not only the consumption of intoxicating beverages but card-playing and the use of tobacco, coffee, and tea. He referred to the chastity of women as "society's most precious jewel," and he insisted that the conventions guarding this jewel could not be abandoned without "a far-reaching heritage of evil." In teaching such doctrines he made no attempt to disguise his indebtedness to Puritanism, but gloried in it. The Puritans, he alleged, derived their great power from the austerity of their practices. In restraint they found strength and the only happiness worth pursuing. The modern man who would attain the same benefits must follow a path as narrow as that of the Puritans, for it is still true that the road which leads to the greatest satisfactions in life is strait and stony, while the path which leads to destruction is broad and flowery.[17]

Theodore Roosevelt's ideal of the strenuous life also bore a close relationship to Puritan morality. He glorified not only the "virile virtues" of strength, hardihood, tenacity, and courage but likewise such qualities as self-restraint, self-mastery, energy, and resolution. "No country can long endure," he affirmed, "if its foundations are not laid deep in the material prosperity which comes from thrift, from business energy and enterprise, from hard, unsparing effort in the fields of industrial activity." [18]

Yet it would be far from the truth to suppose that Puritan ethics dominated the minds of all Americans. Late in his life Jefferson described himself as an Epicurean, professing his admiration for Epicurus' doctrine of indifference to both hope and fear. Moreover, he was persuaded that the genuine Epicurean philosophy contained everything rational in ethics that Greece and Rome had left us. He believed throughout his life in a moral instinct implanted in man by his Creator, though he did not insist that faith in religious dogma was essential to good behavior. The atheist, he thought, might well be a moral man, and he listed Diderot, d'Alembert, d'Holbach, and Condorcet as among the most virtuous of mortals. Unlike some of his recent admirers, he did not shrink with horror from moral relativism. He admitted that the same act may be virtuous in one country and vicious in another. Instead of deploring this, he sought to explain it by saying that nature has constituted usefulness to man the standard and test of virtue. Conduct useful to the inhabitants of one country may, because of different circumstances and habits, be injurious to the inhabitants of another country. This does not mean that the moral instinct is weak or lacking in the one group of people and highly developed in the other. It merely expresses itself in different ways.[19]

A few other eminent Americans have taught a moral idealism far removed from the ethical doctrines commonly associated with Puritanism. Ralph Waldo Emerson demanded that "government shall not be ashamed to be tender and paternal, but that democratic institutions shall be more thoughtful for the interests of women, for the training of children, and for the welfare of sick and unable persons, and serious care of criminals, than was ever true of any of the best governments of the Old World." [20] As president of Princeton, Woodrow Wilson asserted that a poor nation in the right is "more formidable to the world than the richest nation in the wrong." "There is nothing so self-destructive," he added, "as selfishness, and there is nothing so permanent as the work of hands that are unselfish. You may pile up fortunes and dissolve them, but pile up ideals and they will never be dissolved." As the war of 1914 threatened to draw the United States into its terrible vortex, he told a conference on Americanization in Washington: "No nation can live without vision, and no vision will exalt a nation except the vision of real liberty and real justice and purity of conduct." Two days after the sinking of the *Lusitania* he reminded a troubled audience in Philadelphia: "There is such a thing as a man being too proud to fight. There is such a thing as a nation being so right that it does not need to convince others by force that it is right." [21] Although Wilson was a Presbyterian who seems never to have questioned his Calvinist heritage, he was not always an implacable foe of unrighteousness, ready to crack down ruthlessly upon those who disagreed with him.

Finally, we should take note of those distinguished Americans who traveled so far in the opposite direction from Calvinism that they repudiated the entire gospel of self-denial and renunciation. One such, we have seen, was Theodore Parker. Another was Simon N. Patten. Still a third was Wendell Phillips. In 1859 Phillips told a Boston audience that the money-making proclivities of our ancestors were a gift of Providence to enable them to conquer a continent and to dot the wilderness with cities and towns. Such functions could be discharged only "under the keen stimulus of a love of pecuniary and material gain. God gave it to us for that purpose." But now that we had built our London, Paris, and Rome, the time had come "to crowd them with art, to flush them with the hues of painting, and fill them with museums of science." [22]

More vehement in his rejection of the ascetic element in Puritanism was the sociologist Lester Frank Ward. In the opinion of Ward, "all happiness consists in the gratification of desire." Every faculty of man, he contended, "experiences a natural want to be exercised, and that want is a desire." Therefore, the road to progress must take the form of increasing and refining opportunities for exercising human faculties and satisfying human desires.[23] Nothing could have been more shocking to the prudish American conscience of the 1880's, but it was Ward's protest against the hide-bound conventions of the Victorian Age and the privation that stalked him during most of his life.

EDUCATION FOR THE PROMOTION OF RELIGION AND MORALITY

With their firm conviction that the mission of America depends upon piety and virtue, proponents of the ideal must look for means of attaining these goals. Such means they characteristically discover in education. Contrary to general opinion, the aims of American education have not been primarily materialistic. The major prophets of our national ideals have not urged American youth to seek wisdom and understanding as royal roads to wealth. In a few instances they have encouraged the pursuit of knowledge as an end in itself or as a means to comprehension of life and the universe. But in a far larger number of cases they have conceived of the learning process

Until the twentieth century, village schools, such as this one in Vermont, provided all the education that most Americans received. *Standard Oil Co. (N. J.)*

as an aid to the churches in maintaining religion and morality or as an instrument of the state for political objects. Colonial New Englanders established colleges because they considered an uneducated ministry an insult to God. Statesmen and orators of later times recommended that institutions of learning be harnessed to the purposes of democracy, the promotion of good citizenship, the improvement of morals, or the glorification of national ideals. More than once it became a grave question where indoctrination was supposed to end and true education begin.

The first eminent exponent of education as an implement and sheet anchor of democracy was Thomas Jefferson. In drafting plans for an educational system for the state of Virginia, he devoted himself to the great objects of producing a citizenry sufficiently well informed to choose its leaders wisely and training a body of philosopher-rulers to exercise the chief functions of governing. Instruction in the elementary schools, according to his plan, was to be given in reading, writing, "common arithmetick," and history. A knowledge of the last, he believed, would enable the people at large to recognize ambition "under all its shapes" and to take prompt action to defeat its purposes. Through primary education the ordinary citizen would acquire an understanding of his duties to his neighbors and country and an ability to exercise the rights he retains, and to choose and judge "with discretion the fiduciary of those he delegates." The curriculum of the grammar schools would include the Latin and Greek languages as well as history and "the higher part of numerical arithmetick, to wit, vulgar and decimal fractions, and the extrication of the square and cube roots." [24]

But it would be the colleges and the university that would provide most of the enlightenment for future rulers. In addition to the more orthodox disciplines, the subjects to be studied there would include "ideology, ethics, the law of nature and of nations; law, municipal and foreign; the science of civil government and political economy." The university, in particular, would have as its province the exposition of the principles and structure of government, some further study of municipal and international law, and the inculcation of a sound spirit of legislation which would provide for the few absolutely necessary restraints on individual action and leave men free to do whatever does not violate the equal rights of another. Through such methods it would preside over the formation of the "statesmen, legislators and judges, on whom public prosperity and individual happiness are so much to depend." The whole program was based upon the assumption that neither the state of the individual nor that of society was unalterably fixed, but that both were susceptible of *indefinite* improvement. To effect such improvement it would be necessary merely to educate each citizen to the extent his abilities warranted. Even a very modest degree of education, Jefferson believed, would suffice to convince the masses that it was to their interest to preserve peace and order. But whatever the amount, it must be provided, for "they are the only sure reliance for the preservation of our liberty." [25]

Jefferson's conception of an enlightened democracy resting upon an educated citizenry governed by an intellectual aristocracy went into eclipse soon after his death. Frontier influences combined with romanticism from Europe led to a distrust of intellect and a deification of the common man. The chief virtue of the latter, other than his innate goodness, was supposed to be common sense, and all the education he needed was training in a few practical skills. The idea of book learning as essential to governing was particularly despised. As a consequence, until after the Civil War, there were few who were even willing to entertain the suggestion that educated minds might be assets to democracy. In Fourth of July addresses William H. Seward intimated that the most effectual way to banish aristocracy was to extend the advantages of knowledge to the many. "Just so far and so fast as education is extended," he asserted, "democracy is ascendent." Perhaps his conception of education was made clearer when he linked the schools with the churches and the steam engine as the best instrumentalities for the advancement of the nation.[26]

The twentieth century witnessed a modest return to the Jeffersonian ideal of intelligence as the foundation of both personal morality and effective government. Though as staunch a votary of popular sovereignty as Jefferson himself, Robert M. LaFollette insisted that democracy must be based upon knowledge. That the people should know about their government and the policies and principles of their public servants he considered to be absolutely vital to popular rule.[27] These principles he exemplified by his successful advocacy in his own state of a legislative reference bureau and the utilization of the resources of the state university to provide expert assistance for governing officials.

A broader and more cogent defense of education for democracy came from the pen of John Dewey. He decried all reliance upon a priori assumptions in politics and also the trial and error methods of the "practical" statesman. He insisted upon extensive investigation by trained researchers, the careful accumulation of data, and the drawing of conclusions dictated by the weight of evidence. This meant, of course, the use of the scientific method and the determination of policy by social scientists. But Dewey insisted with equal emphasis upon the diffusion of the scientific attitude among the people themselves. He recognized the possibilities for evil inherent in the development of modern science. It had placed at the disposal of dictators, methods of controlling opinion and action vastly more powerful than any available to earlier tyrants. By reiterating their doctrines and alleged information over and over, in season and out, they had produced such a condition of mass hypnosis as to lend an appearance of plausibility to their claim to rule by popular consent. Dewey refused to believe that the common people are incapable of adhering to the scientific attitude. He maintained that it is easy to exaggerate the amount of intelligence necessary to produce respect for the process and results of scientific inquiry. As long as prejudice, propaganda, and sheer ignorance hold sway in the realm of social problems, it is impossible to tell how capable of intelligent judgments the masses may be. Capacities are limited by the objects and procedures available. They are even more limited by habits, traditions, and interest, to say nothing of the quantum of knowledge already accumulated in a given field. The spread of the scientific attitude is the sole guaranty against wholesale manipulation of minds by propaganda. Moreover, it is the only assurance of a public opinion intelligent enough to deal with modern problems.[28]

Commencement at Swarthmore College. With a faculty of over 100 and a student body of less than 1,000, Swarthmore is one of the strongholds of liberal education in America. *Friends Historical Library of Swarthmore College*

That the establishment of a regime in which the masses would adhere to the scientific attitude and accept the leadership of social scientists would be a colossal undertaking, Dewey clearly recognized. It would involve nothing less than revolutionizing the traditional system of education. Dewey contended that instruction in the existing schools was dedicated mostly to imparting ready-made information, along with producing the skills of literacy. "The methods used in acquiring such information are not those which develop skill in inquiry and in test of opinions. On the contrary, they are positively hostile to it." Even science, he maintained, was taught on the whole as a collection of facts and as a basis of training in technical skills. It was not taught as a "supremely humanistic subject" but as if it had nothing to do with human problems or human relations. All of this, Dewey believed, must be radically changed if mankind is not to be overwhelmed by the perversion of knowledge for destructive purposes. The natural sciences must be taught as furnishing in their method the very pattern of all intelligent conduct. In addition, there will need to be a marked expansion of the social sciences. Already some progress has been made as a result of application of the scientific method to problems of human conduct. The death penalty is no longer inflicted for the alleged crime of witchcraft, and the mentally ill have ceased to be abused as victims of demonic possession. Development of the social sciences with a corresponding diffusion of the scientific attitude will make possible in a future day the conquest of such social maladies as delinquency, crime, poverty, and war. Sufficient knowledge exists already to furnish a basis for the eradication of some of them, but ignorance of the scientific attitude prevents its application to the remainder.[29]

By no means all Americans believing in education for a purpose have advocated its use for strengthening democracy. Some have had less commendable objectives. The racists and imperialists of the last century conceived of it largely as an instrument of nationalism. The Reverend Josiah Strong, for instance, taught that the public school in the United States had a peculiar function, viz., "to Americanize the children of immigrants." By means of the common school, he said, "the strange and dissimilar races which come to us are, in one generation, assimilated and made Americans." He seemed to think that the heterogeneous population of America, especially in the large cities, was a threat to the integrity of the nation.[30]

Albert J. Beveridge held similar opinions but was more lyrical in expressing them. "Education," he said, "is the finest thing in the world if it increases interest in the Nation—if it produces pure, brave, and effective citizens." The school, therefore, "must be the great nourisher of the Nation. The Nation, the Nation, always the Nation! The school for the Nation! All education for the Nation! Everything for the Nation!" He admonished university students that all their intellectual activities must reveal and declare the glory of America, whom "God had been preparing through all the ages." Even in the very "gases of the laboratory" they must see our nation—"God's great agent of righteousness in the world." [31]

Woodrow Wilson also seemed to think it justifiable that learning should be directed to national ends. "Nations, as well as individuals," he wrote, "must seek wisdom." And scholarship, though it must everywhere be dedicated to the pursuit of truth, "may select the truths it shall search for and emphasize. It is this selection that should be national." [32]

Closely allied with those who have applauded the school as an implement of national greatness have been the prophets of education as a bulwark of national defense. Conspicuous among them was Harry S. Truman. In the midst of the "cold war" with Russia, he described education as "our first line of defense," the hope of America and the entire free world. Through education alone, he said, can free men combat the tenets of Communism. The unfettered souls of such men offer "a spiritual defense, unconquered and unconquerable." Totalitarian government, he argued, could not survive examination by educated men and women. For these reasons he urged that the federal government take steps to assure to every American youth "the highest level of training by which he can profit." [33] In an earlier connection he had seemed to be saying that this training should be chiefly scientific. "No government," he asserted, "adequately meets its responsibilities unless it generously and intelligently supports and encourages the work of science in university, industry, and in its own laboratories." [34] Whatever the nature of the instruction, the idea that education will lead to a prompt renunciation of Communism is one of remarkable tenacity. It was revived only recently by Allen W. Dulles, Director of the United States Central Intelligence Agency. He indicated to the Alumni Federation of Columbia University that Soviet citizens would lose their faith in the Communist system of thought control when present trends in Russian education became fully effective.[35]

Ideas of the purpose of education have not only been numerous but almost infinitely varied. Grover Cleveland thought that an educational program that failed to contribute to the cultivation and maintenance of "a high standard of American citizenship" was of little value.[36] For Lester Frank Ward a knowledge of man's physical environment was the source of both happiness and progress and the key to the solution of all baffling problems. Henry Wallace maintains that the chief object of schooling should be the training of young people to work together "in the service of the general welfare." Education heretofore has placed too much emphasis upon the competitive individual, imbuing him with the notion that his chief responsibility is to cherish his own rights and advance himself at the expense of others. Individual smartness has been overvalued and the development of character largely ignored. A major consequence has been the growth of "pressure group" government within the nations and "power politics" internationally. To redress the balance there must be more stress upon character teaching and cooperative efforts for the general good. Both are "fundamental to the very life of Western civilization." [37]

That this nation has a religious and moral duty to rescue and uplift the backward peoples of the earth has been one of the most freely propounded of our national dogmas. To voice a conviction that America is not only a ward but an instrument of divine Providence seems almost a duty for anyone aspiring to national leadership. The religiousness of our nation is confidently assumed to exceed that of every other people. Indeed, Americanism itself has been virtually transformed into a religion. It is the equivalent of godliness as opposed to the godlessness of Soviet Communism.

At the same time, purity of morals has also been widely acclaimed as a symbol of our national superiority. This purity has little in common with that freedom from evil desires preached by the Founder of Christianity. Rather, it has meant abstinence from sensual pleasures as a means of promoting efficiency. Indulgence in alcohol or in erotic delights is time consuming and therefore inimical to the pursuit of pecuniary success. Almost the only diversions considered thoroughly legitimate during the greater expanse of our history have been hunting, fishing, baseball, football, basketball, and track. These are supposed to produce hardihood, manliness, keenness of perception, and coordination. It is not a waste of time for youth to indulge in them, for they inculcate the very qualities most conducive to personal efficiency.

Much of this rationalizing of national virtues has carried over into American attitudes toward other peoples. We arrange nations in a kind of hierarchy, depending upon how closely they conform to the habit patterns of our own society. Such prejudices have underlain nearly all our immigration and naturalization laws enacted since 1918. They were reflected also in the attitudes of American soldiers in Europe during and after the two world wars. It was relatively common for our troops to praise the Germans for their industry, cleanliness, efficiency, and manliness; and at the same time to express contempt for the French for their indifference to modern improvements and especially for their "decadence" and moral looseness.

NOTES TO CHAPTER EIGHT

1. C. F. Adams, ed., *The Works of John Adams, Second President of the United States* (Boston: Little, Brown and Co., 1856), IX, 636.
2. Jonathan Elliot, ed., *The Debates in the Several State Conventions on the Adoption of the Federal Constitution* (Washington: Printed by and for the editor, 1863), III, 330.
3. Saul K. Padover, ed., *The Complete Jefferson* (New York: Duell, Sloan and Pearce, 1943), p. 939.
4. *The Works of William E. Channing* (Boston: American Unitarian Assoc., 1877), pp. 187-88, 545.
5. George E. Baker, ed., *The Works of William H. Seward* (New York: Redfield, 1853-54), III, 474; *The Works of Daniel Webster* (Boston: Little, Brown and Co., 1869), VI, 167.
6. *Our Country* (New York: The Baker and Taylor Co., 1885), pp. 14-15.
7. *Lessons of the War with Spain and Other Articles* (Boston: Little, Brown and Co., 1899), pp. 210-24.
8. *Congressional Record*, 56th Cong., 1st Session, XXXIII, 704, 711 (1900).
9. *The Price of Freedom* (Washington: The National Home Library Foundation, 1940), p. 48.
10. *Vital Speeches*, Vol. XVI, No. 10 (March 1, 1950).
11. *Ibid.*, Vol. XIX, No. 8 (February 1, 1953).
12. H. A. Cushing, ed., *The Writings of Samuel Adams* (New York: G. P. Putnam's Sons, 1904), III, 235.
13. Philip S. Foner, ed., *The Complete Writings of Thomas Paine* (New York: The Citadel Press, 1945), I, 231.

14. J. C. Fitzpatrick, ed., *The Writings of George Washington* (Washington: U. S. Government Printing Office, 1931), XXX, 186.
15. J. C. Hamilton, ed., *The Works of Alexander Hamilton* (New York: J. F. Trow, 1850-51), I, 257; III, 207-09.
16. George F. Parker, ed., *The Writings and Speeches of Grover Cleveland* (New York: Cassell Publishing Co., 1892), p. 251.
17. "Drugs and Intoxicants," *The Independent*, LII (April 26, 1900), 1009; *The Strength of Being Clean* (San Francisco: Viavi Press, 1898), pp. 9, 12-13.
18. E. E. Morison, ed., *The Works of Theodore Roosevelt* (New York: Charles Scribner's Sons, 1925), XV, 272.
19. Padover, ed., *The Complete Jefferson*, pp. 1032-34, 1036-38.
20. R. W. Emerson, *Complete Works*, Riverside ed. (New York: Houghton Mifflin Co., 1883-88), XI, 422.
21. *Robert E. Lee, an Interpretation* (Chapel Hill, N. C.: University of North Carolina Press, 1924), pp. 39-40; R. S. Baker and W. E. Dodd, eds., *The New Democracy* (New York: Harper and Brothers, *ca.* 1926), I, 321; II, 252.
22. *Speeches, Lectures, and Letters*, Second Series (Boston: Lee and Shepard, 1905), pp. 316-19.
23. *Dynamic Sociology* (New York: D. Appleton and Co., 1883), II, 177.
24. Padover, ed., *The Complete Jefferson*, pp. 1048-49, 1052, 1097.
25. *Ibid.*, pp. 1082-99; Albert E. Bergh, ed., *The Writings of Thomas Jefferson* (Washington: Thomas Jefferson Memorial Assoc., 1907), VI, 392.
26. George E. Baker, ed., *The Works of William H. Seward*, III, 210, 238.
27. *LaFollette's Autobiography* (Madison: The Robert M. LaFollette Co., 1913), p. 64.
28. *The Public and Its Problems* (New York: Henry Holt and Co., 1927), pp. 208-10; *Freedom and Culture* (New York: G. P. Putnam's Sons, 1939), pp. 125-27.
29. *Freedom and Culture*, p. 149; *Problems of Men* (New York: The Philosophical Library, 1946), pp. 30-31.
30. *Our Country* (New York: The Baker and Taylor Co., 1885), p. 92.
31. From *The Meaning of the Times and Other Speeches* by Albert J. Beveridge, copyright © 1908, 1936, used by special permission of the publishers, The Bobbs-Merrill Company, Inc., Indianapolis, pp. 239-41.
32. R. S. Baker and W. E. Dodd, eds., *College and State* (New York: Harper and Brothers, *ca.* 1925), I, 247.
33. *Vital Speeches*, Vol. XV, No. 11 (March 15, 1949).
34. *Ibid.*, Vol. XI, No. 23 (September 15, 1945).
35. New York *Times*, June 2, 1955.
36. Albert E. Bergh, ed., *Addresses, State Papers and Letters* (New York: The Sun Dial Classics Co., 1908), p. 417.
37. *Sixty Million Jobs* (New York: Reynal and Hitchcock, 1945), pp. 207-08.

Chapter Nine

War as an Instrument of National Mission

At the beginning of the Mexican War of 1846-1848, John C. Calhoun described the feeling of the American people as "much excited and very high." He declared that there was no country in the world, not even France, with a stronger inclination to war. The people were like a young man of eighteen, "full of health and vigour and disposed for adventure of any description," but without wisdom or experience to guide them.[1] Nearly seventy years later, with America threatened by another war, John W. Burgess characterized his fellow citizens as "an adventurous, warlike, and vainglorious people." They were not only "belligerent and boastful" but "restless, nervous, and at times hysterical." They had just the qualities "to answer the call of a Napoleon in the Presidency." No inborn depravity had made them thus, but the circumstances of their history. "The continuous conquest of a new country from the savage, the wild beast, and the jungle" should never have been expected, according to the venerable constitutional lawyer, to produce anything other than a bellicose and irritable nation.[2]

The judgments of Calhoun and Burgess were written during periods of emotional tension and were doubtless exaggerated. Yet they may be more generally veracious and applicable to normal times than is commonly believed. There is simply no proof that the United States has been a peace-loving nation, engaging in war at rare intervals with extreme reluctance. True, she has had her pacifists, of greater or less consistency. So did Germany under the Kaisers and Russia under the Tsars. But it would be difficult to

"View of the Triumphal Arch, and the manner of receiving General Washington at Trenton, on his Route to New-York, April 21st, 1789." Attributed to the eighteenth century engraver, I. Trenchard.

name a militarist dogma commonly associated with the saber-rattlers of Europe that was not duplicated on this side of the Atlantic. The philosophical Emerson, whom nobody would accuse of being a fire-eater, declared: "War civilizes, re-arranges the population, distributing by ideas—the innovators on one side, the antiquaries on the other. It opens the eyes wider. . . . It lifts every population into an equal power and merit." [3] The equally philosophical Theodore Parker glorified war as an instrument of a higher morality and a liberating force in world history. "Sometimes," he said, "there is a contest between a falsehood and a great truth; a self-protecting war for freedom of mind, heart, and soul; yes, a war for a man's body, his wife's and children's body, for what is dearer to men than life itself, for the unalienable rights of man, for the idea that all are born free and equal. It was so in the American Revolution; in the English, in the French Revolution." [4]

Philosophers and molders of opinion in later times also conceived of war as in some degree a medicine for the human race. Although William James deplored the barbarous aspects of international conflict, he could never purge his mind of the idea that war has ennobling and vitalizing effects. Apropos of the American imbroglio with Spain in 1898, he wrote: "These excitements and ambitions are of course the forces that make nations great (when they do not ruin them), and it may be that war is to be the only force that can hammer us into decency, as it is the great force that has hammered the European states." [5] Much more vehement was the attitude of Theodore Roosevelt. He exhorted the members of the Lincoln Club of New York on February 13, 1899: "If we ever grow to regard peace as a permanent condition; if we ever grow to feel that we can afford to let the keen, virile qualities of heart and mind and body be lost, then we will prepare the way for inevitable and shameful disaster in the future."

These and similar statements reflected to some extent, no doubt, an attempt to rationalize the conflict with Spain and the imperialism that followed; but they were also, perhaps, as much of a cause as they were an effect. They were expressions of such dogmas as race superiority and the benefits of competition and conflict that had whetted the appetite for war and empire in the first place.

THE BENEFITS AND DANGERS OF WAR

Recognition of war as a beneficent institution was almost unknown in America prior to the nineteenth century. The Puritans and their immediate descendants saw fighting as merely another evidence of the depravity of man. For Roger Williams and the Quakers, war conflicted with the basic principle that all men are brothers, regardless of their nationality, status, or color of skin. The men of the Enlightenment conceived of international war as both inhumane and irrational and therefore unworthy of civilized beings who professed to follow the system of nature. But the French Revolution, and to some extent the American Revolution also, introduced into the world a fanatical idealism which recognized bloodshed as a desirable means of attaining ends. It became sweet and proper to die for one's country, for the rights of one's class, or to extend the blessings of liberty to all mankind. Fanatical nationalism was born, and every war became a people's war, with whole nations fighting against each other in self-defense or for some hallowed purpose. Whereas the wars of the eighteenth century had been chiefly wars of maneuver, with limited armies striving to win by superior strategy, the post-Revolutionary conflicts became total wars with annihilation their cardinal object.

The attitude of the Founding Fathers toward armed hostilities reflected both the influence of the Enlightenment and of Puritan and secular pessimism. They considered the American Revolution a justifiable struggle for relief from oppression, but they viewed war in general with pronounced apprehension. They feared, however, that it was inevitable and had almost no confidence in measures to prevent it. Alexander Hamilton concluded from his study of history that "the fiery and destructive passions of war" reigned in the human breast "with much more powerful sway than the mild and beneficent sentiments of peace." He believed the causes of hostilities between nations to be innumerable, and that republics were no less disposed to offensive acts than monarchies. The most powerful motives, he thought, were "the love of power" and "the desire of pre-eminence and dominion." So potent were such factors that not even the most pacific policy on the part of a government would preserve it from being engaged in wars "more or less frequently." [6]

James Madison acclaimed peace as "the greatest of all blessings," but he had very little faith that the ideal of a warless world could ever be realized. "A universal and perpetual peace," he said, "is in the catalogue of events which will never exist but in the imaginations of visionary philosophers, or in the breasts of benevolent enthusiasts." Projects for such an ideal, he granted, did great honor to the hearts of their authors but little indeed to their heads. Still, he admitted that "war contains so much folly, as well as wickedness, that much is to be hoped from the progress of reason; and if anything is to be hoped, everything ought to be tried."

It may be doubted, though, that Madison himself did much to aid the "progress of reason" when he found himself confronted by some ugly political realities. He must bear a large share of responsibility for the War of 1812, which he blundered into partly in an effort to cover up his own mistakes and partly under pressure from the War Hawks, who hoped to use a war with Britain as a pretext for conquering Canada. Toward the end of his life he succumbed also to the emotional hysteria which demanded wars all over the globe in behalf of noble causes. In a letter of 1823 he expressed his indignation against Britain for failing to defend the Spanish constitutionalists against the forces of reaction and for declining to rush to arms in support of the Greek Revolution. "No nation," he wrote, "ever held in its hand in the same degree the destiny of so great a part of the civilized world." He suggested that a more glorious use might have been made of the opportunity if "the head of the Nation" had been "worthy of its heart." [7]

Jefferson's views on war differed but slightly from those of his contemporaries. In common with Madison, he regarded peace as the surest reliance for stable prosperity and the happiness of mankind; but he strove more consistently than Madison to prevent the nation from being swept into the holocausts of Europe. His confidence that he could succeed, however, dwindled almost to the vanishing point by the end of his administration. In fact, he had never believed that America could be so fortunate as to enjoy perpetual peace. Such a condition could be achieved only by abandoning oceanic commerce and leaving to the merchant fleets of other countries the transportation of our imports and exports. "This would make us invulnerable to Europe, by offering none of our property to their prize, and turn all our citizens to the cultivation of the earth." As for himself, he looked with favor upon such a proceeding, but he thought the habits of his countrymen attached themselves so firmly to commerce that they could not be diverted from it. Wars then would be bound sometimes to occur; and all the wise could do would be "to avoid that half of them which would be produced by our own follies and our own acts of injustice; and to make for the other half the best preparations we can." [8]

Under the influence of Utopianism, nationalism, and sentimental idealism, war ceased to be regarded as an inevitable calamity and came to be thought of as a kind of rainbow of promise. Even the wicked wars of the past were often justified as agents of progress, an assumption which left the door open for unstinted praise of modern wars for culture and freedom. Emerson applauded the invasion and conquest of the East by Alexander as one of "the most bright and pleasing pages of history." It had the effect of uniting into one great community the divided commonwealth of Greece, and instilling new and enlarged public views into the minds of her statesmen. "It carried the arts and language and philosophy of the Greeks into the sluggish and barbarous nations of Persia, Assyria, and India." War, he maintained, sharpens the senses, develops the will, perfects the physique, and "brings men into such swift and close collision in critical moments that man measures man." [9]

Emerson's forerunner as a Transcendentalist philosopher, William E. Channing, depicted in even more glowing terms the benefits resulting when a nation goes into war clad with the breastplate of righteousness. "A nation in declaring war," he wrote, "should be lifted above its passions by the fearfulness and solemnity of the act. It should appeal with unfeigned confidence to heaven and earth for its uprightness of purpose. It should go forth as the champion of truth and justice, as the minister of God, to vindicate and sustain that great moral and national law, without which life has no security, and social improvements no defence." To protect a state against lawless and unprincipled violence is a sacred duty and holy function; and protection may often be found only in war.[10]

Like all wars, the American War Between the States heightened the feeling that war for a noble purpose is pregnant with possibilities for good. But in view of the amount of theorizing to such effect before the war, it would have been almost a miracle if the conflict had not occurred. In 1859 Henry Thoreau referred to John Brown's raid as "the best news that America has ever heard."[11] Apropos of the same event, Theodore Parker affirmed: "It may be a natural duty for the freeman to help the slaves to the enjoyment of their liberty, and as means to that end, to aid them in killing all such as oppose their natural freedom."[12] But the outbreak of armed conflict generated much greater enthusiasm for the glorious consequences that victory promised. "Boys are heroes," Emerson exulted in 1863; "slavery is broken irretrievably." For such a gain, he thought, "one generation might well be sacrificed." In so doing, the whole continent would be purged of evil and a new era of equal rights would "dawn on the universe." Three months after Appomattox he informed the faculty and students of Harvard College that the war was "within the highest right" and was a "marked benefactor in the hands of Providence." He found his proof in the lift it had given to the national morale. It restored integrity "to this erring and immoral nation." It instilled new power into peaceful and amiable men, who hitherto had regarded conflict as abhorrent. "What an infusion of character," he fondly exclaimed, "went out from this and other colleges!"[13]

In speaking his odes of praise for the blessings of war, Emerson anticipated by about thirty years similar pronouncements by Oliver Wendell Holmes, Jr. The future Supreme Court Justice served as a lieutenant in the Union army. Though he remembered many of his experiences as decidedly unromantic, he seemed, as the years passed, to invest the conflict itself with an aura of beauty and holiness. On Memorial Day, 1895, he told the graduating class of Harvard that the message of war is divine. He hoped we should not soon be called again to sit at that master's feet. "But some teacher of the kind we all need." We need it in order to be ready for danger, to be free from "individualist negations," to have faith in the worth of heroism, to appreciate the value of discipline, and to realize that there are some things in this world of greater consequence than ease and comfort and the fleshpots of luxury. He deplored the fact that many, both poor and rich, no longer had any interest in love of country or much faith in anything else. Their patriotism had been supplanted by loyalty to a labor union; or, under the mask of cosmopolitanism, they were engaged in a "rootless, self-seeking search" for a place of maximum enjoyment at minimum cost. With a strange disregard for consistency he admitted that he also was beset by doubt and uncertainty. He knew neither the substance of truth nor the meaning of the universe. But "in the midst of doubt, in the collapse of creeds," there was one thing that he was sure of, and that was "that the faith is true and adorable which leads a soldier to throw away his life in obedience to a blindly accepted duty, in a cause which he little understands, in a plan of campaign of which he has no notion, under tactics of which he does not see the use."

In hallowing war as a purifying and redeeming institution, Holmes seems not to have been aware of his indebtedness to the prevailing economic and social dogmas. The Social Darwinists hypothesized a world of eternal competition and conflict. They conceived of this perpetual struggle as a process of natural selection, in which the weak and unambitious were weeded out and the strong and more ruthless survived. By such means the cosmic forces that governed the universe were striving to produce a better race, stronger nations, and a more competent and self-reliant species of human beings. The fact that countless individuals had to be liquidated in the process was a matter of no concern. They were the necessary sacrificial victims who had to be offered up on the altar of human improvement. Under the law of evolution nature cares nothing for the individual but bestows all her attention on the perfection of the species.

That Holmes accepted these dogmas is attested by a number of his most celebrated dicta. He remarked in the address quoted above that "the struggle for life is the order of the world, at which it is vain to repine." He could "imagine the burden changed in the way in

Interior of Fort Sumter after the bombardment by General Beauregard, April 12, 1861. Photo by S. R. Seibert. *Library of Congress*

which it is to be borne," but he could not conceive of its ever being lifted from men's backs. He rebelled against the idea of regarding every human being as an end in himself and not as a means, for in wartime we march conscripts up to the front "with bayonets in their rear to die for a cause in which perhaps they do not believe." His conception of World War I he boiled down to the simple formula: "When the Germans in the late war disregarded what we called the rules of the game, I don't see there was anything to be said except: we don't like it and shall kill you if we can." In a fatalistic way he believed that "every society is founded on the death of men," and he saw no method of lessening the crude and wasteful process short of a drastic limitation of births.[14] At the age of eighty-seven he wrote to his friend Sir Frederick Pollock that war is not only not absurd but inevitable and rational.[15] More and more, he appeared to talk like a skeptic who could not endure the logical implications of his own philosophy. Finding an attitude of negation uncomfortable, he embraced an uncritical faith in evolution and in the sanctity of the nation to fill the emotional vacuum left by "the collapse of creeds."

Many another American, in the late nineteenth and early twentieth centuries, went out of his way to eulogize war. In praising the Romans for establishing and maintaining the *Pax Romana* by force of arms, John Fiske drew the conclusion that "for a very long time the possibility of peace can be guaranteed only through war." [16] William Graham Sumner was equally lavish in his praise of the Romans, but he denied that universal peace could *ever* be attained. War was a part of the general pattern of competition which characterized the whole world of nature. It always had existed and always would. But

Military intelligence in the Civil War. The man with the cigar is Allan Pinkerton, intelligence officer of the Army of the Potomac. Despite his fame as a detective, his overestimation of the strength of the enemy seems to have been partly responsible for the excessive caution of General McClellan. Photo by Brady or assistant. *Library of Congress*

it was far from being an unmixed evil. Military inventions were the foundation for industrial improvements. Gunpowder, for example, was the basis for all our peacetime explosives, without which our canals and railroads could never have been built. The Wars of Napoleon tore down the relics of medievalism and freed the nations of Europe from the fetters of tradition. In a similar way the Crusades broke up the stagnation of the Dark Ages, destroying "what was barbaric and deadening" and fostering new hopes by stimulating thought and knowledge.[17]

Both the Spanish-American War and World War I elicited apologies and panegyrics for the iron dice. Theodore Roosevelt described the first-named conflict as not merely "the most righteous foreign war undertaken by any nation during the lifetime of the present generation" but one which "welded this country once and for all into an undivided nation."[18] On November 15, 1900, Alfred T. Mahan read a paper bearing the title "War from the Christian Standpoint" before a church congress in Providence, Rhode Island. His paramount purpose was to refute the contention that war is irreconcilable with Christianity. He admitted that war is an evil, but he insisted that it is "a remedy for greater evils, especially moral evils." When such evils exist, he argued, taking up arms to destroy them is not only not a sin, but to *fail* to do so is "distinctly an *unrighteous* deed." To wars of the past he credited the birth of the United States, the transformation from good into evil of "the devastating fire of the French Revolution and Napoleon," and the extirpation of slavery. To the Spanish-American War he assigned such "benefits" as the destruction of a tyrannical empire, the planting of American power in Asia, and the rending of the veil "which prevented the English-speaking communities from seeing eye to eye, and revealing to each the face of a brother."[19]

Not only for Woodrow Wilson did World War I symbolize a crusade for the enhancement of democracy; John Dewey also thought the "relative eclipse" into which democracy had passed would be "reversed" by an Entente victory. Whether the reversal would be permanent, he said, would depend upon the originality and intelligence of the victors.[20] To the militant economic collectivists Simon N. Patten and Richard T. Ely the war of the two rival alliances would provide a wholesome antidote for many of the social evils that afflicted the world of that time. The former thought it

Battle of Tarawa. The struggle for the Island of Tarawa, the "Gibraltar of the Pacific," was one of the bloodiest battles of World War II. *Official U. S. Marine Corps Photo*

would initiate a moral uplift which would lead to the suppression of extravagance, vice, dissipation, and race suicide.[21] Richard T. Ely looked for a revival of Americanization, which he defined as "loyalty to country based upon the profound emotional experience which is called love." He found the nation to be plagued by "a class of disloyal men who prate loudly about a supernational loyalty which obliterates loyalty to native country, or the country of one's adoption." He hoped for a reinstitution of nothing less than the ancient slogan, *Dulce et decorum est pro patria mori.*[22]

Hopes for a Paradise born out of the Hell of war were less numerous during the second world conflict of our century. The fruits of disillusionment produced by World War I saved most of our leaders from the naïveté that had afflicted their fathers. In the main, World War II was conceived as a struggle *against* such evils as fascism, oppression, and slavery, rather than as a quest for the Holy Grail of permanent peace or universal democracy. Few grandiose ideals were set forth in the speeches of the major war leaders. The Atlantic Charter was a diluted version of Wilson's Fourteen Points. The Declarations and Agreements issued from Cairo, Yalta, and Potsdam dealt almost exclusively with the specific conditions to be imposed upon the vanquished. A partial exception was the Teheran Declaration, which recognized the responsibility of the victors to make a peace which would "banish the scourge and terror of war," not permanently, but "for many generations." The victory of America and her allies probably convinced most of her chieftains that the overthrow of fascist power was a sufficient compensation for the anguish and carnage. But no one assumed that the millennium had been achieved or that a bright new day was about to dawn. The fear of an unstable peace, the lack of enthusiasm for the United Nations, and the haunting specter of a third world war to be fought with weapons many times more deadly than those available in 1939 precluded such rose-colored dreams.

As for the dangers of war, few Americans who have contributed to the shaping of national ideals have ever said much about them. The Founding Fathers present an exception. They were such keen students of the downfall of nations and were so profoundly conscious of the close connection between war and despotic government that they could not refrain from giving their countrymen some stern warnings. Even Hamilton thought it necessary to remind the people of New York that the violence and anxieties of war would "compel nations the most attached to liberty to resort for repose and security to institutions which have a tendency to destroy their civil and political rights." [23] Madison's admonitions were even more emphatic. "Of all the enemies to public liberty," he wrote, "war is, perhaps, the most to be dreaded, because it comprises and develops the germ of every other. War is the parent of armies; from these proceed debts and taxes; and armies, debts, and taxes are the known instruments for the domination of the few over the many." Other perils to republicanism, he said, "may be traced in the inequality of fortunes, and the opportunities of fraud, growing out of a state of war, and in the degeneracy of manners and morals engendered by both." He concluded with the categorical assertion: "No nation could preserve its freedom in the midst of continuous warfare." [24]

Another exception to the generality of American spokesmen who have tended to minimize the dangers of war was Woodrow Wilson. True, he believed in taking up the sword of righteousness and waging crusades after the manner of knight-errantry. On May 7, 1911, he said in Denver that there are times when nations must accept the challenge of battle "in order to vindicate spiritual conceptions. For liberty is a spiritual conception, and when men take up arms to set other men free, there is something sacred and holy in the warfare." Yet no one recognized the evils in international conflict more clearly than he. The night before he delivered his war message of 1917 to Congress he summoned Frank Cobb of the New York *World* to the White House and poured into his ear all of the tragic consequences he feared would be likely to flow from the step he was about to take, "Once lead this people into war," he said, "and they'll forget there ever was such a thing as tolerance. A majority of them will go war-mad, quit thinking, and devote their energies to destruction. To fight you must be brutal and ruthless, and the spirit of ruthless brutality will enter into every fibre of our national life, infecting Congress, the courts, the policeman on the beat, the man in the street." According to Cobb, the President went on to express his fears that the Constitution would not survive the war, and that free speech and the right of assembly would go down into oblivion. At San Diego, on September 19, 1919, he predicted that if another war came, it would make the terrors of the one just ended seem like the nightmares of a child. The weapons the Germans used would be mere toys compared with the implements of horror that would be invented before and during the next war.

PLOWSHARES AND PRUNING HOOKS INTO
SWORDS AND SPEARS

If there was one fond hope of the Founders of the American republic, it was to keep it a nation dedicated to the arts of peace. They feared that wars would have to be fought, but they were determined to do everything in their power to prevent the growth of a dominant military clique or a habit in the people of looking to force or conquest for a solution of their problems. For this reason they insisted upon subordinating the military to the civil authority, empowering the legislature rather than the executive branch to issue declarations of war, and limiting the term of military appropriations to two years.

It was for this reason also that the Fathers condemned large standing armies. Hamilton denounced such forces as "a source of more real danger to our liberties than all the powers that could be conferred upon the representatives of the Union." [25] In the Federal Convention, Madison characterized large standing armies as "the greatest danger to liberty." "The means of defense against foreign danger," he added, "have been always the instruments of tyranny at home." He doubted that even the best organized despotisms of the Old World could maintain themselves without stirring up alarms of foreign danger every now and then to "tame the people to the domestic yoke." Britain alone was an exception. Her insular position rendered defense less necessary, "and admitted a kind of defense which could not be used for the purpose of oppression." [26] In *Federalist* No. 41 he repeated his doleful assertions that the liberties of Europe had been sacrificed to her military establishments. Even the smallest standing army, he declared, has its "inconveniences." "On an extensive scale its consequences may be fatal."

The antimilitarism of the Fathers began to waver a bit in the 1790's as a result of the French Revolution and the threat of a war with France. On March 8, 1794, Hamilton wrote to Washington, advising him that if it should be made known "that the government has an efficient active force in its disposal for defense or offense on an emergency, there will be much less temptation, and much more hesitation to provoke us." This, of course, was merely a polite way of saying that we should preserve peace by flexing our muscles. The preceding December Washington himself had communicated to Congress essentially the same doctrine. "There is a rank," he said, "due to the United States among nations, which will be withheld, if not absolutely lost, by the reputation of weakness. If we desire to avoid insult, we must be able to repel it; if we desire to secure peace, one of the most powerful instruments of our rising prosperity, it must be known that we are at all times ready for war." This assumption, that preparedness for war is the effective means of preserving peace, soon became one of the cardinal premises of American political thinking.

Since the middle 1800's a powerful ground swell of opinion has rolled over this country in favor of armed strength as the safest reliance for peace and security. In 1842 Orestes Brownson declared that the United States needed "as a peace establishment a standing army of at least 100,000 men, and a navy nearly as large as that of England or France." Less would be insufficient, he argued, to preserve henceforth the rank of a first-class power, to maintain "the hegemony of the New World," and to hold in our hands, "to a great extent, the peace of Europe." [27] In *The New Era*, published in 1893, Josiah Strong cautioned his readers that the time had not yet come when nations would consent to be controlled entirely by right and reason. It was still true that the argument was "on the side of the heaviest battalions; still true among nations that the weight of an opinion depends much on the fighting weight of the government which utters it." He hoped devoutly that "the various branches of the Anglo-Saxon race" would cooperate to such an extent in the future that their overwhelming superiority of power would "compel the world's peace and deliver the nations from the vampire of militarism." [28]

The leading apostles of militarism in the United States are generally considered to have been Admiral Mahan and his worshipful admirer Theodore Roosevelt. The former wrote so ingratiatingly, and with so many appeals to Christian morality, that he seemed to some people to be the very soul of charity and peace. But no one went further in glorifying force—not even von Treitschke or Marx. In the view of the great admiral, force was "a faculty of national life; one of the talents committed to nations by God." It must be wisely used, but it could not be renounced or abandoned without incurring the condemnation meted out to the unprofitable servant of the Bible, who hid his talent in the earth. Force was the midwife of all progress, the instrument which had lifted European nations to their present plane, and which "still supports our political systems, national and international, as well as social organization." The obligation "to maintain right by force if need be" rested with special gravity upon the large states with the means to use it effectively, for "much is required of those to whom much is given."

Mahan repudiated with particular vehemence the doctrine that preparedness is a provocation to war. The immense armaments of Europe, he insisted, were "a cheap alternative" to the frequent disastrous wars that had occurred before "the era of general military preparation." It was perhaps an act of poetic justice that he should have been permitted to live for a few months after the beginning of World War I, and so to realize the egregious fallacy in this argument. Mahan also rejected the doctrine that nations should prepare for defensive wars only. It is vain, he contended, to maintain a military or naval force "which cannot, first or last, go out, assail the enemy, and hurt him in his vital interests." Moreover, defensive force "is of small account in diplomatic relations, for it is nearly useless as a deterrent from war." With the construction of the Panama Canal, Mahan foresaw an increasing entanglement of the United States in world affairs. Big armies and navies would become the instruments to bluff our rivals in the poker game of power politics.[29]

No master ever had a more faithful disciple than Mahan found in the young and effervescent Theodore Roosevelt. In fact the pupil outdid the master in proclaiming the virtues of military action. He was himself a perennial volunteer, in constant quest of opportunities for "derring-do." When President Cleveland became involved in a dispute with Great Britain over the boundary between Venezuela and British Guiana, Roosevelt was hysterical with joy. He thought it must surely lead to war and to a chance to conquer and annex Canada. After the Battle of San Juan Hill he proudly reported that he had killed a Spaniard with his own hands, "like a jackrabbit." In 1917, at the age of fifty-nine, he clamored for the privilege of leading an expeditionary force against the Germans. His doctrines were completely in accord with the events of his life. "All the great masterful races have been fighting races," he told the Naval War College in 1897.

Though Roosevelt accepted the Nobel Peace Prize in 1910, and conceded that "peace is generally good in itself," he believed that this end could be obtained by a single method: by confronting a potential enemy with such overwhelming power that he would not dare to attack. "It is only the warlike power of a civilized people," he said, "that can give peace to the world." Most of the time, however, he seemed to think that there was something disgraceful about a prolonged absence of hostilities. He told the Hamilton Club of Chicago in 1899 that "it is only through strife, through hard and dangerous endeavor, that we shall ultimately win the goal of true national greatness." He had a horror that the nation might lose its "fighting edge," and roundly denounced "sentimentalists" like Carl

The United States Atomic Energy Commission's original Gaseous Diffusion Plant at Oak Ridge, Tennessee, for the manufacture of atomic bombs. *USAEC Photo by J. E. Westcott*

Schurz and President Eliot of Harvard for advocating the settlement of international disputes by arbitration and conciliation. "No nation can hold its place in the world," he maintained, "or can do any work really worth doing, unless it stands ready to guard its rights with an armed hand. That orderly liberty which is both the foundation and the capstone of our civilization can be gained and kept only by men who are willing to fight for an ideal." [30]

Few theories have gained wider application in official policy than the military doctrines of Mahan and Roosevelt. Some people would argue that these doctrines have been vindicated by the events of recent years. Others would disagree. But whether vindicated or not, they have been generally accepted. It is assumed that our diplomats must always lead from strength, and that overwhelming force is the only language our potential enemies understand. A third world war has been averted thus far solely by the fact that the United States has the advantage over Russia in the possession of and in the ability to deliver devastating bombs.

Opinions of this sort were freely expressed by President Truman. In his first year in office he advised Congress: "The surest guaranty that no nation will ever again attack us is to remain strong in the

only kind of strength an aggressor can understand—military power."
Four years later he admitted that it was unusual for America to
maintain substantial armed forces in time of peace. But he insisted
that it was an absolute necessity as long as there is a threat to the
existence of peace. "Any uncertainty," he said, "as to the ability or
the willingness of the free nations of the world to defend themselves
is an invitation to aggression." [31]

That Truman's successor would follow policies based upon the
same doctrines was made clear even before he became President.
In 1945 General Eisenhower declared: "To be strong nationally is
not a sin, it is a necessity." He considered it a necessity, first of all,
to defend ourselves, "and secondly, to give the necessary dignity
and influence to the words of our leaders as they labor to perfect
machinery by which the world may settle its difficulties." [32] The
resemblance between the latter purpose and Mahan's idea of diplomacy backed by the mailed fist is more than superficial.

PACIFISM—WITH EXCEPTIONS

Devotion to peace was regarded by Henry Adams as one of the
most deeply rooted of American characteristics. Perhaps he was
right. Certainly the champions of peace in the United States have
equaled in number and fervor those of any other country. Every
one of our wars was vehemently opposed by men of prominence,
at least before it started, while three of them—the War of 1812, the
Mexican War, and the Spanish-American War—continued to be
condemned while they were in progress and for long afterward.
No country has had more organized peace societies or produced
more plans and panaceas for the prevention and cure of war. It is
noteworthy, also, that among all the recipients of the Nobel Peace
Prize, by far the largest number have been Americans.

Yet to discover consistent and unequivocal pacifists among American political and intellectual leaders is not an easy task. Critics of
war can be found by the hundreds, but devout and uncompromising
opponents of slaughter as a barbarous and irrational method of settling disputes can be counted on the fingers of one hand. The list
would include William Lloyd Garrison, Jane Addams, and possibly
David Starr Jordan.

From all the available evidence, Garrison never deviated from the
path of stern opposition to military measures. He would not even

sanction a war for righteousness. "The history of mankind," he said, "is crowded with evidences, proving that physical coercion is not adapted to moral regeneration; that the sinful disposition of man can be subdued only by love; that evil can be exterminated from the earth only by goodness . . . that it is only the meek who shall inherit the earth, for the violent who resort to the sword, shall perish with the sword." [33]

Jane Addams, founder of Hull House and Chairman of the Women's Peace party, saw no justification whatever for taking the sword. War, according to her view, was not only barbarous but "juvenile," a silly pastime of aging men who knew no better way of expending their energies. She put it into the same class with dueling and bear-baiting. The remedy, she believed, lay in a transvaluation of values. The social feelings of sympathy, humanitarianism, and neighborliness must somehow be made to take the place of bloodthirstiness, vengeance, and hatred. She believed that the social instincts of man were just about as strong as the antisocial, and could be brought into supremacy by the proper education and environmental influences. She recommended, also, the development of an enlightened industrialism to divert men's energies into peaceful pursuits and at the same time eliminate the poverty and hunger which provide the excuse for aggression.[34]

David Starr Jordan may also be described as a consistent pacifist during most of his life. According to his own testimony, he became a crusader for peace when he discovered facts which convinced him that the Spanish-American War was being promoted for private profit. Soon afterward he was elected a vice-president of the Anti-Imperialist League, along with Carl Schurz and Andrew Carnegie. In 1909 he became chief director of the World Peace Foundation. Following his retirement as president of Stanford University in 1913, he devoted his energies almost exclusively to the cause of peace. He waged a determined struggle for more than two years to keep America neutral in World War I. He tried to convince President Wilson that the peoples everywhere were tired of the conflict, and that even the governments of the belligerent nations would welcome a way of escape from the nightmare of carnage. To the mind of Jordan, war was the acme of abominations. In the last speech he ever delivered he described it as "murder, robbery, trickery." Military conflict unleashed all the evil passions of human nature, the most bestial and the most sordid displays of lust and greed. He admitted that war might be better than slavery, but he contended that "every war involves widespread degradation and spiritual enslavement to a greater or less degree." So-called defensive wars and holy wars possessed no more merit, in his judgment, than aggressive wars or wars of conquest. No holy or righteous war, he said, was ever carried on except by the most unrighteous methods.

Yet Jordan cannot be classified as an absolute pacifist. He was more consistent than the majority of other leaders in the peace movement, but he did admit that the Civil War was "necessary," and he eventually gave his benediction to America's participation in World War I, though with profound reluctance and deep misgivings. He preferred to classify himself as a "pragmatic pacifist," who appraises war scientifically from the standpoint of its practical effects. Such appraisals, he believed, would generally lead to the conclusion that war destroys freedom, promotes hate, vitiates democracy, and undermines civilization by the destruction of superior manhood. Nevertheless, such scientific studies would not rule out the possibility that *some* wars are justifiable as "wars to end wars" or to deliver peoples from oppression. They would show that though war is never righteous, in rare instances it may still be honorable as the last resort of "mangled, murdered liberty." [35]

Some other Americans have been more generously acclaimed as champions of peace than any of the three already discussed. But whether deservedly or not is open to question. Henry Thoreau, for example, became so well known for his stress upon conscience and the moral law that he still stands, in the opinion of many, as a symbol of opposition to the use of force in adjusting the affairs of men. His *Essay on Civil Disobedience* served as a Bible to Tolstoy and Gandhi. Yet Thoreau saluted John Brown as a deliverer of humanity for his raid at Harpers Ferry. And when the Civil War broke out, the dying ascetic at Concord felt himself uplifted at the prospect of moral regeneration to accompany the conflict.

Of almost equal fame, perhaps, as a proponent of peace was James Russell Lowell, who referred to war in "The Biglow Papers" as "murder," and pointedly asked,

> Wut's the use o' meetin' goin'
> Every Sabbath, wet or dry,
> Ef it's right to go amowin'

Feller-men like oats or rye?
I dunno but wut it's pooty
Trainin' round in bobtail coats,—
But it's curus Christian dooty
This 'ere cuttin' folk's throats.

But Lowell had no qualms whatever about "cuttin' folk's throats" over the issues of slavery and secession. He declared that reconciliation from the first was impossible, and "that to attempt it was unwise, because it put the party of law and loyalty in the wrong." He thought a "ten years' war would be cheap that gave us a country to be proud of, and a flag that should command the respect of the world because it was the symbol of the enthusiastic unity of a great nation." [36]

Probably no American has contributed more to the development of a psychological basis for pacifism than William James. As noted previously, he found war to be an outgrowth of subliminal instincts of pugnacity and love of glory and excitement. Behind the façade of civilized human nature lurked a savage beast, ready to break through at the first opportunity. Our ancestors bred pugnacity into our very bones; centuries of peace would not suffice for its elimination. The people want war, and would be bored by the dullness and insipidity of perpetual peace. Unless some substitute is found which will provide the thrills and excitement, the heroism and contempt for danger, the appeals to idealism and self-sacrifice that are the fruits of military conflict, pacifism will rest upon flimsy foundations. It will fail and will deserve to fail.

According to James, the virtues of militarism must be preserved to prevent the evolution of a nation of mollycoddles. He therefore urged the adoption of "a moral equivalent of war." He recommended that this take the form of conscripting the whole youthful population to wage war against the evils and injustices of nature. Some of our "gilded youths" would be drafted to work in the coal mines; others would engage in dish-washing, road-building, or tunnel-making; still others would go into foundries and stoke-holes, to freight yards, or to fishing fleets in December. All would "get the childishness knocked out of them," and would "come back into society with healthier sympathies and soberer ideas." By such methods, James believed that the values of war and the military life could be preserved without the blood-letting. But he was still un-

U.S.S. *Nautilus*, first of the atomic-powered submarines. *General Dynamics Corporation*

willing to concede that blood-letting was entirely devoid of advantages. In the past, war had been "the gory nurse" that had "trained societies to cohesiveness," and he thought it might well continue to do so in the future. Civilization and all its blessings, he contended, "have grown up in the shadow of the wars of antiquity." [37]

It is interesting and perhaps significant that some of the strongest condemnations of war have come from the Presidents who took the nation into its most recent conflicts. Three days after the sinking of the *Lusitania* threatened to plunge the United States into a war of vengeance against Germany, Woodrow Wilson sought to counteract the influence of interventionists by reminding his fellow citizens: "The example of America must be the example not merely of peace because it will not fight, but of peace because peace is the healing and elevating influence of the world and strife is not." Franklin D. Roosevelt declared during the campaign of 1940, "I hate war," and avowed that he had one supreme determination—to do all in his power to keep war away from American shores. At Chautauqua in 1936 he assured an admiring audience: "We believe in democracy; we believe in freedom; we believe in peace. We offer to every nation of the world the handclasp of the good neighbor." President Truman had been in office little more than two years when he affirmed that "the only security for the United States, or for any other nation . . . lies in the abolition of war." In 1948 he informed the American Legion that "the Government of the United States utterly rejects the concept of war as a means of solving international differences." The spirit of the American people, he insisted four years later, "has never been warlike. Our people came to this country to find peace and freedom. That's what we have always wanted. That's what we want now, and that is what our national policy is designed to preserve." [38]

There was doubtless not the slightest insincerity in any of the statements quoted above. The Presidents who made them seem to have been convinced in their own minds that in leading their country into war in 1917, 1941, and 1950 they were doing the most logical thing in the world to hasten the day when international strife should be no more. If they were deluding themselves, they were no more deluded than the vast majority of their countrymen. The idea that resort to force is the most efficient means of disposing of baffling problems is one of the strongest of our national myths. Force has likewise always been considered a justifiable instrument for the attainment of those noble purposes which Destiny has thrust upon us. As the Israelites of the modern world we could hardly think otherwise. The Chosen People have a God-given right to put to the sword those who would prevent us from extending the sphere of our blessings. Though recent years have brought some abatement of this ethnic conceit, it still must be reckoned with by optimists who believe that the United States is the world's best hope for peace.

NOTES TO CHAPTER NINE

1. J. Franklin Jameson, ed., *Correspondence of John C. Calhoun* (Washington: American Historical Assoc., 1900), II, 692.
2. *The Reconciliation of Government with Liberty* (New York: Charles Scribner's Sons, 1915), p. 373.
3. R. W. Emerson, *Complete Works,* Riverside ed. (New York: Houghton Mifflin Co., 1883-88), XI, 105.
4. S. B. Stewart, ed., *Sins and Safeguards of Society* (Boston: American Unitarian Assoc., n.d.), p. 310.
5. R. B. Perry, *The Thought and Character of William James* (Boston: Little, Brown and Co., 1935), II, 309.
6. *The Federalist,* Modern Library ed. (New York: Random House, n.d.), Nos. 6, 34; J. C. Hamilton, ed., *The Works of Alexander Hamilton* (New York: J. F. Trow, 1850-51), V, 379.
7. *Letters and Other Writings of James Madison.* Published by Order of Congress (Philadelphia: J. B. Lippincott Co., 1865), II, 132; Gaillard Hunt, ed., *The Writings of James Madison* (New York: G. P. Putnam's Sons, 1900), VI, 88-89; IX, 179.
8. Saul K. Padover, ed., *The Complete Jefferson* (New York: Duell, Sloan and Pearce, 1943), pp. 540, 684.

9. *Complete Works*, Riverside ed., XI, 180-81.
10. *The Works of William E. Channing* (Boston: American Unitarian Assoc., 1877), pp. 662-63.
11. *The Writings of Henry David Thoreau* (Boston: Houghton Mifflin Co., 1906), XVIII, 438.
12. *Writings*, Centenary ed. (Boston: American Unitarian Assoc., 1907-16), XIV, 423.
13. *Complete Works*, Riverside ed., XI, 319-20.
14. Max Lerner, *The Mind and Faith of Justice Holmes* (Boston: Little, Brown and Co., 1946), pp. 392, 428, 431.
15. Mark DeWolf Howe, ed., *The Holmes-Pollock Letters* (Cambridge: Harvard University Press, 1941), II, 230.
16. *American Political Ideas, Viewed from the Standpoint of Universal History* (Boston: Houghton Mifflin Co., 1911), pp. 100-01.
17. Albert G. Keller, ed., *War and Other Essays* (New Haven: Yale University Press, 1913), pp. 10-11, 32-33.
18. E. E. Morison, ed., *The Works of Theodore Roosevelt* (New York: Charles Scribner's Sons, 1925), XVI, 535.
19. *Lessons of the War with Spain and Other Articles* (Boston: Little, Brown and Co., 1899), pp. 230-32.
20. *Characters and Events* (New York: Henry Holt and Co., 1929), II, 607.
21. *Culture and War* (New York: B. W. Huebsch, 1916), pp. 32-33.
22. *The World War and Leadership in a Democracy* (New York: The Macmillan Co., 1918), p. 109.
23. *The Federalist*, Modern Library ed., No. 8.
24. *Letters*, Cong. ed., IV, 491-92.
25. J. C. Hamilton, ed., *Works*, II, 373.
26. Max Farrand, ed., *Records of the Federal Convention* (New Haven: Yale University Press, 1911), I, 464-65.
27. *The American Republic: Its Constitution, Tendencies and Destiny* (New York: P. O'Shea, 1866), pp. 389-90.
28. *The New Era or The Coming Kingdom* (New York: The Baker and Taylor Co., 1893), p. 74.
29. *Lessons of the War with Spain*, pp. 232, 286-87; *The Interest of America in Sea Power, Present and Future* (Boston: Little, Brown and Co., 1898), p. 104.
30. Morison, ed., *Works*, XV, 244, 281, 291; XVIII, 411.
31. *A New Era in World Affairs* (Washington: Department of State Publications 3653, 1949), p. 18.
32. *Vital Speeches*, Vol. XII, No. 4 (December 1, 1945).
33. *Selections from the Writings and Speeches of William Lloyd Garrison* (Boston: R. F. Wallcut, 1852), p. 75.
34. *Newer Ideals of Peace* (New York: The Macmillan Co., 1907), pp. 3-30.
35. The ideas attributed to Jordan in the foregoing paragraph are taken from E. M. Burns, *David Starr Jordan: Prophet of Freedom* (Stanford, Calif.: Stanford University Press, 1953).
36. *Works* (New York: Houghton Mifflin Co., *ca.* 1892), V, 90; VIII, 46.
37. *Memories and Studies* (New York: Longmans, Green and Co., 1912), pp. 271-72, 276-77, 290-92, 301-04.
38. *Vital Speeches*, Vol. XIII, No. 17 (June 15, 1947); Vol. XVIII, No. 17 (June 15, 1952).

Chapter Ten

Empire and World Leadership

S ince the beginning of their history as a nation, Americans have struggled to reconcile two sharply conflicting views of their relations with the rest of the world. On the one hand, they have considered themselves a peculiar people, separated by thousands of miles from the homeland of their fathers, and hating the wicked and irrational ways of Europe. In accordance with this line of thinking, the Old World has been synonymous with oppression, tyranny, and crafty and cynical diplomacy. On the other hand, Americans have conceived of their republic as the handmaid of Destiny, as a chosen nation with a mission to guide and instruct and even to rule "savage and senile" peoples. To accomplish such a mission it would be necessary for America to express her sympathy with the victims of repression, to intervene to assist them, and even to overthrow autocratic and militaristic regimes that stood as obstacles to the spread of liberty and civilization. Arguments of this sort have frequently been used to justify our intervention in the rivalries and contentions of Old World politics.

THE LURE OF EMPIRE

It would scarcely be an exaggeration to say that America became an empire before she became a state. At least she developed imperial ambitions. These were manifested in the claims of several of the colonies to lands extending to the Mississippi River and even in some cases to the Pacific Ocean. They were exhibited also in the speeches and writings of a number of the Founders. As early as 1778 George Mason avowed that the Union would not be complete "until the inhabitants of all the territory from Cape Breton to the Mississippi" were included in it. As long as Britain possessed Canada and West Florida she would be continually inciting the Indians against the whites, and as long as she held the harbors of St. Augustine and Halifax Americans would not be able to protect their trade from depredations.[1] In 1799 Hamilton wrote that "we ought certainly to look to the possession of the Floridas and Louisiana, and we ought to squint at South America."[2] Even Jefferson confessed to looking with covetous eyes upon Cuba "as the most interesting addition which could ever be made to our system of States." It would round out our control over the Gulf of Mexico and "fill up the measure of our political well-being." He realized, however, that it could not be obtained without war, and that was a price he was unwilling to pay.[3]

Neither the success nor the failure of expansionist projects in the early nineteenth century seemed to have much effect upon imperialist ambitions. In 1803 the Union more than doubled its size by the purchase of Louisiana. But some leaders were not satisfied. John Quincy Adams advised his father eight years later that the whole continent of North America appeared "to be destined by Divine Providence to be peopled by *one* nation," speaking one language and adhering to the same principles and social usages. For their common happiness, peace, and prosperity he considered it "indispensable that they should be associated in one federal union." The War of 1812 seemed to place the stamp of failure and hopelessness upon dreams of annexing Canada. Yet belief in the possibility of future success continued to flourish. It found lodgment in the minds of some Americans as late as 1911, when Champ Clark, Speaker of the House of Representatives, brazenly announced that he hoped "to see the day when the American flag will float over every square foot of the British-North American possessions clear to the North Pole."[4]

But designs upon Canada were only one element in a comprehensive pattern of expansionist ambitions. Theodore Parker could think only in terms of the whole hemisphere. "Then what a nation we shall one day become. America, the mother of a thousand Anglo-Saxon states, tropic and temperate on both sides of the equator, may behold the Mississippi and the Amazon uniting their waters . . . may count her children at last by hundreds of millions. . . .

The fulfillment of this vision is our province; we are the involuntary instruments of God. Shall America scorn the mission God sends her on? Then let us all perish, and may Russia teach justice to mankind." [5] To his credit it should be said that he approved of expansion by purchase only, and not by conquest.

Parker's younger contemporary, Parke Godwin, Fourierist and idealist, was not so discriminating. He justified both the forcible ejection of the Indians from their lands and the conquest of territory from Mexico. "A small, but savage and intractable race suddenly surrounded by a powerful and civilized people, whose laws and customs it cannot or will not accept, but whose vices are readily spread among them, has no other destiny but to die of its corruptions, to perish in arms, or to be removed by gentle methods to some more remote and untroubled hunting grounds." In such summary fashion he disposed of the Indian problem. The dispossession of Mexico of half her territory caused him no greater qualms. "It was a regular war, begun in vindication of the clearest national rights, which had been outraged." Moreover, it was carried on with a strict regard for "honorable principles," and it was concluded by a "deliberate treaty" which provided generous payment for everything taken. But payment or no payment, "an instinct in the human soul, deeper than the wisdom of politics . . . impels the people on, to the accomplishment of that high destiny which Providence has plainly reserved for our race." Cuba, Canada, Mexico, South America, the islands of the seas, all will be ours if we condescend to take them. Every one of them should "rise up to meet us at our coming, and the desert and the solitary places be glad that the hour for breaking their fatal enchantments, the hour of their emancipation, had arrived." [6]

The planter aristocrats of the South are often accused of having instigated the Mexican War for the purpose of bringing more slave states into the Union, and of being rabid imperialists in other directions for the same reason. Undoubtedly some of them had such ambitions. In 1846 John C. Calhoun dreamed of an America with one foot on the Atlantic Coast and the other on the Pacific. He coveted the possession of Mexico, although both he and Alexander H. Stephens opposed its conquest by force. Jefferson Davis longed for the acquisition not merely of Mexico but of Cuba and other tropical territories. Proclaiming expansion as "the most settled policy of the United States," he affirmed the Machiavellian doctrine that nations which do not grow, inevitably wither and die. He hoped that growth might always be accomplished by peaceful methods, but when the vital interests of humanity and civilization commanded the United States to annex more territory, the methods were of little consequence.[7]

The imperialism of northerners in this period was scarcely less audacious. Although William H. Seward expressed his disapproval of a war to conquer Cuba, he echoed the conviction of John Quincy Adams that the United States must never allow the Pearl of the Antilles to pass under the dominion of any power that was then, or could become, a rival or enemy.[8] Even lower depths of brashness were reached by Edward Everett and James Buchanan. The former argued that Cuba lay at our very door and was "almost essential to our safety." The latter was one of the authors of the so-called Ostend Manifesto, declaring that if Spain refused to sell Cuba for a maximum price of $120,000,000, it should be wrested from her, in accordance with "every law, human and divine."

Post-Civil War imperialism is generally more familiar to students of American history than is the ante-bellum variety. Moreover, it is commonly associated with specific struggles and controversies, like those growing out of the acquisition of the Philippines. Actually, the growth of imperialist sentiment in the United States paralleled that in European countries. Just as in England and France, after 1870, men with aspirations for position and power came forward to trumpet the advantages of colonies, so on this side of the Atlantic prophets of empire made their appearance years before the outbreak of the War with Spain. First in chronological order was Josiah Strong, who in his celebrated essay *Our Country*, published in 1885, set forth his firm conviction that God was not only preparing in Anglo-Saxon countries the die with which to stamp all the other peoples of the earth, but that He was "also massing behind that die the mighty power with which to press it."[9] A few years later he expressed the hope that Britain and America would bring China "thoroughly" under their influence, impregnating her with a new life and giving her a "political and religious regeneration." The fact that she and some other backward countries had governments of their own made no difference. The popular idea that no people can be rightfully governed without their consent "was formed when

"Uncle Sam—By gum, I rather like your looks." This cartoon of 1898 gives expression to the surging pride in overseas empire. *Rocky Mountain News, Denver*

world conditions were radically different, and peoples could live separate lives." But the world has grown smaller, and plague spots in any part of it are a menace to all the rest.[10]

More brutally frank even than Strong was John W. Burgess, well known as a constitutional lawyer and champion of the Teutonic genius as the chief agent of human progress. The Teutonic nations, Burgess alleged, have a mission to carry political civilization into those parts of the world inhabited by "unpolitical and barbaric races." The latter, it seemed, occupy the greater portion of the earth's surface. The civilized states have a right to insist that the uncivilized populations become civilized. If they cannot do so by their own efforts, "they must submit to the powers that can do it for them." Not only does the civilized state have the right to conquer barbaric peoples, but if they remain recalcitrant in their barbarism, the civilized state "may clear the territory of their presence and make it the abode of civilized man." The latter need not be troubled in his conscience about the morality of such a policy "when it becomes manifestly necessary." No rights are thereby violated which are not petty and trivial in comparison with the "transcendent right and duty" of the civilized state "to establish political and legal order everywhere." No one can deny that it is in the interest of world civilization "that law and order and the true liberty consistent therewith shall reign everywhere upon the globe." The civilized states should, of course, refrain from hasty and irresponsible action in seizing power, but they have no obligation to await an invitation from misgoverned or incompetent states. They themselves are the best judges of the proper time and occasion for intervening "for the execution of their great world duty." To shirk their responsibility in this matter is to be recreant to their mission as the uplifters and guardians of the human race.[11]

The outbreak of war with Spain in 1898 and the vistas of imperial grandeur it opened up for the United States resulted in further bombastic outbursts in justification of colonial expansion. The most voluble of its new apostles was Albert J. Beveridge. Six days after the declaration of war upon Spain, he pronounced the American people "a conquering race," who must obey their blood and "occupy new markets and, if necessary, new lands." God had ordained it so. He had made it a part of His infinite plan that "debased civilizations and decaying races" should disappear "before the higher civilization of the nobler and more virile types of man." Two years later in his "Star of Empire" speech, he proclaimed that every people who had achieved greatness had done so in part as colonizers and subjugators, and that the sovereignty of the Stars and Stripes could be nothing but a blessing to any land and any people. History shows, he maintained, that civilization can be extended only by the small number of superior peoples among the nations of the world. They are God's anointed, chosen by Him as trustees of the progress of mankind. And most of all among those chosen, He has marked the American people to lead finally in the regeneration of savage and degenerate races. This is their destiny, and they have no alternative but to accept it.

As one would expect, the associates of Beveridge in acclaiming the Spanish-American War as an epochal event in the divine pattern of the universe were also apostles of imperialism. Admiral Mahan, for instance, could not understand the long chain of colonial conquests by Great Britain on any other basis than manifestations of a Supreme Intelligence, "acting through all time, with purpose deliberate and consecutive, to ends not yet discerned." The great admiral was not always so mystical, however. Generally he was content to find justification for empire in such mundane sources as the importance of sea power. Control of the sea, as "the world's great medium of circulation," he regarded as the chief material element in the power and prosperity of nations. It followed that a nation should not hesitate to take possession, "when it can be done righteously," of such maritime positions as will "contribute to secure command." The pious clause, "when it can be done righteously," was not much of a limitation. Like John W. Burgess, Mahan made political capacity and the interests of civilization the tests of a people's right to retain their independence. The right of any people to self-government is not an indefeasible right but is subordinate to "the natural right of the world at large that resources should not be left idle, but be utilized for the general good." Failure to contribute to this larger result justifies, according to Mahan, "compulsion from outside." Nor need any tenderness be shown to corrupt or incompetent governments. Should necessity demand it, they should be "discontinued" as unworthy institutions by the bearers of the higher civilization.[12]

Few Americans have justified imperialism for definite reasons of economic aggrandizement. Senator Beveridge made occasional oblique references to "China's illimitable markets" and to nuggets of gold which could be plucked from the streams of the Philippine Islands. But, mostly, he and his compatriots talked in terms of mission, race, and civilization.

An outstanding exception to the practice mentioned above was Brooks Adams, lawyer, philosopher, and member of one of the most distinguished families that ever embellished the pages of American history. In 1900 Adams published a fatalistic little essay entitled *America's Economic Supremacy,* in which he described an increasingly savage competition among the powers of the world for control of markets and vital resources. All of the great powers were caught as in a maelstrom. None could remain stationary. To fail to move with the current spelled destruction. The explanation stemmed from the fact that every industrialized nation was glutted with products. Its prosperity and even survival depended upon finding markets to absorb the surplus. But since all were in the same predicament, and since the potential markets were limited, every major nation faced the prospect of a deadly war just as soon as the tensions became serious enough to produce an explosion. The prize to be won would be the most dazzling in the imagination of man, but failure would mean the fate of Carthage after the Punic Wars or of Spain after the defeat of the Armada. America must either elect to compete for this prize and prepare to fight Germany, Japan, Russia, and possibly Britain, or resign herself to the example of France, limiting her birthrate and practicing frugality to the point of penury. By so doing she might save her existence, but she would lose her national vitality. Rather than endure such a loss, Adams quite obviously preferred that America should continue the scramble for colonies and markets even at the risk of almost certain war.

Support of imperialism in the United States has obviously been far from unanimous. Every great orgy of conquest has brought out a small group of dissenters. Henry Clay, Albert Gallatin, and John C. Calhoun condemned the demand that Mexico be held as a conquered province when her defeat seemed imminent in 1847-48. Calhoun, especially, protested that such action would be contrary to the genius and character of our government, and "subversive of our free institutions." It would transfer all sovereignty to the Union and reduce the states to mere counties. It would enable the executive branch to aggrandize itself at the expense of the legislative. It would create such a multitude of jobholders and place-hunters as to open the door to wholesale corruption. The struggle to obtain the Presidency would become so hard-fought and desperate as to destroy the freedom of elections. The end result would be anarchy or despotism.[13]

Equally vehement and more numerous protests accompanied the Spanish-American War, with its threats of a more dangerous imperialism. William Graham Sumner wrote a little book which he sardonically entitled *The Conquest of the United States by Spain*. Spain had had her brief moment of grandeur and power in the time of Charles V and Philip II, and then had succumbed to greed and luxury and to the unprofitable pursuits of a master race. America was imitating her foolish example.

During the Boer War and the war for the conquest of the Philippines, William James and William Jennings Bryan voiced their characteristic sympathies for the underdog and bewailed the tendency of the strong among nations to devour the weak. James hoped that the Boers would "give fits" to the British, and that similar discomforts would be inflicted by the Filipinos upon the Americans.[14] Bryan compared the slaughter and despoiling of defenseless Fili-

Enlightened economic imperialism in Central America. Indian mother consults doctor at clinic of company hospital in Guatemala. *Courtesy of United Fruit Co.*

pinos with the robbing and killing of a cripple by an armed thug.[15]

The most emphatic denunciations of the quest for empire came from Carl Schurz and David Starr Jordan. Both were vice-presidents of the Anti-Imperialist League, organized in 1898 to prevent the United States from being drawn into the scramble for overseas possessions. Schurz blasted the imperialists for turning a proclaimed war of liberation and humanity into a war of "criminal aggression and subjugation," thereby branding the United States as "a nation of hypocrites and destroying our moral credit with the world." They had "put to contempt and ridicule the fundamental principles of our democracy" and were undermining the ideals of right, justice, and liberty. Their example was teaching the people that "might makes right" and similar lessons, which would "transform the political life of our democracy into wild, unscrupulous and eventually, anarchistic struggles of selfish passions and greedy interests."[16]

Jordan's opposition to imperialism rested upon three assumptions. He regarded it, first of all, as the antithesis of democracy. The Constitution of the United States, he contended, was made for citizens, not for subjects and slaves. Governments can have no powers except what they derive from the consent of the governed, and where such consent cannot be given, democracy is out of the question. His second objection to imperialism grew out of his fear that it would lead to war. Alien and rebellious peoples, he maintained, can be held in subjection only by force. The result is the necessity for great military and naval establishments, which inspire fear and arouse the antagonism of other nations. Finally, Jordan condemned imperialism on the ground that it saps the foundations of civilization. All the great empires of the past, he believed, brought ruin upon themselves because they insisted upon extending their rule over alien peoples. Conquest brought habits of luxury and idleness, fostered slavery, impoverished the small farmer, corrupted the government, and transformed the ruling classes into domineering tyrants. He saw evidence that modern empires, pursuing the same ambitions, were headed for an identical fate.[17]

INTERNATIONALISTS AND INTERVENTIONISTS

The suggestion of a relationship between imperialism and what ordinarily passes for internationalism would probably impress most Americans as illogical. Yet such a relationship exists. The reason is that internationalism in this country has commonly taken the form of interventionism. Prophets of the internationalist gospel have generally demanded for America a role of world leadership, to be achieved by a vigorous foreign policy which will retain the initiative and the power of taking the offensive in American hands. To the extent that such a policy is dependent upon powerful alliances, upon weapons of aggressive warfare, upon military bases thousands of miles from our homeland, and upon satellites and protectorates, it does not differ essentially from ruling over colonies and subjugating alien territories.

Ideas of a foreign policy based upon sufficient strength to dictate to other nations and to protect our vital interests in all parts of the world can be traced as far back as the time of the Fathers. In 1788 Alexander Hamilton warned his countrymen against placing too much confidence in the wide ocean that separates the United States from Europe. Improvements in the art of navigation, he said, had "rendered distant nations in a great measure, neighbors." He emphasized especially the danger that two or more of the great maritime powers might combine to attack us.[18] His purpose was to call attention to the need of a strong Union which could build a powerful navy to protect our commerce and cope with aggressors before they reached our shores.

Hamilton's warnings have been reiterated many times since and in almost identical language. The twentieth century, particularly, has seen the revival of the dogma that the oceans are not bulwarks of defense but highways. Contemporary leaders have also sought to impress upon us the idea that hostile combinations of powers across the seas are likely to attack us, and that for our own protection we must prevent the formation of such combinations or enter into alliances to resist them. One of the chief formulators and expositors of this doctrine has been Walter Lippmann. He expounded it, first of all, in *The Stakes of Diplomacy*, published in 1915. He warned at that time that isolation had become a myth and that America must either assume a role of active leadership in world affairs or resign herself to passive acceptance of international disorder. For him there was only one possible choice. The United States should create interests which would justify its participation in world politics. It should invest and trade in the backward countries. It should weight its diplomacy with armaments of sufficient potency to make its voice heard by the Great Powers. Above all, it should abandon its traditional dislike of European alliances. He admitted that this was a "terrifying" program, but he considered it the only alternative if America was to become an important factor "in the stabilizing of mankind." By 1943 Lippmann was envisioning a new terror that America might be isolated by a hostile world. The thing to do now was to forestall this by forming alliances of our own. To be a member of an alliance "which can be depended upon to act together, and, when challenged, to fight together," is to achieve the highest degree of security attainable, in a world composed of sovereign states. If the alliance is as strong as it should be, its members will either have peace without fighting for it, or they will have peace following a victorious war.[19] He did not seem to contemplate the possibility that the strength of the opposing alli-

The Big Three at the Crimean (Yalta) Conference, February, 1945. Here plans were made for the distribution of conquered territories, for the establishment of the United Nations, and for the maintenance of world peace under American, British, and Russian leadership. *U. S. Army Photograph*

ance might be both an unknown and a decisive determining factor.

The Lippmann doctrines bear a marked similiarity to a number of basic foreign policies enunciated by recent statesmen. Not the least of the resemblances occurs in Franklin D. Roosevelt's plan for keeping the peace after World War II. In 1942-43 he wrote privately of his scheme for postponing a formal peace settlement for three or four years after the end of hostilities. During this transition period, the United States, Great Britain, Russia, and China would act as "sheriffs" for the maintenance of order. The rest of the nations would be required to disarm. If any of them should be caught arming, they would be threatened with a quarantine; and if that did not work, they would be bombed. For some curious reason, Russia would be charged with keeping the peace in the Western Hemisphere, and China and the United States in the Far East.[20] There is evidence that Roosevelt continued to set great store by this plan for making the major Allied powers responsible for the peace of the world. Even the United Nations, as he conceived it, appears to have been essentially an alliance of the Big Three with some assistance from China and France.

After Roosevelt's death the policy of seeking peace and security by counteralliances was continued by his successors. The containment policy and the establishment of the North Atlantic Treaty Organization during the Truman administration were the best examples. Though the Eisenhower government indicated at first some interest in "liberating" countries recently brought under the Communist yoke, it soon reverted to the policy of cooperating with allies to hold the Communists in check. In pursuance of this policy, NATO was strengthened, West Germany was permitted to rearm, and Chiang Kai-shek was put back on a leash and discouraged from attacking the mainland.

Second only to the policy of alliances as a means of maintaining American leadership is the practice of direct intervention. Characteristic instances have been crusades to make the world safe for democracy, or interference in the politics of other areas to advance our own interests. The most vocal exponent of interventionist policy was probably Admiral Mahan. Writing in the 1890's, he sought to impress upon Americans the idea that they should begin to look outward. Public sentiment, increasing production, and the position of the United States between two great oceans demanded it. Just as religions which rejected missionary enterprise were doomed to decay, so with nations that failed to look beyond their borders. Whereas, once, to avoid European entanglements was essential to the development of America as an infant nation, "now to take her share of the travail of Europe is but to assume an inevitable task, an appointed lot, in the work of upholding the common interests of civilization." To pursue such a course would aid in preserving the martial spirit and in reviving the sense of nationality, "which is the true antidote to what is bad in socialism." Moreover, it would equip the nation in some future time to deal successfully with the threat imposed by "the teeming multitudes of central and northern Asia." This menace looms large on the Western horizon, and against it the only barrier "will be the warlike spirit of the representatives of civilization." It was typical of Mahan that he should have argued a few years later in favor of repudiation of that part of the Monroe

Doctrine which pledges the United States to remain aloof from the broils of Europe. America could not tolerate henceforth, he contended, a substantial change in the European balance of power.[21] It was a thesis which seems to have occupied ever since a central place in the shaping of our foreign policy.

Interventionism was also the gospel of some lesser known Americans. Parke Godwin, idealistic editor and reformer, seemed to think that the United States should roam the world like a Don Quixote of democracy seeking forlorn damsels to protect. At the very least, we should express our unreserved sympathy for every people struggling for liberation, give immediate recognition to their independence, and guarantee that independence, when once established, against the forceful interference of other nations. Only thus could America be true to the great tradition of Anglo-Saxon love of liberty. Godwin doubted that intervention in this form would lead to hostilities; but if war should come, "in what more just or magnanimous battle could a great people engage?" It would be "a glorious struggle for liberty, justice, and humanity," for the rights of small nations, for the majesty of law, and for the golden precepts of Christian civilization.[22]

At the end of the nineteenth century Henry Demarest Lloyd, socialist and archfoe of monopolies, championed the idea of intervention not only in Cuba but in Greece and in South Africa. We should intervene everywhere for good, he said, but nowhere for evil. It was our solemn duty, if we wanted to be a "gentleman" among the nations. Since we won our freedom and prosperity in the first place by seeking and accepting the help of others, we could keep our self-respect only by giving help to those who needed it now. Washington's advice to keep clear of European politics was not intended to apply when we should become great and rich and able to assist other peoples "struggling for life and liberty and the honor of their women."[23]

From the examples given it should be clear that genuine internationalism is not synonymous with any of the conceptions just discussed. It is not the equivalent of alliances, of attempts to maintain a balance of power, of intervention, liberation, or containment, of economic imperalism, or of the establishment of military and naval bases in all parts of the world. It can scarcely be identified even with collective security, since most programs of that sort are devices mainly for self-protection. They are schemes for saving one's own skin with the help of others who have similar interests. True internationalism, or cosmopolitanism, it might better be called, must rest upon the assumption that the human race is a unit, that people are not natural enemies merely because they happen to live on different sides of a boundary line, that the public welfare is indivisible and cannot be enhanced for one group of people by beggaring its neighbors economically or destroying them militarily, and that sovereignty is not the exclusive possession of separate national units.

Internationalism has won but few converts in American history. This is paradoxical in view of the fact that Americans invented a system of government, the federal system, which could be adapted more easily than any other to true international organization. Most American leaders also have been aware of the fundamental defects in the confederate type of government, which derives its authority not from the people themselves but from sovereign units such as the thirteen states under the Articles of Confederation. Since the government of the Confederation was an agent or trustee of the states, it could exercise its authority only upon them. Alexander Hamilton emphasized these defects in urging adoption of the Constitution. The "great and radical vice" of the Confederation, he said, is legislation "for STATES or GOVERNMENTS, in their CORPORATE or COLLECTIVE CAPACITIES, and as contra-distinguished from the INDIVIDUALS of which they consist." But such legislation must be enforced by military action, or else it will remain in the character of mere recommendations. There is no means whereby a league of sovereign states can punish individuals for violating its laws. But to coerce a state would be one of the "maddest projects" ever suggested. It would mean nothing less than civil war. Suppose Massachusetts should be accused of a violation, and the central government should march troops against it. Would not Massachusetts be able to enlist the sympathy and support of other states, perhaps even of a majority? The central government would then have to choose between ignominious surrender and splitting the confederacy wide open by armed conflict. How long would reasonable men support such a government when it became obvious that it could maintain its existence only by the sword? [24]

Although most of the Fathers, along with Hamilton, recognized the unsuitability of the confederate form of government on the national scale, few Americans indeed have perceived its inadequacies as an international system. One was the scientist, educator, and philosopher David Starr Jordan. As a critic of modern machinery for preventing wars, Jordan had a low opinion of the League of Nations. He regarded it as essentially an alliance of the victors to preserve the *status quo* and hold the vanquished in subjection. It suffered from a membership less than universal, for both Germany and Russia were excluded. Worse still, the fact that it had authority to coerce member states gave it a character little different from that of a concert of powers. It was fundamentally a continuation of the old state system, whose members had always been free to organize "grand alliances." The crying need of the twentieth century was not a concert of powers but "a concert of peoples, an assembly of good men devoted to the common welfare." What Jordan fervently hoped to see was a world that would exemplify the ideal of Goethe: "Above all nations is humanity." In an interdependent world, nations had become obsolete. They should cease to be "powers" and take on the character of mere areas of jurisdiction. Boundary lines would then no longer be lines of suspicion and contention and would become, like the boundaries of provinces, mere conveniences for judicial and administrative purposes. Jordan did not expect that a fully developed world republic would emerge overnight. He preferred that it should be a product of growth, of an increasing consciousness of world community. Even in its final form he hoped to keep political machinery down to a minimum. He wanted no centralized world state with overweening authority, but rather a series of regional parliaments and courts of appeal, which would deal at first with international equity and lay down a body of precedents which would crystallize eventually into a body of law. But this law would be applicable to persons only and not to states.[25]

A second noted American who perceived the defects in conventional forms of international organization was John Dewey. In common with Jordan, Dewey was also sharply critical of the League of Nations, mainly because of its power to invoke military and naval sanctions. The nation against which sanctions are used, he argued, "would feel that it had yielded not to the claims of justice but to superior force, quite as much as if it had been defeated in war."

International aid for underdeveloped countries. An International Cooperation Administration trainee demonstrating the characteristics of a new variety of cotton to a class in Pakistan. *ICA*

In fact, he contended, the employment of sanctions *is* war, no matter
by what name it may be called. It involves the use of armies and
navies, artillery and high explosives, blockades, and the bombing
of cities. It is not possible to make the use of such measures any the
less war by giving it the polite name of police action. The application of police power against an obstreperous individual is radically
different from the use of military measures against a nation. In the
former case violation of a law is universally recognized as a crime.
Agencies representing society have made it so and have provided
the instruments for judicial trial, conviction, and punishment. But in
the international sphere there are no such agencies or instruments.
Resort to violence by dissatisfied nations is legitimate and is sanc-
tioned by the only law that exists. This condition, Dewey maintained, points the way to the only logical solution: the adoption of
a universal agreement by which every nation would outlaw war,

and the establishment of a world court to try and sentence violators. The latter, of course, would be individuals, since, under the agreement, war-making activities would be a crime the same as any other preparations for violence.[26]

It is pertinent to add that Dewey worked zealously for the adoption of the Pact of Paris of 1928, by which the nations of the world did formally renounce war as an instrument of national policy. He failed to foresee, however, the ingenious reservations which some of the politicians would devise to preserve the war system, despite their promises to abandon it. The pact was a dead letter even before it was ratified.

A few other distinguished Americans gave evidence of a cosmopolitan turn of mind in at least some of their writings. A famous slogan of Thomas Paine was "My country is the world, to do good my religion." In drafting a Declaration of Sentiments for the Peace Convention of 1838, William Lloyd Garrison expressed a similar doctrine: "Our country is the world, our countrymen are all mankind. We love the land of our nativity only as we love all other lands. The interests, rights, and liberties of American citizens are no more dear to us than are those of the whole human race. Hence we can allow no appeal to patriotism, to revenge any national insult or injury." Charles Sumner, in *The True Grandeur of Nations*, pleaded the cause of a higher patriotism than loyalty to one's native country. All the people of the earth, he affirmed, derive their blood from a common source, and are members of a single family. "Discord in this family is treason to God; while all war is nothing else than *civil war*."

The least sentimental of those who wrote from a cosmopolitan viewpoint was probably Thorstein Veblen. For him almost nothing was important except the smooth and efficient working of the industrial system. Life and material well-being were bound up with it. This system had an international or cosmopolitan character. The nation was obsolete and simply stood in the way of a proper functioning of the industrial order. Since no civilized country's economic system would work at all, if confined within national frontiers, the sooner such relics of a primitive past were abolished, the better. The world should then be turned over to "reasonably unbiased" production engineers and technical specialists who know what is needed to make the economic organization function for the benefit of all mankind.[27] Though a product of tough-mindedness and economic realism, Veblen's proposal had little more chance of realization than the other internationalist ideals. Presumably all must await the operation of revolutionary forces which will destroy not only the fact of national independence but the belief in its value as well.

THE PERSISTENCE OF ISOLATIONISM

By popular theory the history of the foreign policy of the United States falls into two periods—a period of isolation from 1776 to 1898 and a period of intervention in world affairs from 1898 to the present. Insofar as actual events are concerned, this theory is essentially correct; but it falls short of the truth with respect to the opinions of national leaders. There were interventionists and internationalists as far back as 1789, and isolationists have continued to flourish since 1898. In both periods the same men have been isolationists at one time and internationalists at another. Those who thus vacillated were, generally speaking, isolationists in tranquil times and interventionists or internationalists when they felt that danger threatened. For the most part they were able to find convenient principles to justify either position.

The isolationism of the Fathers is well known, though it was probably more deeply embedded than. is generally believed. It was motivated both by pride in the achievement of independence and determination to build in America a citadel of freedom uncontaminated by the corruption and degeneracy of Europe. It stemmed also in part from a curious fear and contempt that Americans of this period felt toward foreigners. George Mason wrote in 1783 that "nature having separated us, by an immense ocean, from the European nations, the less we have to do with their quarrels or politics, the better." [28] Ten years later Rufus King mourned that the history of mankind had shown "that foreign influence is the most subtle and fatal poison that can be communicated to a nation." Great and once happy states, under its operation, "have either expired in violent convulsions, or been reduced to a deplorable state of debility and insignificance." [29] James Madison was less emotional but equally fearful of designing foreigners. He advised the Virginia ratifying convention that we ought not to engage in European politics or

European wars. He warned, however, that in spite of all our caution we could not eliminate the risk of being drawn into Europe's wars. Our only hope lay in a united nation possessed of "respectable" strength.

The most firmly convinced isolationists among the Founders of the republic seem to have been Jefferson and Hamilton, though the latter was not consistent. As noted in an earlier chapter, Jefferson would have been willing for the nation to abandon the ocean altogether if necessary to keep out of war, and to turn all our citizens to cultivating the earth as their sole means of livelihood. In his first inaugural he called for "peace, commerce, and honest friendship with all nations—entangling alliances with none." Even during the War of 1812 he was optimistic enough to contend that in the near future America would be invulnerable to sparks of war kindled in other parts of the globe. In fifty years she would have the strength of fifty million inhabitants to add to the advantage of the insulated position nature had given her. But she must also cultivate a "separate system of interest, which must not be subordinated to those of Europe." [30]

At times Hamilton expressed isolationist views apparently derived from his pessimism and from fears that America would be contaminated by the French Revolution. But, his conclusions were remarkably similar to Jefferson's. In 1795 he wrote that if the United States would consult her true interests, her "motto could not fail to be '*Peace* and *Trade* with *all Nations*—beyond our present engagements, *political connection* with *none*.'" He went on to condemn the idea of exposing our peace and interests by means of alliances to all the shocks with which the "mad rivalship and wicked ambition" of European nations "so frequently convulse the earth." [31] Hamilton also spoke through the mouth of Washington, for the famous farewell address of the latter was largely the work of his one-time Secretary of the Treasury. In it he repeated his warnings against "the insidious wiles of foreign influence," which "history and experience prove is one of the most baneful foes of republican government." He reiterated also the advice to have, beyond present engagements, political connections with no foreign nations. The time would soon come when we should be able to defy external annoyance, and our neutrality would be scrupulously respected. Why jeopardize so fortunate a situation? "Why quit our own to stand upon foreign ground? Why, by interweaving our destiny with that of any part of Europe, entangle our peace and prosperity in the toils of European ambition, rivalship, interest, humour, or caprice?" It was advice which has had a strong appeal ever since.

Isolationist principles found frequent reaffirmation through the course of the nineteenth century. They received a classic formulation in the Monroe Doctrine of 1823. The doctrine declared that any attempt by European powers to extend their system to the New World would be regarded by the United States as "dangerous to her peace and safety." But it also contained the self-denying ordinance that America would refrain from taking part in any of the wars of European powers, "in matters relating to themselves," and would not interfere in the internal concerns of any of these powers. Andrew Jackson believed that the advice against entangling alliances should be extended to political connections with South American countries as well.[32] Long before he became President, Abraham Lincoln emphasized the geographic and military impregnability of the United States. "All the armies of Europe, Asia, Africa combined with all the treasure of the earth (our own excepted) in their military chest, with a Bonaparte for a commander, could not by force take a drink from the Ohio or make a track on the Blue Ridge in a trial of a thousand years." He insisted that if destruction should ever overtake our country, it would have to come as a result of our own misdeeds.[33] Perhaps the language of his later years would not have been so brash, but there is nothing to indicate any change in his sentiment.

Although both the Civil War and the Spanish-American War involved the United States in diplomatic entanglements with foreign powers, neither resulted in any marked abatement of isolationist thinking. As early as 1862, William Dean Howells, who was then United States consul in Venice, wrote that he was getting disgusted "with this stupid Europe" and was growing to hate it. He described European society as socially rotten and was particularly censorious of the "filthy frankness" of the Germans. He contended that the less we knew of Europe, "the better for our civilization." [34]

In his *Triumphant Democracy*, published in 1886, Andrew Carnegie demanded that the United States should diligently cultivate internal perfection instead of chasing the will-o'-the-wisp of international trade or world power. Above all, let her avoid the accumulation of monster ships and engines of war to frighten her neighbors, for that is the surest way to make enemies. True, she may be attacked, just as any individual who walks down Broadway may be beaten and robbed by a thug, "but no one suggests that we walk about, therefore, in coats of mail." Not a single port exists in America which could not be effectively closed against an assailant before he had time to reach it. Besides, there is little chance that the country will ever have an assailant if she remains unarmed.[35]

A few years later William James advanced the same argument and berated President Cleveland and his Secretary of State for threatening Britain with war over the Venezuelan boundary dispute. Insisting that the United States had absolutely nothing to fear from invasion, he contended that the "party of civilization" ought to begin immediately "to agitate against any increase of army, navy, or coast defense." He regarded such action as the one form of protection "on which we can most rely."[36]

The most formidable protagonist of isolationism in the latter half of the nineteenth century was Carl Schurz, liberal Republican Senator from Missouri and later Secretary of the Interior in the cabinet of President Hayes. Schurz made use of every intellectual weapon in the isolationist armory: the content of Washington's farewell address, the marvelous growth in the prosperity and power of the republic through adherence to a noninterventionist policy, the frightening effect upon our neighbors in this hemisphere of a policy of power politics, and the alleged impregnability of the United States.

Schurz rejected the thesis that the United States must play the role of Sir Galahad to the rest of the world, assuming responsibility for all the injustices suffered by weak nations at the hands of the strong. He did not deny that America had her world responsibilities, but he suggested that before undertaking the office of dispenser of justice and righteousness abroad, she should set her own house in order. He was willing that his adopted country should become a great power, not by swaggering about with a chip on her shoulder, shaking her fist under everybody's nose, but by being patient and forbearing, respecting her neighbors, and conducting her foreign relations so justly and fairly and without arrogance that whenever a mediator was wanted to settle international differences, the United States would immediately appear to be the logical choice. She would then be in the noblest sense a real world power—"indeed, the grandest world-power mankind has ever known." With the attainment of such an objective in the foreign sphere, and with the perfection of democracy at home, the republic would achieve its true mission of benefactor of the human race.[37]

To a far greater extent than the events of the nineteenth century, those of the twentieth should have given alarm to the isolationists. The 1900's began with America involved in the conquest of the Philippines and partially committed to the maintenance of a balance of power in both Europe and Asia. As the century advanced these commitments increased. In 1905 President Theodore Roosevelt intervened in the Russo-Japanese War to induce the belligerents to lay down their arms and sign a treaty of peace. He acted at a juncture favorable to Japan because he believed that a victory for Russia would upset the balance of power in the Far East. In 1906, with Germany and France threatening to leap at each other's throats in a dispute over Morocco, Roosevelt used his good offices to bring the two countries together in the Algeciras Conference. Two representatives from the United States participated, and Roosevelt, who had strong pro-French sympathies, boasted that he stood the Kaiser on his head "with great decision." In succeeding years the same President authorized agreements with Japan, giving her a free hand in Korea and receiving in return Japanese recognition of American annexation of the Philippines and promises to respect the integrity of China.

Yet none of these events muted the voices or dampened the enthusiasm of the isolationists. The Progressive movement, whose development paralleled the new ventures in foreign policy, was almost wholly nationalist. Even Albert J. Beveridge, vociferous apostle of America's mission to dominate the earth, emerged, among Progressive leaders, as a caustic antagonist of everything international. Robert M. LaFollette, George W. Norris, Hiram Johnson, William E. Borah, and a score of others, persisted in their isolationism throughout the life of the Progressive movement. LaFollette was their chief fount of inspiration. To the doughty Senator from Wisconsin the war that began in Europe in 1914 was simply another in a long series of power struggles for control of that continent. America had nothing to gain from supporting either side, for all the belligerents were tarred with the same brush. If, compared with

Britain, Germany was an autocracy, Russia, fighting as an ally of Britain, was even more an autocracy. As for the movement to force American intervention in the struggle, it was simply a greedy plot on the part of Wall Street bankers to protect their loans to the Entente allies.

Following the defeat of Germany, LaFollette centered his attack upon the peace settlement. He denounced the Treaty of Versailles as unjust and vindictive, and he condemned the Covenant of the League of Nations as a scheme to keep us forever embroiled in the quarrels of Europe. Joining the league, he protested, would require us to surrender "our right to control our own destiny as a Nation." We would be compelled "to emasculate, if not destroy, our form of government by recognizing the right of some assembly or council of nations, in which we have small voice, to interfere with our most vital concerns." We should have to scuttle our traditional policy of avoiding entangling alliances and "become a party to every political scheme that may be hatched in the capitals of Europe or elsewhere in this world of ours." [38] To his credit, it should be added that his criticisms were not wholly destructive. In place of Wilson's league, which he contended was a league for war, he proposed a "League for Peace," comprising all the nations of the world that would accept agreements, with proper guaranties, to abolish compulsory military service and reduce all armaments "to the strict requirements of a purely police and patrol service." [39]

During the period when Progressive ideals held sway over his mind, Woodrow Wilson was almost as much of an isolationist as LaFollette. The chief difference lay in the greater originality of Wilson's arguments. On the eve of the war in Europe he expressed his opposition to entangling alliances on the unique ground that no other country had yet set its face in the direction America was traveling. He contended also that only the weak need alliances, and that nations, like individuals, are weak when they are in the wrong, when they are not true to themselves. In 1915 he described his country's duty as summed up in the motto, "America First"—not in any selfish way, however, but in order that America might be fit to be the friend of other nations when the day of tested friendship should come. The true test of friendship, he continued, is not sympathy for one side or the other "but getting ready to help both sides when the struggle is over." He rejected the suggestion that neutrality is indifference or self-interest. Instead, it is sympathy for mankind. It is fairness and good will. It is impartiality of spirit and of judgment.[10]

As everyone knows, the end of the war brought disenchantment and a vengeful determination to have as little as possible to do with the world overseas. War weariness, war debts, the secret treaties, disillusionment with the peace, and postwar depressions combined to produce in the majority of Americans a desire to shake the dust of Europe off their feet and consign her to the perdition her wicked militarism and stubborn conservatism seemed to deserve. The new mood was expressed not only by spiteful opponents of Wilson but by Progressive Senators like Norris, LaFollette, and Borah and by liberal journals like the *New Republic* and the *Nation*.

The new attitude received its most carefully reasoned support, perhaps, from the philosopher John Dewey. Dewey admitted that isolation is not a high ideal, but he insisted that it "denotes a better state of things than one of meddling which involves the meddler in unpleasant complications and does no one else any good in the end." He affirmed his sympathy with the idea of cooperation, but he contended that Europe did not want cooperation except on its own terms. The League of Nations, he thought, was mainly a scheme whereby Britain and France hoped to get the cooperation of the United States in maintaining their own hegemony. He conceded that European statesmen probably did not want war, but neither did they wish to avoid it enough "to lead them to reduce armaments, balance budgets, straighten out their affairs, and try to create a decently stable and amicable Europe." He criticized the league also because it was a league of governments and not of peoples, because it was tied up with the inequities of the Treaty of Versailles, because it contained no provision for effective solution of the "war-breeding issues" of Europe, and because it provided for the application of military and naval sanctions against nations. He repudiated the implication of a parallel between the use of coercion by the municipal police against individuals and the proposed use of force by the league against whole nations. The latter action, if resisted, would mean nothing less than civil war, and would be the most effective means imaginable for preventing the growth of a sense of community and a climate of opinion based upon the voluntary acceptance of law and order. Dewey believed at this time that America should continue her policy of aloofness until the liberal parties of European countries brought their foreign offices under the control of democratic principles and until Americans themselves gained more knowledge of the devious ways of international politics.[41]

The economic collapse of 1929-1933 seemed to intensify the determination of Americans to turn their backs upon Europe. Some went so far as to blame the depression, or at least the most serious phases of it, upon unsettled conditions in Europe. Herbert Hoover maintained that the United States would have recovered quickly from the stock market panic of 1929 had it not been for the bank failures in Austria and Germany and the abandonment of the gold standard by Britain. During the campaign of 1932, Franklin D. Roosevelt, in response to a demand from William Randolph Hearst, promptly repudiated his earlier support of the League of Nations. In 1935 he informed an audience at the San Diego Exposition that "despite what happens in continents overseas, the United States of America shall and must remain, as long ago the Father of our country prayed that it might remain—unentangled and free." Although he did not like its mandatory embargo provisions, he signed

"Samuel! You're not going to another lodge meeting!" Or the persistent conflict between our desire for knight errantry and our longing for preoccupation with our own problems. Herbert Johnson in *The Saturday Evening Post*, January 8, 1938. *Reproduced with permission of Mrs. Herbert Johnson*

the Neutrality Act of 1935; and when the Spanish Civil War broke out in 1936, he asked Congress to amend the act to cover civil conflicts, thereby helping to guarantee a victory to Franco's Fascist Insurgents. Despite a few private expressions of concern over the ambitions of Nazi Germany, Roosevelt showed no clear indications of a turn toward collective security until he delivered his Chicago "quarantine" speech in October, 1937, soon after the beginning of the "China Incident" which was to usher in World War II. With a warning eye on Japan, he proposed that the peace-loving nations of the world should unite in quarantining aggressor nations. By this means they might hope to check the spread of "international anarchy."

But the major prophet of isolationism in these years was Charles A. Beard, historian and political scientist, whom many people accused of treason to the best traditions of his profession. Beard rarely, if ever, used the term isolationist. Instead, he preferred to think of himself as a "continentalist." By this he meant a concentration of interest by the United States "on the continental domain and on building here a civilization in many respects peculiar to American life and the potentials of the American heritage." Specifically, he meant non-intervention in the controversies and squabbles of Europe and Asia and "resistance to the intrusion of European or Asiatic powers, systems, and imperial ambitions into the western hemisphere." Beard maintained that this had been the traditional policy of our government, and he saw no reason why it should be abandoned. He identified it with Jefferson more closely than with anyone else, but he would doubtless have argued that Jefferson was simply extending, with a humanitarian emphasis, the essential policy of Washington and Hamilton. Like most other men who followed the same pattern of thought, Beard rejected the accusation that his theory would preclude or hinder international cooperation. He argued that, on the contrary, it would promote it. Cooperation could be most fully realized when all nations should put their own houses in order, repress their predatory interests, renounce war, and organize their domestic economies in such a way that exchange could be carried on on a basis of mutual benefit.[42]

As Beard conceived it, a policy of continentalism would be distinguished by several features. It would include a return to correct and restrained diplomacy. It would become the duty of public officials to refrain from abusing or denouncing any state with which this country was at peace. If protests were necessary, they would be couched in the language of dignity. No swaggering or boasting would be tolerated; our leaders would speak softly, but none would ostentatiously carry a big stick. The Department of State would avoid dissertations on the manners and morals of other nations and their rulers, and would accord recognition to any government successful in maintaining its authority. If some conqueror ran amuck in Europe or Asia, America would have nothing to fear. "Enthroned between two oceans, with no historic enemies on the north or south," she could be defended against almost any conceivable foe.

But more important, the policies America would follow would remove all but a minor possibility of her ever being attacked. She would eschew trade wars and offer to exchange "honest goods for honest goods" without any threats or coercion. She would abandon both imperialism and dollar diplomacy, and "surrender forever the imbecilic belief" that it was her duty to "defend every dollar invested everywhere and every acquisitive merchant seeking his private interests everywhere." She would sell no munitions to belligerents, would lend them no money, and "would sit in no diplomatic game played in the old style for old ends." Instead, she would offer to the world "the strange sight of a national garden well tended," and thereby "teach the most effective lesson—a lesson without words." [43] Perhaps Beard was also dreaming of a cuckoo-land as difficult to realize as the interventionists' ideal of perpetual peace through international trade, alliances, and a balance of power.

It seems evident that American imperialists, internationalists, interventionists, and isolationists have all been exponents of national mission. The difference among them has been a matter not so much of degree as of the area in which they would carry on their activities. The first three would project their operations abroad, some with sword or Bible in hand, others through the methods of diplomacy, loans and donations, courting allies, training and equipping their armies, or by organizing machinery for collective security or international government. The isolationist would confine our activities to our own homeland or at least to our own hemisphere north of the Bulge. He believes that the example of a regime of peace and justice within our own borders, of a house set in order and a garden well tended, would have more effect in regenerating the rest of the world than all the efforts of Sir Galahads since the beginning of time. Though a reduction in the scope of activities would almost certainly result in a reduction of intensity also, the isolationist is really about as firmly committed as any of his opponents to the idea that America has a call to rescue a suffering and benighted humanity. His basic disagreement with them concerns not so much the goal as the methods of heeding and answering the call.

NOTES TO CHAPTER TEN

1. Kate M. Rowland, *The Life of George Mason, 1725-1792* (New York: G. P. Putnam's Sons, 1892), I, 294.
2. J. C. Hamilton, ed., *The Works of Alexander Hamilton* (New York. J. F. Trow, 1850-51), V, 283.
3. Saul K. Padover, ed., *The Complete Jefferson* (New York: Duell, Sloan and Pearce, 1943), p. 175.
4. *Congressional Record*, 61st Cong., 3rd Session, XLVI, 2520 (1911).
5. *Writings*, Centenary ed. (Boston: American Unitarian Assoc., 1907-16), XII, 194-95.
6. *Political Essays* (New York: Dix, Edwards and Co., 1856), pp. 152-53, 156-57, 160-62.
7. Dunbar Rowland, ed., *Jefferson Davis, Constitutionalist, His Letters, Papers and Speeches* (Jackson, Miss.: Dept. of Archives and History, 1923), IV, 63, 85.
8. George E. Baker, ed., *The Works of William H. Seward* (New York: Redfield, 1853-54), III, 610.
9. *Our Country* (New York: The Baker and Taylor Co., 1885), p. 165.
10. *Expansion under New World Conditions* (New York: The Baker and Taylor Co., 1900), pp. 202-03, 241-42.
11. *Political Science and Comparative Constitutional Law* (Boston: Ginn and Co., 1890), I, 44-48.
12. *The Interest of America in Sea Power, Present and Future* (Boston: Little, Brown and Co., 1898), pp. 52-53, 307-08.
13. Richard K. Cralle, ed., *The Works of John C. Calhoun* (New York: D. Appleton and Co., 1856), IV, 411-12.
14. Henry James, ed., *The Letters of William James* (Boston: The Atlantic Monthly Press, 1921), II, 106.
15. *The Commoner Condensed* (New York: The Abbey Press, 1902), p. 186.
16. Frederic Bancroft, ed., *Speeches, Correspondence and Political Papers of Carl Schurz* (New York: G. P. Putnam's Sons, 1913), V, 241-42, 293-94.
17. *Imperial Democracy, passim;* "War Selection in Western Europe," *The Popular Science Monthly*, LXXXVII (August, 1915), 153.
18. *The Federalist*, Modern Library ed. (New York: Random House, n.d.), No. 24.
19. *U. S. Foreign Policy: Shield of the Republic* (Boston: Little, Brown and Co., 1943), pp. 105-06.

20. Elliot Roosevelt, ed., *F. D. R. His Personal Letters* (New York: Duell, Sloan and Pearce, 1947-50), IV, 1366-67, 1446-47.
21. *The Interest of America in Sea Power*, pp. 49, 122-24; *The Problems of Asia and Its Effect upon International Policies* (London: S. Low, Marston and Co., 1900), pp. 16-17.
22. *Political Essays*, pp. 115-18, 124-27.
23. *Mazzini and Other Essays* (New York: G. P. Putnam's Sons, 1910), pp. 118-20.
24. *The Federalist*, Modern Library ed., No. 15; Jonathan Elliot, ed., *The Debates in the Several State Conventions on the Adoption of the Federal Constitution* (Washington: Printed by and for the editor, 1863), II, 232-33.
25. *The Days of a Man* (Yonkers-on-Hudson: World Book Co., 1922), II, 653-54; *War and Waste* (Garden City, N. Y.: Doubleday, Page and Co., 1914), p. 7.
26. *Characters and Events* (New York: Henry Holt and Co., 1929), II, 653-54, 658.
27. *Essays in Our Changing Order* (New York: The Viking Press, 1934), pp. 388-89, 419-20.
28. Rowland, *The Life of George Mason*, II, 52.
29. C. R. King, ed., *Life and Correspondence of Rufus King* (New York: G. P. Putnam's Sons, 1894), I, 458.
30. Albert E. Bergh, ed., *The Writings of Thomas Jefferson* (Washington: Thomas Jefferson Memorial Assoc., 1907), XIII, 22-23.
31. J. C. Hamilton, ed., *Works*, VII, 172.
32. J. S. Bassett, ed., *The Correspondence of Andrew Jackson* (Washington: The Carnegie Institution, 1926), p. 300.
33. John G. Nicolay and John Hay, eds., *The Complete Works of Abraham Lincoln* (New York: Francis D. Tandy Co., 1905), I, 36-37.
34. Mildred Howells, ed., *The Life in Letters of William Dean Howells* (New York: Doubleday, Doran and Co., 1928), I, 59.
35. *Triumphant Democracy or Fifty Years' March of the Republic* (New York: Charles Scribner's Sons, 1886), pp. 209-10.
36. Henry Adams, ed., *The Letters of William James* (Boston: The Atlantic Monthly Press, 1920), II, 29.
37. Bancroft, ed., *Speeches*, V, 209, 257, 495-96; VI, 373-74.
38. *Congressional Record*, 66th Cong., 1st Session, LVIII, 8428 (1919).
39. Belle Case and Fola LaFollette, *Robert M. LaFollette* (New York: The Macmillan Co., 1953), II, 993.
40. R. S. Baker and W. E. Dodd, eds., *The New Democracy* (New York: Harper and Brothers, *ca.* 1926), I, 109, 303-04.
41. *Characters and Events*, II, 619, 622-24, 626-28; Joseph Ratner, ed., *Intelligence in the Modern World* (New York: The Modern Library, 1939), p. 590.
42. *A Foreign Policy for America* (New York: Alfred A. Knopf, 1940), pp. 12, 32-33; *The Open Door at Home* (New York: The Macmillan Co., 1934), pp. 273-74.
43. *The Open Door at Home*, pp. 318-19.

Chapter Eleven

The Decline and Fall
of America

B y a strange paradox many of the men who have been most
vocal in their affirmations of the resplendent mission of
the American republic have also believed in the inevitability of its
decline and fall. They have generally assumed that the mission
would be realized in large measure, but that soon afterward some
Nemesis would overtake the nation and bring it to certain destruction. A number have based their reasoning upon defects in the
American character, but others upon philosophical premises or upon
precedents drawn from history. Republics of the past, they have
pointed out, succumbed to decay and death. How could America
escape?

In 1832 John Quincy Adams expressed his disbelief that the Federal Union would last for twenty years, and he doubted its con-
tinuance for five.[1] In the same year John C. Calhoun lamented that
"the growing symptoms of disorder and decay" were discernible on
every hand. "In the midst of youth, we see the flushed cheek, and
the short and feverished breath, that mark the approach of the
fatal hour."[2] Theodore Parker wrote that after forty years of national
history without catastrophe, he knew not what lay before us. He
was sure, however, that it must be some calamity, for America, like
other nations, must have her time of troubles, her day of disaster,
when she would sit "with ashes on her head" and mourn the sins
of her past. "Mankind will one day bury the American State," he
philosophized further, "as gladly as the Babylonian, or Egyptian,
or Roman was gathered to its fathers."[3]

In contrast with these doleful predictions, a few other prominent Americans have refused to admit that the greatest republic on earth could ever sink into decay and oblivion. The boldest and most scholarly example was Charles A. Beard. After years of study and contemplation of the philosophy of history he was ready to conclude in 1928 that Western civilization was in no danger of extinction. Its disappearance by conquest, he contended, could be safely excluded. No barbarian hordes from Asia or Africa were ever likely to acquire the scientific and mechanical skill necessary to make such a conquest possible. Even if they should acquire the knowledge and complete the conquest, Western civilization would not be destroyed but would merely shift its geographic basis.

The economic debacle of 1929 and the outbreak of a second world war did not undermine Beard's confidence. In *The Republic,* published in 1943, he raised the question, "Will there always be an America?" and answered it with a buoyant affirmative. As ground for his assurance, he argued, first, that the analogy of Rome was "utterly inapplicable" to the United States. Rome at its zenith was not a nation but a collection of nationalities ruled by an emperor, "a commander in chief with unlimited power." All along her northern boundary were barbarians armed with weapons just about as deadly as those of the Romans themselves. Beard affirmed, in the second place, that history does not repeat itself. "Rome did not repeat the history of Egypt, Babylonia, or the Alexandrian empire." Nor has any nation since repeated the history of Rome. What basis then is there for assuming that America must pass through a cycle of growth, development, stagnation, and death? Finally, Beard contended that "our universe is not all fate; we have some freedom in it. Besides fate or determinism, there is *creative intelligence* in the world, and there is also *opportunity* to exercise our powers, intellectual and moral." America is abundantly equipped with such powers, and evidence of the sort of apathy and retreat from reason that characterized Rome in the fifth and sixth centuries is simply nonexistent.[4]

LESSONS OF GREECE AND ROME

From the Founding Fathers until late in the nineteenth century the downfall of Rome provided an object lesson of the fate that was likely to be in store for republics. The example of what happened to the Greek states exerted a lesser influence. The Fathers themselves set the precedent for neglecting the history of Greece. Perhaps they learned to read Latin with more facility and therefore with greater pleasure than they did Greek. Undoubtedly the Greek classics were less concerned with legal and juristic problems than were those of the Romans and consequently did not make so strong an appeal to a generation of lawyers. But the principal reason seems to have been that Greek political history stamped itself upon the American mind as a record of failure. According to James Wilson, the Greek republics were products of inexperience and lack of political maturity.[5] Hamilton declared that "no friend to order or to rational liberty" could read "without pain and disgust, the history of the commonwealths of Greece." They were a constant scene, he said, "of the alternate tyranny of one part of the people over the other, or of a few usurping demagogues over the whole." They were a prey to "frequent revolutions and civil broils," and for want of a solid union fell victims of their aggressive neighbors.[6] In the opinion of both Hamilton and William R. Davie of North Carolina, the Greek commonwealths suffered from the fatal defect that they lacked the principle of representative government. Authority was exercised by "tumultuous assemblies of the collective body of the people, where the art or impudence" of demagogues prevailed rather than the utility or justice of the measures.[7]

To the Fathers of the American republic, Roman history by contrast with Greek contained an abundance of profitable lessons. Quite a number of features of Roman life and institutions excited their admiration. Alexander Hamilton thought that "the Roman republic had attained to the utmost height of human greatness."[8] Charles Pinckney praised the Romans for "making the temple of virtue the road to the temple of fame."[9] Oliver Ellsworth believed that the world owed Rome a debt of gratitude for demonstrating the benefits of unity.[10] Others of the Fathers admired the Romans for their emphasis upon the virtues of discipline and obedience, for their stress upon the importance of law, for their ideals of stability and order, and for various features of their constitution designed to provide effective curbs upon power without opening the floodgates of anarchy.

But there were numerous incidents of Rome's development which the Fathers regarded as grim warnings to later republics. The very bigness of the Roman empire impressed Madison as an omen of

Jefferson believed that "the mobs of great cities add just so much to the support of pure government as sores do to the strength of the human body." The section of New York depicted here, and known as "Bandits' Roost," would have confirmed his opinion. Photograph by Jacob A. Riis. *Jacob A. Riis Collection, Museum of the City of New York*

disaster, for, in his judgment, all overgrown states "must fall to pieces." [11] Hamilton found cause for alarm in the demagoguery that afflicted the Roman states. Every republic at all times, he feared, would have its Catilines and its Caesars. Men of this brand are really scoffers at the principles of liberty, and are arbitrary, persecuting, and intolerant. Moreover, they are extravagant, mercenary, dissipated, corrupt, and interested in no cause but their own and that of their party. Yet in their harangues they profess themselves the most zealous friends of liberty, continually "making a parade of their purity and disinterestedness," and attempting to fasten upon others the guilt which they know belongs to themselves. In order to hide their own plots and conspiracies, they flatter the prejudices of the people in the hope of throwing affairs into confusion and bringing on civil commotion. According to Hamilton, liberals and radicals are more addicted to the demagogic arts than are conservatives. He thought it significant that Cato was the Tory and Caesar the Whig of their day. "The former frequently restricted; the latter always flattered the follies of the people." Yet Cato perished with the republic; Caesar destroyed it. [12]

Jefferson also considered demagoguery one of the besetting evils of ancient Rome, but he regarded Caesar as only the last in a long line of corrupters and destroyers. The Roman people, he contended, had not had good government "from the rape of the Sabines to the ravages of the Caesars." They were "steeped in corruption, vice, and venality," and even such leaders as Cato, Cicero, and Brutus had no idea of government "but their degenerate Senate." Jefferson saw no way in which the Romans could have saved their republic except through a drastic process of re-education. The people themselves would have had to be rescued from their demoralized and depraved condition by being instructed from the ground up as to what was right and what wrong. It was characteristic of Jefferson that he did not suggest turning to enlightened Tories to save the republic in time of crisis. He never lost confidence that the ultimate power of an educated citizenry is the surest reliance for good government. If the Roman people had been like the American, "enlightened, peaceable, and really free," the government could have found obvious solutions to its problems: Restore independence to all its foreign conquests, relieve Italy from the domination of the city mob, consult the people "as a nation entitled to self-government, and do its will." [13]

Emphasis upon the lessons of Rome continued through the nineteenth century, though the example of Greece was not ignored. An astonishing variety of alarms and portents was found in the history of both civilizations. Theodore Parker deplored their indifference to the higher law, "which results in the destiny of nations being left to political Jesuits—the end justifies the means." [14] Henry Thoreau maintained that "even music may be intoxicating," and that such apparently slight causes had destroyed Greece and Rome, and would ultimately destroy England and America.[15] Josiah Strong traced the downfall of the two great cultures to "moral failure," which he attributed in turn to the growth of cities. An agricultural life had instilled in the people temperate and virtuous habits, but the influx into the cities had made much more difficult the maintenance of moral standards. Strong obviously considered this an evil omen for modern nations.[16]

Equally pessimistic were those who were impressed only by the example of Rome. William Lloyd Garrison demanded to know what should save us from the fate of the Romans, a fate brought on by their vanity, licentiousness, intemperance, infidelity, and slavery.[17] William E. Channing avowed that all communities fall by the vices of the prosperous ranks, and cited the dissoluteness, brutality, and greed of the Roman patricians to prove his point. For decades they had "glutted Rome with the spoils of the pillaged world," fed the idle population of the city from the public treasures, and corrupted them by public shows.[18] In the opinion of John C. Calhoun, Rome fell because of the decay of patriotism. Large standing armies thus became necessary, and the citizens who were unwilling to render military service adequate to the defense of their rights soon found a master. Calhoun considered this a universal source of danger to free states.[19]

Economic causes of the decline of ancient empires appear to have been given comparatively slight recognition by most Americans. Jefferson Davis was distressed by the fact that hundreds of thousands of Roman citizens received a dole or subsidy from the state, which required no services in return. This destroyed their independence and left them craven and discontented.[20] For Brooks Adams the cardinal weakness of the Romans was their lack of economic versatility. They had neither the instinct of the Greeks for commerce nor that of the Hindus for manufactures. They were essentially landowners, until their acquisitive faculties made some of them usurers. At an early date Roman society divided into creditors and debtors. The former increased their pressure upon the latter and made their situation so hopeless that they lost interest in prolonging the struggle. Reproduction slackened, disintegration set in, and the state itself was gradually smothered in irreversible decay.[21] William Graham Sumner and Josiah Strong discovered the maldistribution of wealth to have been the principal cause of Rome's undoing. The former believed that, in some fashion, military duty and taxes were steadily making the rich richer and the poor poorer, and he denied that any society consisting of the two extreme classes could be in a sound and healthy condition.[22] Strong conceded that the splendor of Roman riches dazzled the world, but he argued that it was the wealth of only a corrupt and indolent few. He feared that our own "wonderful material prosperity" might hide "a decaying core."[23]

In view of the evidence of ancient history, it is a surprising fact that no man in a position of eminence in America referred to imperialism as a major cause of Rome's downfall. Perhaps most of them were deriving too much satisfaction from the expansionist activities of their own country and could not easily entertain the suggestion that it was heading for the abyss. They found it more comfortable to confine their thoughts to such superficial cankers as variety, vice, intemperance, race suicide, and the increasing inequality of wealth.

A possible exception to the foregoing practice was Elisha Mulford, a Protestant Episcopal clergyman of the mid-nineteenth century. Mulford lived the sequestered life of a scholar and was little known in his lifetime. A disciple of Hegel and Bluntschli, he deified the nation as an organism with a personality responding to ethical ideals. He described it as nothing less than God in history, working to a purposeful end. But there was one activity in which nations could engage only at their peril. That was imperialism. The decline of ancient Rome began at the moment when she ceased to be a nation and became an empire. The acquisition of an empire destroyed her public spirit. As she grew more and more unwieldy, her people became apathetic and fatalistic. Their state was so huge that they were obsessed with a feeling of bewilderment and incapacity. Since everything that happened appeared to be the result of remote, external factors, they lost all sense of responsibility for the evils weighing upon them. With the exclusion of the people from public affairs came the decay of public conscience and the disappearance of energy and effort for the reform of abuses. The government arrogated more and more power to itself, invading the sphere of private interest, destroying individuality, and regulating the affairs of the citizen so minutely as to deprive his life of nearly all significance.[24] No doubt Mulford was concerned primarily with the effects of imperialism in destroying the organic unity of a nation, since it would bring in hordes of unassimilable peoples: but the other points in his indictment were just as valid.

THE MAJOR PITFALLS AND PERILS

If the downfall of America ever happens in accordance with the predictions of her leaders, it will occur as a result of internal causes. Upon this, agreement has been practically unanimous. Not a single writer of distinction has assumed that the factor producing the final collapse will be Toynbee's "external proletariat." But with respect to conditions of internal causation the theories have been infinitely varied. Possibly the one most commonly emphasized has been the effects of luxury. This was a popular theme of the Founders of the republic. Hamilton proclaimed it a "universal maxim that luxury indicates the declension of a state."[25] Both Hamilton and Madison believed that as the country filled up with inhabitants, wealth would become concentrated in fewer hands. Commerce, also, would pile up riches for the few much more rapidly than agriculture, and would encourage opulent tastes and contempt for simplicity of manners. In Madison's judgment, the results would be wholly evil. The wretchedness and artificiality of cities, he said, produce, on the one hand, Bridewells and Bedlams and, on the other, "impertinent fops," who breed in densely populated places "as naturally as flies do in the shambles."[26] Hamilton agreed that the insolence, vicious luxury, and licentiousness of morals stemming from commerce and riches would "corrupt the government, enslave the people, and precipitate the ruin of a nation," but he had little enthusiasm for preventive measures. No statesman, he argued, would reject the immediate benefits of commerce and riches because of the fear of ultimate evil.[27] Curiously, Jefferson said almost nothing about the effects of luxury upon the health of the state. His thoughts can only be divined from his opposition to primogeniture and entails, his contempt for cities, and his advocacy of agrarianism, the minimized state, and an aristocracy of virtue and talent.

Numerous leaders of later years also condemned the growth of luxury. William Graham Sumner complained in the 1880's that "the thirst for luxurious enjoyment" had taken possession of us all. This craving he thought particularly dangerous when brought into connection with ideas of rights, power, and equality, and when dissociated from notions of industry and frugality. When connected in the manner described, it generates the idea that a man is deprived of justice if he does not get everything he wants, that he is denied equality if anyone has more than he has, and that he is a fool if, having the power in his hands, he allows this state of things to continue. "Then we have socialism, communism, and nihilism; and the fairest conquests of civilization . . . may be scattered to the winds in a war of classes, or trampled underfoot by a mob which can only hate what it cannot enjoy." [28]

Many of Sumner's contemporaries were just as pessimistic. Wendell Phillips maintained that the evil of debt was the fatal disease of republics, "the first thing and the mightiest to undermine government and corrupt the people." [29] It was the solemn conviction of Albert J. Beveridge that regardless of the strength of our army and navy or the extent of our natural resources, "if an unregulated extravagance corrupt individual or national character we are a lost people." Extravagance, he thundered, is immoral; it is a theft of the future, an evidence of dishonesty of character. Its effects he recounted as "loose habits of thinking instead of exactness and clean-mindedness; slippered slovenliness of conduct instead of booted, erect and ready action; resources wasting and desires increasing, with nothing to take the place of what we spend." [30] It seemed not to occur to him that the imperialist policies he advocated would contribute quite a little to some of these effects, especially the last.

The most voluble of all the Jeremiahs who pointed to the perils of luxury was Josiah Strong. From poverty to riches, from riches to luxury, and from luxury to enervation, corruption, and decay, he regarded as an almost inevitable cycle in the history of nations. For this reason, nations actually go down in their prime. They do not sink into a slow dissolution from the infirmities of age, but become soft and effeminate and, at the very peak of their cultural progress, an easy prey for barbarians. He alleged that this had been true of Spain, of ancient Israel, and even of Rome. But there was at least one aspect of this problem which he thought did admit of correction. This was the concentration of luxurious living as an advantage of the few. He deplored the growth of huge fortunes in the United States. It was easy, he contended, in 1885 to make up a list of one hundred persons averaging $25,000,000 each, in addition to ten averaging $100,000,000 each. Such persons were in a position to spend recklessly or to waste enough in a week to buy the necessaries of life for a dozen families for a year. Such inequalities could only breed discontent and ultimately sedition. But the only remedy Strong could suggest was to inculcate in the rich man an increasing power of self-control, a stronger sense of justice, and a more intelligent understanding of his obligations.[31]

The most recent of eminent Americans to deplore luxury as a danger to the republic seems to have been Justice Brandeis. Testifying before the Clapp Committee in 1911, he produced a newspaper clipping stating that Elbert H. Gary, chairman of the board of the United States Steel Corporation, had given his wife a $500,000 pearl necklace for Christmas. This to Brandeis was a crime against society. In view of the discontent prevailing throughout the country, it was almost an open invitation to class war. "Is it not," he inquired, "just the same sort of thing which brought on the French Revolution?"[32]

It is pertinent to add that not all distinguished Americans have agreed with the thesis that where wealth accumulates, men and nations decay. It was rejected implicitly by Abraham Lincoln when he affirmed that it is best to leave each man free to acquire property as fast as he can and opposed limitations on the amount acquired. It was rejected also by Simon Patten when he scorned the ideals of the age of privation and called for a frank acceptance and a positive enjoyment of the age of plenty.[33] It was repudiated even more explicitly by Theodore Parker. Though he referred to the "peril of exclusive devotion to riches," he refused to take it seriously. One of the great needs of mankind, he averred, has always been "power over the material world as the basis for the higher development of our spiritual faculties." Wealth is indispensable, he insisted. "No nation was ever too rich. . . . The human race still suffers from poverty, the great obstacle to our progress."[34]

Interior of a New York tenement in 1910. From James Madison to our own day, extreme poverty has been recognized as a cause of the downfall of nations. Photographer: probably Jessie Tarbox Beals. *Jacob A. Riis Collection, Museum of the City of New York*

Related to the idea of waste and extravagance in general has been the doctrine that prodigality in the use of natural resources is a major cause of the downfall of nations. Interestingly enough, one of the first Americans to bring this doctrine to the fore was Henry Thoreau. The great civilized nations of history, he wrote, survived as long as the fertility of their soil was not depleted. But "little is to be expected of a nation," he added, "when the vegetable mould is exhausted, and it is compelled to make manure of the bones of its fathers." [35]

A similar conception was advanced by Henry C. Carey, who found the theory of soil exhaustion neatly adapted to his gospel of economic nationalism. Civilization grows, he taught, in proportion to the ability of a country to reduce its dependence for income upon the exportation of the raw products of plantations and farms. It must learn to refine and fabricate these products and return their

A popular theory of today traces the decline of nations to exhaustion of soil and other vital resources. Wasteful lumbering methods cause not only destruction of forests but flooding of lowlands and washing of valuable top soil down to the sea. *U. S. Forest Service*

refuse to the soil—"thus augmenting the productive power of the land, and enabling more and more people to live together." A persistent failure to do this is the surest way to promote the encroachment of barbarism. The existing system in America, Carey wrote in 1858, pointed to almost certain disaster. More and more land was being planted in wheat, cotton, and tobacco for sale in foreign markets. The result was a waste of capital, a virtual selling of the soil for an immediate cash income. Exhaustion of old lands brought an insatiable hunger for new. Thus Louisiana was acquired, then Florida, and finally Texas, New Mexico, Arizona, and California. Soon it would be necessary to increase the size of the army and to build a big navy, with a view to new and more difficult conquests in the future. The combined effects of soil exhaustion, militarism, and the increase of nonproductive speculators and middlemen to

Efficient lumbering methods call for logging by patches, which are then replanted or allowed to reseed before the intervening areas are cut. *U. S. Forest Service*

handle the growing volume of foreign trade would soon put this country on the broad path that leads *away* from civilization instead of toward it. If the present trend continues, he shouted, "the hour is surely fixed when America, Greece, and Rome will stand together among the ruins of the past." [36]

Warnings of disaster from the waste of natural resources have continued down to the present. Soon after the turn of the century, sociologists like Edward A. Ross were ringing the changes on the fact that the free land of America was gone, and that henceforth the fate of the nation would be that of European countries. Although Theodore Roosevelt gained a reputation while President as the outstanding apostle of conservation, he seems actually to have been perturbed more deeply by the alleged evils of un-Americanism, race suicide, and class conflict. He did say, however, that if in a given community unlimited rule of the masses resulted in waste and destruction of natural resources, it was a sure sign that that community was not fit for self-government.[37]

A more articulate spokesman on the subject was Henry Wallace. During the era of the Dust Bowl and after, Wallace cautioned that soil decadence, then spreading over a large portion of the earth's surface, is inevitably followed by social and political decadence. Conservation, he argued, is the key to continued progress in democracy and high standards of living. Rich soil and plenty of it was the main factor which made this nation different from all others. "Freeholders in a wide land of fabulous fertility, guarded by great oceans from foreign invasion, could erect separate strongholds of individual enterprise, free speech, and free conscience." It is not too much to say, he maintained, that liberty and equality were "a natural outgrowth of our great gift of soil." Now a large portion of this magnificent gift has been blown away or washed into the sea. Nothing short of intelligent and extensive planning will save the rest. America should learn some lessons from the example of Sweden, where regulatory laws prevent wasteful exploitation of the nation's heritage. Swedish forest laws require that lumber companies replace the timber cut from a given area with new stock. Mining interests are obligated to consider the permanent good of persons employed in their industries by establishing welfare funds to provide for workers and their families who would otherwise be left destitute by the exhaustion of the mines in a particular locality. The United States, Wallace contended, was far behind Sweden in these respects, and must seriously consider emulating her example or go into a swift and irreversible decline.[38]

A third of the deadly perils confronting republics, according to distinguished commentators, is disunity, especially in the form of conflict between economic classes. Again this was a factor heavily emphasized by the Founding Fathers. It underlay their opposition to parties and factions and was a prime motivation of their concern for stability. Gouverneur Morris warned in the Constitutional Convention that the time was not distant when the country would abound with mechanics and laborers who would receive their bread from their employers. Such men would be perpetually discontented. If given the suffrage, they would sell their votes to the rich and thereby contribute to the growth of an aristocracy. Madison expressed similar fears. In future years, he asserted, the majority of the people would be without land or any other form of property. They would then either combine under the influence of their common wretchedness and attack the interests of property; or, more probably, they would "become the tools of opulence and ambition" and rally around the standard of some wealthy tyrant. In either case, the turbulence and danger surrounding such activities would provide poor nourishment for a republic.[39] Factions, divisions, internal dissensions, he told the Virginia ratifying convention, have demolished civil liberty more frequently "than a tenacious disposition in rulers to retain any stipulated powers."[40]

The perils of disunity and instability also alarmed some recent minds. As early as 1893 Theodore Roosevelt was referring to "the anarchic violence of the thriftless and turbulent poor." In his fifth annual message as President, he avowed that the most direful influence sapping the foundations of republics had ever been the growth of the class spirit, "the growth of the spirit which tends to make a man subordinate the welfare of the republic as a whole to the welfare of the particular class to which he belongs." Though he insisted that both reactionaries and revolutionaries are a menace, the former to order and the latter to liberty, he generally seemed more concerned with berating "revolutionaries" than with reproving "reactionaries." He deplored the domineering of unscrupulous rich men, but he condemned "the Debs type of socialist" for pointing the way to national ruin "as surely as any swindling financier or corrupt politician." During the Pullman strike he wrote to his friend Brander Matthews that he liked "to see a mob handled by the regulars, or by good State-Guards, not over-scrupulous about bloodshed."[41] His real attitude, as explained by Richard Hofstadter, probably reflected a desire to maintain the authority of the state over all elements. As a member of the governing class, Roosevelt conceived of himself as representing that authority and as vested with an obligation to maintain it unimpaired.[42]

Still another kind of dangerous internal conflict has been recognized by leading Americans, perhaps all too seldom. This is racial and religious conflict. It, too, received some attention from Theodore Roosevelt. He predicted that if we come to look upon one another "not as brothers but as enemies divided by the hatred of creed for creed or of those of one race against those of another race," our great democratic experiment on this continent will crash in ruins. Most of the time, however, he seemed to advocate a kind of enforced uniformity to compel immigrant nationalities to abandon their old loyalties and dedicate themselves with unswerving devotion to becoming "good Americans." [43]

At least one of his successors in the White House gave wiser counsels. To Franklin Roosevelt it was self-evident that no democracy could long survive which did not accept "as fundamental to its very existence the recognition of the rights of its minorities." He flayed doctrines that set groups against groups, creed against creed, race against race, class against class, "fanning the fires of hatred in men too despondent, too desperate to think for themselves." Such doctrines were used as "rabble-rousing slogans" by Hitler in destroying the German republic. But the danger was also one, according to Roosevelt, which America could not safely ignore. He denounced selfish and partisan groups in this country that wrapped themselves "in a false mantle of Americanism" for their own advantage, "trying to weaken us by setting our own people to fighting among themselves." [44]

In modern nations, especially, racial and religious conflict and intolerance of minorities have often been used to conceal exploitation or to make it more palatable. Obscure and insignificant folk in Nazi Germany were encouraged to despise and persecute the Jews as a means of building up illusions of superiority in persons who had no genuine basis for such feelings. It was hoped that thereby they would forget their own humble status and poor economic condition. According to some Americans, the same danger also exists in the United States. Theodore Parker maintained that nations come to an end because of their injustice. There are rights which nations must keep, "or they shall suffer wrongs." There is a God "who hurls to earth the loftiest realm that breaks His just, eternal law . . . justice is the unchanging, everlasting will to give to each man his right." [45]

The noted apostle of the single tax, Henry George, deprecated what he thought was a trend toward rapidly increasing economic exploitation in this country. The rich, he believed, were growing much richer, the poor more helpless and hopeless, and the middle class more nonexistent. Such conditions, he contended, had destroyed every previous civilization in history. Increasing political democracy would have saved none of them; for "where there is gross inequality in the distribution of wealth, the more democratic the government, the worse it will be." To give votes to tramps, to paupers, to men who must beg, steal, or starve, is to invite destruction.[16] It seemed to be his thought that such men would regard their votes as of little value and would quickly sell them to the highest bidder. Gouverneur Morris had drawn the same conclusion a hundred years earlier, but with a different motivation.

Contemporary writers and statesmen have also been vocal on the subject of class exploitation. During the 1930's Henry Wallace wrote that an enduring democracy can be maintained only by promoting a balance among major economic groups in such a way as not to build up "a small, inordinately wealthy class." A chief weakness in democracies, he thought, is their tendency to succumb to pressures from either the extreme left or the extreme right. The same legislators may allow themselves to be stampeded toward reaction by frightened capitalists, or less frequently in the opposite direction by scared workers. Objectives of social welfare may be completely forgotten under the influence of pressures of the moment.[17] In his celebrated Commonwealth Club speech in 1932, Franklin D. Roosevelt sounded the keynote of an important aspect of the New Deal when he complained that the economic life of the United States was dominated by about six hundred corporations, controlling two thirds of American industry. Ten million small businessmen divided the remaining third. He warned that if the process of concentration continued at the same rate, by the end of the century American industry would be controlled entirely by a dozen corporations, run by perhaps a hundred men. He feared that we were steering a steady course toward economic oligarchy, if indeed we were not already there.

Exclusive of the philippics of socialism, the sharpest criticisms of economic inequality and exploitation were contained in the speeches of Robert M. LaFollette. The Wisconsin Progressive went so far as to say that only one great issue had ever confronted the nations of the world. That was the issue between those who labor and those who attempt to control labor "through slavery in one form or another." All the great nations of the past, he declared, went down in ruin because they attempted to make slaves of the masses of men. When a powerful privileged class attempts to benefit itself at the expense of the masses of the people, it ultimately brings down upon itself the justice of God Almighty. He feared that America was already on the road that other nations had traveled. Monopolists and profiteers, taking advantage of opportunities created by World War I, had produced an inequality of wealth without parallel in the history of the world. If the poorest of our people were not yet as wretched as the starving paupers of other countries, this was only because of the much greater abundance of America's resources. Profiteers and exploiters had discovered long ago that the road to unlimited pelf and power lies through control of the government. They learned that a man may work all his life with his hands or his brain and have little more at the end than he had at the beginning. But they found that by using the government to create privileges, wealth in excess of their fondest dreams could be amassed in a few years. For this reason they have been zealous to gain control of the national conventions of both parties, the Presidency, Congress, and especially of the Supreme Court.[48] LaFollette could envisage no remedy except to abolish monopoly and privilege and restore government to the control of the people.

Closely allied with exploitation through special privileges is political corruption, though not so universally recognized as a cause of the decline of nations. The Fathers generally thought of it as a consequence of other evils, which in themselves would be sufficient causes of destruction. But as early as 1836 John C. Calhoun affirmed that "a state of boundless corruption" is the one condition from which there can be no recovery. He thought it a demonstrable lesson of history that almost any great evil—piracy, robbery, violence of every description—may be followed by virtue, patriotism, and national greatness. But where, he demanded, is the example of "a degenerate, corrupt, and subservient people" who have ever escaped destruction?[49] In his third annual message, Theodore Roosevelt declared that democratic government will perish from the face of the earth "if bribery is tolerated." Seven years later as temporary chairman of the New York Republican State Convention he pronounced corruption in every form as "the arch-enemy of this Republic, an even more dangerous enemy than the open lawlessness of violence, because it works in hidden or furtive fashion." There can be no doubt that he meant this, for with his high opinion of public authority he regarded anything that weakened the power of the state as the equivalent of treason.

Senator LaFollette's attitude was no less uncompromising. During the first revelations of scandals following World War I, he described "corruption from within" as "the gravest danger menacing the life of the American Democracy." The responsibility for corruption he laid almost exclusively at the door of the big corporations. The evil, he said, dates from the time that corporations began to take charge of the development of the country. The great railroads and mining and manufacturing companies soon learned that it was to their interest to bring business and government into close contact. They sent their agents to the national and state capitals to organize powerful lobbies and to tempt the representatives of the people with bribes and favors. Soon they began buying seats in the legislatures and judicial positions. In return they obtained protective tariffs, invaluable franchises, and grants of land, to say nothing of court decisions that made almost every governmental restriction a deprivation of property without due process.[50] For LaFollette it was again the old problem of curbing the monopolies by law and strengthening the rule of the people by direct democracy and stringent limitations on the power of the bosses.

Some formulators of opinion in America have looked with grave apprehension upon the growth of population and its concentration in cities. We have already noted the Malthusianism of some of the Fathers, especially Madison. Jefferson had similar views. "When we get piled upon one another in cities, as in Europe," he wrote, "we shall become corrupt as in Europe, and go to eating one another as they do there."[51] But the most relentless of American Malthusians was the dour sociologist from Yale, William Graham Sumner. To Sumner the laws of population growth worked out by the famous English rector were a virtual Apostles' Creed. "When men are too numerous for the means of subsistence," he pontificated, "the struggle for existence is fierce." Every crime that has ever stained the pages of history then becomes possible, for the simple reason that a man whose whole soul is absorbed in a struggle to get enough to eat will give up his manners, his morals, his education, and will stoop to any hideous deed that may be necessary simply to maintain existence. With a whole society thus forced to compete for a livelihood, the bonds of civilization are quickly loosened. Selfishness triumphs; superstitions flourish; vices otherwise inconceivable become prevalent; education and the arts and sciences slowly but steadily perish.[52] From so dismal a fate Sumner suggested no way of escape, other than an implicit endorsement of the prudential restraints recommended by Malthus.

That some Americans would vigorously repudiate a Malthusian interpretation of the nation's prospects goes almost without saying. Henry George and Henry C. Carey turned fiercely on the doctrine that the growth of population brings nothing but misery. Can it be, the latter demanded, that the Creator has been inconsistent with himself? How explain the command to be fruitful and multiply and replenish the earth if the inevitable consequence is to be the descent of men into a sordid struggle for existence, fighting like animals over morsels of food? Carey's alternative, we have seen, was mutual dependence, with multitudes living together supplying each other's wants.

The optimistic Josiah Strong also rejected the gloomy defeatism of Malthus. Though he recognized the dangers of urban congestion and deplored the replenishment of populations by the "ignorant and degraded" classes, he did not consider the outlook hopeless. The way to obviate the evil, he said, is "to elevate the lower classes." The higher classes themselves should assume the obligation, "in self defense," of raising the level of the lower. This, he contended, would provide the really effective antidote to the Malthusian law. "Elevate the masses, and the rate of increase of the race will be correspondingly reduced." [53]

The most rabid, and at the same time the least critical, anti-Malthusian in America was undoubtedly Theodore Roosevelt. Though he also considered overcrowding in cities a dangerous symptom, he by no means opposed a rapidly increasing population. On the contrary, he was a vociferous enemy of what he called "race suicide." In season and out he clamored for larger families *among all classes.* "The race cannot go ahead," he insisted, "unless the average man and woman who are married and who are capable of having children have a family of four children." Upon such people rests the whole future of the nation and of civilization itself. "If a race does not have plenty of children," he said in a later connection, "or if the children do not grow up, or if when they grow up they are unhealthy in body and stunted or vicious in mind, then that race is decadent," and no quantity of wealth or splendor of material prosperity can make much difference. [54] He did not seem to take account of the fact that without a substantial material prosperity for the

Great wealth and display of luxury have been regarded by many leading Americans as a menace to the existence of the republic. William K. Vanderbilt's marble "cottage" at Newport, R. I., was built in 1892 at a cost of $9,000,000. *Preservation Society of Newport County*

families concerned, a numerous progeny would be very likely indeed to grow up "unhealthy in body and stunted or vicious in mind."

A sizable number of thoughtful Americans castigated imperialism as a major threat to the civilization of the United States. Notice has already been taken of the objections of John C. Calhoun and Albert Gallatin to the expansionism growing out of the Mexican War, and of Edwin L. Godkin and William James to the lust for empire incident to the War with Spain. Others saw in imperialism of any description a danger to the continued existence of the American republic. William H. Seward warned about 1850 that ambition for martial fame and the lust of conquest had entered the warm, youthful heart of the nation. The whole continent and its islands seemed ready to fall within our grasp, and fabulous wealth would flow through the country like a mighty river. But no public virtue could withstand "such seductions as these." [55] At the end of the century William Graham Sumner complained bitterly that imperialism meant giving the lie to the origin of our own national existence and throwing the Constitution into the gutter. We could not deny the protection of the Constitution to subjects in conquered territories, he alleged, without ultimately denying it to our citizens at home. Expansion by conquest, therefore, would be a deadly blow to democracy.[56]

An even broader and more forceful criticism of imperialism emanated from Carl Schurz. A nation cannot "play the King over subject populations," he insisted, "without creating in itself ways of thinking and habits of action most dangerous to its own vitality." America could not permanently govern by arbitrary power millions of people with the status of subject populations "without doing ruthless violence to the spirit of our Constitution and to all the fundamental principles of democratic government." Such a repudiation of democracy would germinate conditions of demoralization and corruption surpassing any the country "has ever seen, even in the palmiest days of the carpet-bag governments in the South after our civil war." Moreover, expansion into other continents would lead to involvement in the quarrels and jealousies of Old World nations. We should soon be in the position of the Great Powers of Europe that have lost the ability to determine their own foreign policies. We should be forced to watch nervously reports from abroad telling us that this nation is increasing the number of its battleships, or that another is enlarging its army or multiplying its garrisons in far-away places; and we should have to follow suit. Not our own wishes but the actions of our rivals would determine how much money we should spend and how high our taxes should be. And thus our great and glorious republic, which once prided itself upon marching in the vanguard of progressive civilization, would deliberately go to the rear and take its place among the strongholds of reaction and enemies of liberty.

Schurz was particularly dismayed by that pathological phenomenon under which northern nations were so frequently obsessed by romantic longing for the south. One country after another had frittered away golden opportunities for domestic development in pursuing the mare's nest of tropical or subtropical empire. America, he feared in 1898, was about to succumb to the same foolish enterprise.

She, too, was in danger of throwing away a glorious destiny in a region "where the very sun hatches out the serpents' eggs" of enmity to republican institutions.[57]

The most imposing theories of decline ever developed in America were those of the two philosophical pessimists of the House of Adams. The older brother, Henry Adams, worked out his philosophy of history in the early 1900's. He began with the premise that the essential ingredient of civilization is energy. Every human activity, every human achievement, whether physical, emotional, or intellectual, requires an expenditure of energy. On the basis of types of energy or power available, Adams divided the history of the world into four periods. From the beginning to about A.D. 1600 was the period of human power, when little but clubs, spears, fire, and a few domesticated animals supplemented the power of human muscle. From 1600 to about 1900 was the age of mechanical power when the laws of Galileo and Newton made possible the development of the water wheel, the steam engine, and the machines to utilize their power. The period of mechanical power gave way about 1900 to the age of electricity, based upon the invention of the dynamo. The age of electricity would be followed about 1918 by the age of ethereal power, made possible by the discovery of radium. But every expenditure of energy resulted in a diminution of the total quantity available in accordance with the law of entropy, or the second law of thermodynamics. Adams therefore concluded that the world would run down in a few more decades. He estimated that by 1932, at the latest, the industrial civilizations of Europe and America would have lost their momentum and would be hurtling rapidly down the road toward impotence and extinction. He saw evidence of this in falling birth rates, decline of the rural population, growth in alcoholism and drug addiction, and increase in nervous exhaustion, suicides, and insanity. He found solace in his old age in dreaming of the twelfth century, when unity and simplicity reigned under the influence of the cult of the Virgin. The worship of Our Lady symbolized to Adams the triumph of humanism and charity over the stern realities of the laws of nature. Her womanly sympathy and understanding made life livable in a capricious and unintelligible world.[58]

Brooks Adams developed a philosophy of history related in only moderate degree to that of his brother. He utilized the same principle of dissipation of energy but in a much more limited way. Instead of a single Western civilization divided into periods in accordance with the particular form of power available, he recognized a number of civilizations, in different areas of the world, each undergoing development through two successive stages. The exhaustion of the particular type of energy characteristic of each stage results in its termination. According to Adams, the initial stage in the evolution of every civilization is a stage of decentralization. The ruling classes in this period are warriors and priests, and the keynote in terms of the energy employed is *fear*. Fear generates superstitions, and this is the stage when religions multiply, with elaborate ceremonies, dogmas, and creeds. But fear also stimulates the imagination, and consequently the arts receive encouragement and generally flourish. Artist, priest, and warrior—cathedral, shrine, and castle —these were the emblems par excellence of the medieval period, the golden age of decentralization.

The point is eventually reached, however, when the fear emanating from warriors and priests loses its magic. The status of the warriors declines as the attack in war masters the defense, and the combative instinct becomes less necessary for the preservation of life. Meanwhile, increasing materialism germinates skepticism, which rapidly corrodes the myths of the priests. Decentralization soon gives way to a stage of consolidation or centralization. The dominant note of the new stage is *greed*, and its rulers are a class of financiers, speculators, and industrial and commercial capitalists whom Adams called the *usurers*. Everything is now subordinated to the economic motive. All individuals are made equal before the law, and are forced to compete with each other for the means of subsistence. Birth rates decline, luxury increases, and crime becomes rampant. But eventually under the stress of intense competition, even the power of greed loses its force. The exhausted nation sinks into inertia "until supplied with fresh energetic material by the infusion of barbarian blood." [59]

The younger Adams conceived of a world in which the centers of civilization were constantly shifting in accordance with the growth and decay of industry and commerce. The Roman Empire declined when "adverse exchanges carried the bullion of Italy to the shores of the Bosphorus." Byzantium fell as the Italian cities rose, and they in their turn withered when Portugal established direct communication with India. The opening of the ocean as a highroad to the New World established the supremacy of Spain and the Netherlands and prepared the way for the Industrial Revolution. The latter centralized the world at London, but only for a time. Thus "empires rise and fall, philosophies are born and die, art and poetry bloom and fade, as societies pass from the disintegration wherein the imagination kindles, to the consolidation whose pressure ends in death." Since 1870, Adams maintained, consolidation has been the order of the universe. As competition quickens, men consolidate in larger and denser masses, for the simple reason that the administration of the largest mass is the cheapest. Just as the working of this law has produced trusts and other gigantic accumulations of capital, so it has produced political agglomerations such as Germany, the British Empire, and the United States. Writing in the years 1900 to 1902, Adams foresaw the decline of Britain and France and the rise of Germany, Russia, the United States, and Japan. He envisaged a coming struggle for supremacy in which America would line up with Britain against some combination of the others. At the end of the first stage of the struggle two great competing systems would be left pitted against each other. America, because of her vast resources, would be one of them. Germany or Russia would be the other. He assumed that in the final stage, the garlands of victory would go to America—but not for long. Nations will exhaust their energy in the future as they have done in the past, and centers of commerce and industry will continue to shift, carrying civilization with them. Perhaps the seeds of empire and culture are already being planted on the shores of Asia.[60]

It is often said in our day that Americans as a nation are rushing as heedlessly as Gadarene swine toward certain destruction. If this is true, it is not because of lack of warnings. Probably no people in history has ever been so freely admonished that pride goeth before a fall, that corruption and licentiousness degrade a nation, that class conflict destroys free government, and that lust for wealth and power corrodes the national soul.

Perhaps too much stress has been laid, however, upon the consequences of moral failure. Possibly our leaders would have done better to direct our attention more to China, India, and Egypt and not so much to ancient Rome. Perhaps licentiousness, corruption,

With the depletion of oil resources beneath the land area, many producers are turning to drilling operations in the off-shore regions of the Gulf of Mexico and the Pacific Ocean. Shown here is seismographic testing for oil in the Gulf of Mexico. *Texas Company*

greed, crime, and other social pathologies are not the real causes of decay but are merely surface manifestations of something that lies deeper. Such was the conception advanced by a few of our prophets of impending trouble, notably Henry C. Carey and Henry Wallace. It has been brought out much more forcefully, however, by contemporary conservationists and Neo-Malthusians like William Vogt, Fairfield Osborn, and Karl Sax. They deplore what Aldo Leopold calls the Abrahamic conception of land as something given to man to be exploited. They deplore even more the destruction of forests, the reckless plowing up of lands unfit for cultivation, and the spawning of human offspring in such numbers as to produce a threat of "standing room only." They foresee, on the one hand, vast areas turned into desert as happened to Mesopotamia and North Africa, and, on the other, great empires like India and China, swarming with such multitudes of people that everyone is reduced to a miserable subsistence. They consider one or both of these fates as the major pitfall of nations, America not excluded.

NOTES TO CHAPTER ELEVEN

1. C. F. Adams, ed., *Memoirs of John Quincy Adams* (Philadelphia: J. B. Lippincott Co., 1874), VIII, 360.
2. Richard K. Cralle, ed., *The Works of John C. Calhoun* (New York: D. Appleton and Co., 1856), VI, 192.
3. *Writings*, Centenary ed. (Boston: American Unitarian Assoc., 1907-16), V, 251.
4. *Whither Mankind* (New York: Blue Ribbon Books, 1928), pp. 16-20; *The Republic* (New York: The Viking Press, 1943), pp. 340-42.
5. Max Farrand, ed., *Records of the Federal Convention* (New Haven: Yale University Press, 1911), I, 343.
6. J. C. Hamilton, ed., *The Works of Alexander Hamilton* (New York: J. F. Trow, 1850-51), I, 153; II, 188.
7. *Ibid.*, II, 188; Jonathan Elliot, ed., *The Debates in the Several State Conventions on the Adoption of the Federal Constitution* (Washington: Printed by and for the editor, 1863), IV, 59.
8. *The Federalist*, Modern Library ed. (New York: Random House, n.d.), No. 34.
9. Farrand, ed., *Records*, II, 490.
10. Elliot, ed., *Debates*, II, 185.
11. *Letters and Other Writings of James Madison*, Published by Order of Congress (Philadelphia: J. B. Lippincott Co., 1865), III, 239.
12. J. C. Hamilton, ed., *Works*, VI, 637-38.
13. Albert E. Bergh, ed., *The Writings of Thomas Jefferson* (Washington: Thomas Jefferson Memorial Assoc., 1907), IV, 233-35.
14. *Writings*, Centenary ed., XII, 361.

15. *The Writings of Henry David Thoreau* (Boston: Houghton Mifflin Co., 1906), II, 240.
16. *The Twentieth Century City* (New York: The Baker and Taylor Co., 1898), pp. 71-73.
17. *Selections from the Writings and Speeches of William Lloyd Garrison* (Boston: R. F. Wallcut, 1852), p. 48.
18. *The Works of William E. Channing* (Boston: American Unitarian Assoc., 1877), p. 169.
19. Cralle, ed., *Works,* II, 146-47.
20. *Rise and Fall of the Confederate Government* (New York: D. Appleton and Co., 1881), I, 504.
21. *The Law of Civilization and Decay* (New York: The Macmillan Co., 1895), p. 62.
22. Albert G. Keller, ed., *The Challenge of Facts and Other Essays* (New Haven: Yale University Press, 1914), pp. 69, 71.
23. *Our Country* (New York: The Baker and Taylor Co., 1885), p. 173.
24. *The Nation* (Boston: Houghton Mifflin Co., 1890), pp. 346-51.
25. J. C. Hamilton, ed., *Works,* II, 14.
26. Gaillard Hunt, ed., *The Writings of James Madison* (New York: G. P. Putnam's Sons, 1900), I, 11, 12; VI, 97-99.
27. J. C. Hamilton, ed., *Works,* I, 237.
28. Albert G. Keller, ed., *War and Other Essays* (New Haven: Yale University Press, 1913), pp. 190-91.
29. *Speeches, Lectures, and Letters,* First Series (Boston: Lothrop, Lee and Shepard Co., 1891), p. 421.
30. *Work and Habits* (Philadelphia: Henry Altemus Co., 1908), pp. 91-92.
31. *Our Country,* pp. 120, 173-74.
32. A. T. Mason, *Brandeis: A Free Man's Life* (New York: The Viking Press, 1946), p. 361.
33. See above, p. 56.
34. *Writings,* Centenary ed., XII, 353-54.
35. *Writings,* V, 229.
36. *Letters to the President on the Foreign and Domestic Policy of the Union, and Its Effects* (Philadelphia: M. Polock, 1858), pp. 49, 55, 150, 157.
37. E. E. Morison, ed., *The Works of Theodore Roosevelt* (New York: Charles Scribner's Sons, 1925), IV, 228-29.
38. *The American Choice* (New York: Reynal and Hitchcock, 1940), p. 54; *Whose Constitution? An Inquiry into the General Welfare* (New York: Reynal and Hitchcock, 1936), pp. 106-07, 114. (Quoted by permission of Harcourt, Brace and Company.)
39. Farrand, ed., *Records,* II, 202.
40. Elliot, ed., *Debates,* III, 90.
41. Morison, ed., *Works,* XVII, 335; XXI, 383.
42. *The American Political Tradition and the Men Who Made It* (New York: Alfred A. Knopf, 1948), p. 215.
43. Morison, ed., *Works,* XX, 457, 471.
44. Samuel I. Rosenman, compiler, *The Public Papers and Addresses of Franklin D. Roosevelt* (New York: Random House, 1938-50), IX, 9.
45. *Writings,* Centenary ed., XII, 128-30.
46. *Progress and Poverty,* Modern Library ed. (New York: Random House, n.d.), pp. 528, 530-32.

47. *New Frontiers* (New York: Reynal and Hitchcock, 1934), p. 21.
48. *Congressional Record,* 66th Cong., 1st Session, LVIII, 4755 (1919); 66th Cong., 2nd Session, LIX, 527 (1919); 67th Cong., 2nd Session, LXII, 1770 (1922).
49. Cralle, ed., *Works,* II, 569.
50. *Congressional Record,* 64th Cong., 1st Session, LIII, 1673 (1916); 67th Cong., 2nd Session, LXII, 13549 (1922).
51. Saul K. Padover, ed., *The Complete Jefferson* (New York: Duell, Sloan and Pearce, 1943), p. 123.
52. Keller, ed., *The Challenge of Facts,* pp. 12-21.
53. *The New Era or the Coming Kingdom* (New York: The Baker and Taylor Co., 1893), pp. 36, 187.
54. Morison, ed., *Works,* XIV, 159; XVII, 265-66.
55. George E. Baker, ed., *The Works of William H. Seward* (New York: Redfield, 1853-54), III, 23-24.
56. Keller, ed., *War and Other Essays,* pp. 314-15.
57. Frederic Bancroft, ed., *Speeches, Correspondence and Political Papers of Carl Schurz* (New York. G. P. Putnam's Sons, 1913), II, 115, 117-18; V, 487; VI, 10-11, 22-23.
58. *The Education of Henry Adams* (Boston: Houghton Mifflin Co., 1930), pp. 493-97; *The Degradation of the Democratic Dogma* (New York: The Macmillan Co., 1919), pp. 155-56, 186-87.
59. *The Law of Civilization and Decay,* pp. 61, 335, 338-39.
60. *Ibid.,* pp. 285-86; *America's Economic Supremacy* (New York: Harper and Brothers, 1947), pp. 80-81, 84-85, 99-100; *The New Empire* (New York: The Macmillan Co., 1902), pp. 207-08.

Chapter Twelve

The America of the Future

It has seemed to the majority of apostles of the mission of America that they should not only affirm their faith in the ideal but also recommend some means of giving it reality. Quite a few have gone beyond this and drafted plans or produced models of a structure of society designed to bring justice and liberty to all and thereby to fulfill the national destiny. Some of these dreamers have turned for inspiration to European thinkers; others have constructed their plans almost entirely from materials peculiar to the American environment. But whatever their source, the schemes developed have been as numerous and as fruitful as those produced by any other people.

Perhaps the most conspicuous fact that emerges from any consideration of views of the future America is the small part that Marxian or revolutionary socialism has played in them. On the whole, Americans have remained fundamentally capitalistic. They have agreed with Henry Wallace in visualizing an America wherein all can become members of the middle class, with even the humblest worker enjoying the bourgeois benefits of central heating, modern plumbing, electric refrigeration, vacation trips, and a college education for his children. To be sure, there have been exceptions. James Russell Lowell wrote, in 1884: "Communism means barbarism, but Socialism means . . . the practical application of Christianity to life, and has in it the secret of an orderly and benign reconstruction." [1] Some thirty years later the sociologist Edward A. Ross aplauded socialism as "simply the later phase of the world-wide drift toward democracy." [2] At the end of World War I, Robert M. LaFollette announced that he was willing to give individual initiative "its fair chance." If that failed, he would then go after government ownership of all "basic essentials." In the meantime, he would not hesitate about government control and ownership of all transportation and all lines of communication.[3]

The noted American who made the closest approach to orthodox Marxism was probably Thorstein Veblen. The great image-breaker wrote at times as if he believed that communism, of a pattern similar to the Russian model, held the golden key to the solution of all economic problems. He thought that, with the abolition of private property, the characteristic of human nature which now finds vent in keeping up with the Joneses would be turned into nobler and more socially profitable activities. In his *Engineers and the Price System*, he recommended a Soviet of Technicians to take over the economic affairs of the country and operate them in such a way as "effectually to take care of the material welfare of the underlying population." Guided by consultation with representatives of the main subdivisions of industry, transportation, and distribution, the Soviet would be able to eliminate virtually all unemployment of men and machines, on the one hand, and all local or seasonal scarcity on the other.[4]

But Veblen was not quite consistent in his attitude toward socialism. He scoffed at some of Marx's favorite dogmas, particularly those pertaining to the class struggle. Denying that class antagonisms are becoming increasingly simplified, he pointed to the fact that big capitalism had not invaded the agricultural field or ground the small businessman down into the ranks of the proletariat in anything like the degree expected by the Marxists. He doubted also that advance toward socialism through victory of the workers against their employers was in any sense inevitable. He thought it just as probable that the workers would continue to be hoodwinked into believing in the equity and excellence of the established system. Besides, the engineers and industrial experts, who alone had the ability to establish a Soviet of Technicians, were "a harmless and docile sort, well fed on the whole, and somewhat placidly content with the 'full dinner-pail' which the lieutenants of the Vested Interests habitually allow them." For these reasons he concluded that an organized attack on the existing system was improbable. Possibly he was just as well satisfied, for it would appear that his real

An urgent problem of the immediate future is accommodating the volume of traffic on the nation's highways. More and more states are constructing turnpikes or thruways. Shown above is the New Jersey Turnpike as it passes under the Pulaski Skyway and over the Passaic and Hackensack rivers. *N. J. Turnpike Authority*

interest lay in industrial efficiency and full employment rather than in a dictatorship of the proletariat leading eventually to a classless society.[5]

DREAMERS OF DREAMS AND SEERS OF VISIONS

In 1936 Franklin D. Roosevelt told the members of the Young Democratic Club of Baltimore that they ought to thank God if any of them were young enough in spirit "to dream dreams and see visions—dreams and visions about a greater and finer America that is to be." Dreaming dreams and seeing visions has always been characteristic of Americans, regardless of age. To countless thousands America itself has been a dream—of equality, justice, freedom, and plenty. Only the failure to realize these objectives quickly enough has caused some theorists to develop a sense of grievance and to propose radical revisions of the social and economic order designed to usher in immediately a New Jerusalem of happiness and prosperity for all. Many of these glittering Utopias were products of the first half of the nineteenth century, but an even larger number were developed during the age of prodigality and exploitation that followed the Civil War.

The original form of Utopianism in the United States was an importation. It was brought in by its founder, Robert Owen, in 1825, and for a number of years was an important ingredient in American thinking. Owen, a successful manufacturer of cotton goods in New Lanark, Scotland, turned his attention to the miseries of the unemployed in the depression that followed the Napoleonic Wars. He came to the conclusion that the chief cause of their sufferings was the profit system. The collection of profit by the owners of industry makes it impossible, he maintained, for the worker to buy the things he has produced. The result is overproduction, periodic depressions, and unemployment. As a solution, Owen undertook the establishment of "cooperative villages," in which workers would pool their talents and produce goods for each other's needs. At specified times the net income would be divided among all the members in proportion to their actual hours of labor. He hoped to obtain government assistance for the creation of such villages in all parts of the country. Failing in this, he migrated to the United States. In 1825 he organized at New Harmony, Indiana, what he hoped would become a shining example to all the world of a self-sufficient, cooperative economy, entirely invulnerable to the fluctuation of the business cycle.

Though the New Harmony project failed, chiefly as a consequence of sectarian and doctrinal disputes, its founder left a legacy of social and economic contributions since recognized as important additions to American thought. First was the doctrine that the individual's character is "shaped for him and not by him." This means that he is a product of environment much more than heredity, and consequently the remedy for vice and crime must be found in education and in reform of institutions rather than in sacraments, punishments, and futile attempts to change human nature. The other of Owen's contributions was his doctrine that underconsumption is the primary cause of depressions. This theory was adopted in part by the Marxists and became a cardinal element in the economic gospel of the New Deal.

Of lesser importance than Owenism, but of greater renown, was the second form of Utopianism in America, which derived at least part of its inspiration from the Fourierist movement in France. Charles Marie Fourier, in the early nineteenth century, worked out a scheme for cooperative communities, or phalansteries, in which the members would live in hotels with common facilities for cooking and laundry, and would find employment in various enterprises operated by the community. The members would be encouraged to buy stock in the community, and the net proceeds of their labors would be divided in the proportion of $\frac{5}{12}$ to labor, $\frac{4}{12}$ to capital, and $\frac{3}{12}$ to management. Fourier hoped that eventually the whole world would be organized in accordance with his plan. There would be phalansteries all over the globe, with a central unit, or Grand Phalanstery, in Constantinople. With the population of the earth thus federated on a cooperative basis, Fourier believed that all problems of depressions, poverty, class conflict, and war would automatically disappear.

Two communities flourished briefly in America in accordance with the Fourierist ideal. The first was Brook Farm, established in 1841, at West Roxbury, Massachusetts, nine miles from Boston. Its founder, George Ripley, a Unitarian minister and Transcendentalist, enlisted the support of a distinguished group of writers, including Emerson, Theodore Parker, Bronson Alcott, Orestes Brownson, Nathaniel Hawthorne, Charles A. Dana, and John S. Dwight. Only the last three, however, actually lived at the farm. The project was originally of native origins, an outgrowth of the miscellaneous reform enthusiasms of Unitarians and Transcendentalists. But in 1844 Albert Brisbane, an ardent disciple of Fourier, appeared on the scene and succeeded in converting the community to his master's principles. His success was short-lived, however, for in 1846 a disastrous fire inflicted financial losses from which the enterprise never recovered.

Meanwhile, Brisbane, with the assistance of Horace Greeley, had organized another Fourierist project at Red Bank, New Jersey. Known as the North American Phalanx, it was designed to provide an experience in noncompetitive living for about a thousand people who would derive their livelihood principally from employment in a grist mill. This experiment also ended in failure soon after the destruction of the mill by fire in 1854. Even without the fire it would probably have failed eventually, since Brisbane was an impractical visionary who was so indifferent to the world of reality that he could see no essential distinction between American democracy and the despotism of the Sultan of Turkey.

The seers and dreamers after the Civil War included a motley array of currency reformers, single-taxers, and literary or bourgeois socialists. In the ranks of the currency reformers were Greenbackers and Free Silverites, who believed that the economic troubles of the nation were the result primarily of an inadequate supply of money. Claiming that money in circulation had shrunk from $58 per capita in 1865 to $17 in 1876, they argued that this meant severe hardship for debtors, for farmers especially, who had borrowed money to buy land at inflated prices during or soon after the Civil War. What was needed now and in the future was an increase in the supply of money in proportion to the growth of population. Farmers would then receive better prices for what they produced, and as a consequence would be able to pay off their mortgages and to purchase more of the products of industry. According to the Greenback party, the supply of money should be increased by the simple expedient of printing large quantities of paper currency.

The Free Silverites, who generally called themselves Populists, advocated the remonetization of silver in the proportion of 16 of silver to 1 of gold. But both movements had other objectives. The Greenbackers demanded an income tax, government ownership of railroads and telegraphs, woman suffrage, and the direct election of United States Senators. The Populists added to these the advocacy of postal savings banks and a single term for the President. Both parties went down to defeat, though the combined Populist-Democratic ticket polled about 47 per cent of the popular vote for President in 1896. The major factors responsible for ultimate failure were the discovery of gold in the Klondike and South Africa and the development of the cyanide process for extracting gold from low-content ores. As a result, the currency reformers were no longer able to make the valid claim that the supply of gold was insufficient to provide for the nation's currency needs.

Contemporaneous with the Greenback and Populist movements was the single-tax movement initiated by Henry George. Born in Philadelphia in 1839, George fled from his environment of poverty and hardship and found refuge on a sailing vessel en route to Australia. Upon his return he decided to seek his fortune in California of the gold-rush era. He found no gold, but he got the inspiration for an idea that was ultimately to bring him both fame and fortune. In California in those days men were scrambling all over one another to buy up the titles to the choicest tracts of land, hoping to sell them later at a fabulous profit. Like a flash, it dawned upon Henry George that here was the explanation of increasing poverty alongside of increasing wealth. "With the growth of population land grows in value, and the men who work it must pay more for the privilege." This was the kernel of an economic philosophy that he brought to fruition in *Progress and Poverty*, which he published in 1879. Though it got off to an unpromising start, its sales multiplied until by 1905 they approximated two million copies.

The strength of the appeal of *Progress and Poverty* stemmed both from its eloquence and from the simplicity of the remedy it offered. All that would be necessary would be to levy a confiscatory tax on the unearned increment of land values; that is, on the increase in land values which comes about from social causes, such as the growth of population, the erection of a school, the building of a sewer, or the pavement of a street. Since, according to George, this tax would be sufficient to defray all the expenses of government, the burdens now resting upon industry, trade, and other socially useful pursuits could be entirely removed. Consequently, without socialism or any other painful reorganization or adjustment, prosperity and economic justice would be vouchsafed to all.

Nine years after the publication of *Progress and Poverty*, the most successful of America's Utopian romances came off the press. Its author was Edward Bellamy and its title, *Looking Backward*. The son of a Baptist minister of Chicopee Falls, Massachusetts, Bellamy became impressed with "man's inhumanity to man" on a tour of the great cities and peasant hovels of Europe. In *Looking Backward* he etched the portrait of a paradise of opportunity and efficiency in the year 2000 which was supposed to have been brought into existence by a bloodless revolution about a hundred years before. The economic system was a giant monopoly owned and operated by the state. The citizens were forced to serve in an industrial army, and credit cards secured for them the goods they needed. No person could achieve distinction or power by amassing wealth. Instead, rewards for ability or special effort took the form of medals and honors or titles of higher rank in the industrial army. For refusal to work in accordance with one's faculties the penalty was solitary imprisonment on bread and water. The organization of society was exclusively economic and military, with nothing resembling a political state. Foremen in the factories had the rank of captain, and the superintendents were colonels. Next came the generals of the guilds, representing trades or industries, and above them the major-generals, "or chiefs of the ten great departments, or groups of allied trades." At the top of the structure was the general-in-chief, "who is the President of the United States." But the functions of the latter were administrative only. Nor was there any Congress or State Department or courts or police. The society had no need for legislation since the fundamental principles upon which it was founded had settled for all time the "strifes and misunderstandings" which formerly called for the enactment of laws. Courts and police also had been rendered unnecessary by the elimination of the economic motive responsible for crime.

Though it had not the phenomenal success of *Progress and Poverty,* Bellamy's romance found a place on the shelves of at least a million readers. Moreover, it led to the growth of a Nationalist cult dedicated to the propagation of the author's ideas. The first Nationalist Club was organized in Boston in 1888. Others quickly appeared in many parts of the nation. In two years the leaders of the movement claimed no fewer than one hundred and twenty-seven clubs in cities as far apart as New York and San Francisco and Philadelphia and Minneapolis. But the crest of the wave soon passed. By 1896 the great bulk of the Nationalists had been absorbed into the Populist party. Yet the fact that such a movement could have struck a sympathetic chord in the hearts of millions of Americans is profoundly significant. For Bellamy's socialism came perilously close to being totalitarian. With its compulsory service in an industrial army, its "coordination" of culture, and its abolition of the judiciary, it left very little scope or protection for individual liberty outside the area of freedom of economic opportunity. Disillusionment with capitalism, however, seems to have been sufficiently deep to have caused many people to attach more importance to equality of economic opportunity than they did to freedom of mind or freedom of expression.

When *Looking Backward* was published in 1888, one of the first to acclaim it was William Dean Howells, who was destined to produce in later years some Utopian works of his own. Howells was the son of a poorly paid, Ohio antislavery editor. Under the necessity of working to supplement the family income from the age of nine, and with very little formal education, he rose by sheer brilliance to become editor of the *Atlantic Monthly* and one of the foremost novelists of his generation. Not until the 1890's, when he was past fifty years of age, did he become a socialist. He published his two socialistic novels, *A Traveler from Altruria* and *Through the Eye of the Needle,* in 1894 and 1907, respectively. But it was a socialism far removed from the Marxist variety. It involved no sympathy for the class struggle or for the interests of laborers apart from those of the rest of society. During the Homestead Steel strike, Howells wrote to his son that the workers were "playing a lawless part, and that they must be made to give up the Carnegie property." Expressing pity for the "poor wretches of Pinkerton detectives," who were "so shockingly used" after their surrender, he thought it would have been "much better if the Homesteaders could have suffered the Pinkertons to shoot them down unarmed." Then they would have had "the power of martyrs in the world." [6]

The socialism of Howells owed far more to William Morris and to Bellamy than it did to Marx. The influence of Morris is reflected in a distaste for the ugliness of the Industrial Revolution. In Altruria, for example, the use of steam was abolished, and the water wheel was the exclusive source of power. The resemblances between Altruria and Bellamy's dreamland of A.D. 2000 were numerous. Both would come into existence through a peaceful revolution. Accumulation and concentration would be carried so far that only a single economic combination would remain. Perceiving the illogic of leaving this in private hands, the people would vote to transfer it to the state. Both Bellamy and Howells believed in the principle of payment in accordance with needs, which for all practical purposes would mean equality. Both conceived of an essentially noneconomic society, with competition for financial gains eliminated, and with distinctions rewarded by a sense of duty performed or by badges and decorations.

But the land of Altruria lacked the compulsive elements of Bellamy's paradise. There would be no industrial army with its military discipline and imprisonment on bread and water. Howells assumed that men would work cheerfully, willingly, and even eagerly at the tasks which all would share for the production of common necessities. He seems also to have placed a higher premium upon leisure and enjoyment than did the author of *Looking Backward*. In Altruria the working day was only three hours. After that the citizen was free to devote himself to pleasure and sport or to intellectual and artistic pursuits. Nearly everyone lived in country villages, and traveled to the city on special business by electric expresses operating at a speed of 150 miles an hour. Mills and shops were beautiful as well as useful. They looked like temples rising from leafy boscages beside the streams which furnished their power.

SOCIAL ENGINEERING—THE PLANNED SOCIETY

As previously indicated, American political and social thinking underwent a revolutionary transformation about 1880. Previous to that time the dominant note had been the importance of the free individual pursuing his own happiness in a competitive world. His rights, privileges, and opportunities were generally regarded as preeminent over everything else. To be sure, the welfare of society was also a consideration. But this was supposed to result as a by-product of the pursuit by individuals of their enlightened self-interest. The more actively they competed with one another for the choicest morsels at life's banquet, the greater would be the enhancement of the common good. Of the utmost importance was the reduction of the state to a minimum role in this process. It should be little more than an umpire or referee to enforce the rules while the multitude of competitors pursued their game of getting there first and seizing the most.

The new attitude developed by liberals and reformers about 1880 proposed to change all of this. From being acclaimed as the law of life, competition was degraded to a law of death. More important, the state was given an expanded role. Instead of being limited to the negative functions of preserving order and protecting life, liberty, and property, it was exalted to the positive role of an agency for social engineering and economic planning. Its functions as a policeman would pale into insignificance compared to its activities as educator, protector of the weak and unfortunate, and promoter of prosperity and the general welfare.

This revolutionary change was symbolized by the organization of the American Economic Association in 1885, with its platform repudiating economic individualism and endorsing positive assistance by the state as an indispensable condition of human progress. But it was still necessary that someone should develop an underlying philosophy or basic pattern for the new attitude. This office was fulfilled by two distinguished thinkers of the nineteenth and twentieth centuries, who provided the rationale for new governmental policies and gave voice to the hopes and needs of bewildered citizens. The first of such philosophers was Lester Frank Ward, and the second was John Dewey. Both were apostles of social engineering. They believed firmly in progress and in the ability of man to conquer his problems by exercising his intelligence upon them. Their deity was science and their gospel the scientific method. They argued that nature is one, and that the entire universe is governed by identical laws. The principles that guide the astronomer, physicist, or chemist in his researches are fully applicable to the social, political, and economic realms.

Lester Frank Ward was a good exemplar of his own precepts. Though possessed of an education of dubious value, he became an authority in such disparate fields as sociology, geology, psychology, and paleobotany. He had no sympathy whatever for the negative attitudes of the classical economists. Intelligent men, he contended, have never followed the practice of letting nature take its course. The artificial is infinitely superior to the natural, and the whole tendency of civilization is to render everything artificial, "which means more and more perfect." The transfer of functions from private to public control is a process, he added, which has been going on from the earliest stages of history. And of all, the enterprises brought under the control of the state, every one has been managed more wisely than it had been before under private interests. Ward was far from insisting upon complete socialism. "The question in each case," he said, "must always be, Is the age ripe for this change?" He suspected, however, that the strength of established custom would nearly always mean that the change would be too long postponed. He feared no loss of freedom from the extension of government control. In fact, he maintained that individual freedom could come only through social regulation. This, he argued, was inevitably the case, since unrestrained competition invariably led, sooner or later, to powerful and greedy monopolies.[7]

In order to achieve the purposes of social engineering, Ward believed that an entirely new form of political organization would have to be devised. This would be what he called *sociocracy,* and he maintained that it would be superior not only to autocracy and aristocracy but even to democracy. The chief trouble with democracy was that it was largely party government. Contests for control of the government became a kind of game, in which the interests of the party were placed uppermost and the public welfare largely forgotten. Sociocracy would put an end to this childish play. Measures would be considered in a businesslike way without fear, favor, or bias. Every proposal would be subjected to a strictly scientific investigation, which would actually settle the question of its merits or demerits. "In a word, society would do under the same circumstances just what an intelligent individual would do."

Ward seemed to ignore the fact that the individual is a much more homogeneous unit than society is likely to be under any conditions. He was supposing, however, a far higher level of general education than obtains at present. This would be brought about through the abolition of poverty and economic insecurity, so that every family would have the means to educate its children to the full limit of their capacities. The standard of living would be raised by a marked increase of both production and consumption. No redistribution of existing wealth would suffice, but production would need to be multiplied ten, twenty, or even a hundredfold. This could be done by systematic planning and the use of machinery. Ward did not shrink from the implications of his materialist philosophy. To a large extent he interpreted both individual happiness and social progress in terms of comforts and the satisfaction of wants. He urged the abandonment of what he called the old *privative* ethics of want and pain and the substitution of a *positive* ethics of plenty and security. Only then would it be possible to dream of abolishing the great social evils of ignorance, crime, and war.[8]

John Dewey began writing on social and political problems about fourteen years after Ward's death in 1913. Like Ward, he believed devoutly in progress, but he denied that it is automatic. It depends for its actuality upon human intent and human achievement. He deprecated especially the complacent attitude which trusts the management of human affairs to "nature, or Providence, or evolution," on the assumption that no matter what we do, some benign power will underwrite the future for us. He was just as critical of the laissez faire attitude in economics. He contended that economic individualism had failed by the end of the nineteenth century, and no longer existed except in name. Social control is already upon us in the form of giant organization of business. Our only choice is between accepting the capitalistic control that already exists and establishing a new one that will operate in the public interest.

Although Dewey at one time looked hopefully toward Soviet Russia as the Moses that would lead the world out of the wilderness of economic confusion, he later decided that neither communism nor fascism had anything to offer as models of planning. Both claimed to be planned societies; but he argued that a tremendous difference marks off the *planned* society from a *continuously planning* society. The former requires fixed blueprints handed down from above, and imposed by physical and psychological force upon the entire nation. The latter involves a process of continuous inquiry and investigation to discover the best methods of solving present and future problems. The former makes use of "the frozen intelligence" of some past thinker, sect, or party cult. The latter regards all theories and accumulations of knowledge as tentative until verified by scientific investigation."

The styling administration building and the styling auditorium of the country's largest automobile manufacturer. *General Motors Corp.*

Unlike Ward, Dewey made no suggestion of a newfangled political system to carry on the work of social engineering. On the contrary, he considered democracy as almost perfectly adapted to that end. "The very heart of political democracy," he wrote, "is adjudication of social differences by discussion and exchange of views." Democratic procedure, he contended, necessarily involves experimentation, investigation, and analysis and testing of results; in other words, a close approximation of the scientific method. Determination of policies arbitrarily or in accordance with some gospel or tradition of the past is not democracy but authoritarianism.

Nevertheless, Dewey believed that adherence to the scientific method by democratic states is persistently hindered by the refusal of so many people to abandon their devotion to the prejudices instilled in them by some secular or religious cult. He maintained that adequate knowledge already exists for dealing scientifically with such problems as crime and war. But we persist in thinking of such things in "prescientific moral terms." Instead of acting upon the knowledge we have of human behavior, we categorize people as "good" or "evil" and long to keep the former on our side and to punish the latter. Punishment, revenge, retribution, however, are antiquated concepts with no foundation in science. The urgent need, according to Dewey, is for training the citizens of a democracy in an appreciation and understanding of the scientific attitude. Then only will the scientific revolution which began three hundred years ago be brought to fulfillment. Great as have been the social transformations of the past, "they are not to be compared with those which will emerge when our faith in scientific method is made manifest in social works." [10]

The germ of the idea of government intervention to promote prosperity or to foster the development of some particular branch of a nation's economy is an old one. A few years before he died, Madison wrote that canals, railroads, and turnpikes were not only the criteria of a wise policy but causes of national prosperity. He thought that a government that failed to provide them was recreant to its duty. [11] Hamilton considered a large public debt as the invigorating principle of a nation. Since it would exist in the form of bonds, it would provide extra capital as a spur to economic activity. Trade, manufacturing, and agriculture would all benefit from it, since there would be more capital to carry them on. A United States

Bank, he contended, would serve similar purposes. Gold and silver used simply as money are essentially "dead stock," but when deposited in banks, to become the basis of a paper currency, "acquire life, or, in other words, an active and productive quality." Hamilton estimated that a bank can procreate as money two or three times the quantity of gold and silver in its vaults. The reason for this is that every loan which a bank makes is listed as a credit to the borrower on its books. In many cases the borrower does not collect the money, but transfers his credit to some other person to whom he has a payment to make. In this way "the credit keeps circulating, performing in every stage the office of money." [12]

Hamilton's doctrine gained general acceptance, if not in his own time, at least a century later. An interesting reaffirmation of it came from the pen of William Allen White in 1916. In one of his editorials he said: "Kansas is the only state in the Union that is out of debt—and should be ashamed of it. . . . The credit of a great state like Kansas should not lie dormant, unused, so long as any permanent improvement necessary to the wellbeing of its citizens remains unachieved." [13]

Advocacy of positive governmental action even to the extent of economic planning has punctuated nearly every period of United States history. It was an element, of course, in the American System of Henry Clay and in the philosophies of Henry Carey, Simon Patten, and Thorstein Veblen. It was a staple ingredient in the platforms of the Greenback, Populist, and Progressive parties. Yet advocacy on an extensive scale did not assume capital importance until the depression of 1929. The great debacle of that year and the years following revealed the hopeless inadequacy of the negative state and brought to the fore a galaxy of critics of the old economics and proponents of remedies for the unexpected disaster. Many were officials in the new administration that came into power in 1933; but at least one occupied a completely independent position as an intellectual authority in his own right. He was Charles A. Beard.

After resigning from Columbia University in 1917, in protest against administrative tyranny, Beard had produced books and articles by the score on political and economic subjects. As early as 1932 he advanced the contention that modern nations must of necessity resort to planning. Technology is the basic factor in their civilization, and technology can make no headway at all without first establishing a goal or purpose. Beard denied that there was anything Russian about the origin or nature of planning. He asserted, on the contrary, that planning was anathema to the Bolsheviks until, facing the task of averting starvation and restoring their broken industrial system, they abandoned Marx, adopted the scientific management of Frederick W. Taylor, "and borrowed foreign technology to save their political skins." Planning was already well established in the United States. It was exemplified by the rise of the budget system, the work of the Bureau of Standards, and the thousands of boards or commissions for municipal planning in progressive American cities.[14]

Beard did not stop with mere advocacy of an idea. He went on to suggest a means of implementation. He recommended the institution of a National Economic Council, under the authorization of Congress. Represented in the council would be all the great industries that have attained a high degree of concentration, together with the various organizations in agriculture, labor, wholesale and retail trade. The original function of the council would be to serve as a kind of federal convention, like that of 1787, to draw up an economic constitution for the approval of the voters. To facilitate the establishment of the program, the Sherman and Clayton acts would be repealed. All industries of a high degree of concentration, or approaching that status, would be classified as businesses "affected with a public interest" and therefore subject to the same extent of regulation as is already required for public utilities. Associated with the National Economic Council would be a Board of Strategy and Planning, whose prime function would be to survey the resources and productive capacity of the country and plan the production of consumers' and capital goods. Such would be the central or over-all arrangement.

Each industry associated with the National Economic Council would also have its own organization. It would be set up as a syndicate of affiliated corporations, resembling a holding company, "with large directorial and service powers." Dividends would be limited, and any surpluses earned would be used to pay bonuses and to provide reserves for unemployment resulting from accidents, temporary shutdowns, technological changes, and depressions, "if any." In some fashion, idle and absentee stockholders would be induced or required to exchange·their shares for 3 per cent bonds, and the capital stock would be transferred largely to the directors, managers, and employees of the several corporations. Beard maintained that this program could be put into operation "without violating a single American economic tradition." Indeed, he thought more generous treatment could be given to stock-and-bond-holders than is usual in cases of bankruptcy and reorganization—as if divesting stockholders of their shares in the largest and most flourishing corporations in America could be compared to a proceeding in bankruptcy.[15]

The popular and dynamic President who assumed the reins of power in 1933 was an exponent not so much of economic planning as of the welfare state. He had a deep conviction that the government must do something to mitigate the sufferings of the underprivileged, but his mind did not run to fixed economic blueprints. He preferred the method of trial and experiment from day to day, comparing himself to the quarterback who knows what the next play is going to be but does not know the one after that or any of its successors. As late as 1936 he informed the people in a fireside chat that "private enterprise is necessary to any nation which seeks to maintain the democratic form of government." Nevertheless, he did pay homage to the general idea of planning. Even before he became President he told a Governors' Conference at French Lick, Indiana, in 1931, that "in the long run, State and national planning is an essential to the future prosperity, happiness and the very existence of the American people." He continued to advise caution, however. In his Commonwealth Club address in 1932, he said that the government should assume the function of economic regulation "only as a last resort," to be tried when private initiative "has finally failed." Later in the same year he expressed the hope that government interference to stabilize business and industry could be kept to a minimum, "limiting itself perhaps to wise dissemination of information."[16] In the first months of his administration he still seemed to think little more would be required for restoring health to the economy than curtailment of agricultural production, spreading the work in industry, and currency-tinkering to raise the prices of raw commodities.

Most of the ideas on economic planning that distinguished the New Deal came not from Mr. Roosevelt but from his subordinates and advisers. Indeed, it is astonishing to note the extent to which they disagreed with him, especially on restricting production and sharing the work. Perhaps the boldest and most original of the advocates of economic planning was Jerome Frank. In two works, bearing the titles of *Save America First* and *Fate and Freedom*, Frank warned of the danger that an unregulated economy would end in chaos or in some form of totalitarianism. But one example of regulation he sternly rejected. This was redistribution of existing national income without any attempt to increase production. This he denominated the fascist method. Instead of it, he would raise production above the 1929 level and raise it again with each succeeding year, allocating the major portion of the increase to those with meager incomes. Like Charles A. Beard, he would establish an economic parliament or council through which the necessary cooperation of business in planning production for the future would be secured. He would supplement this by constant lowering of prices, by government construction of public works at high wages to prevent the supply of labor from glutting the market, and by government purchases and distribution to counterbalance insufficient earnings and wages. By such expedients he believed it would be possible to create a good life for all Americans without upsetting political democracy, without destroying producers' property in small factories, shops, and farms, and even without affecting the property rights of "ordinary investors in giant corporations." By the exercise of intelligence, he believed that we could steadily reduce the working hours of the great majority of our citizens and arrive at a goal resembling the leisure society of which Sir Thomas More dreamed. He admitted the remote possibility that this might destroy social discipline. If it did so, he was then prepared to advocate the conscription of young men and young women for a battle against the evils and hardships of nature in the manner recommended by William James.[17]

That the Department of Agriculture, during the early New Deal, should have been the branch of the government most deeply conscious of the need for planning is not surprising. Agriculture had suffered from chronic depression even during the fat years of the 1920's, when the rest of the economy was booming. Roosevelt's first Secretary of Agriculture was as familiar with the problems of the farmer as anyone else, from his long experience as a plant breeder and editor of a farm journal. Henry Wallace, however, did not regard agricultural problems as existing in a vacuum. He thought of them more and more as susceptible of solution only in relation to the economy as a whole. To relieve depression in agriculture, the best of all methods, he argued, would be the creation of sixty million jobs in industry. Not only would this increase the demand for agricultural products, but it would entice surplus farmers away from the land and enhance the opportunities of those who remained. Moreover, by raising the economic status of the poorest ten million families it would ensure an annual market for fifteen billion dollars' worth of goods and services.

To provide for sixty million jobs by 1950, Wallace admitted, would necessitate a considerable amount of planning and ·a small degree of regimentation. But he denied that either would be sufficient to justify alarm. A certain amount of government control and even government operation is as inevitable in a maturing economy as is the subconscious functioning of the lungs or heart in a complex organism. The issue of vital importance is not government control of economic affairs but "which group will be in control of the government, and whether or not that group will have ulterior purposes to serve." On at least one point Wallace sharply disagreed with

Seeding a Kansas farm at the rate of 150 acres in ten hours. *Caterpillar Tractor Co.*

Jerome Frank. He did not believe that a life of leisure should become the paramount object of economic reform. Too large a proportion of the people lacked the necessaries of life, he contended, to justify our dreaming of a lotus-land of ease and pleasure for the foreseeable future.[18]

For four years, from 1933 to 1937, Henry Wallace had as his Under-Secretary in the Department of Agriculture Rexford Guy Tugwell, one of the original Brain Trusters of the New Deal. Tugwell had been a student of Simon Patten and had imbibed copious draughts from his master's fount of wisdom on such subjects as the worthlessness of a competitive economy. Tugwell came to the conclusion that a large share of the blame for American economic troubles could be ascribed to our efforts to enforce free competition. By 1900 it had become apparent that democracy and strict individualism were not compatible. But we refused to recognize the fact. As fast as cooperative combinations appeared, we denounced them as trusts and attempted to put them out of business. The result was simply to force them into subterranean channels, where they could not be regulated for the common welfare. We thereby compelled business to be lawless, or at least hypocritical. On the one hand we produced a vast concentration of corporate power, operating in the dark, for private benefit; and on the other, dire poverty, the result of unregulated exploitation.

Because of such gross maladjustments, Tugwell considered planning all the more urgent. He would repeal the laws against trusts and allow business to follow its ineluctable tendency toward concentration. Soon there would be an aggregate of giant combinations comparable to the great railroads and the telephone system. And they would be just as strictly regulated. Although there would be no government ownership, it would be made clear to every businessman that it was industry's responsibility "to provide continuous employment for all and to distribute purchasing power which will enable the public to buy its goods." Nor would agriculture be neglected. Tugwell envisaged a gradual resettlement of America. Vast areas of marginal and semiarid land would be taken out of farming and returned to pastoral use. Middle and more western regions would be planted in trees, "perhaps wide belts of them to turn the wind and temper the climate." Farms would be larger and more highly mechanized, and many families now struggling for a bare livelihood on poor lands would be absorbed into industrial employment. But this would not mean urban congestion. The government would foster the extension of electric power lines and the building of highways so that industry could be decentralized and factories could spring up in the villages. It was a shining dream, and perhaps more of it has been realized than even Tugwell hoped for when he expounded it in 1935.[19]

THE WELFARE STATE

Without question a close relationship exists between the planned or planning society and the welfare state. Yet they are not the same. It would seem accurate to say that every advocate of a planned society is also an advocate of the welfare state, since the professed purpose of social planning is to promote the general welfare. But to many who have believed that the state should function as an agency to advance the common good, the idea of national planning has been anathema. They have criticized it either as impractical or as so dangerous to individual liberty that it should never be tolerated. As good a spokesman of their point of view as it is possible to find is Walter Lippmann. In various works published between 1914 and 1935, Lippmann acclaimed the provision of economic security as "the central task of government, the very heart of statesmanship." Democracy will be satisfied with nothing less, he contended, for if capitalism is combined with popular sovereignty, the people will turn to the government for help whenever capitalism fails to satisfy their expectations. "A really imaginative program of Americanization," he wrote in another connection, "must include a comprehensive, nation-wide system of health, accident, maternity, old age and unemployment insurance." [20]

Even so, Lippmann repudiated a planned economy as an instrument of tyranny. Though he told the graduating class of the University of California in 1933 that "deliberate direction of human affairs is necessary and unavoidable," further reflection and insight appeared to convince him otherwise. By 1934 he was ready to conclude that a democratic people cannot embrace a system of planning. Insofar as they attempt to do so, they must abandon democracy. He thought it no accident that wherever planned collectivism had been instituted, during World War I and in the postwar dictatorships, it had required censorship, espionage, and terrorism to make it work. Not only did he regard the regimented society as impractical; he maintained that it was not even theoretically conceivable. Be the blueprint as grandiose a work of genius as Plato's *Republic*, he said, it cannot be made effective. A directed society implies that men will remain satisfied in the station to which some ruler or rulers have assigned them. But in real life "men rest content in their station only if their interests have been successfully reconciled: failing that, they do not fit the design until they have been dosed with castor oil, put in concentration camps, or exiled to Siberia." [21]

The germ of the welfare state is an old one in American history. It goes back at least to Roger Williams in the seventeenth century. The liberal founder of the Rhode Island colony conceived of the state as something vastly different from a secular arm of the church or a carnal weapon of God to maintain the true religion. To Williams it was a public service corporation, a servant of the people to provide for their needs. Accordingly, he prohibited primogeniture, stipulated that the land should be equally divided among families, and decreed that prices should be fixed for the necessaries of life in time of scarcity. To the government was assigned the responsibility not only of caring for the poor and dispensing charity to the incapable and to widows and orphans but also of procuring work for the able-bodied.[22] From all the evidence Williams seems to have been as far advanced in his political and social doctrines as he was in his espousal of religious freedom. Except for the archaic language, his treatises resemble disquisitions of the twentieth century more closely than they do the writings of his contemporaries. Not only did he profess ideals of democracy distinctly modern—including popular sovereignty, universal suffrage, the separation of church and state, and the initiative and referendum—but he taught advanced conceptions of international relations. He insisted upon the sanctity of treaties, condemned imperialism, and urged conciliation, arbitration, and mediation as substitutes for war.

Although the Founding Fathers are generally classified as exponents of an individualist philosophy, they carried over enough relics of mercantilism to enable them to approve of a considerable measure of government intervention for the public good. Such was especially true of Hamilton. As a leader of the conservative revolution that brought the Constitution into being, Madison did not favor government assistance to the less fortunate members of society. Compassion was due them, he graciously conceded, but not direct beneficence. He feared that the persistent tendency of the lower classes to increase their own numbers with every improvement of their economic condition would wreck any permanent plan of government intervention for their benefit. But the passing of the years seemed to mellow his attitude. In 1820 he wrote: "To provide employment for the poor, and support for the indigent, is among the primary, and at the same time, not least difficult cares of the public authority." He thought the task particularly arduous in densely populated countries. In favored America, where food and employment were less subject to failures and deficiencies, government assistance would not often be necessary. But some degree of interposition of the public authority "is at all times and everywhere called for." [23]

Examples of belief in the welfare state through the remainder of the nineteenth and during the early twentieth centuries could easily be multiplied. Even Emerson was swept off his feet at one time by the collectivist ferment of the 1840's. "All this beneficent socialism," he proclaimed, "is a friendly omen, and the swelling cry of voices for the education of the people indicates that Government has other offices than those of banker and executioner." He deplored the fact that in the scramble of parties for offices and plunder, the main duties of government were being neglected. These duties he enumerated as instructing the ignorant and supplying the poor with work and with "good guidance." [24]

A few years before he became President, Abraham Lincoln set forth what appeared to be a definite enlargement of the province of government. "The legitimate object of government," he said, "is to do for a community of people whatever they need to have done, but cannot do at all, or cannot so well do, for themselves, in their separate and individual capacities." Among the things requiring the combined action of the state he listed public roads and highways, public schools, charities, pauperism, and orphanage. Though none of these would represent a wide departure from the orthodox canons of individualism, it is interesting to observe his contention "that if all men were just there still would be some, though not so much, need of government." [25]

A few other individualists of the nineteenth century wrote from time to time in a manner suggestive of the welfare state. The too-often maligned prophet of the Gospel of Wealth was one of them. In discoursing upon the origin of wealth, Andrew Carnegie presented views reminiscent of those of Thomas Paine. The obvious creator of wealth, he said, is the community. This comes about through increase in the population. Without steadily increasing population, there can be no great fortunes. "Where wealth accrues honorably, the great are always silent partners." The railroad magnate could never gather his harvest of riches except through expansion of settlement into frontier regions and increasing need for the shipment of goods. The owner of a steel mill would go into bankruptcy were no new railroad lines extended, bridges built, or hotels and office buildings constructed. Carnegie modestly refused to deny that the men who conceive and administer the factories and railroads are exceptional men. He conceded also that their gathering of millions is an evidence of ability, foresight, and assiduity above the average. For these reasons he would not hamper or restrict their money-making proclivities during their lifetime. The millionaire himself is usually one of the least expensive bees in the industrial hive, and should not be disturbed while gathering honey. But when he dies, most of the product of his activity should be returned to the general hive, under a drastic system of taxation which will prevent wealth created by the community from falling into the hands of wastrels and drones.

Though generally upholding free competition, Carnegie was broad-minded enough to see some advantages in government ownership. There is much evolutionary socialism, he declared, which "we Progressives have long welcomed." Municipalization of public utilities he described as "certainly a step in the right direction." It is a proved fact, he said, that cities can advantageously own, operate, or lease for definite periods their water, gas, and electric works, street railways, and so on.[26] He would, of course, see no such advantages in government ownership, operation, or even leasing of blast furnaces, coal mines, or railroads, but it is significant that he would make a few dents in the ironclad armor of ruthless competition.

As one would expect, the collectivists of the nineteenth century were foremost champions of the welfare state. A few exceptions, however, must be noted. Both the orthodox Marxists and the Utopian socialists maintained that the systems they advocated would usher in such a golden age of justice and harmony that no welfare measures on the part of the state would be necessary, save as temporary expedients. Actually, in most of these systems the state as we know it would disappear. With the elimination of greed and competition, men would cooperate voluntarily, and no instruments either of coercion or direction would be needed. The majority of the collectivists, however, recognized the state as a beneficent institution and intended not only to keep it but to maximize its functions. For example, John P. Altgeld, Governor of Illinois from 1893 to 1897 and influential Populist at the Democratic Convention of 1896, described government as not merely an essential but a noble institution. Its functions, he said, are "to protect the weak, to restrain the vicious, to see that justice is done, to perform economic and industrial functions for the benefit of all, to labor for the elevation of all." As a statesman, he sponsored some of the earliest laws regulating the labor of women and children, abolishing sweatshops, requiring employers to compensate injured workmen, and providing for inheritance taxes, factory inspection, and municipal ownership of public utilities. Since the happiness and even the lives of the citizens depend on these utilities, he held that they should be owned by the people themselves, and not left in the hands of a few private individuals for their own gain.[27]

The full development of the welfare state did not come, of course, until the twentieth century. A few milestones were erected under the Square Deal of Theodore Roosevelt and the New Freedom of Woodrow Wilson. The former witnessed the enactment of the Pure Food and Drug Act of 1906, a Federal meat inspection law, and important measures for the conservation of natural resources. The New Freedom was exemplified by a graduated income tax law, an eight-hour law for railroad workers, the Clayton Anti-Trust Act, a workmen's compensation act for government employees, subsidies for agricultural and vocational education, and the establishment of the Federal Reserve System. But not until the advent of the New Deal did the welfare state become a household phrase and gain general acceptance as a necessary and desirable program. And no one did more to promote such results than the great standard-bearer of the New Deal himself.

For Franklin D. Roosevelt the welfare state was almost synonymous with the word security—a fact which is certainly not surpris-

A supreme achievement of the New Deal was the Tennessee Valley Authority, inspired by Senator George W. Norris and sponsored by President Roosevelt. Shown here is the Fontana Dam on the Little Tennesse River. It is the highest dam east of the Rocky Mountains. *TVA*

ing when one takes into account the condition of the country when he became President. But he did not mean security in the narrow sense of old-age pensions and unemployment insurance. He identified it rather with the broader idea of confidence on the part of the masses that they would not have to worry about losing their homes, about being ill-fed or ill-clad, or becoming objects of charity. It meant also that Americans would have "full opportunity for education, for reasonable leisure and recreation, for the right to carry on representative Government and for freedom to worship God in their own way." Despite many speeches on the subject, Roosevelt never went much beyond this simple but eloquent conception. At the end of the campaign of 1940, with a second world war threatening to draw us into its vortex, he portrayed his ideal of the future America in terms which still revealed a deep preoccupation with social and economic security. No words could better describe this preoccupation than the ones he employed himself in setting forth his ideal:

I see an America where factory workers are not discarded after they reach their prime, where there is no endless chain of poverty from generation to generation, where impoverished farmers and farm hands do not become homeless wanderers, where monopoly does not make youth a beggar for a job.

I see an America where small business really has a chance to flourish and grow.

I see an America of great cultural and educational opportunity for all its people.

I see an America where the income from the land shall be implemented and protected by a Government determined to guarantee to those who hoe it a fair share in the national income.

An America where the wheels of trade and private industry continue to turn to make the goods for America. Where no business man can be stifled by the harsh hand of monopoly, and where the legitimate profits of legitimate business are the fair reward of every business man—big and little—in all the nation.

I see an America with peace in the ranks of labor.

An America where the workers are really free and—through their great unions undominated by any outside force, or by any dictator within—can take their proper place at the council table with the owners and managers of business, where the dignity and security of the working man and woman are guaranteed by their own strength and fortified by the safeguards of law.

An America where those who have reached the evening of life shall live out their years in peace and security. Where pensions and insurance for these aged shall be given as a matter of right to those who through a long life of labor have served their families and their nation as well.

I see an America devoted to our freedom—unified by tolerance and by religious faith—a people consecrated to peace, a people confident in strength because their body and their spirit are secure and unafraid.[28]

Molders of opinion on political economy in the United States have always been in danger of falling between two stools. On the one hand, they have attempted to preserve the individualist tradition of free enterprise with its emphasis upon the sanctity of property as a condition essential to the maintenance of liberty. On the other hand, they have been anxious to encourage the development

Both public and private agencies are striving to provide adequate health facilities for the growing population. The University of Pittsburgh has developed one of the large health centers, integrating the Medical School with teaching hospitals and clinics. The building on the left is the Veterans Administration Hospital. *University of Pittsburgh*

of the country, to promote prosperity, and to foster the welfare of particular classes or favorite interests. Few have ever advocated a comprehensive program to remake the social and economic structure for the benefit of the whole society. If they have advocated economic nationalism, it has been done with a disregard for the interests of all but the financiers and manufacturers. If they have sponsored agrarian legislation, they have been concerned almost exclusively with the welfare of farmers.

America alone among the principal nations of the Western world has never had a strong socialist movement. Even the Christian socialism of 1885-1910 has virtually disappeared. These facts are not traceable solely to the sparse population of the country or to its abundance of cheap land. They are offshoots also of a stubborn tradition that the individual is sovereign and that to limit his economic freedom is both dangerous and immoral. Our reformers have never been able to make up their minds in the difficult choice between the economic liberty of a pioneer age and the public control essential in a complex economy. Thus we have had advocates of the welfare state proclaiming their devotion to capitalism, and New Dealers clamoring simultaneously for suspension of the Sherman Act and protection of small business. No doubt loyalty to the individualist tradition has had positive advantages in strengthening civil liberties; yet it is not without significance that America lagged far behind the nations of Europe in taxing swollen incomes and in providing the elemental safeguards against the hazards of unemployment, sickness, and disability for the least fortunate but most numerous members of her population.

NOTES TO CHAPTER TWELVE

1. *Works* (New York: Houghton Mifflin Co., *ca.* 1892), VI, 35.
2. *Changing America* (New York: The Century Co., 1919), p. 30.
3. *Congressional Record,* 66th Cong., 2nd Session, LIX, 4758 (1920).
4. *The Engineers and the Price System* (New York: B. W. Huebsch, 1921), pp. 143-44; *The Place of Science in Modern Civilization* (New York: The Viking Press, 1934), pp. 399-400.
5. *The Place of Science in Modern Civilization,* pp. 441-42, 450-51; *The Engineers and the Price System,* pp. 134-35.
6. Mildred Howells, ed., *The Life in Letters of William Dean Howells* (New York: Doubleday, Doran and Co., 1928), II, 25.
7. *The Psychic Factors of Civilization,* 2nd ed. (Boston: Ginn and Co., 1906), pp. 275-76, 286-87; *Dynamic Sociology* (New York: D. Appleton and Co., 1883), II, 578-79.
8. *The Psychic Factors of Civilization,* pp. 325-27; *Applied Sociology* (Boston: Ginn and Co., 1906), pp. 326-29.
9. *Characters and Events* (New York: Henry Holt and Co., 1929), II, 827; *Individualism, Old and New* (New York: Minton, Balch and Co., 1930), pp. 119-20; Joseph Ratner, ed., *Intelligence in the Modern World* (New York: The Modern Library, 1939), pp. 421-32.
10. *Problems of Men* (New York: The Philosophical Library, 1946), p. 157; *Philosophy and Civilization* (New York: Minton, Balch and Co., 1931), pp. 329-30.
11. Gaillard Hunt, ed., *The Writings of James Madison* (New York: G. P. Putnam's Sons, 1900), IX, 437.
12. J. C. Hamilton, ed., *The Works of Alexander Hamilton* (New York: J. F. Trow, 1850-51), III, 6-7, 108-09.
13. *The Editor and His People* (New York: The Macmillan Co., 1924), p. 169.
14. *America Faces the Future* (Boston: Houghton Mifflin Co., 1932), pp. 117-19.
15. *Ibid.,* pp. 124-30.
16. Samuel I. Rosenman, compiler, *The Public Papers and Addresses of Franklin D. Roosevelt* (New York: Random House, 1938-50), I, 495, 755, 783; V, 337.

17. *Save America First* (New York: Harper and Brothers, 1938), pp. 250-51, 342-43, 357, 373-74, 401; *Fate and Freedom* (New York: Simon and Schuster, 1945), pp. 194, 201-02.

18. *Sixty Million Jobs* (New York: Reynal and Hitchcock, 1945), p. 17; *The Price of Freedom* (Washington: The National Home Library Foundation, 1940), p. 29; *Technology, Corporations and the General Welfare* (Chapel Hill: University of North Carolina Press, 1937), pp. 24-25.

19. *The Battle for Democracy* (New York: Columbia University Press, 1935), pp. 55-56, 65-66, 313.

20. *The Method of Freedom* (New York: The Macmillan Co., 1934), p. 36; *The New Imperative* (New York: The Macmillan Co., 1935), p. 3; "Integrated America," *The New Republic*, VI (February 19, 1916), 67.

21. *The Method of Freedom*, pp. 44-45; "Piecemeal Collectivism," *The Atlantic Monthly*, CLIX (February, 1937), 228; *An Inquiry into the Principles of the Good Society* (Boston: Little, Brown and Co., 1937), pp. xi-xii, 366.

22. See J. E. Ernst, *The Political Theory of Roger Williams* (Seattle, Wash.: University of Washington Press, 1929).

23. *Letters and Other Writings of James Madison*, Published by Order of Congress (Philadelphia: J. B. Lippincott Co., 1865), III, 162.

24. F. I. Carpenter, *Ralph Waldo Emerson, Representative Selections* (New York: American Book Co., 1934), pp. 161-62.

25. John G. Nicolay and John Hay, eds., *The Complete Works of Abraham Lincoln* (New York: Francis D. Tandy Co., 1905), II, 186-87.

26. *Problems of Today* (New York: Doubleday, Page and Co., 1909), pp. 21, 29-30, 128.

27. *The Cost of Something for Nothing* (Chicago: The Hammersmark Publishing Co., 1904), pp. 33, 107.

28. Rosenman, comp., *Public Papers and Addresses*, IX, 551-52.

Chapter Thirteen

The Mission as Ideal
and Actuality

It is appropriate that we should now bring together the various conceptions which have made up the American ideal of mission and see to what extent they have been realized in practice. Looking at the dominant threads which have run through our history, we discover that the following have been considered as the basic elements constituting our myth of purpose and destiny:

First: It is our duty to proclaim liberty throughout the world and to all the inhabitants thereof. We must even strive on occasion to extend the blessings of liberty to people less fortunate than we, especially if they happen to be the victims of an oppressor in an opposing economic or ideological camp.

Second: The glory of America is to set an example of equality to all nations. We are not as other men are, for we have no royalty, hereditary aristocracy, relics of feudalism, or traditions of servility and dependence. Here the son of the charwoman or itinerant peddler has an equal chance with the scion of plutocracy to rise to the limit of his ambition and talents.

Third: America is the home of the truest and most complete democracy to be found in the world. The democratic achievements of other peoples were simply foundation stones for the construction of the magnificent American edifice. God preserved the American continent from discovery until sufficient progress had been made in Europe to enable the beginnings to be brought to final perfection across the sea. But a nation thus favored has the duty and privilege of reading democratic lessons to her backward neighbors, of setting them right when they go astray, and of fighting to defend the democratic heritage whenever it is threatened.

Fourth: America is the most peaceful and nonmilitaristic of the leading nations. It has been so from the beginning. The Founding Fathers sounded a warning against large military establishments in time of peace. With few exceptions, Americans have not glorified war or followed the example of degenerate Europeans in extolling the military virtues. When they have found it necessary to fight, they have gone into battle armed not merely with swords and guns but with breastplates of righteousness and shields of justice. And with the end of hostilities, they have set a noble example of treating their enemies humanely and even generously—except, maybe, for such benighted peoples as the Mexicans in 1848 and the Filipinos around 1900.

Fifth: America is the exemplar of the highest standard of living the world has ever known. This is a source of great satisfaction, for it proves our superiority over those nations that still blindly prefer the arts and crafts of their ancestors to modern mechanical improvements. Comfort and luxury open the door to a high civilization, if they are not the very essence of it. Americans have demonstrated this, and therefore have a call to confer such blessings upon the rest of mankind.

Belief in the uniqueness of the American nation and the consummate value of its mission seems almost as strong in our own time as in any other period of our history. During the campaign of 1952 Adlai Stevenson declared: "God has set for us an awesome mission: nothing less than the leadership of the free world." [1] In a recent book on contemporary affairs Elmer Davis bemoans the horrible prospects of a possible nuclear war and ends his jeremiad on a grim and fateful note. "Whatever happens," he writes, "we must not surrender. That war, if it comes, will be for all we have and are; if we value that, we can't give it up, in any circumstances. If we can't go on being Americans, we might as well not be at all." [2] In a sophisticated age that boasts of its world-mindedness, such ideas sound strange and not a little parochial. Moral relativism may be pernicious, but to speak in terms of such absolutes as fighting "for all we have and are" is to open the door to mutual destruction. To insist that we must choose between being Americans and not being at all seems equally presumptuous and unrealistic. Any number of alternatives short of preserving our existence as Americans would be better than nonexistence. We certainly do not have to go to the extent of total victory over our enemy in order to avoid enslavement. Such has been the opinion for a long time of the Swiss, the Swedes, and the Indians, and it is not without considerable support in other countries much closer to the threat of foreign invasion than the United States.

To what extent has America realized her high sense of mission as a guide to suffering and oppressed humanity and as a renovator of the world? The most accurate answer would probably be: As well as any other modern nation. Great Britain's achievement in carrying the White Man's Burden has not been a signal success, nor has France's *mission civilisatrice.* The efforts of Soviet Russia to win recognition as a socialist fatherland for workers all over the world have fallen far short of their sponsors' hopes. Indeed, since the brutal repression of the Hungarian revolutionists, this dream has practically vanished into the shadows of history. Not every conception of national destiny, of course, is worthy of realization. The Nazi ambition of Aryan supremacy and the Italian nationalist dream of making the Mediterranean an Italian lake would fall into this category, as would the Japanese dream of a Greater East Asia Co-prosperity Sphere and the British boast that the sun never sets on the British Empire. Ambitions that reflect greed, racial chauvinism, or the desire for power or domination are, properly speaking, not ideals at all; yet they have often had a potent influence in shaping the course of a nation's history.

Turning to a consideration of the specific ideals composing the American conception of mission, we find difficulty in concluding that any have been realized in a degree approaching perfection. Liberty, for example, has come to be sicklied o'er with shades of interpretation vastly different from the meaning it had during the formative period of the republic. To the authors of the Bill of Rights, freedom meant primarily freedom of speech and of the press and freedom of religion. These were indefeasible rights, belonging to every individual by virtue of his being a reasoning creature. Freedom of the press, at least, was assumed to be absolute. In the viewpoint of Madison, a supposed freedom of the press which admitted of exceptions was not freedom at all. Jefferson took the stand on several occasions that liberty to express opinions on any subject should never be restricted unless they break out into overt acts against peace and good order.

But much of this has been changed in more recent years. Men are now punished for "conspiring to teach and advocate," or for the expression of ideas which might have a "tendency" to foment revolution, to cause riots, or to incite assassination. Freedom during our early history also implied reverence for man, a conception of the individual as a being entitled to respect, as a creature of dignity and worth. But during World War II hundreds of native-born citizens of the United States were torn from their homes and forced into relocation camps solely because of their Japanese ancestry. They had committed no crimes, but their presence on the Pacific Coast was considered a "potential" danger. Richard B. Morris and Jerome Frank have shown how difficult it is for any accused person, under conditions of national hysteria, to obtain an impartial trial based upon scientific evaluation of evidence. It is not simply emotionalism and prejudice that stand in the way, but the survival of antiquated procedures and an increasing failure to respect the safeguards provided by our constitutional system.[3]

If there is one star in the American constellation which gleams more brightly in the eyes of foreigners than any other it is equality. In this country, it is assumed, there are no classes, no hidebound traditions of servility and dependence, no ancient customs barring the way to success in proportion to talent or perseverance. America is the land of opportunity, where everyone, regardless of the circumstances attending his birth, has an equal chance to obtain the highest honors and rewards that the nation can bestow.

That the recent history of our country gives evidence of some progress along this line, scarcely anyone would deny. Great fortunes and large incomes have both undergone a substantial leveling since the lush days of the early 1900's and even since 1929. The latter year could boast of 513 persons with annual incomes of $1,000,000 or more. By 1953 the number had dwindled to 145. In 1900 Andrew Carnegie had a net income of $23,000,000 from his steel interests alone. At the present time not even the most fabulous of Texas oil kings could duplicate that figure after paying his taxes. One after another the baronial castles of our large cities and our magnificent country estates have been converted into art galleries or charitable foundations, or their buildings have been torn down to make way for business establishments or housing developments. The grand balls and cotillions of yesteryear, costing as much as a quarter of a million dollars apiece, seem to have become a rarity. The top hat has been replaced by the Homburg, the cutaway and striped trousers by the business suit. The synthetic beads from the five-and-ten look almost as good as the dowager's pearls, while a Cadillac at a moderate distance is not easy to distinguish from a Chevrolet.

But the proportion of myth in the American ideal of equality is at least equal to the proportion of fact. It is simply not true that the surest requisite for the Presidency has been birth in a log cabin. Of the thirty-three chief executives to date, only five—Jackson, Fillmore, Lincoln, Johnson, and Garfield—were born in circumstances that could be described as poverty-stricken. At least thirteen were the scions of either moderate or extensive wealth—Washington, Jefferson, Madison, Monroe, J. Q. Adams, the two Harrisons, Tyler, Polk, Taylor, Buchanan, and the two Roosevelts. The remainder descended from families of about average economic condition. Their children knew no luxury and had to struggle for a place in life, but they suffered few hardships. A study of the men who have risen to the top in almost any other field would probably reveal a similar picture. Lester Ward contended that more than 80 per cent of the individuals of eminence in every country sprang from the 15 or 20 per cent of the population able to provide their offspring with the advantages of education, culture, and travel. The primary remedy for this imbalance is a system of public education which would give the children of both rich and poor an equal chance to make the most of their endowments. But America still denies a college education to nearly 50 per cent of her gifted young men and women because they and their parents are too poor to pay for it.

It has long been the proud boast of those who have presumed to speak on behalf of the nation that America is the true home of democracy. What they have meant by the term has most of the time been perfectly plain. Democracy is a system of political rule combining popular sovereignty with reverence for the individual and respect for the rights of minorities. Such was the meaning it had for Roger Williams, for Jefferson and Madison, for Lincoln and Emerson, and for Justice Holmes, John Dewey, and Franklin Roosevelt. Only from a few agitators and radical reformers like Wendell Phillips, William Jennings Bryan, and Robert M. LaFollette did the idea of a literal sovereignty of the majority receive strong endorsement. But all three were consumed by such a passion for remaking society that they could feel little interest in the rights of individuals; nor could they show much solicitude for the civilized process of eliciting truth from the clash of competing ideas. Even then, they were not always consistent. Phillips based his crusade for the abolition of slavery in large part upon the doctrine of the Declaration of Independence that all men have inalienable rights, while LaFollette and his collaborators looked with some favor upon proportional representation. The latter device, by giving a voice to every substantial minority, would certainly not strengthen the supremacy of the majority.

Judged by recent developments in our history, democracy in realization can scarcely be regarded as a perfect epitome of the American dream. Reference has already been made to the attenuation of liberty by our courts under the argument of national danger and to judicial sanction of laws trespassing upon the freedom of individuals. In comparatively few countries outside the dictatorial sphere are the rights of persons so lightly regarded as in the United States. Perhaps nowhere else in the free world does the belief persist so strongly that it is the duty of the government to save people from themselves, not merely from evil deeds but even from evil thoughts. Comstockism, for instance, still allows our Post Office Department to exclude from the mails *Lysistrata* and the works of James Jones, John Steinbeck, and James Joyce. It appears at times that we tolerate almost everybody except certain foreigners and unpopular minorities. Despite the Fifth Amendment, which many people seem to forget is a part of the Bill of Rights, we deprive men of their jobs if they decline to answer questions imputing a past affiliation with some Communist organization. Notwithstanding our plethora of laws, which increase to a staggering total with each passing year, we are one of the most lawless of nations. We permit all sorts of private organizations to intimidate law-abiding citizens and to employ vigilante tactics against them. Racketeers bully and threaten labor unions and frequently employers as well. Ecclesiastical authorities prescribe the content of books and plays to both authors and publishers and maintain a censorship which operates not merely for their own members but for the public at large. Even our Presidents commit flagrant violations of the speed limits, endangering their own lives and the lives of others who use the highways.

The most serious failure in connection with realization of the American democratic dream involves the insistence upon racial inequality. In recent years this concept has undergone considerable moderation, but for upwards of a century and a half it held sinister sway over the minds of scores of our leaders. They did not often proclaim it in public addresses, but in their letters and other more intimate writings they admitted their allegiance to it. Even such generous and humane spirits as Thomas Jefferson, Theodore Parker, and Abraham Lincoln were not immune from its influence. Under the effects of Social Darwinism in the late nineteenth and early twentieth centuries it became fashionable, and Josiah Strong, Edward A. Ross, and Theodore Roosevelt shouted it from the housetops. The efforts of anthropologists and other social scientists to combat the absurd prejudice availed little. The need for millions of men, regardless of race, in the armed services during two world wars accomplished somewhat more. The courage of the Supreme Court in pronouncing void the old "separate but equal" doctrine in public education gave reason to hope that the day might ultimately come when inequality would be a relic of the past. Yet many obstacles remain unconquered. The treatment of the American Indian is a standing disgrace. The son of the former governor of Formosa was "depledged" by a fraternity in one of our most respected universities solely because his membership in the "Chinese race" made him an undesirable associate for his Caucasian "brothers." Negroes in both North and South are often forced to inhabit the shabbiest and most undesirable residence areas and to limit their ambitions to the more menial occupations. As for the prospects of desegregation in education, a number of the southern states have threatened to abolish their public school systems entirely rather than permit the Supreme Court's order to be applied in the territories over which they rule.

In the opinion of most of her citizens, no ideal is more characteristic of America than devotion to peace. Four years after World War II had ended, President Truman pronounced the amiable judgment: "We are not a militaristic country. We do not glorify the military way of life. Some nations," he went on, "have taken greater pride in their military victories than in any other national achievements, but it has never been so with us. When we think of war, it is with a prayer that the sacrifices our dead have made will

Despite its weaknesses, the United Nations remains the primary agency for world cooperation and the settlement of international disputes. The low, domed building in the center is the General Assembly, and the glass and aluminum skyscraper on the left is the Secretariat. *United Nations*

never have to be repeated." Though he doubtless believed these statements, their truth may be seriously questioned. We do take more pride in our military victories than in any other national achievements, with the possible exception of inventions. Our military victories are commemorated by statues and monuments. They are celebrated in school histories and on patriotic holidays. After every one of our wars, with the single exception of World War I, a military hero was chosen President. We do not, as a nation, pray that the sacrifices our dead have made will never have to be repeated. Instead, we pray that "these honored dead shall not have died in vain," that is, that the cause for which they died shall remain triumphant. But it is still noble and glorious to die for one's country. We still think, as Emerson did, that the sacrifice of a generation of youth is not too high a price to pay for the defense of the nation or to guarantee victory for some noble endeavor.

Such views of war did not always predominate. The Founding Fathers deplored armed conflict as the most dangerous of all threats to national existence. Traces of their attitude survive in the general contempt for the military that characterizes American sentiment, especially in periods between wars. It is doubtless significant that the majority of our most popular novels and plays, from *What Price Glory?* to *Mister Roberts* and *From Here to Eternity,* have pilloried army and navy life and scoffed at the usages of rank and the whole body of traditions of the officer caste. But the outbreak or even the threat of war in recent times has been followed by the same unquestioning assumptions of national righteousness that prevail in less idealistic countries. And while the conflict rages, and usually for some time afterward, the air is filled with doctrines of the health-giving and ennobling effects of war—doctrines as bizarre as any that ever emanated from the fire-eating militarists of Europe. No one who professes to a knowledge of the intellectual history of America can ignore the glorifications of war as an instrument of moral and political progress contained in the writings of Theodore Parker, Justice Holmes, Alfred T. Mahan, and Theodore Roosevelt.

Unfortunately, what most acclaimers of America as the personification of peace have wanted has not been peace, but security and national advantage. Not a few have conceived it as our mission to impose peace upon the rest of the world. Such was the dream of John Fiske, of John W. Burgess, of Albert J. Beveridge, and of Theodore Roosevelt. It was the hope also of Woodrow Wilson and Franklin D. Roosevelt that America might become the leader of an alliance of victors to maintain law and order throughout the earth. The latter, especially, had an almost childlike faith in the ability of the United States and Russia to cooperate harmoniously and to serve as "sheriffs" in stamping out lawlessness and aggression wherever they might show their heads. When the Russians balked and developed aggressive designs of their own, the idea of the Big Three as "sheriffs" of the world gave way to the "containment" policy of the Truman regime. But the dream of active intervention to negate the results of conquest and to liberate subjugated peoples did not die. As recently as February, 1957, our chief delegate to the United Nations issued a declaration that the United States refused to accept with indifference the situation which Russia had created in her satellite states. The American people, he asserted, would not reconcile themselves to "the relentless Soviet assault on human dignity and freedom." A few months earlier, when revolt flared in Hungary, numerous Americans found themselves chafing in frustration because their country was not able to play a militant role in breaking the yoke of oppression.

Probably the element in the American concept of mission which has come nearest to fulfillment is the goal of a standard of living unparalleled in the rest of the world. When one looks at the statistics of averages, one can hardly avoid the impression of amazing progress. The gross national product, for example, increased from 104 billion dollars in 1929 to over 400 billions in 1956. In 1929 the national income was 88 billion dollars and in 1955 more than 320 billions. Of these totals, labor received 58 per cent in 1929 and 69 per cent in 1955.[4] Making full allowance for the decline in purchasing power of the dollar, it is estimated that the average individual was 53 per cent better off in 1955 than he was in 1929. Yet even this

Many Americans believe that the hope of the world lies in raising standards of living in underdeveloped countries. Shown here is the Hirakud River dam in India, for which technical assistance has been provided by the United States. It will eventually irrigate 2 million acres. *ICA*

pleasing picture was not without some blemishes. A recent survey by the Industrial Commissioner of the State of New York shows that one family out of eleven in the United States has an income of $1,000 per year or less, while one out of five receives $2,000 or less. Included in the latter category are some 30 million persons. To be sure, many of the heads of such families are disabled and unemployable. A still larger number are farmers. But one half are employed wage-earners who must struggle to support their dependents in cities and towns in the face of a steadily rising cost of living.

Despite the criticisms enumerated above, there is little intrinsically wrong with the ideals themselves that make up the American concept of destiny and greatness. They are objectionable mainly to the extent that they imply a swaggering conceit and consciousness of superiority over other peoples. Almost any exaggerated vision of a glorious destiny or noble calling is likely to result in fostering illusions. The world has recently witnessed the spectacle of British statesmen attempting to salvage imperial interests by methods reminiscent of the gunboat diplomacy of the nineteenth century—just as if the Union Jack still waved over three fourths of the globe, and nationalism were a relatively civilized force confined to the continent of Europe. America is no less immune from illusions that cloud her vision. After every orgy of foreign intervention, she must reckon with isolationists who yearn for policies of self-containment and withdrawal from involvements with perfidious Europe. Equally self-deluded are the exponents of a "tough" policy who believe that force is the only language our opponents can understand. Their constant fear seems to be that Uncle Sam will be "played for a sucker." They would therefore limit foreign aid to the provision of weapons for our allies and to the establishment of bases from which we can threaten potential aggressors.

All such illusions are the natural fruit of an excessive emphasis upon national pride and sense of mission. As long as we believe that we are God's anointed and therefore endowed with superior virtue, we are likely to close our eyes to current realities and return to some dream world of a glorious past. While some of us fancy that we can ignore the squalor and misery in the rest of the world and build a surging prosperity within our own borders, others dote on the idea that we can dictate to other nations and stand for no nonsense from powerful rivals. The two groups are about equally oblivious of the revolutionary changes resulting from the decline of our friends in Western Europe, the bid of Russia for world supremacy, and the revolt against privation and foreign domination in Africa and Asia.

That a strongly developed sense of mission should blind a people to numerous realities seems almost unquestionable. So firmly convinced have we been of the rightness of our ideals that we delude ourselves into believing that our prejudices have validity also. The authors of our Bill of Rights and the Declaration of Independence were slaveholders. Our Great Emancipator could express almost in the same breath his abhorrence of slavery and his repudiation of social equality of Negroes and whites. Our attitudes to this day, on many fundamental issues, are contradictory and ambivalent. We insist upon democracy in government but ignore its importance almost everywhere else. The average employee of a corporation, for example, or the average teacher in a school or college, is as completely at the mercy of an oligarchy as if Jefferson or Madison had never lived. We take for granted freedom of publication of novels and plays but accept a rigorous censorship of the mails and of TV and the movies. We boast of our devotion to the ways of peace but give medals of honor to our champion killers and spend more than half of our national revenue in preparation for new wars. The ambiguity of our national position was perhaps never more glaringly illustrated than at the second inauguration of President Eisenhower on January 21, 1957. In his inaugural address the President lauded peace as the foundation of our foreign policy and proclaimed it our sacred mission to lead the way toward a warless world. A few hours later he rode at the head of a parade bristling with the newest lethal weapons, which seemed obviously designed to impress the world with our military might and our will to use it whenever we think necessary.

Purged of its dross of conceit and illusion, the mission of America remains one of the noblest expressions of idealism that any nation has embraced. What it needs most of all is more wisdom and tolerance in carrying it out. Intelligently applied, its elements of liberty, equality, democracy, and peace are the prime essentials to give the substance of hope to a tortured humanity. But we must mean what we say if our slogans are to have lasting value. We must banish discrimination, curb lawlessness, enlarge freedom, provide for real equality of opportunity, reduce disparities of wealth and income,

Atomic energy has enormous possibilities for peacetime industry. Here, an atomic power plant is under construction by private industry at Shipping-port, Pennsylvania. In the center is a nuclear reactor. *Westinghouse Electric Corporation*

and make a wiser use of our material and intellectual resources. We must abandon all sympathy and association with imperialism, whether practiced by the British on Cyprus, by the French in North Africa, or by our own minions in Guatemala. We must support internationalism zealously, whether or not it suits our convenience, and go out of our way to devise and use every conceivable means for peaceful settlement of disputes even if it necessitates some sacrifice of "vital" national interests. For example, if we are to demand internationalization of the Suez Canal, we must be ready to accept a similar disposition of the Panama Canal. At the same time we must avoid the encouragement of militant nationalisms that would sooner or later eventuate in expansion and conflict. Both nationalism and imperialism are obsolete in the contemporary world.

In this world of anxiety and conflict, no need is more urgent than that of disarmament. In the final analysis the most effective means to this end is an international regime of law and order. Few nations will consider disarming in the face of uncertainty and danger. But the perfection of world organization can scarcely be expected in the proximate future. Short of it, some country must set the example of a bold initiative even at the risk of impairing some fancied security. Words like "security" are largely meaningless anyway when two powerful enemies possess substantial equality in weapons capable of blowing each other off the map. If either decides to use them, virtual annihilation will be the fate of both. To go on testing and adding to our stockpile more and more horrible instruments of slaughter is simply to keep the nerves of the world on edge and to magnify dangers. As long as competition in the development of such instruments continues, there is always the possibility that some nation will be goaded by fear or desperation into making use of them. Surely, the conclusion of water-tight agreements for the control of

Through the Golden Gate, America looks out toward the Orient. For many years the Pacific Ocean imposed a limit to Manifest Destiny. But since the Spanish-American War, Asia has been added to Europe and South America as an area in which Uncle Sam has vital interests. *Fairchild Aerial Surveys, Inc.*

these weapons should not be impossible. All weapons and engines of war are sources of international tension, and means must be found for scaling them down to rational levels. If we fail to do so, we invite wholesale depletion of our national resources, impoverishment of our people by inflation and high taxes, and perhaps eventual destruction of freedom and democracy. Though no amount of disarmament will eliminate all wars, any steps that can be taken to substitute diplomatic or judicial settlement for the arbitrament of the sword will reduce the fears and suspicions that are the chief breeders of conflict.

Finally, it behooves America to recognize the social and political revolution now sweeping over Asia and Africa and give it an enlightened direction by providing economic and intellectual assistance to enable the distressed nations to solve their problems. They need the services not merely of agronomists and engineers but of sanitation experts, teachers, physicians, and birth control clinicians. Famine, disease, ignorance, and excess population are simply different elements in a single pattern of evils. To try to eliminate the first two without correcting the others would yield short-term gains but would ultimately plunge the countries concerned into deeper trouble than ever. We must grasp the truth that the time has gone by when the white race can enjoy a monopoly of prosperity while the colored peoples languish in squalor and poverty. To complete undertakings of the sort described would involve the expenditure of perhaps half the cost of our current armaments program; but it would bring us more genuine security than all the atom and hydrogen bombs ever manufactured. It would be a venture truly in keeping with the spirit and traditions of our nation—a mission with at least a respectable chance of making the name of America an inspiration to men forever.

NOTES TO CHAPTER THIRTEEN

1. *Major Campaign Speeches, 1952* (New York: Random House, 1953), p. 262.
2. *Two Minutes till Midnight* (Indianapolis: The Bobbs-Merrill Co., 1955), pp. 19, 50.
3. Richard B. Morris, *Fair Trial* (New York: Alfred A. Knopf, 1952); Jerome Frank, *Courts on Trial* (Princeton: Princeton University Press, 1949).
4. *The American Workers' Fact Book* (Washington: United States Department of Labor, 1956), p. 112.

Suggested Supplementary Readings

GENERAL

Baldwin, Leland D. *The Meaning of America: Essays Toward an Understanding of the American Spirit.* Pittsburgh, Pa.: University of Pittsburgh Press, 1955.

Beard, Charles A. and Mary R. *The American Spirit.* New York: Macmillan Co., 1942.

——— *The Rise of American Civilization.* New York: Macmillan Co., 1946.

Clough, Shepard B. *The American Way.* New York: Thomas Y. Crowell Co., 1953.

Commager, Henry S. *The American Mind.* New Haven: Yale University Press, 1950.

Curti, Merle. *The Growth of American Thought.* New York: Harper and Brothers, 1943.

Faulkner, Harold U. *The Quest for Social Justice, 1898-1914.* New York: Macmillan Co., 1931.

Gabriel, Ralph H. *The Course of American Democratic Thought.* New York: Ronald Press, 1956.

Hartz, Louis. *The Liberal Tradition in America.* New York: Harcourt, Brace and Co., 1955.

Hofstadter, Richard. *The Age of Reform, from Bryan to F.D.R.* New York: Alfred A. Knopf, 1955.

———. *The American Political Tradition and the Men Who Made It.* New York: Alfred A. Knopf, 1948.

Mosier, Richard D. *The American Temper.* Berkeley: University of California Press, 1952.

Parrington, Vernon L. *Main Currents in American Thought.* 3 vols. New York: Harcourt, Brace and Co., 1927.

Riley, Woodbridge. *American Thought from Puritanism to Pragmatism.* New York: Henry Holt and Co., 1915.

Rossiter, Clinton. *Conservatism in America.* New York: Alfred A. Knopf, 1955.

———. *Seedtime of the Republic.* New York: Harcourt, Brace and Co., 1953.

Schneider, Herbert W. *A History of American Philosophy.* New York: Columbia University Press, 1946.

Wish, Harvey. *Society and Thought in America.* 2 vols. New York: Longman's, Green and Co., 1950-1952.

THE NATIONAL HERITAGE

Barrow, Lyons. *Tomorrow's Birthright.* New York: Funk and Wagnalls Co., 1955.

Mudge, Eugene T. *The Social Philosophy of John Taylor of Caroline.* New York: Columbia University Press, 1939.

Osborn, Fairfield. *Our Plundered Planet.* Boston: Little, Brown and Co., 1948.

Perry, Ralph B. *Puritanism and Democracy.* New York: Vanguard Press, 1944.

Pinchot, Gifford. *Breaking New Ground.* New York: Harcourt, Brace and Co., 1947.

Potter, David M. *People of Plenty: Economic Abundance and the American Character.* Chicago: University of Chicago Press, 1954.

Sax, Karl. *Standing Room Only.* Boston: Beacon Press, 1955.

Vogt, William. *Road to Survival.* New York: William Sloane Assoc., 1948.

DEMOCRACY

Adams, Randolph G. *Political Ideas of the American Revolution.* Durham, N. C.: Trinity College Press, 1922.

Beard, Charles A. *The Republic.* New York: Viking Press, 1943.

Biddle, Francis. *Mr. Justice Holmes.* New York: Charles Scribner's Sons, 1942.

Bowen, Catherine D. *Yankee from Olympus*. Boston: Little, Brown and Co., 1944.

Bowers, Claude G. *Beveridge and the Progressive Era*. Boston: Houghton Mifflin Co., 1932.

Brant, Irving. *James Madison*. 5 vols. New York: Bobbs Merrill Co., 1941-1956.

Burns, James M. *Roosevelt: The Lion and the Fox*. New York: Harcourt, Brace and Co., 1956.

Corwin, Edward S. *The Constitution and What It Means Today*. Princeton: Princeton University Press, 1954.

———. *The Doctrine of Judicial Review*. Princeton: Princeton University Press, 1914.

———. *The Higher Law Background of American Constitutional Law*. Ithaca, N. Y.: Cornell University Press, 1955.

Donald, David. *Lincoln Reconsidered: Essays on the Civil War Era*. New York: Alfred A. Knopf, 1956.

Frank, Jerome. *Law and the Modern Mind*. New York: Tudor Publishing Co., 1949.

Friedel, Frank. *Franklin D. Roosevelt*. 2 vols. Boston: Little, Brown and Co., 1952-1954.

Goldman, Erich F. *Rendezvous with Destiny*. New York: Alfred A. Knopf, 1952.

Haines, Charles G. *The American Doctrine of Judicial Supremacy*. New York: Macmillan Co., 1914.

Hamilton, Alexander, John Jay, and James Madison. *The Federalist*. (Modern Library ed.) New York: Random House, n.d.

Hyman, Sydney. *The American President*. New York: Harper and Brothers, 1954.

LaFollette, Belle Case and Fola. *Robert M. LaFollette: June 14, 1855-June 18, 1925*. 2 vols. New York: Macmillan Co., 1953.

Lerner, Max (ed.) *The Mind and Faith of Justice Holmes*. Boston: Little, Brown and Co., 1946.

Mitchell, Broadus. *Alexander Hamilton, from Youth to Maturity, 1755-1788*. New York: Macmillan Co., 1957.

Pound, Roscoe. *An Introduction to the Philosophy of Law*. New Haven: Yale University Press, 1954.

———. *Social Control Through Law*. New Haven: Yale University Press, 1942.

Pound, Roscoe. *The Spirit of the Common Law.* Boston: Marshall Jones Co., 1921.

Randall, James G., and Richard N. Current. *Lincoln the President: Last Full Measure.* New York: Dodd, Mead and Co., 1955.

Schachner, Nathan. *The Founding Fathers.* New York: G. P. Putnam's Sons, 1954.

Schilpp, Paul A. (ed.). *The Philosophy of John Dewey.* Evanston, Ill.: Northwestern University Press, 1939.

Schlesinger, Arthur M., Jr. *The Age of Jackson.* Boston: Little, Brown and Co., 1945.

Tocqueville, Alexis de. *Democracy in America.* 2 vols. New York: Alfred A. Knopf, 1945.

Weyl, Walter. *The New Democracy.* New York: Macmillan Co., 1912.

FREEDOM AND EQUALITY

Barth, Alan A. *The Loyalty of Free Men.* New York: Viking Press, 1951.

Beale, Howard K. *Are American Teachers Free?* New York: Charles Scribner's Sons, 1936.

Chafee, Zechariah. *Free Speech in the United States.* Cambridge, Mass.: Harvard University Press, 1941.

Commager, Henry S. *Freedom, Loyalty, Dissent.* New York: Oxford University Press, 1954.

Davenport, Russell W. *U.S.A. Permanent Revolution.* New York: Prentice-Hall, 1951.

Ernst, Morris L. *The First Freedom.* New York: Macmillan Co., 1946.

Fraenkel, Ormond. *Our Civil Liberties.* New York: Viking Press, 1944.

Hofstadter, Richard, and Walter P. Metzger. *The Development of Academic Freedom in the United States.* New York: Columbia University Press, 1955.

Morris, Richard B. *Fair Trial.* New York: Alfred A. Knopf, 1952.

Myrdal, Gunnar. *An American Dilemma.* New York: Harper and Brothers, 1944.

Pritchett, C. Herman. *Civil Liberties and the Vinson Court.* Chicago: University of Chicago Press, 1954.

Ratner, Joseph (ed.) *Intelligence in the Modern World: John Dewey's Philosophy*. New York: Random House, 1939.

Smith, James Morton. *Freedom's Fetters: The Alien and Sedition Laws and American Civil Liberties*. Ithaca: Cornell University Press, 1956.

INDIVIDUALISM

Beard, Charles A. *The Myth of Rugged American Individualism*. New York: John Day Co., 1932.

Dewey, John. *Freedom and Culture*. New York: G. P. Putnam's Sons, 1939.

———. *Individualism, Old and New*. New York: Minton, Balch and Co., 1930.

Fromm, Erich. *Escape from Freedom*. New York: Rinehart and Co., 1941.

Hocking, William E. *The Lasting Elements of Individualism*. New Haven: Yale University Press, 1937.

Kallen, Horace M. *Individualism: An American Way of Life*. New York: Liveright, Inc., 1933.

Lippmann, Walter. *The Method of Freedom*. New York: Macmillan Co., 1934.

Mills, C. Wright. *The Power Elite*. New York: Oxford University Press, 1956.

Perry, Ralph B. *Shall Not Perish from the Earth*. New York: Vanguard Press, 1940.

———. *The Thought and Character of William James*. Cambridge, Mass.: Harvard University Press, 1948.

Riesman, David. *Individualism Reconsidered*. Glencoe, Ill.: Free Press, 1954.

NATIONALITY AND RACE

Handlin, Oscar. *Race and Nationality in the United States*. Boston: Little, Brown and Co., 1957.

Higham, John. *Strangers in the Land*. New Brunswick, N. J.: Rutgers University Press, 1955.

Hofstadter, Richard. *Social Darwinism in American Thought, 1860-1915*. Philadelphia: University of Pennsylvania Press, 1945.

EDUCATION, RELIGION AND MORALITY

Hopkins, Charles H. *The Rise of the Social Gospel, 1865-1918.* New Haven: Yale University Press, 1940.

Kandel, Isaac L. *The New Era in Education.* Boston: Houghton Mifflin Co., 1955.

Knight, Edgar W. *Fifty Years of American Education.* New York: Ronald Press, 1952.

Pfeffer, Leo. *Church, State and Freedom.* Boston: Beacon Press, 1953.

Schneider, Herbert W. *Religion in Twentieth Century America.* Cambridge, Mass.: Harvard University Press, 1952.

Sweet, William W. *The Story of Religion in America.* New York: Harper and Brothers, 1950.

WAR AND PEACE

Addams, Jane. *Newer Ideals of Peace.* New York: Macmillan Co., 1907.

Adler, Mortimer J. *How to Think about War and Peace.* New York: Simon and Schuster, 1944.

Beard, Charles A. *A Foreign Policy for America.* New York: Alfred A. Knopf, 1940.

Curti, Merle. *Peace or War: The American Struggle, 1636-1936.* New York: W. W. Norton and Co., 1936.

Einstein, Albert. *The World As I See It.* New York: Philosophical Library, 1949.

Gelber, Lionel M. *Reprieve from War: A Manual for Realists.* New York: Macmillan Co., 1950.

Hibben, John Grier. *The Higher Patriotism.* New York: Charles Scribner's Sons, 1915.

Kennan, George F. *Realities of American Foreign Policy.* Princeton: Princeton University Press, 1954.

Morgenthau, Hans. *In Defense of the National Interest.* New York: Alfred A. Knopf, 1951.

Reves, Emery. *The Anatomy of Peace.* New York: Harper and Brothers, 1946.

Roosevelt, Theodore. *Fear God and Take Your Own Part.* New York: George H. Doran Co., 1916.

Warburg, James P. *Peace in Our Time?* New York: Harper and Brothers, 1940.

———. *The United States in a Changing World.* New York: G. P. Putnam's Sons, 1954.

Wright, Quincy. *A Study of War.* Chicago: University of Chicago Press, 1942.

THE AMERICA OF THE FUTURE

Berle, Adolf A., Jr. *The Twentieth Century Capitalist Revolution.* New York: Harcourt, Brace and Co., 1954.

Calverton, Victor F. *Where Angels Dared to Tread.* Indianapolis: Bobbs Merrill Co., 1941.

Croly, Herbert. *The Promise of American Life.* New York: Macmillan Co., 1909.

Destler, Chester M. *American Radicalism, 1865-1901.* New London, Conn.: Connecticut College, 1946.

Frankel, Charles. *The Case for Modern Man.* New York: Harper and Brothers, 1955.

Galbraith, John K. *American Capitalism; The Concept of Countervailing Power.* Boston: Houghton Mifflin Co., 1952.

Hertzler, J. O. *The History of Utopian Thought.* New York: Macmillan Co., 1926.

Hicks, John D. *The Populist Revolt.* Minneapolis: University of Minnesota Press, 1931.

Morgan, Arthur E. *Nowhere Was Somewhere.* Chapel Hill, N. C.: University of North Carolina Press, 1946.

Nordhoff, Charles. *Communistic Societies in the United States.* New York: Harper and Brothers, 1875.

Owen, Robert. *A New View of Society.* New York: E. P. Dutton and Co., 1949.

Quint, Howard H. *The Forging of American Socialism.* Columbia, S. C.: University of South Carolina Press, 1953.

Index